Also Available

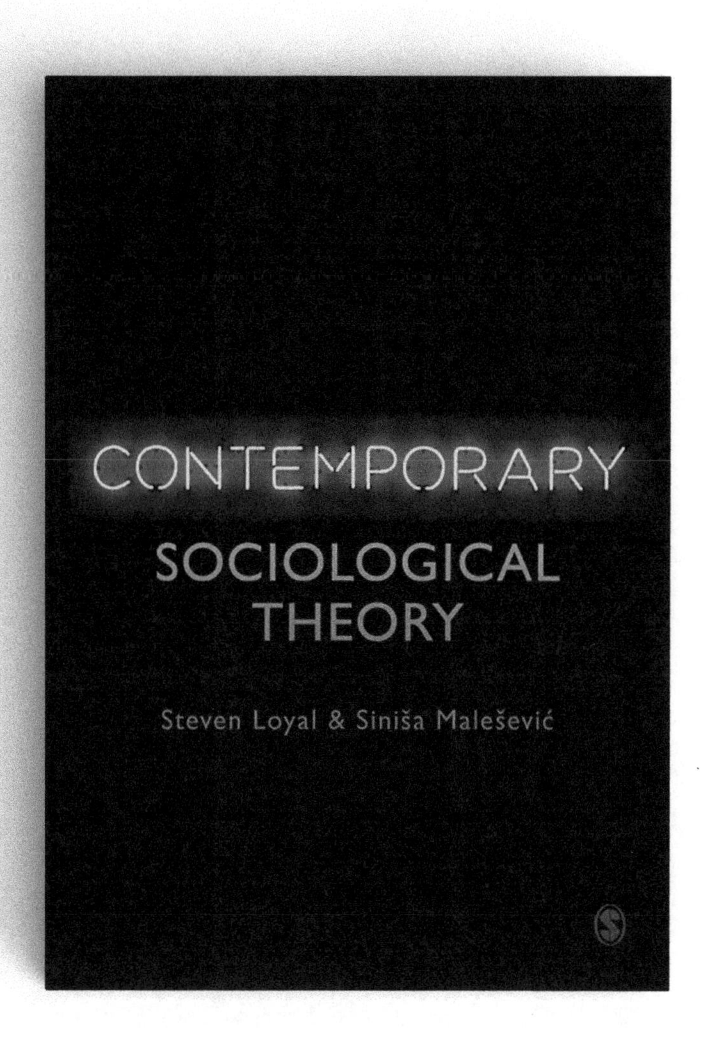

Sara Miller McCune founded SAGE Publishing in 1965 to support the dissemination of usable knowledge and educate a global community. SAGE publishes more than 1000 journals and over 800 new books each year, spanning a wide range of subject areas. Our growing selection of library products includes archives, data, case studies and video. SAGE remains majority owned by our founder and after her lifetime will become owned by a charitable trust that secures the company's continued independence.

Los Angeles | London | New Delhi | Singapore | Washington DC | Melbourne

CLASSICAL SOCIOLOGICAL THEORY

Steven Loyal

I would like to dedicate this book to my former teachers who served as exemplary academic role models, István Mészáros and Barry Barnes.

Sinisa Malesevic

I dedicate this book to John A. Hall, a wonderful scholar, my teacher and a lifelong friend.

CLASSICAL SOCIOLOGICAL THEORY

Steven Loyal & Siniša Malešević

Los Angeles | London | New Delhi
Singapore | Washington DC | Melbourne

Los Angeles | London | New Delhi
Singapore | Washington DC | Melbourne

SAGE Publications Ltd
1 Oliver's Yard
55 City Road
London EC1Y 1SP

SAGE Publications Inc.
2455 Teller Road
Thousand Oaks, California 91320

SAGE Publications India Pvt Ltd
B 1/I 1 Mohan Cooperative Industrial Area
Mathura Road
New Delhi 110 044

SAGE Publications Asia-Pacific Pte Ltd
3 Church Street
#10-04 Samsung Hub
Singapore 049483

Editor: Natalie Aguilera
Assistant editor: Eve Williams
Production editor: Katherine Haw
Copyeditor: Neville Hankins
Proofreader: Camille Bramall
Indexer: Charmian Parkin
Marketing manager: George Kimble
Cover design: Francis Kenney
Typeset by: C&M Digitals (P) Ltd, Chennai, India
Printed in the UK

© Steven Loyal and Siniša Malešević 2021

First published 2021

Apart from any fair dealing for the purposes of research or private study, or criticism or review, as permitted under the Copyright, Designs and Patents Act, 1988, this publication may be reproduced, stored or transmitted in any form, or by any means, only with the prior permission in writing of the publishers, or in the case of reprographic reproduction, in accordance with the terms of licences issued by the Copyright Licensing Agency. Enquiries concerning reproduction outside those terms should be sent to the publishers.

Library of Congress Control Number: 2019956917

British Library Cataloguing in Publication data

A catalogue record for this book is available from the British Library

ISBN 978-1-5297-2572-8
ISBN 978-1-5297-2571-1 (pbk)

At SAGE we take sustainability seriously. Most of our products are printed in the UK using responsibly sourced papers and boards. When we print overseas we ensure sustainable papers are used as measured by the PREPS grading system. We undertake an annual audit to monitor our sustainability.

CONTENTS

ACKNOWLEDGEMENTS

This book and its accompanying volume, *Contemporary Sociological Theory*, took many years to complete. Initially we envisaged writing one shorter volume focusing on both classical and contemporary social thought, but soon realised that we had to cover many more sociological theories and theorists than we originally planned. Since sociological thought is so rich and diverse, including thousands of scholars who have made a significant contribution to the development of sociology, it became apparent that a single volume could not do justice to all forms of sociological thinking. Hence after completing 32 chapters and discussing it with our editors at SAGE, it was agreed to split the original manuscript into two separate books – *Classical Sociological Theory* and *Contemporary Sociological Theory*. The original manuscript was also substantially shortened in this process, the principal aim of which was to make the two books as accessible as possible to students. Both authors have contributed equally to these two volumes. In *Classical Sociological Theory*, Loyal was responsible for writing Chapters 1, 4, 5, 11 and 12 and Malešević wrote 2, 3, 6, 7, 8, 9 and 10. In *Contemporary Sociological Theory*, Loyal was the lead author for Chapters 2, 4, 5, 6, 7, 8, 11, 12, 13, 14 and 15 while Malešević was responsible for Chapters 1, 9, 10, 16, 17, 18, 19 and 20, with the Introduction and Chapter 3 a product of joint work.

We would especially like to thank Roddy Condon for his invaluable work in producing the boxed pedagogical material and compiling the references. We would also like to thank Chris Rojek for encouraging us to write this book and also for commissioning the project. Thanks also to Tim Mooney for helpful comments on Chapter 1, and Kieran Allen for comments on Chapter 5. We are also very grateful to everyone at SAGE for their goodwill and enormous patience with the numerous new deadlines that we never met. Finally, we would like to thank our families for their support during the very long and sometimes arduous, but mostly enjoyable, writing process.

ABOUT THE AUTHORS

Steven Loyal is Associate Professor at the School of Sociology at University College Dublin, Ireland. His areas of interest include sociological theory, migration, the sociology of knowledge, social stratification and historical sociology.

Siniša Malešević is a Full Professor of Sociology at the University College, Dublin. His recent books include *Grounded Nationalisms* (CUP, 2019), *The Rise of Organised Brutality* (CUP, 2017) and *Nation-States and Nationalisms* (Polity, 2013). His work has been translated into 12 languages.

INTRODUCTION: THE RISE OF SOCIAL THOUGHT

In 1971 Lewis Coser wrote an unusual, and later highly successful, textbook *Masters of Sociological Thought: Ideas in Historical and Social Context*. The book differed from the standard social science textbooks of its time. Instead of summarising the main concepts, ideas and theories of various thinkers, as other textbooks have done, Coser aimed to frame these intellectual developments within the wider social and historical context. While other books would usually provide only a few biographical and historical paragraphs, Coser's work devoted almost as much attention to the history, social environment and biography as it did to the key sociological contributions of respective scholars. He justified this strategy in the following terms:

> We have a great number of books that attempt to elucidate what Marx or Weber or Pareto *really* meant but only few and scattered efforts to use the tools of the sociologist to investigate the role of sociological theorists within the social structure in which they are variously placed. There has been no sustained attempt to show how social origins, social position, social network, or audience found a reflection in the problems that a theorist addressed himself to or in the overall orientation of his life's work. (Coser, 1971: xiv)

This unusual approach proved popular with the audiences and many students found Coser's textbook enlightening, informative and accessible. Most of all, this approach made it possible for students to contextualise the development of sociological thinking. Instead of de-contextualised abstract concepts and theories created by some distant experts, one encountered real human beings struggling to make a sense of their own world. By focusing on individual biographies and the wider social, political and historical contexts, Coser made the classics of sociology alive and relevant to one's own times. Nevertheless, despite the textbook's success as a teaching tool, Coser's example was not followed by the majority of authors and publishers and they continued to produce social theory textbooks that lacked a historical, social and biographical grounding.

Classical Sociological Theory and the accompanying volume *Contemporary Sociological Theory* follow firmly in Coser's footsteps aiming to situate the rise and transformation of social thought within its historical, cultural, political and economic background. Moreover, we also aim to locate the development of specific ideas, concepts and theories within the unique biographical experiences of the respective theorists. Like Coser, we too aspire to understand social thought not as a system of fixed ideas and postulates but as a processual phenomenon deeply rooted in the social structures and vagaries of their own time and place. By zooming in on this 'social ecology of sociological ideas' (Coser, 1971: xiii) one can make sociological thinking relevant for understanding the social dynamics of the contemporary world. Furthermore, this analytical strategy allows us to see how novel ideas and approaches are created, disseminated and popularised.

As Collins (1998) showed in his monumental *The Sociology of Philosophies*, original and influential ideas do not just pop up in somebody's head but are regularly a product of long-term social interaction. In other words, novel and sophisticated concepts and theories are usually created through dialogues, disputes, disagreements and conflicts within the established intellectual networks. It is no coincidence that all major philosophical traditions owe their existence to such active networks of thinkers who developed their new ideas not as solitary individuals but as energetic members of specific schools of thought. For example, the highly influential school of German idealist philosophy (Kant, Fichte, Schelling, Hegel, Hölderlin, Novalis, Schlegel and Jacobi) developed among individuals who all lived and moved in the same location (mostly Jena and Weimar), developed strong networks of personal connections (with some of them even living in the same street), studied and worked in the same universities and published with the same publishers (Collins, 1998). As we show in this book a similar principle applies to the major schools of social thought as many thinkers developed as a part of already established networks of intellectuals. A second perspective that influenced our approach is drawn from the sociology of knowledge, but deriving more so from Marx than Durkheim, finds its exemplary manifestation in the work of Karl Mannheim, and highlights the political and ideological character of much social thought. In our analyses we draw on both perspectives.

This 'social ecology of sociological ideas' helps us identify the profiles of the leading classical and contemporary thinkers. What comes across instantly is that the classical sociologists typically share a very narrow social background – they tend to be almost as a rule white, middle to upper class, heterosexual males who lived and worked in large and powerful Western European imperial states. They would also write and publish almost exclusively in three languages only – English, French or German. This in itself indicates that classical social thought was deeply shaped by the dominant social and political strata of its own time. This has been expressed in contemporary sociological cum political concerns to decolonise and highlight gender imbalances in the sociological curriculum and 'canon', though class determinations have strangely been ignored. They have, nevertheless, usefully highlighted the question of what constitutes a sociological canon or a classic. Issues which we can only superficially touch on here. At the end of the nineteenth and in the early twentieth century when sociology became established as a fully fledged academic discipline its key thinkers largely represented the power dynamics of the social world they inhabited.

It is no big surprise that academia resembled other sectors of society where there was little or no place for women, ethnic and sexual minorities, working classes, farmers or individuals with disability. Even those who ticked the class, gender and whiteness boxes but were outside of the European centres of power, lived on the imperial and national peripheries, or did not belong to the main linguistic communities, were likely to be excluded or severely underrepresented. Hence there is no doubt that sociology was created by the narrow circle of relatively privileged intellectuals based in Germany, France and the UK. In this sense one could also argue that their sociological perspectives were significantly influenced by their own biographical, social, economic and political backgrounds. It is no accident that many classical sociologists were preoccupied with the issues that affected their own gender, social class, nation and other categories of identification. Since this was a deeply hierarchical, patriarchal, Eurocentric, imperialist, heterosexual and racist world, no classical sociologist could remain completely immune to these hegemonic views of their time and place. At the same time women, lower social classes, minorities of various kinds and the people outside the metropolitan centres and other groups largely had no voice in the articulation of sociology as a discipline. This is a hard and cold reality of sociology's origin that one has to face when analysing the contributions of its classics. While in this book we identify some classical thinkers who did not belong to this narrow circle of white middle-class European heterosexual men (i.e. Confucius, Ibn Khaldun and Martineau)[1] and merit inclusion on the originality of their work, the key names that have shaped early sociological thought are inevitably dominated by the establishment.

In a world where most of the population were illiterate and where many groups had few if any rights it was almost impossible to succeed if one was not part of the dominant group. Hence any attempt to find the key pre-twentieth-century sociological thinkers outside the establishment is unlikely to succeed because an overwhelming majority of the world population had no access to the privilege of education, research and scholarship. In this context any attempt to project our contemporary parameters of social inclusion into the past and reframe some religious and communal leaders as early sociologists would really be counterproductive, resembling what Hobsbawm and Ranger (1983) referred to as 'the invention of tradition'. The fact that the overwhelming majority of key social thinkers come from the same narrow social background is a potent indicator of this particular group's political, social and economic hegemony over the centuries.

Nevertheless, recognising that most early social theorists and sociologists represented the privileged strata should not take away from the quality of their contributions. On the contrary it is necessary to emphasise that many early sociologists have managed to overcome their narrow backgrounds and have produced theories and approaches that offer universalist explanations of the social world. It is precisely because they were able to see beyond their own class, gender, religion, nation or ethnicity that they could develop sophisticated explanatory models that have resonated with many sociologists for the past several centuries. It is their analytical concern with the universal issues that affect all human beings that made classical sociological thought possible and it is this universalism that makes these theories still relevant today. As Mouzelis (1995: 245–6) convincingly argues, the classics of sociology were not imposed on us by some kind of dictatorial decree but their work has been accepted and utilised on the basis of its 'cognitive potency, analytical acuity, power of synthesis and imaginative reach and originality'.

The Layout of Chapters

The main aim of this book and its companion volume, *Contemporary Sociological Theory*, is to provide a critical and contextual introduction to social thought. In this context we analyse contributions of the key thinkers who have shaped and continue to influence sociological theory today. Hence the book contains 12 chapters focusing on the most influential representatives of different approaches within social theory. Some chapters are devoted to exposition of a single theorist, while other chapters analyse the contributions of two or more scholars who tend to be part of the same intellectual tradition. Since each chapter also explores the key contemporary influences of various theoretical perspectives, we briefly present the contributions of many other social thinkers. Thus, this book and its companion volume explore the work of over 100 social thinkers who have made substantial contributions towards advancing sociology as an explanatory and theoretical project. Even though we have attempted to be as comprehensive as possible we could not possibly cover all aspects of social thought and all theorists whose contributions could merit inclusion in this book. The latter remains an open possibility for others to pursue.

This volume explores the work of classical social thinkers starting with the pre-sociological and proto-sociological approaches of Plato, Aristotle, Confucius, Ibn Khaldun, de Tocqueville, Martineau and Hegel. Our aim here was to trace the intellectual sources that have shaped thinking about the social world before and in the immediate aftermath of modernity. The first part concludes with the chapters zooming in on the four key classical theorists who have influenced the formation of sociological thought in the late nineteenth and early twentieth century – Marx, Weber, Durkheim and Simmel. In addition, we also analyse two sociological perspectives that had enormous influence for the birth of sociology as an academic discipline but have largely been ignored by the late twentieth- and early twenty-first-century scholars – the elite theory (Pareto, Mosca and Michels) and the bellicist theory (Hintze, Gumplowicz and Ratzenhofer).[2] Although classical theory derives for the most part from Continental Europe, two key North American figures, DuBois and Mead, are also discussed.

Each chapter is intentionally structured in a similar way so that the reader can get the sense of the time, place and key structural influences that have shaped individual theorists. Thus, we explore the biographical and intellectual context of the theorists and then focus on the wider historical, social and political environment in which respective scholars have lived and worked. Each chapter also discusses the central ideas and arguments associated with a specific theoretical approach and then looks at the contemporary relevance and applications of their ideas. The chapters end with the criticisms of each perspective and we also provide lists of references for each theorist.

One of the key ambitions of this book is to contextualise sociological thinking and to do this it is paramount to situate each theoretical contribution within its social, economic, political, historical and biographical context. Since sociology is an intellectual endeavour that is continuously shaped by its own social environment, it is crucial that the knowledge we produce, use and disseminate to others is understood within this wider context in which it is forged. Unlike physics, which perhaps can advance with the use of abstract and de-contextualised knowledge, sociology is a social and historical project that can never be completely removed from the time and place in which it is created.

Notes

1 Even these three 'non-establishment' scholars, as will be evident in the book, were relatively privileged in their own societies.

2 On the reasons for this, mostly deliberate, neglect of these two classical perspectives, see Malešević (2010: 17–49).

References

Collins, R. (1998) *The Sociology of Philosophies: A Global Theory of Intellectual Change*. Cambridge, MA: Harvard University Press.

Coser, L. A. (1971) *Masters of Sociological Thought: Ideas in Historical and Social Context*. New York: Harcourt Brace Jovanovich.

Hobsbawm, E. J. and Ranger, T. O. (1983) *The Invention of Tradition*. Cambridge: Cambridge University Press.

Malešević, S. (2010) *The Sociology of War and Violence*. Cambridge: Cambridge University Press.

Mouzelis, N. P. (1995) *Sociological Theory: What Went Wrong? Diagnosis and Remedies*. London: Routledge.

1

PLATO AND ARISTOTLE

It may seem odd to begin a book on sociological theory as far back as ancient Greece, but what is distinctive about Western thought and rationality – the view that the world has fundamental properties and processes accessible to the human mind – finds its origins there (Rossides, 1998: 2). Given the limited development of the division of labour the Greeks did not comprehend society in a compartmentalised way as contemporary thinkers do. Although the word 'sociology' does not appear until the eighteenth century with Comte, the ancient Greeks provided a number of terms that we now take for granted and use in the social sciences and humanities generally. These include the word theory *theória* (θεωρία), from the Greek contemplation, often contrasted with the word 'practice' (*praxis*, πρᾶξις) – for doing. But other indispensable concepts including science, art, criticism – for judging, as in a court case, or at a theatrical performance – also derive from ancient Greece. In addition to his philosophy Plato was one of the first thinkers to reflect systematically upon political society or the polis, and on the idea of what a just society should look like. However, it was with Aristotle that a more general analysis of human association became possible especially through his discussion of *koinonia*, which simultaneously included the notions of association, community and society since these were not conceived as separate (Frisby and Sayer, 1986: 13–14).

However, language as a practice is always embedded in broader social practices and relations (Wittgenstein, 1968), and there were fundamental differences between the ancient Greek structure of language, thought and life and modern ways of thinking. The writings of Plato and Aristotle, two thinkers whose thought not only directly shaped subsequent philosophy, but also, indirectly, sociological thinking and theorising, are indeed deeply rooted in the social, political, economic and cultural context of their time. This shaped and served as a frame of reference for many of the questions they asked about the human condition, and their diagnoses of the problems they faced, through philosophy (*philosophia*, φιλοσοφία), meaning 'love of wisdom', and the images and metaphors with which to think about humans and human societies.

Plato

Life and Intellectual Context

Some of the biographical facts concerning Plato's life are based on disputed evidence and much of what we know comes from the doxographer Diogenes Laërtius. Plato was born in 428 BCE in Athens to a highly distinguished aristocratic family during a period in which the Peloponnesian War was already underway. The family was steeped in politics: Ariston, his father, was said to be a direct descendant of the last king of Athens, while his mother, Perictone, was reputed to have been related to the famous law-maker Solon (638–558 BCE), who is credited with laying the foundations of Athenian democracy. When Plato's father died his mother remarried, to Pyrilampes, a close acquaintance of Pericles. Plato, had two brothers, Adiemantus and Glaucon, a sister, Potone, and a half-brother, Antiphone. It is reputed that Plato's birth name, Aristocles, was replaced by the nickname Plato, referring to his broad shoulders. As a child he studied music, rhetoric, mathematics and poetry at a gymnasium owned by Dionysios and Palaistra of Argos. He served and fought in the military three times between 409 and 404 BCE. In 407 he met and became a pupil of Socrates (470/469–399 BCE) who would be of central influence for the rest of his intellectual life, and whose thought is difficult to disentangle from his.

Peloponnesian War

In 404 BCE, following the defeat of Athens in the Peloponnesian War against Sparta (431–404 BCE), Plato witnessed an oligarchic revolution, led by his uncles Critias and Charmides. Many of these oligarchs, who became known as the 'Thirty Tyrants', blamed the system of democracy for the defeat. However, after their removal, Socrates was executed on the grounds of impiety and corrupting the minds of the youth. Plato abandoned politics and left Athens, travelling and studying for a dozen years or so. During his travels he first went to Megara, Theodorus in Cyrene, then to Sicily and lastly to Egypt. In Syracuse in Sicily, as well as under Archytas at Taras, in the south of Italy, he studied Pythagorean philosophy.

Steeped in politics Plato travelled to Syracuse on three occasions in the hope of educating its tyrants, Dionysius I and II, to become philosopher kings, and to facilitate an end to the malaise of the times by unifying Greece against Persian influence (Gouldner, 1967). His first visit had been arranged by Dion, cousin to Dionysius II, and a favourite disciple of Plato's and possibly an object of his love. However, Dionysus I, unwilling to listen to his advice, sold him into slavery. He nevertheless returned to Syracuse several years later. In between these visits he established the Academy in Athens in 387 BCE, one of the earliest places of higher educational learning. The Academy trained future statesmen, or 'philosopher rulers', in addition to those who would help create constitutions for future newly founded states – law-givers. Subjects taught there included mathematics, arithmetic, astronomy, geometry, music, law and philosophy. Following the Pythagoreans, numbers and ratios possessed almost a divine quality for Plato. It is rumoured that the portals of the Academy were inscribed: *medeis agometrtos esisito* ('let no one without geometry enter here'). Plato spent the rest of his years teaching and writing at the Academy. He died in 347 BCE, at the age of 80, while attending a wedding.

The Ionian and Italian Schools of Natural Philosophy

In the sixth century there emerged two schools of natural philosophy, the Ionian and the Italian. The Ionian or Milesian School is represented by Thales, Anaximander and Anaximenes, who were all natives of the same city of Miletus. In their philosophies they sought something permanent and persistent through the chaos of apparent change. For Thales it was water, for Anaximenes it was air, while for Anaximander it was not a substance as such but the balance of opposite qualities – hot and cold, wet and dry. By contrast, the Italian School was associated with the name of Pythagoras. An early form of social movement, it sought to revive a pre-existent social order whose virtues centred on austere simplicity in the individual and social cohesion within the group. Pythagoreans argued that the soul passes through various reincarnations and, as the higher, exalted part of humans, remained imprisoned in the body.

Further intellectual influences on Plato included the arguments of Heraclitus (544–484 BCE) for whom two principles were central: everything was born of strife, and everything was in constant flux.

The Ionian rationalists and Pythagoreans had focused on the natural world rather than the values of the human community. It was not until the close of the fifth century BCE that a philosophy of human conduct based on a systematic co-ordination of knowledge and theory emerged. This arose from the work of the Sophists and Socrates. Central to the former's perspective was the opposition between the concept of *physis* (nature) and *nomos* (convention). They questioned conventional beliefs and the notion of *nomos*, meaning both 'law' and 'custom'. For the Sophists, the multiplicity of *nomoi* in different cultures revealed a diversity that suggested that local customs were the product of tradition rather than of abstract unchanging principles of right and wrong. Laws and moral codes were not divine, but human made and imperfect. Thus for Protagoras, the central figure in the Sophist school, 'man was the measure of all things'.

Socrates (470–399 BCE) was undoubtedly the greatest influence on Plato's thinking and, as we noted above, it still remains unclear where the former's work ends and the latter's begins. Socrates was the son of a middle-class stonemason and a midwife who, as an Athenian citizen, fought as a hoplite soldier in the Peloponnesian War. His thinking delves into questions concerning action, morality and the best way to live for humans. According to Socrates, individuals cannot talk about acting wisely, justly or well, unless they know what wisdom, justice and goodness are in the first place, and this needs to be established. The best way to develop ideas was through the give and take of conversation – the dialectic – and the best way to educate people was to ask them a series of what appear innocuous questions (the method of *elenchus*). This usually began by pressing individuals for a definition of a term until they recognised that they did not really have an adequate answer.

A sharp critic of Athenian democracy as an ideal and actuality, Socrates argued that democratic government, in which anyone's opinion counted as much as anybody else's, could be swayed by rhetorical display within a volatile assembly. Just as an individual would ask a doctor about their health, so only he or she who knows about governing should govern. Taking the example of the useful crafts, Socrates argued that the *arête* (skill) of a shoemaker and what made them good at their job depended first and foremost on the knowledge of what a shoe was and what its use was. Given a proper understanding of the end, knowledge of the means would follow. If there was any legitimate sense in which individuals could talk about *arête* there must be an end or function which all humans have to perform. The first task was to discover what the function of man was.

Historical, Social and Political Context

Ancient Greece has often been regarded as the birthplace of Western civilisation (Rossides, 1998). However, there existed no single entity or country that could be called 'ancient Greece'. Instead, between the second half of the first millennium BCE and the first three centuries CE about 1,000 mostly small, independent city-states or *poleis* pertained (Cartledge, 2011: 4). Moreover, although cities play a central role in ancient Greece, the vast majority of the population, up to 90%, lived in the countryside (Cartledge, 2011: 2).

The Restrictions of Citizenship in Greece

By the time of Pericles (495–25 BCE) the full power of the polis derived from the people, specifically male citizens, the *demos*, rooted in the Assembly. Greek democracy entailed each male having one vote. The basic principle underlying political leadership was that no one was better qualified than anyone else – by breeding, intellect or training – to direct public policy. The Assembly met regularly, usually four times a month but more in times of emergency, in the open air on the hill known as the *Pnyx*. During Pericles' time, perhaps nearly every 10 days. Although initially a full-time bureaucracy did not exist, with much administrative work done on a voluntary basis, as the number of offices increased in public affairs it required the attention of about one-third of the citizenry: 500 boule, 6000 heliastai (jury members) sitting in people's courts known as *dicastries*, 500 wardens of the arsenal and around 10,000 citizens who performed a host of other duties. Pericles initiated payment for carrying out these administrative political duties, for example paying citizens 1 *obol* a day for service on juries.

In such a context ordinary citizens did not think of the state abstractly as a distinct generic establishment standing over them, but rather as a community of male citizens. Nor were there any hard and fast distinctions between state and society or public and private. Somewhat paradoxically, as Anderson notes 'Athens, which had known the most untrammeled democracy of the Ancient World, produced no important theorists or defenders of it' (1978: 73).

Shifts in the social structure of Athens and policies designed to reduce class tensions led to a reconfiguration rather than disappearance of class conflicts within the Athenian polis and between it and other *poloi*. The conflict between the rich and poor over taxation rested on the demos's political power in the Assembly. This in turn led the rich to oppose democracy and aim to supplant it with an oligarchy – rule by a small number of rich individuals. Economic pressures and status tensions were exacerbated by wars, especially the Peloponnesian War with Sparta. It has been argued that the Greek class system was conducive to war and that the demos was more inclined to military adventures and war since these provided much of the state's surplus from which it derived its direct economic support (Gouldner, 1967). Through war the upper classes found themselves economically drained and politically damaged, yet they needed war as a way of diverting the demos from taxing them further. Warfare was a fact of everyday life for the ancient Greeks. During the century and a half from the Persian Wars (490 and 480–79 BCE) to the Battle of Chaeronea (338 BCE) Athens was at war, on average, more than two years out of three, and never enjoyed a period of peace for over ten consecutive years (Garlan, 1976: 15).

In addition to the warrior code and martial values, various commentators have tried to identify other values important to Greek culture (Adkins and Adkins, 1998; Gouldner, 1967; MacIntyre, 1998). These include the disposition to punish one's enemies and reward one's friends; high levels of competition, which also affected interpersonal relations; a need for friends but also a crisis in intimacy (Gouldner, 1967); and envy as a normalised emotion. Greeks were also attracted to the body, to its health, its youth, its beauty, and physical prowess was associated with all-round virtue. They also foregrounded and placed great emphasis on the notion of immortality.

Slaves, Foreigners and Women in Athens

During Pericles' time about 50,000 male citizens lived in Athens. When slaves, foreigners (*metics*) women and children were included the population varied between 200,000 and 300,000 people. Neither the poorest peasant nor the richest philosopher could conceive a world without slaves since both benefited enormously from the institution. The largest individual holdings of slaves in Athens were workers in the mines; it is estimated that about 30,000 slaves worked in the Athenian silver mines in Laurium. Others were in domestic service held by Greeks. Most of the leisure class owned slaves. Plato mentioned 5 in his will whereas Aristotle had 14 when he died. At all times and in all places Greeks relied on some form of dependent labour to meet public and private needs. The ideal of being a citizen in Athens was one who could hold public office, discuss politics, vote and sit on juries. In the context of Greek values and practice, slavery was generally seen as a natural and unquestioned phenomenon in ancient Greece. The slave was seen as a non-person, an unfree body of human stock, and the chief market day for cattle was the same as for slaves. Very few challenged the moral basis of slavery. The exact number of slaves in Athens is a matter of dispute. Finley (1991: 72) argues for a figure between approximately 60,000 and 80,000 slaves. Anderson argues for a slightly higher figure of 80,000–100,000 so that the ratio of slaves to free men in Periclean Athens was approximately 3:2 and that although the slave mode of production was the central productive force in Hellenic society, other producers included free peasants, dependent tenants and urban artisans (Anderson, 1978: 21–2).

If adult males were responsible for politics, which, as Aristotle noted, required a man of leisure (*schole*), this presupposed a large amount of menial work being undertaken by slaves but also by women and foreigners. Women were not an undifferentiated mass and their position varied according to their economic and social status. Although women of all classes went to festivals and funerals, those who were citizens were expected to marry and have children but not engage in the public sphere of politics yet remain in the private sphere of the *oikos* leading spatially secluded lives. In her book *Goddesses, Whores, Wives, and Slaves: Women in Classical Antiquity*, Pomeroy notes:

> Socrates blunt dismissal of his wife Xanthippe from his deathbed and his desire to die among his male companions is a dramatic, if exaggerated, indication of the emotional gulf between husband and wife. The distance between husbands and wives extended to other spheres... While men spent most of their day in public areas such as the marketplace and the gymnasium, respectable women remained at home. In contrast to the admired public buildings, mostly frequented by men, the residential quarters of Classical Athens were dark, squalid, and unsanitary. Women stayed home not only because their work did not allow them much chance to get out but because of the influence of public opinion. Many families were likely to own at least one female slave, but even a woman with slaves was tied down by the demands of her household, husband, and infants. (1995: 79)
>
> [Republished with permission of Blackwell, from *The Blackwell Companion to Major Social Theorists*, G. Ritzer, 2000. Permission conveyed through Copyright Clearance Center, Inc]

The democratic experiment reached its peak under Pericles, and Plato wrote at a time when Athens was at a crossroads following a huge military loss in the Peloponnesian War. The war lasted over 25 years, led to the death of nearly half the population and cast a huge shadow over Athens and its cultural achievements. Plato saw all this as a consequence of democracy, amateur rule and misrule. In addition, he witnessed constant and inconclusive fighting between the numerous Greek city-states and as a result often called for Greek unity.

Against Democracy

Plato's thinking constitutes a worldview, a political vision aimed at transforming the world. However, this does not necessarily mean that his ideas and concepts are bereft of value. Wood and Wood (1978) argue that Plato's thought constitutes the ideological standpoint of a declining landed aristocracy. Prior to and following the death of Pericles, aristocratic values no longer held sway in Athenian politics, exacerbating the sense of injustice caused by the loss of large swathes of land during the Peloponnesian War. In such a context, the aristocracy became increasingly conscious of their identity and sought to distance themselves from the growing numbers of traders, manufacturers, artisans, shopkeepers and wage labourers. According to Wood and Wood they constituted:

> 'gentlemen' (*kalot kagalhoi*) and the 'better sort' (*chrestoi*) in contrast to 'bad men' (*poneroi*), prosperous business men (*agorawi*), and the *nouveau riche* of the commercial and manufacturing world or *neoploutoi*, a term beginning to be used frequently during the period. (1978: 2)

In the context of a humiliating defeat in the Peloponnesian War, Socrates and Plato as part of the *kalot kagalhoi*, or beautiful people, sought to reform and revitalise aristocratic values to provide a new foundation for civic and political life, a counter-revolutionary ideology, that although not fitting wholly aristocratic values, nevertheless shared in their condemnation of the rule of the lower classes.

That Plato and the members of his Academy were neither disinterested nor uninvolved in the practical politics of their time is illustrated by their intervention in Syracuse. The Academy was not only a teaching and research institution but, according to Gouldner (1967), the first intellectual colloquium of rational policy development. It was, Gouldner argues, 'the RAND corporation of Antiquity' (1967: 157), though such a reductionist view of Plato's political position has been challenged by others (Saunders, 1986; Euben, 1980). It has been argued that, for example, Plato was not simply a proponent of aristocratic values but championed forms of communism, austere living, and a rejection of material objects that were incompatible with an aristocratic value system.

Arguments and Ideas

The Republic (1945) is perhaps the book that captures best the breadth and depth of Plato's philosophical, political and proto-sociological outlook. In his multiple dialogues, which constitute a central modality for expressing Plato's ideas (Strauss, 1978: 52), Socrates[1] argues that governing is a specialised art or craft that, like other useful crafts (medicine, shoemaking, building, navigation), requires certain skills and knowledge that has definite ends. Governing is a practice, a sense of 'know-how', or specialised knowledge, containing excellence and virtue or what the Greeks termed *arete*. Like other crafts, the art of ruling embodies specific capacities and skills and uses them to do the best work possible to serve the interest of subjects in much the same way that a shepherd tends and cares for his sheep, or a doctor heals his or her patients. Like these crafts, it is generally done for others and not for one's own ends. Moreover, objects and individuals not only have specific functions, but also possess a peculiar excellence or virtue that enables them to work well. This applies equally to living, which is the function of the soul. Since the virtue of the soul is justice, only the just man, according to Socrates, can be happy since when the soul does not have virtue it cannot work well.

For Socrates, as for Plato, unless something is grounded in nature; it cannot serve as an objective standard and a sound basis of knowledge and action. The notion of what is 'Good', or right, is not a subjective interpretation as democratically inclined Sophists may argue, but rather an objective fact. In addition, Plato believed, some would argue naively, that if we know the Good we will automatically act according to its principles. The idea of the Good represents the most important of the Forms, and it is the theory of the Forms that underpins all Plato's thinking. The Theory of Forms constitutes his attempt to deal with the relation between universals and particulars. The tangible objects we see are debased inferior copies of unseen ideas. In this sense Plato was an idealist. Similar, though by no means identical, conceptions were later used by Weber in his notion of ideal types, Hegel in his notion of the concept, and Schutz in his notion of typifications.

The Ideal State and the Division of Labour

For Socrates humans have a multiplicity of needs and a state comes into existence in order to meet these mutual needs 'because no individual is self-sufficing; we all have many needs' (Plato, 1945: II.368). When people coalesce in a certain location to meet one another's needs, this forms a state. It is also on this basis that the division of labour develops. Although discussion of the division of labour is often attributed to Adam Smith and Émile Durkheim, it has its first systematic, though condensed, discussion, in Plato's work.

According to Plato, individuals are born with different natural capacities, aptitudes and talents that subsequently need to be developed and perfected through training. They are also naturally suited to perform one type of activity rather than many. Since 'no two people are born exactly alike', this permits them to be funnelled into specific types of job. Society and the individuals that compose it are thereby better off by restricting themselves to one trade or vocation: a farmer should remain a farmer, a craftsman a craftsman, etc. This specialisation of tasks and roles, given by nature, leads to greater efficiency and excellence: 'more things will be produced and the work be more easily and better done, when every man is set free from all other occupations to do, at the right time, the one thing for which he is naturally fitted' (Plato, 1945: II.370). Justice at the level of a city-state is thereby grounded in a such a mutually beneficial, co-operative division of labour based on differing natural aptitudes in which each individual follows just one task. When individuals follow their naturally given endowments and assume their allotted role in a complex interdependent division of labour, a just and harmonious social order ensues.

Plato's definition of political justice in the city-state is, *prima facie*, rather odd. It does not refer to behavioural criteria or individual actions. Instead, it is grounded on each individual assuming a specialised place in a structural allocation of roles based on their natural aptitude. It is based on a specific hierarchical configuration of social relations drawing on the principle of individual differentiation, of remaining in one's function and effectively 'minding one's own business' and not interfering in others – 'a man should possess and concern himself with what properly belongs to him' (Plato, 1945: IV.433). Justice, *dikaiosyne*, the state of the man who follows *dikē*, is no more than minding your own business or following the way that is properly your own, and not mixing yourself up in the ways of other people.

Embellishing this conception, Plato argues for the establishment in the Ideal state of a tripartite class-system of philosopher rulers, warrior–soldiers, and producers and merchants. Justice then is when each individual is allocated to a position within an interdependent socio-economic class order consisting of producers, auxiliaries and guardians in which each individual and class keeps 'to its own proper business in the commonwealth and does its own work' (Plato, 1945: IV.434). Some men are naturally suited to philosophising, others to fighting, and others to producing and trading things. By remaining in these fixed roles the cumulative effect is to produce the best overall outcome for society – a harmonious social order ruled by the best.

Criticism

Given *The Republic*'s influence and centrality to the Western canon and its revolutionary ideas it is no surprise to know that it has been subjected to a vast amount of criticism. The most infamous critical attack was probably that of Karl Popper, who in *The Open Society and its Enemies* (2012 [1945]), written shortly after the Second World War and the Nazi atrocities, accuses Plato of attempting to establish a totalitarian system of rule and justify its existence. Such criticism has itself been questioned as overstated, unhistorical and anachronistic for judging a work from the standpoint of modern liberal democratic societies (Voegelin, 2000; Klosko, 2012: 109). The concept of the individual as such, as a unique bounded entity, did not exist in early forms of society. Nevertheless, Popper's criticism does contain a kernel of truth to the extent that the individual's worthiness was measured in terms of how they served the city-state as a whole. Plato's belief in the benevolence of the Guardians and their ability to rule, and produce or determine who is wise and who will become a future Guardian, has also been questioned.

Aristotle also makes a number of criticisms of Plato's proposals concerning the abolition of private property. These, he argued, were unworkable since:

> the greater the number of owners, the less the respect for common property. People are much more careful of their personal possessions than of those owned communally; they exercise care over communal property insofar as they are personally affected. Other reasons apart, the thought that someone else is looking after it tends to make them careless of it. (1261b32)

Aristotle also questioned Plato's Theory of Forms, which assumed the existence of a hypothetical realm of Forms that existed independently of the real world. Reversing Plato's argument, Aristotle argued, rather than the general explaining the particular, it is the particular that gives us access to what is universal. The reality of things can be seen in the world around us, and is inherent in everyday objects, and it is from our experience of these particular things that we derive our universal concepts. Aristotle therefore criticises Plato for ignoring the role of experience in assessing knowledge and for being too preoccupied with rationalism and reasoning based on mathematics and geometry.

Aristotle

Life and Intellectual Context

The historian Geoffrey de Ste. Croix has described Aristotle as 'the greatest of ancient sociologists and political thinkers' (1981: 4). Ste. Croix continues:

> It is natural to begin with Aristotle, who was in a class by himself among the political theorists and sociologists of antiquity: he studied the politics and sociology of the Greek city more closely than anyone else; he thought more profoundly about these subjects and he wrote more about them than anyone. There could be no greater mistake than to suppose that because Aristotle was primarily a philosopher he was, like most modern philosophers, either incapable of, or uninterested in, extensive and accurate empirical investigation. (1981: 69)
>
> [Republished with permission of Cornell University Press from *The Class Struggle in the Ancient Greek World: From the Archaic Age to the Arab Conquests,* G. E. M. de Ste Croix, 1981]

Aristotle was born in the city of Stagira in Chaldice in northern Greece in 384 BCE. His father Nicomachus was the physician of King Amyntas (393–70 BCE) of Macedon, himself father of Philip II (382–36 BCE). Macedonia at the time was an oligarchy composed of kingdoms and with a huge army and population of about 800,000. As the son of a physician Aristotle was probably taught dissection and this background may have contributed to his lifelong interest in biological studies and his belief in biology as the paradigm for the sciences. Both his parents died before Aristotle reached 17. At the age of 18 he attended Plato's Academy, remaining there until he was 37. Although it is not known why he left the Academy, it may have been because of increasing anti-Macedonian feeling in Athens following the rise to power of Philip of Macedon, who opposed democracy. Aristotle moved to the court of Hermias of Atarneus located in Assus, before going to Mytilene on the island of Lesbos, with his assistant Theophrastus, in order to carry out research in zoology and botany. After marrying Pythias, Hermias's niece and adopted daughter, he was invited in 343 BCE by Philip II of Macedon to tutor his 13-year-old son Alexander, who became Alexander the Great, and to head the Royal Academy in Macedon. Returning to Athens in 335 BCE together with Theophrastus, he founded his own school, *the Lyceum*, where he taught for a dozen years or so and gathered a number of research students around him – *peripatetics*. Since he was a metic (foreigner) in Athens he was unable to own property, including land. Living in a rented house, he collected many books, which later became part of the library of the Lyceum. It was here that Aristotle composed most of his major works, many of which have been destroyed, while others remain only as fragments or in the form of sketches or lectures for his students. Anti-Macedonian resentments re-emerged after Alexander the Great's death in 322 BCE, forcing Aristotle to leave Athens for a second time and move to Chalcis. He died later the same year in Euboea from a stomach disorder.

The relation between Plato and Aristotle, his foremost pupil at the Academy, is a matter of some controversy, with some seeing him as diametrically opposed to Plato (Nisbet, 1976), while others see him as completing the project that Plato had begun (MacIntyre, 1998). There is no doubt, however, that both continuities and discontinuities exist between their writings. Some of the major differences in their understanding of the social world result from the contrasting paradigmatic models they draw on – namely, mathematics and biology, respectively.

Historical, Social and Political Context

In his representation of Plato and Aristotle in the School of Athens, the Italian painter Raphael portrays them as diametric opposites. Plato, an exponent of idealism and rationalism, holds a copy of the *Timaeus* and points upwards towards the heavens, while Aristotle, a steadfast empiricist and materialist, gestures towards the earth clasping a copy of the *Ethics*. From a sociology of knowledge perspective, it is clear, however, that both thinkers lived through what can be called the great experiment of direct democracy and were fervently anti-democratic intellectuals. Their politics differ, however, in terms of the emphasis on an anti-democratic position. To an extent this reflected the different historical situation in which Aristotle was working, in some cases writing almost half a century later than Plato. The latter wrote during the end of the Peloponnesian War, blaming democracy for the defeat of Athens and looking to the constitution of Sparta as a solution to class and Athenian international dilemmas. By contrast Aristotle, who had close ties with the Macedonian monarchy, looked to Philip II as a solution to the problems that democracy threw up. The victory of Philip as conqueror and unifier of all Hellas in 338 BCE intimated that the city-state composed of morally equal free citizens based on the rule of law and consent was on the wane and monarchical forms of constitution on the rise. As Kelsen notes with reference to the Macedonian monarchy and the Athenian polis:

> This monarchy claimed the right to establish itself over democracy, not indeed completely to abolish the latter but to strip it of its most important functions, which it arrogated to itself. Aristotle's doctrine of the state reflects most clearly this change. Only by keeping this change in view does the political significance of the Aristotelian conception of God and of the moral ideal of a purely contemplative life become comprehensible. Let it be sufficient here to recall that the glorification of the contemplative life, which has renounced all activity and more especially all political activity, has at all times constituted a typical element of the political morality set up by the ideologies of absolute monarchy. For the essential tendency of this form of state consists in excluding the subjects from all share in public affairs. (1937: 15)
>
> [Republished with permission of Chicago University Press from 'The Philosophy of Aristotle and the Hellenic-Macedonian Policy', *International Journal of Ethics,* H. Kelsen, 1937]

In a context where Greek democrats regarded political activity and freedom as connected, Aristotle's foregrounding of contemplation as the supreme value attempts to challenge this norm.

Nevertheless, they both wrote in a period of acute class conflict. Both theorists then attempt to synthesise different political systems which they confronted. For Plato this is Sparta and Athens; for Aristotle, Athens and Macedonia (Kelsen, 1937).

It has been argued that, like the writings of Socrates and Plato, Aristotle defended and provided an attempt to revitalise and regenerate the social position and values of a declining landed Aristocracy. Wood and Wood (1978) argue that if Plato was the architect of the 'anti-Polis', Aristotle was the 'tactician of conservatism' whose moderation was an ideological attempt to ensure the survival of aristocratic values. Though less excessive than Plato, he was nevertheless anti-democratic and authoritarian. Aristotle's conceptualisation of the truly happy and virtuous life is only possible for the well born and wealthy who avoid working for wages or selling goods in the marketplace. Although this again may be too reductive an analysis, it certainly points to some important aspects of Aristotle's thinking. He presupposed and naturalised slavery and its existence as a given, unable like many thinkers to transcend his social and political horizons. A slave belongs to his master *tout court*: 'any human being that by nature belongs to another whenever, in spite of being a man, he is a piece of property i.e. a tool having a separate existence and meant for action' (Aristotle, 1254a9). In effect, the slave is a mere 'animate tool' (*empsychon organon*) or talking tool (*instrumentum vocale*).

Challenging the view that slavery is a convention based on force, Aristotle instead saw it as an outgrowth of a natural process. There are always rulers and ruled and this is necessary both in nature and in society. The slave has the function to use his or her body and to be directed by the mind and reason of the master.

In an extraordinary rationalisation and justification of slavery as an economic institution, and given his teleological and functional view of the world, slaves he argued are born physically strong, with curved backs to work in fields. This contrasted with their master's upright stature required for political discussions:

> It is then, nature's purpose to make the bodies of free men to differ from those of slaves, the latter strong enough to be used for necessary tasks, the former erect and useless for that kind of work, but well suited for the life of a citizen of a state, a life which is in turn divided between the requirements of war and peace. (Aristotle, 1998: 1254b16)

Arguments and Ideas

Metaphysics

In his *Metaphysics* Aristotle, as we have noted above, criticised Plato's Theory of Forms from an empirical perspective. The form of a thing was not just a sum of the physical characteristics pertaining to it, but also included what it *did* – its function (*ergo*). By studying and observing specific plants and animals in nature, Aristotle developed a more rounded picture of what makes them similar and different to other plants or animals. Such a comparative method points towards *empiricism* – knowledge depends upon what we can see.

Just as a craftworker gives a piece of wood form by making a table according to a plan, or an aim or end, so too does nature work according to a plan or end. Aristotle posits, however, a fundamental difference between the change in artificial objects, which comes from outside the objects themselves, and the change in nature, which comes from within. Nature (*phusis*) not only is complex and highly efficient, but also works towards an end, that is towards a purpose or *telos*. For example, an acorn has a natural and constant tendency to become an oak, a lamb to become a sheep, a puppy to become a dog. In each case what is *actual* – a puppy – will change according to a inherent *potentiality* – becoming a dog. All things not only move towards ends but also have a purpose that they are designed to serve. A chair has the purpose to allow us to sit, a cup to drink from, a house to provide shelter. By knowing a thing's purpose, we can understand it in terms of how good or bad it is in terms of its function – a good chair is comfortable, a bad cup leaks, a warm house provides shelter, etc. This allows us to move from description to making judgements or normative explanation about a thing in terms of its excellence in fulfilling the function for which it was designed.

Teleology – the study of the ends or purpose of a thing or entity – plays a central role in all of Aristotle's thinking, especially as part of his explanation of *causality*. Everything in the world is explained by four major causes that account for why a thing exists. These are: (1) the *material* cause, what a thing is made of; (2) the *formal* cause, the arrangement or shape of a thing; (3) the *efficient* cause, how a thing is brought into being; and (4) the *final* cause, the function or purpose of a thing. In the example of constructing a house, the material cause would be the materials needed to build the house, the formal cause would be the plan or design of the house, the efficient cause would be building the house and the final cause would be to provide shelter or a home to live in.

On the basis of classifying according to observed shared characteristics and marked differences, on what makes a thing unique, Aristotle undertakes a complete classification of things from the simplest organisms to complex human beings, including objects and processes in the world – from literature and poetry to the organisation of states. The essential quality or distinctive function that differentiates humans from plants and makes them unique among animals is the fact that they have *reason*. That is, they are reasoning creatures for whom rationality underpins their actions. This places them at the top of the animal hierarchy.

The Nicomachean Ethics

Aristotle conceives ethics as part of what he calls the 'practical sciences' – which also include politics. These are separated from the *theoretical* and *productive* sciences in terms of their ends and objects. His aim in the *Nicomachean Ethics* is not to teach for the sake of knowing, which is the aim of the theoretical sciences, but a practical aim, so that men can lead good, happy, lives. It is to tell people how to act in the world, akin to providing a skill as in artistic production. The methodology and approach used in the practical arts must be also commensurate with the subject matter being dealt with. Here scientific precision and exact knowledge are, for Aristotle, impossible since 'noble and just actions' exhibit 'much variety and fluctuation' so that one can only 'speak about things which "are only for the most part true" that is roughly and in outline' (Aristotle, 2014: 1094b).

It was noted earlier how the principle of self-sufficiency was a central value in Greece. Drawing on his principle of hierarchy, Aristotle argues that the highest good must be wanted for itself, and not as a means to something else; it must be self-sufficient, and lack nothing. Although all actions aim at some purpose or good, some goods or ends are means for seeking higher goods or ends, of which one is the final chief good, 'that for whose sake of everything else is done' (Aristotle, 2014: 1097b).

It is, he argues, generally agreed by both 'the general run of men and people of superior refinement', including Plato, that the ultimate goal of all our actions is happiness so that people identify 'living well and faring well with being happy' (Aristotle, 2014: 1095a19). In Greek the term *eudaimonia* has a much broader objective connotation than the modern subjective notion of happiness, and can also be translated as flourishing, blessedness, living well (*eu zên*) or fulfilment, which imply behaving well and faring well in terms of physical, material and psychological well-being. Happiness is the supreme good because it is chosen for its own sake and not for the sake of something else, and all other goods are chosen to achieve it. It is in other words a first principle, for it is for the sake of happiness that we do everything else.

Humans need to fulfil their 'rational element' to its maximum 'since man is born for citizenship, he is a *politikon* zoon (political animal)' (Aristotle, 2014: 1097b). Here Aristotle introduces a crucial sociological concept: of humans as fundamentally social and political beings. The terms 'born for citizenship' can also be translated as 'is a political animal' and the term 'political' also encapsulates what in modern societies we would refer to as 'social'. Humans also possess the capacity for language, which allows them to communicate and reflect on what is just and unjust.

The importance of happiness and virtue does not reside in the state of mind of the individual, but in his or her *activity* or practice, since virtue in the mind can produce no 'good result'; it is akin to a man being asleep or inactive. It is only by doing just acts that someone can become just, and temperate acts become temperate. For Aristotle the life of those who lead a virtuous life will also be a pleasant life since pleasure is a state of the soul.

Aristotle, while acknowledging happiness as ' a virtuous activity of soul, of a certain kind' (2014: 1099b), does, however, presuppose the existence of a certain amount of sufficient resources which he refers to as 'proper equipment' or 'external goods' – instruments for carrying out noble actions. These include material goods and wealth, power and friendship. Moreover, the absence of certain things or qualities diminishes one's happiness; this includes good birth, goodly children and beauty. Happiness, though it requires a degree of 'study and care', also requires an element of chance and good fortune in life.

According to Aristotle, individuals need to act 'in accordance with correct reason', more specifically, than they do so by choosing to act in accordance with a mean, rather than incorrect or inappropriate feelings. The 'mean' refers to a rule or principle of choosing actions appropriately in different situations based on a criterion that avoids two opposite extremes: one of deficiency and the other of excess. For example, courage constitutes the virtuous mean between cowardice and rashness. This emotionally laden social skill of acting according to the mean, that is the ability to do the right or the appropriate thing in each different circumstance, is generally acquired through habit, upbringing and practice rather than learned through explicit teaching. Having devoted a large part of the book to discussing the importance of moral virtues and the importance of practical wisdom in realising these, Aristotle concludes, perhaps as a result of countervailing political reasons, by arguing that the happiest life is not one centred on an ethical life of practice and activity, as found in democracy, but on a life devoted to contemplation and study (*theorie*). It is in fact the life of a philosopher.

The Politics

Aristotle begins *The Politics* by discussing the state as the highest form of association, aiming at the highest of all goods. He offers a hypothetical theory of state formation rooted in nature and teleological explanation, as the final and highest form of association that is self-sufficient. The private counterpart to the public association of citizens – the *polis* – that aims at securing the good life, is the household – *oikos* – which meets daily needs, and a collection of which constitutes a village. In the household, the man as master naturally dominates the women as he does the slave and children. This contrasts with the domination in the political sphere, which is by free individuals or citizens over one another both through their acquiescence and through just law (Frisby and Sayer, 1986: 15).

There is, for Aristotle, a natural and unnatural way of acquiring a good or object. Though they share with animals the acquisition of goods from their surrounding environment, humans also possess different ways of living through their natural productive labour: as nomads who move with their domesticated animals; as hunters and pirates; and by agriculture. Some peoples combine all three types of existence. Just as these modes of acquisition are given by nature, so too is the food chain. This includes acquiring animals, but also other peoples; war itself is a result of nature.

There is, however, a second method of acquiring goods. In what was to become central to Marx's argument in his distinction between use-value and exchange-value in *Capital*, Aristotle argues that pieces of property have a double use, one of which is the proper use, the other for exchange. For example, a shoe can be put on a foot, its proper use, or become an object of exchange, an improper use. The latter emerges as a result of the mutual needs of many individual households having too much of one good and not enough of the other. Exchange is not contrary to nature since it aims to re-establish nature's own equilibrium of self-sufficiency. It is on this basis that money-making arose. Trade was initially a simple affair but became more complex as people became aware of where the greatest profits could be made from exchanges. However, when trade goes beyond the self-sufficiency required by a community it becomes unnatural since the unlimited acquisition of wealth becomes an end in itself for some people.

For Aristotle the constitution is the citizen-body and constitutions can be distinguished according to the numbers of those who rule. Hence in democracies the masses are sovereign while in oligarchies it is only the few. There are three correct constitutions which can be differentiated in terms of numbers and that aim at the common good – *monarchy* (kingship), *aristocracy* and *'polity'*. In the first one man has virtue; in the second, the best few rule; in the last, some, but not all rule since it is difficult for a large number to gain virtue except in military terms. Corresponding to these there exist three deviant constitutions that aim at the private advantage of the rulers – tyranny, *oligarchy*, and *democracy*. These constitutions are ranked with hereditary monarchy being the best, aristocracy next, followed by polity, democracy, oligarchy, with tyranny rooted at the bottom. However, Aristotle then modifies this view of constitutions by arguing that we in fact need to look at economic factors for distinguishing constitutions rather than simply numerical criteria: 'what really differentiates oligarchy and democracy is wealth or the lack of it. It inevitably follows that where men rule because of the possession of wealth, whether their number be large or small, that is oligarchy, and when the poor rule, that is democracy' (Aristotle, 1998: 1279b26).

Criticisms

Aristotle's work has been criticised in a number of respects. His analysis of causal and functional explanation has been seen as especially problematical. It is not clear why he assumes animate and inanimate objects, including humans, only have one unique function. His theory of ethics and acting in relation to the golden mean has also been criticised for being too vague since it may tell us that the right acts are between two extremes but little else, or more precisely it fails to guide how individuals ought to act in actual situations. His analysis in the *Nicomachean Ethics* also has Greek aristocratic values and virtues underpinning it (MacIntyre, 1988).

His politics has also been criticised for its discussion of slavery and its naturalisation. However, these were views shared widely in Greek society at the time. There is also a vacillation running throughout his political work between a desire to emphasise the importance of politics and political activity for humans as part of their rational aspect on the one hand, which is central to democratic thinking, and a desire to emphasise the contemplative life (Kelsen, 1937).

Contemporary Relevance

The influence of Plato and Aristotle on Western thought has been profound. This is in a two-fold sense. In a general sense their ideas have filtered down to pervade Western forms of thinking in art, literature, politics and philosophy, and in Aristotle's case physics and biology.

PLATO'S PHILOSOPHER KINGS

In *The Republic*, Plato elaborates a theory of expert rule by 'philosopher kings' as an alternative to majoritarian democracy. Through the Ship of State metaphor, governance is likened to the command of a sea-going vessel, such that only those suitably qualified should be considered fit to captain. The implication is that public rule is a less effective steering mechanism than knowledgeable leadership, and that ruling requires suitable skills. The ideal statesman is thus a specially trained philosopher, dedicated to the good of the city-state rather than political ambition. As an enlightened ruler, the philosopher king courts true knowledge over the whims of the masses. This exceptional leader should then be granted absolute power, safeguarded by his virtuous, benevolent and incorruptible character. Fundamentally anti-democratic, this idea was influential in the Roman Empire, with Marcus Aurelius approximating the ideal, as well as in early modern monarchical Europe. Today, the idea of enlightened leadership is carried in the ideology of technocracy, which advocates governance by technical experts rather than elected officials.

In a more particular sense, their ideas were central to the teachings of classics which most nineteenth- and some twentieth-century sociologists undertook as part of their educational training. Those who we consider today as the paradigmatic sociological thinkers, for example, Marx, Weber and Durkheim in their discussion of alienation, rationalisation and anomie, all drew on analyses of ancient Greece and antiquity as well as critical engagements with the Enlightenment. Sometimes this was direct; in other cases mediated by the work of Hegel, Nietzsche and Montesquieu, respectively. As Ste. Croix notes:

> Marx read extensively in Classical authors, in particular Aristotle, of whom throughout his life he always spoke in terms of respect and admiration which he employs for no other thinker, except perhaps Hegel. As early as 1839 we find him describing Aristotle as 'the acme [Gipfel] of ancient philosophy' (MECW 1.424); and in Vol. I of Capital he refers to 'the brilliance of Aristotle's genius' and calls him 'a giant thinker' and 'the greatest thinker of antiquity'. (1981: 24)
>
> [Republished with permission of Cornell University Press from *The Class Struggle in the Ancient Greek World: From the Archaic Age to the Arab Conquests,* G. E. M. de Ste Croix, 1981]

Marx's critique of the market draws on Aristotle's political writings, while the development of a rational communist society, and the distinction between how things appear and how they really are, from Plato. Durkheim's discussion of the political forms of the collective consciousness draw from his understanding of the Greek Polis, his discussion of the division of labour, derive from both Plato and Aristotle, his discussion of functionalism from Aristotle, while his discussion of education is rooted in Plato. Weber's discussion of the iron cage and the difference between ancient and modern forms of commerce, and the division between reason and instincts, also draws on Greek thought. The influence of the classical thinkers on the classical sociologists was evident not only in the latter's critique of political economy, the origins of capitalism, and the formation of collective consciousness and social solidarity, but also in their science and method. All three held the role of social science to be moral – to foster self-realisation, rational discourse or democratic community. McCarthy argues:

> From this perspective, sociology is distinctive among the social sciences since its intellectual foundations rest in the remembered landscape of Attica. Modern social theory, science, and critique were formed by a synthesis of empirical and historical research methods with classical Greek assumptions about the nature of knowledge, community, virtue, political freedom, and social justice. By blending together the ancients and moderns, nineteenth century sociology became the most unusual of the social sciences because it self-consciously attempted to integrate empirical research and philosophy, science and the humanities, as no

> other discipline before or since. However, this distinctive element has been all but lost and forgotten today. (2003: 2)
>
> [Republished with permission of State University of New York Press from *Classical Horizons: The Origins of Sociology in Ancient Greece,* G. E. McCarthy, 2003]

This forgetting was a consequence not only of the Parsonian influence in the development of sociological thought, transforming it into a utilitarian, positivistic form of thought based on explanation and prediction, but also of foregrounding only Enlightenment forms of rationality. As a result an Aristotelian conception which highlights civic virtue and practical wisdom (*phronesis*) at the expense of a singular emphasis on the technical and utilitarian science (*techne*) of explanation and formal causality, disappeared.

Plato's and Aristotle's influences have not been restricted to just the classical sociologists; as we shall see they are also present in the work of modern social theorists including Foucault, Habermas and Bourdieu. For example, in the latter we see the concepts of *doxa, phronesis, habitus* and *hexis*. Their thought then is a central foil against which sociological theory develops. More recently social scientists such as Flyvbjerg (2001) have attempted to develop a contemporary interpretation of Aristotle's notion of *phronesis* by using it as a way to understand social practice and bypass readings of social science and theory, which reduce it to either *episteme* or *techne*. The social sciences deal with reflexive actors, values and interests rather than predictive theory.

Conclusion

Although ordinarily seen as philosophers, both thinkers developed what we may refer to as proto-sociological concerns in their work, especially Aristotle, who was more empirically minded. Their thought and thinking as well as the images and metaphors used have continued to influence classical and modern sociological thinking in a variety of ways. However, in order to understand their arguments and assess their explanatory power they need to be contextualised within ancient Greek society.

Note

1 In his books Socrates often expresses Plato's views in dialogue with others.

References

Adkins, L. and Adkins, R. A. (1998) *Handbook to Life in Ancient Greece.* Oxford: Oxford University Press.

Anderson, P. (1978) *Passages from Antiquity to Feudalism.* London: Verso.

Aristotle (1998) *Politics.* C. D. C. Reeve, trans. Indianapolis, IN: Hackett.

Aristotle (2014) *Nicomachean Ethics.* R. Crisp, trans. Revised edition. Cambridge: Cambridge University Press.

Cartledge, P. (2011) *Ancient Greece: A Very Short Introduction*. Oxford: Oxford University Press.
Euben, J. P. (1980) Review. *Political Theory*, 8(2), pp. 245-9.
Finley, M. I. (1991) *The Ancient Greeks*. London: Penguin.
Flyvbjerg, B. (2001) *Making Social Science Matter: Why Social Inquiry Fails and How it Can Succeed Again*. S. Sampson, trans. Cambridge: Cambridge University Press.
Frisby, D. and Sayer, D. (1986) *Society*. New York: Tavistock.
Garlan, Y (1976) *War in the Ancient World*. London: Chatto & Windus.
Gouldner, A. (1967) *Enter Plato: Classical Greece and the Origins of Social Theory*. New York: Basic Books.
Kelsen, H. (1937) The Philosophy of Aristotle and the Hellenic-Macedonian Policy. *International Journal of Ethics*, 48(1), pp. 1-64.
Klosko, G. (2012) *History of Political Theory: An Introduction, Volume 1: Ancient and Medieval Political Theory*, 2nd edition. Oxford: Oxford University Press.
MacIntyre, A. (1988) *Whose Justice? Which Rationality?* Notre Dame, IN: University of Notre Dame Press.
MacIntyre, A. (1998) *A Short History of Ethics: A History of Moral Philosophy from the Homeric Age to the Twentieth Century*, 2nd edition. Notre Dame, IN: University of Notre Dame Press.
McCarthy, G. E. (2003) *Classical Horizons: The Origins of Sociology in Ancient Greece*. New York: State University of New York Press.
Nisbet, R. (1976) *Sociology as an Art Form*. Oxford: Oxford University Press.
Plato (1945) *The Republic of Plato*. F. M. Cornford, trans. London: Oxford University Press.
Pomeroy, S. B. (1995) *Goddesses, Whores, Wives, and Slaves: Women in Classical Antiquity*. New York: Schocken.
Popper, K. (2012 [1945]) *The Open Society and Its Enemies*. London: Routledge.
Rossides, D. W. (1998) *Social Theory: Its Origins, History, and Contemporary Relevance*. New York: General Hall.
Saunders, T. J. (1986) 'The RAND Corporation in antiquity?' Plato's Academy and Greek Politics. In: J. H. Betts, J. T. Hooker, and J. R. Green (eds) *Studies in Honour of T. B. L. Webster*. Bristol: Bristol Class, pp. 200-10.
Ste. Croix, G. E. M. de (1981) *The Class Struggle in the Ancient Greek World: From the Archaic Age to the Arab Conquests*. Ithaca, NY: Cornell University Press.
Strauss, L. (1978) *The City and the Man*. Chicago: University of Chicago Press.
Voegelin, E. (2000) *Plato*. Columbia, MO: University of Missouri Press.
Wittgenstein, L. (1968) *Philosophical Investigations*. Oxford: Blackwell.
Wood, E. M. and Wood, N. (1978) *Class Ideology and Ancient Political Theory: Socrates, Plato, and Aristotle in Social Context*. Oxford: Basil Blackwell.

11

CONFUCIUS AND IBN KHALDUN

Introduction

There is no doubt that as an academic discipline sociology is a child of the Enlightenment and as such it develops and proliferates only in modernity. However, this does not mean that sociological thought emerges suddenly and out of nowhere. On the contrary, and as argued in the Introduction and Chapter 1 to this book, sociological thinking has deep roots in the ancient world. In many respects the latter-day intellectual movements such as the Renaissance, Rationalism and the Enlightenment, owe a great deal to the ancient social philosophers and scholars who provided elaborate conceptual frameworks aiming to understand and change the social world. While the traditional accounts have emphasised the role ancient Greek and Roman thinkers had in the development of social and political thought, less weight has been given to the non-European scholars. This chapter focuses on the two leading social thinkers that have made profound impacts on the development of social thought in Asia, the Middle East, North Africa and further afield. Although they lived in different time periods and in very different parts of the world, both Confucius and Ibn Khaldun have made significant marks on the rise of social thought worldwide. This chapter highlights their main contributions and historically traces the broader social contexts that shaped their intellectual development.

Life and Intellectual Context

Confucius (551–479 BCE)

Since over the past centuries Confucius has become a subject of worship and myths it is difficult to differentiate between fact and fiction in the various accounts that describe his life and work. Some sources emphasise his aristocratic lineage (a descendant of the royal Chou dynasty), others insist that he was born in poverty. There is very little trustworthy information on his childhood. Nevertheless, according to most records Confucius (full name Kong Qiu) was born in 551 BCE in Zou, the state of Lu (in today's Shandon province, China). Despite having relatively privileged origins his father's premature death confined the rest of the family to poverty. Confucius's father was an officer in the Lu military, which meant that his family were neither aristocrats nor commoners but were part of the middle social stratum (*shi*).

In addition to losing his father at the age of 3, Confucius also lost his mother at the age of 23. Struggling to avoid utter poverty he worked as a cow herder, a shepherd and later as a keeper of granaries, the director of public pastures, a book-keeper and a clerk. He married his wife Qiguan at the age of 19 and they had two children: a son, Kong Li, and a daughter whose name, indicatively, has not been recorded. Although there is no reliable information on his education the traditional sources indicate that Confucius was a bright, hardworking and inquisitive student and that he studied ritual with the 'fictional Daoist Master Lao Dan, music with Chang Hong, and the lute with Music-master Xiang' (*Stanford Encyclopaedia of Philosophy*, 2010). Upon completion of his studies Confucius became gradually known for his teachings and was apparently followed by a group of disciples. The records indicate his gradual rise in the state administration: in 501 BCE he was appointed to the relatively minor position of the town governor and through time rose to the much more influential and prestigious position of Minister of Crime. After the failed attempt to reform decentralised state power and establish a more legitimate system of aristocratic rule, Confucius created many powerful enemies and as a result was forced into self-imposed exile from Lu. From then on, he and his disciples, undertook a long and torturous series of journeys around the kingdoms of northeast and central China, spending most time in the states of Wei, Chen, Cai and Song. Although Confucius's reputation remained high and he was occasionally welcomed to the courts of these small states, his philosophical principles were largely ignored. Near the end of his life at the age of 68, as the political situation in Lu changed, Confucius returned home. His last few years were spent in teaching the Five Classics set of texts to his remaining 70 or so faithful disciples.

Although Confucianism today is a well-established, and in some parts of Asia dominant, philosophical, and some would argue religious, tradition of thought, for much of Chinese history Confucian ideas were countered by several other philosophical traditions. Among these the most influential were Legalism, Mohism and Daoism. During the Spring and Autumn period (770–480 BCE) and the Warring States period (479–221 BCE) these four intellectual traditions were competing for supremacy. Although initially Mohism and Confucianism were more prominent with the unification of China under the Qin dynasty (in 221 BCE), Legalism was adopted as the official doctrine of the state with Confucianism, Mohism and Daoism being largely suppressed.

Nevertheless, once the Han dynasty gained power over the Qin dynasty (206 BCE to CE 220), Confucianism replaced Legalism as the dominant belief system of the Chinese state and, with a few exceptions, Confucian principles remained an official state philosophy until the communist takeover in 1948.

This centuries-long symbiosis between Confucianism and the Chinese state often conceals the complexities and doctrinal conflicts that have shaped the early history of China. The Spring and Autumn period and the Warring state period were highly turbulent, violent and socially dynamic times that stimulated intellectual creativity and ultimately produced highly distinct and competing schools of thought. Even though three out of these four philosophical traditions shared some key principles such as piousness towards rulers, the glorification of Tian (the 'mandate of heaven') and respect for the hierarchical order, they developed very different understandings of social and political life. Legalism, most forcefully articulated by Han Fei and Shang Yang, is a utilitarian philosophy that emphasises stringent obedience to the legal system. In this view state power rests on the transparent and public system of laws that apply equally to all citizens.

Whereas Legalism was a doctrine that appealed to the rulers, military and traditional priesthood, Mohism become more popular with the technical intelligentsia, craftworkers and some merchants who were determined to challenge the status quo. Mozi, the founder of this ethical tradition, is often considered to be China's first philosopher. He condemned the use of offensive warfare and advocated a doctrine of 'impartial care', which was seen in utilitarian terms, long before Bentham and Mill, as something that 'will bring the greatest benefit to the largest number of people' (Mozi, 2003: 10). The concept of impartial care stands for the view that an individual should care equally for all human beings regardless of their actual relationship to that individual (i.e. one's own children should not be loved more than the children of other people). For Mozi, social conflicts arise from the absence of moral uniformity: in the original state of nature a human being cannot differentiate between right and wrong. It is the presence of the state hierarchy and especially the righteous leaders and their followers that guarantees the creation of social harmony able to balance right and wrong. Daoism (or Taoism) shares this focus on establishing harmonious relationships between human beings, but in contrast to Mohism and Legalism, Daoists oppose hierarchy and state power. For Laozi, the intellectual father of this doctrine, Dao (or Tao) is a metaphysical concept that stands for 'the way' or 'the path' behind everything that exists. It is conceived as a powerful force that generates all existence. Unlike Legalists and Mohists (and Confucians) who venerate order, discipline and division of labour, the Daoists advocate simplicity, spontaneity, moderation, humility, harmony with the nature and 'action through non-action' (*Wu-Wei*). As some sources indicate, the young Confucius was a student of Daoism and his teachings originated in dialogue with the key Daoist principles.

Ibn Khaldun (1332–1406)

In contrast to Confucius, whose biographical details are less known and shrouded in mythology, Ibn Khaldun's life and work are well documented. Although Ibn Khaldun was born in Tunis in 1332 (AH 723) his family had aristocratic, Arab-Andalusian, origins. The Banū Khaldūns were part of the ruling elite in ninth-century Seville. Ibn Khaldun's family emigrated to Tunis just before the fall of Seville in the Reconquista in 1248. While most of his male family members held political offices under the Hafsid dynasty in Tunis, Ibn Khaldun's grandfather and father abandoned politics and became members of a mystic order. This highly privileged family background allowed Ibn Khaldun to be educated by leading North African scholars and imams. His main teacher was Al-Abili, a proponent of both the rational sciences and the occult arts. In addition to classical Islamic texts, his early education included Arab linguistics, law and jurisprudence, mathematics, poetry, logic and philosophy. He memorised the Qur'an by heart and was well versed in the works of the world's leading philosophers of his time including Averroes, Avicenna, Razi and Tusi. Similarly to Confucius, Ibn Khaldun lost his parents when he was relatively young (aged 17).

For much of his life Ibn Khaldun was a skilful politician who managed to survive, and navigate, the tides of the complex, chronically unstable and unpredictable world of medieval North Africa and the Middle East. He came to age in the midst of protracted inter-dynastic conflicts in the region where loyalty to a current ruler regularly indicated a high probability of being beheaded by his successor. Ibn Khaldun started as an official at the court of Ibn Tafrakin with responsibility for calligraphic writing, marking and ratification of royal correspondence. Although this position gave him direct access to state secrets, he considered it to be beneath his talents. To further his political career he moved to the city of Fez where he worked at the court of Abu 'Inan. He was soon accused of treachery and imprisoned for nearly two years, to be released upon the king's death. The new king, Abu Salim, appointed Ibn Khaldun to several senior posts, but once the ruler was murdered Ibn Khaldun had to flee the city. Following this he spent several years as a high official at the court of Ibn al-Khatib in Grenada, but after a serious quarrel had to leave the city. For the next nine years Ibn Khaldun travelled around the Maghreb collecting tribal levies and negotiating with the various tribal groupings on behalf of several rulers. It is this period that has proved central for Ibn Khaldun's intellectual development: during one of his expeditions into the Dawawida tribal region he decided to retire to the Sufi shrine, near contemporary Mascara in Algeria, and devote his time to scholarship.

The result of his four-year retreat to this shrine was *The Muqaddimah* (1377), the most significant proto-sociological study written before the modern era. The search for more extensive library resources and ill health forced Ibn Khaldun to move to Tunis in 1378, where he spent the next four years as a teacher and scholar. The persistent court intrigues and intellectual animosities with other scholars and imams led to another period of exile – this time to Alexandria where Ibn Khaldun was appointed a grand Maliki judge at the Mamluk court of Abu Sa'id Barquaq, in 1384. During his stay in Egypt he held several high positions including the Superior at the Baibarsiya Sufi lodge and the professor of Maliki law at Quamhiyyah College in Cairo. However, most of his time was devoted to research and the writing of what he considered to be his main work, to which *The Muqaddimah* was merely an introduction – *The Book of Exemplaries and the Record of Narrative and its Principles concerning Arabs, Persians, and the Berbers, and those Nations of Great Might Contemporary with Them.* During his time in Cairo Ibn Khaldun made pilgrimages to Mecca and Jerusalem and had highly eventful visits to Damascus where he experienced the siege and destruction of the city by Tamerlane. The famous conqueror invited Ibn Khaldun to spend time in his company and to write a geographical report on North Africa. Ibn Khaldun died in 1406 and was buried in the Sufi cemetery outside Cairo's main gates.

At first glance it might seem that, unlike Confucius whose ideas developed in a protracted struggle with competing schools of thought, Ibn Khaldun was an intellectual loner removed from the leading scholarly networks of his day. Some commentators insist that because he was 'remote from the intellectual centres' and 'without significant structural ties of his own' Ibn Khaldun's teachings had little impact on the development of Islamic philosophy (Collins, 1998: 428). It is true that, unlike Confucius, Ibn Khaldun did not have any recognisable followers and that his work has largely been forgotten for centuries (Lacoste, 1984: 1). Nevertheless, the creativity of his social thought did not emerge in an intellectual vacuum. On the contrary, for much of his life Ibn Khaldun was in a dialogue with the dominant intellectual perspectives of his time.

In his early years Ibn Khaldun was profoundly influenced by the leading logician Abelli. His education in philosophy and theology was largely built on the works of leading ninth-, tenth- and eleventh-century rationalist philosophers such as Al-Kindi, al-Farabi, Ibn Sina (Avicenna) and Ibn Rochd (Averroes). He was very well versed in historiography, which at that time was a highly developed research field in the Islamic world. In this context much of Ibn Khaldun's work represents a direct or indirect engagement with rationalist philosophy and logic, mysticism, theology and the historiography of his day. Although all his main works are rooted in the rationalist principles derived from the work of Ibn Sina, Ibn Tatmiyah, Ibn Rochd or al-Kindi, he is also a fierce critic of their philosophies. In contrast to the dynastic narratives and hagiographies that dominated the historiography of his day Ibn Khaldun advocated the development of historical science rooted in the principles of causality and rationality. For Ibn Khaldun, history is an empirical endeavour that relies upon observation with a view of generating universalist findings. History is not to be viewed as a branch of literature but 'is firmly rooted in science' (2005: 6). More specifically he distinguishes between conventional views of history and its scientific purpose:

> On the surface, history is no more that information about political events, dynasties, and occurrences of the remote past, clearly presented and spiced with proverbs. It serves to entertain large, crowded gatherings... The inner meaning of history, on the other hand, involves speculation and an attempt to get at the truth, subtle explanations of the causes and origins of existing things, the deep knowledge of the how and why of events. (Ibn Khaldun, 2005: 6)

In a similar vein to Confucius, Ibn Khaldun was deeply responsive to the dominant intellectual currents of his period. He wrote commentaries on the works of leading philosophers such as al Roushd and Razi and he was involved in stringent debates in theology, history, logic and politics. Although he too, just like Confucius, was living in times of civilisational decline characterised by continuous political and ideological conflicts, he was an heir of the highly advanced Islamic civilisation. His ideas and teachings were well known and debated throughout North Africa and the Middle East. Although the rationalist discourses were on defence as much of the medieval Muslim world was gradually moving away from rationalism towards religious mysticism, the cities Ibn Khaldun inhabited, namely Fez, Grenada, Bougie and Cairo, were still important university centres with prolific intellectual life. These intellectual disputes have found their reflection in many of Ibn Khaldun's works where he continuously attempts to reconcile his analytical rationalism with the religious mysticism that was slowly but surely gaining the upper hand all over the Maghreb and the rest of the Islamic world.

Historical, Social and Political Context

Ancient China

As Collins (1998) argues, intellectual creativity is rarely if ever a product of an individual genius. Original and influential thinking is regularly created in direct or indirect collective interaction. Scholars develop new conceptual and analytical models in dialogue with others and in many historical instances the rise of influential and competing schools of thought tend to reinforce each other. Confucianism is no exception as its key principles have developed in creative disagreements with Mohism, Legalism and Daoism. Furthermore, the new ideas also often entail the presence of historically turbulent times. In this context the origins of Confucian ideas owe a great deal to the blustery social and historical context of the Spring and Autumn and Warring States periods. In contrast to the previous age of relative stability, rooted in the dominance of the Western Zhou dynasty that was focused on fighting the 'barbarian tribes' in the north while maintaining peace among its feudal fiefdoms at home, the Spring and Autumn periods initiated a new era defined by protracted violent conflicts. When the 'barbarians' inflicted a decisive blow to the Zhou, the internal geopolitical stability crashed: from 771 BCE onwards a series of wars led to the emergence of several relatively powerful states which had managed to subdue their weaker neighbours and were competing between each other for supremacy. These two long periods were defined not only by incessant warfare and political instability, but also by organisational and intellectual creativity as the competing local powers tried to build a sturdy state and powerful military apparatuses. Hence they all attempted to recruit the best scholars, soldiers, scientists and engineers in order to achieve the ultimate military victory. In the Spring and Autumn periods the key states were Jin, Chu, Qin, Qi, Wu and Yue, most of which also controlled smaller, tributary states in the Central Plains. By the end of this period some states such as Jin had collapsed and others emerged from their ruins. Thus during the Warring States period the key players were Qin, Qi, Wei, Zhao, Han, Chu and Yan. This period was characterised by intensive military, technological and organisational developments including the invention and mass use of the crossbow, the shift from chariots to massed infantry and the establishment of efficient bureaucratic institutions (Tinbor-Hui, 2005).

By the end of the Warring States period Chinese states were world leaders in state formation and in the development of military capacity. The seven leading states were able to field massive armies and provide complex logistical systems, and establish effective bureaucratic structures capable of training, supplying and controlling hundreds of thousands of soldiers. In other words this period was defined on the one hand, by intensive warfare with an unprecedented number of human casualties and, on the other, by substantial organisational advancements, economic growth and significant bureaucratic, legislative and military reforms. Some of these developments, such as the Shang Yang reforms, were instrumental in eventually bringing about a unified and centralised authority for the whole of China. Before unification in 221 BCE, the rulers of the Qin state tended to avoid major conflicts with other states, using their unique and beneficial geographical position to build alliances, trade and play off other states against each other. It is only in the last decades of the Warring States period as the Qin evolved to become the most powerful polity that war was used as the principal device for expansion and control. From 238 BCE onwards the rulers of Qin devised a concrete strategy to conquer the other six states. The key idea behind this plan, devised by Ying Zheng, was to attack and annex each state individually along the principle of 'allying with distant states and attacking nearby ones' (Tin-Bor Hui, 2005).

Medieval North Africa

Just as with Confucius, Ibn Khaldun's intellectual project owes a great deal to the historical, political and ideological turbulence of his times. The fourteenth century was a period of protracted crisis in North Africa, a region which in many respects was unlike the rest of the medieval Muslim world. Since the large-scale rebellion of the 730s, inspired by the egalitarian heretic teachings of Kharijism, the rulers of the Maghreb were politically independent from the caliphs of Baghdad and Damascus. This autonomy was rooted in economic strength, as the region was the epicentre of Middle Eastern and Mediterranean trade for centuries. In addition the rulers of the Maghreb kingdoms controlled the gold trade as they had a monopoly on the routes to the Western Sudan's gold, destined for European and Middle Eastern merchants (Lacoste, 1984: 16). The direct consequence of this trading monopoly was the substantial growth of towns such as Fez, Tlemcen, Bougie, Constantine, Tahert or Kairouan, the centres of prominent medieval kingdoms. However, unlike the relatively centralised imperial orders of the Mamluk Sultanate in Cairo or the Ottoman Empire, the North African kingdoms were largely decentralised entities where the rulers controlled the towns and the main trading routes, while the local tribal groupings maintained a wide degree of autonomy. More specifically, unlike feudal Europe where warrior lords controlled vast swaths of peasantry and were all in turn immersed in personal vassalage relations, in North Africa the tribe was the locus of power and solidarity.

Hence, it was not individuals but 'the tribe that was subject to the chieftain who had granted the right to raise taxes' (Lacoste, 1984: 21). In this context, the power of individual rulers was heavily dependent on their ability to negotiate with the chieftains of different tribes and their power base was firmly rooted in their tribal group. Simply put, the kings were essentially tribal leaders who assumed control of a confederation of several tribes. The rise of the Almohad Empire in the twelfth century temporarily changed the political landscape of North Africa as the Almohad dynasty unified the Maghreb in 1120. The Almohad period was characterised by a degree of cultural renaissance and the establishment of new universities teaching Greek and Roman philosophy, science, geometry, astronomy and the arts, development of novel artistic and architectural forms, and advancements in jurisprudence and Islamic theology. The leading philosophers of the medieval world found their intellectual home in the Almohad Empire including such distinguished neo-Aristotelians as Averroes (Ibn Rusd), and the Jewish philosopher Maimonides. This period was remembered as the golden age of the Maghreb.

Ibn Khadun was coming of age at the time when the well-established stability of the Hafsid dynastic order was dramatically and substantially undermined by the rising Marinid dynasty, and the neighbouring Zayyanid powers, all struggling to establish entire control of North Africa. Furthermore the inter-dynastic claims within the Hafsid royal court triggered internal conflicts which led to the fragmentation of Hafsid territories under different claimants to the throne. This situation triggered a scramble for territories between different political actors including neighbouring kingdoms, distinct dynastic claimants, and nomadic and semi-nomadic tribal groupings inhabiting the Maghreb region. All these radical geopolitical changes created long-term instability with constant shifts in alliances between rival sides. More significantly, the geopolitical volatility brought about new social realities where on the one hand, no single political power could establish its hegemony and, on the other, the rulers were forced to compromise with different social groups and extend some rights and privileges to non-aristocrats. More specifically, various dynastic claimants welcomed to their courts talented individuals, some of which were without patrician credentials.

Arguments and Ideas

Confucian Social Philosophy

Confucius's ideas have occasionally been described as a predecessor of sociological thought. For example, Cho (1996: 112) argues that 'Confucianism was, in a sense, Durkheim's "moral education" and Weber's "ethic of responsibility" combined into a single set of doctrines'. However, unlike nineteenth- and early twentieth-century sociologists whose principal focus was to explain the changing dynamics of social life, Confucius's interests were more prescriptive: to identify the ultimate ethical principles that should govern human conduct. In this Confucius was not unique as nearly all pre-modern thinkers tended to privilege prescription over description and explanation. In a similar vein to Mohists, Confucianism emphasises cosmic harmony between heaven and earth (*tian*) and endeavours to establish such harmonious relationships in social life: 'This equilibrium is the great root from which grow all the human actings in the world, and this harmony is the universal path which they all should pursue' (Confucius, Chung Yung 1, 1991).

For Confucius, the key guiding moral principle was to strive towards achieving and maintaining virtuous behaviour on both the individual and collective level. In his understanding the social and political virtues directly reflect personal virtues, and virtuous society can only be composed of virtuous citizens. In this context, Confucius advocated traditional values including ancestor worship, the preservation of rituals, respect for the elders by their descendants, clearly defined filial and gender duties, and strong family loyalties. Moreover, the family was seen as the cornerstone of society and the ideal government was to resemble family relationships of love, responsibility and mutual interdependence. Nevertheless, in addition to his moral prescriptions, Confucius was also an astute social analyst who developed a highly influential social philosophy that centred on the importance of self-cultivation and discipline, topics that dominate the latter-day sociologies of both Weber and Elias. For Confucius, a superior human being is defined by his or her ability to exercise self-restraint and to engage in permanent self-cultivation. In his own words, 'the gem cannot be polished without friction, nor man perfected without trial' (Confucius, 19 in *The Analects*, 1979).

Discipline and Morality

Self-control is understood to be a precondition of individual and social development. In Confucian teachings the lack of discipline is likely to create conditions leading to corruption, abuse of power, inequity and poverty. The prosperity and well-being of a particular social order are premised on the morality and self-restraint of individuals constituting that social order. Since in this view 'the perfecting of one's self is the fundamental base of all progress and all moral development', there is a great emphasis on education. For Confucius, education involves the acquisition of knowledge which helps develop moral capacity so that individuals can recognise ethical absolutes, and strive towards creating better social order built on such absolutes. Another role of education is to stimulate self-discipline by learning how to observe and enact proper forms of behaviour. In this context, the strict observation of rites (*li*) is seen as the way to overcome the urge towards self-gratification and fulfilment of one's self-interest. Hence the performance of particular rituals is not an empty gesture that indicates one's submission to the rulers or ancestors, but has a specific and functional role: it generates self-restraint and discipline that foster individual and social development. For Confucius, sages are envisaged as the leading lights of moral cultivation. An ideal sage would be someone who constantly aspires towards ethical perfection while also guiding others on the same path towards greater virtuousness. The sage is also understood as a self-critic who espouses the particular ethical principles of Confucianism (which literally means 'the confession of literati') and as such articulates high moral standards for the entire society.

Whereas sages are conceptualised as the moral guardians of people and moral supervisors of the rulers, the gentlemen or literati, were understood to be individuals most likely to influence the everyday lives of most people. In contrast to sages who are exceptional but very rare, the gentleman is a more concrete ethical exemplar. For Confucius the gentleman is defined by his moral excellence, self-discipline and a genuine concern for the welfare of others. In this sense the gentleman is a morally superior person who can command and receive obedience on the grounds of his own morality and ability to help others: 'the nature of the gentleman is like the wind and the nature of the small people is like the grass; when the wind blows over the grass it always bends' (Confucius, 1979: 12, 19).

In this way the literati provide an indispensable service to both the state and civil society: their teachings help hold the behaviour of rulers in (moral) check while aiding the autonomy and continuous ethical development of the civil society groupings. Confucius distinguishes between the office-holding literati, whose role is to make sure that the state is governed according to high ethical principles, and the 'backwoods literati'; that is, sages without an office who act as social leaders for specific local communities (Cho, 1996: 113). Nevertheless, the gentlemen are not born as such; instead anyone has the potential to become a gentleman. In Confucian teachings the educational processes that mould individuals into gentlemen are envisaged as open to all regardless of their origin. Hence one's ability to guide others rests exclusively on one's capacity and willingness to learn and to achieve self-cultivation and self-control.

The rulers too require self-discipline and humility and are more likely to be trusted and followed if leading virtuous lives. The stability of social and political orders depends on the willingness of all citizens (including the rulers) to obey the 'rites' (*li*) and to act morally. As Confucius (1979: 87) emphasises:

> If the people be led by laws, and uniformity sought to be given them by punishments, they will try to avoid the punishment, but have no sense of shame. If they be led by virtue, and uniformity sought to be given them by the rules of propriety, they will have the sense of the shame, and moreover will become good.

Thus, in contrast to Legalism, which highlights the coercive pressure of the laws, Confucianism stresses the emotional and moral sense of responsibility: once duty is internalised, shame is a much more powerful deterrent of vice than the state's threat of violence. Confucian social philosophy perceives social order through the prism of well-established hierarchies where every individual and social strata fulfil their requisite role to the best of their ability.

For Confucius self-discipline ultimately leads to benevolence. In his own words: 'To discipline self to fulfil the rites is benevolence. The day when self-discipline fulfils the rites, all under heaven would be with benevolence. Indeed, the practices of benevolence originate from self and not from others!' (Confucius, 12: 1). Confucian social philosophy prioritises refined and morally superior judgement over knowledge and skill even when that knowledge involves the advanced command of existing rules. Confucius's ideas give clear primacy to organisational form and group morality over knowledge and individual freedom.

Ibn Khaldun as the First Proto-sociologist

Much premodern social and political thought obsessed over normative questions such as: What constitutes a good life? How can group morals be maintained? Or how can a social harmony be achieved? The tendency was also to provide moralistic, usually religiously inspired, answers to such questions. In sharp contrast to these perspectives, Ibn Khaldun focuses on the causal relations between different social processes. Instead of advocating a particular course of action, Ibn Khaldun is one of the first social thinkers who aims to explain how the social world works. Although his studies contain extensive passages that resemble religious sermons or glorify mysticism and anti-rationalism, his main contributions are uniquely couched in the language of what we would today call social science. Drawing on wide historical, geographical and philosophical knowledge, Ibn Khaldun articulated the first proto-sociological theories of state formation, power, solidarity and urban and rural dynamics. Moreover, *The Muqaddimah* is often described as the first sustained work of historical science (Lacoste, 1984: 160; Schmidt, 1967).

At the heart of Ibn Khaldun's project is the ambition to explain long-term social change. In this context, he explores the macro historical processes that impact state development, violent conflicts, urban life, civilisations, religious beliefs, social stratification and power configurations. At the same time he also tackles the micro interactional social world as he assesses the patterns of group solidarity, the role family and kinship play in nomadic and sedentary groups, personality transformations, and the dynamics of sociability.

The Rise and Fall of Civilisations

In *The Muqaddimah* the author presents us with a cyclical philosophy of history that analyses the development of civilisation through the prism of a dialectical relationship between the city and the countryside, both of which are indispensable for long-term social advancement.[1] In this view civilisations gradually rise through the interdependence of two principal and distinct ways of life: (1) sedentary populations able to develop the new skills, ideas, knowledge and economic environment necessary for social development; and (2) nomadic tribes capable of providing the coercive might, solidarity and moral fibre required for the establishment, protection and long-term stability of a particular civilisation.

More specifically, he argues that nomadic warriors are the only group capable of founding or conquering the new states. The social sources of their military might stem from their unique lifestyle: a generally frugal and disciplined existence, sturdy and functional military organisation, and intense bonds of kinship and solidarity. The rigours of nomadic life, perpetual involvement in the violent conflicts, loyalty to their chieftains and tight group attachments enable tribes not only to establish states, but also to maintain the stability of state rule. While the tribal cohesion generates military power and security, city life remains crucial for economic productivity, day-to-day governance, and social and cultural development. Although the nomadic warriors are good at conquering lands, protecting and policing towns, they are quite feeble at generating 'luxury goods, clothing, sophisticated cuisine, refined pleasures, relatively sumptuous houses, and social accomplishment' (Lacoste, 1984: 96). Hence a prosperous and stable civilisation entails a symbiotic relationship between the two principal social strata – tribal warriors and urban dwellers.

Nevertheless, as civilisations advance, they also sow seeds of their own demise. As Ibn Khaldun (2005: 296) emphasises: 'The goal of civilization is sedentary culture and luxury. When civilization reaches that goal, it turns towards corruption and starts being senile, as happens in the natural life of living beings.' Since the state's stability is grounded in asceticism, moral purity, tribal solidarity and loyalty, once the tribal warriors settle in towns their frugality and social cohesion evaporate and they slowly, but surely, become corrupted by the luxuries of sedentary life. Hence all civilisations undergo cyclical transformations with periodic growth, expansion and inevitable decline.

For Ibn Khaldun the rise and fall of civilisations is determined by the complex social relationships rooted in the changing political dynamics. In his view the durable social order entails not only coercion, but also a substantial degree of group solidarity. Life outside the state is dependent on the social cohesion of lineage, kinship and deep friendships. The nomadic tribes living in inhospitable environments where there is a chronic shortage of food and water and constant dangers of raiders, carnivorous animals and natural disasters would not be able to survive without strong group attachments. In his own words: 'Those who have no one of their own lineage feel affection for their fellows. If danger is in the air ... such a man slinks away... Such people, therefore, cannot live in the desert' (Ibn Khaldun, 2005: 98).

Group Feeling

One of Ibn Khaldun's central concepts is *asabiya*, meaning a strong group feeling, often associated with unity, group consciousness, social cohesion and intense solidarity. Although it is frequently rooted in kinship or tribal lineage, it is not reduced to 'blood relations'. On the contrary, for Ibn Khaldun *asabiya* refers to a 'capacity for collective will-formation and commitment to sustained action', which is not necessarily linked with one's family ties but can also include a sense of attachment that resembles blood relations (Arnason and Stauth, 2004: 34; Ibn Khaldun, 2005: 264). As Gellner (1981: 27) emphasises, '"blood" is neither a necessary nor sufficient condition of cohesion; it is merely a way of *talking* about it'. This is explicitly stated in *The Muqaddimah*: 'The affection everyone has for his clients and allies results from the feeling of shame that comes to a person when one of his neighbours, relatives, or a blood relation is in any way humiliated' (Ibn Khaldun, 2005: 273). *Asabiya* is expressed as the intense, mutual interdependence, affection and willingness to help one's comrades. It involves a close-knit group solidarity, unity and determination to sacrifice for one's tribe, clan or a circle of friends and neighbours. As such it generates particular group dynamics often articulated as a superior organisational might: 'Group feeling produces the ability to defend oneself, to protect oneself and to press one's claims. Whoever loses his group feeling is too weak to do any one of these things' (p. 289). Moreover, strong *asabiya*, often created and reinforced in war and military struggle, is the principal source of political power and authority.

As Ibn Khaldun makes clear in one of his most quoted sentences, 'Leadership exists only through superiority and superiority only through group feeling.' In other words, social cohesion generated on the battlefields and in the harsh living conditions of North African deserts fosters a unique form of solidarity, which is an essential prerequisite for political power. Ibn Khaldun identifies the strength of *asabiya* as a crucial reason why the various imperial armies had difficulty in conquering Maghreb lands. In contrast to the Spain and Egypt of his times, which provided little resistance as 'they are now free of tribes and group feelings' (p. 334), the Maghrebian Berber tribes who possess a high degree of *asabiya* were able to repel the imperial powers. *Asabiya* provided a mechanism for social cohesion, and hence military prowess, that no conqueror could easily destroy.

In this context, intense group feelings also tended to overpower other sources of identification, including religion. Although nearly all of the fourteenth-century North African tribes were pious Muslims, when directly confronted to choose between their tribal solidarity and the Islamic universalism of *umma*, the tendency was to opt for the former over the latter. Whereas the cities were the cradle of this civilising universalism, the countryside, was the beacon of diversity and civil virtue.

For Ibn Khaldun the tribal warrior vs. urban dweller dichotomy is at the heart of historical change. The urban centres generate economic growth, prosperity, civilisational refinement, religious and cultural development, but none of these advancements would be possible without the political stability and military protection provided by the tribal warrior groupings. Furthermore, unlike the tribal countryside, which is characterised by a defence-intensive egalitarianism of frugal and uncertain living, urban life is more comfortable but also deeply stratified and hierarchical. Paradoxically, the origins of this social stratification are to be found in the previous conquests of tribal warriors.

It is no coincidence that the cities were regularly established, conquered and ruled by dynasties of militarised tribes and clans. The rulers establish their legitimacy through lineage with the particular tribes, and maintain their power through their tribal links and group solidarities. In other words, *asabiya* is not only a form of group cohesion but also a means of political power exercised by the tribal chiefs. Relying on this social device of group unity, the rulers impose their power in the cities. Nevertheless, as social hierarchies develop and grow in the urban environment, they undermine the egalitarian principles that underpin tribal social cohesion. It is a strong *asabiya* that allows the warrior tribes to acquire military might and it is this same cohesive quality that fosters political domination. However, as social solidarity is built in the harsh conditions of the countryside, once the tribal warriors settled permanently in the cities, the building blocks of social cohesion gradually erode. As the ruling groups embrace a life of luxury, stability, certainty and abundance their moral principles tend to change. Once the rulers lose their tribal ties and become highly corrupt, their political and ideological power is destabilised, leading to internal dissent and ultimately providing conditions for those new tribal invaders who are eager to establish their own dynasty.

Contemporary Relevance and Applications

There is no doubt that Confucius's teachings had much more impact on the state policies and the social behaviour of millions of people, than those of Ibn Khaldun. For one thing Confucianism was an official state doctrine of China for more than 2,000 years. From the second century BCE (during the Han dynasty) until 1948, Confucian teachings were institutionalised as the principal state narrative and as such were integral to the system of education that reproduced the civil service structure of Mandarin bureaucrat scholars who were crucial for the shape of the Chinese state for centuries.

For another thing, in much of East Asia, Confucianism gradually developed into something akin to a religious doctrine and as such it has deeply influenced the behaviour of ordinary individuals for many generations. Even though the Chinese communists were initially hostile to what they regarded as a profoundly conservative ideology, recent years have witnessed a major re-evaluation of Confucius in communist China. The consequence of this top-down revision within the Communist Party of China is much more space being given to Confucius's teachings in the mass media, educational system, cultural diplomacy and even popular culture. The fact that Confucianism has a large and strong following throughout East Asia and continues to influence the behaviour of hundreds of millions of people would indicate that its contemporary relevance is enormous.

SOCIOLOGY, MODERNITY AND EUROCENTRISM

The critique of Eurocentrism reflects the need to go beyond established sociological perspectives in pursuit of a truly cosmopolitan sociology suited to contemporary globalised societies. That classical sociology was justified in assigning world historical significance to specific developments in European societies is not disputed. Instead, the critique of Eurocentrism problematises the generalisation of Western perspectives over other forms of knowing, with its implicit assumption of cultural superiority and exaggeration of difference. This is perhaps most pernicious in the postulates of modernisation theory, as it was developed in the 1950s. With the contemporary field of post-colonialism spearheading movements to 'decolonise' the literature and enable the voice of the subaltern to be heard, sociology may yet embrace non-European forebears.

However, while Confucian teachings have a substantial impact, as a form of state policy and society-wide cultural practice, these ideas had less impact on the development of social science in general and sociological analysis in particular. Although scholars have utilised Confucian concepts and principles to articulate a neo-Confucian sociological tradition (Seok-Choon et al., 2011; Cho, 1996); the deeply normative character of Confucius's writings has prevented development of an original and vibrant sociological school of thought.

In contrast, Ibn Khaldun's contributions have inspired generations of scholars to use and refine his original proto-sociological models and apply them to a variety of social contexts in the contemporary world. Hence scholars have made use of his theories of state formation to analyse the rise and fall of civilisations in Africa, Asia, the Middle East and further afield (Alatas, 1993, 2007, 2014; Arnason and Stauth, 2004; Ortega y Gasset, 2000 [1976]; Gellner, 1981). Furthermore, Ibn Khaldun's concept of *asabiya* has retained much of its sociological relevance throughout the centuries and as such has been deployed to explain the dynamics of social cohesion in North Africa, the Ottoman Empire, Safavid Iran, Syria and Saudi Arabia among others (Abir, 1987; Alatas, 1990, 2014; Gellner, 1969, 1981) as well as to analyse the transformation of micro-level solidarities through time (Al-Azmeh, 1997; Lacoste, 1984; Malešević, 2015). More recently scholars have applied Khaldunian arguments to specific contemporary contexts ranging from issues such as the political legitimacy in Morocco (Cory, 2008), the contrasting state development trajectories in Algeria and South Africa (Wylie, 2008) and the social sources of the political disintegration in post-Gaddafi Libya (Elkeddi, 2015). The recent political fragmentation of Libya is particularly instructive in the sense that a Khaldunian-type analysis can help us explain the speed and direction of this unprecedented state collapse. The regional experts have emphasised how Gaddafi-era Jamahiriya was a rentier state that fostered re-tribalisation as a mechanism to maintain a hold on power. Thus instead of establishing organisational channels for the political participation of Libyan citizens, Gaddafi replaced the existing organisational structures with direct ties to the tribal leaders (Tabib, 2014). Hence, the Libyan polity had a very feeble organisational core while local power remained in the hands of the tribal chefs. Consequently, the collapse of the Gaddafi regime was paralleled by state fragmentation along tribal lines, with the paramilitary units representing different tribal groupings, just as Ibn Khaldun would predict. Ibn Khaldun's work has also been used to explore the social dynamics of the frontier experience within and outside the Islamic cultural sphere (Newby, 1983).

Criticisms

Both Confucius and Ibn Khaldun were scholars of a pre-modern world and as such their ideas reflected in part their own times. Judging from a safe historical distance one can easily dismiss their contributions as being patriarchal, staunchly elitist, overly moralist, or state-centric. However, this type of criticism would be ahistorical in a sense that it would apply contemporary moral yardsticks to the ancient past. A much more beneficial form of critique would be to assess how sociologically adequate are the concepts and ideas developed by Confucius and Ibn Khaldun. In other words, can we still deploy some of these ideas to understand the social world? In this light it seems that Ibn Khaldun has to offer more than Confucius. While Confucius provides some insightful analyses on the social origins of virtuous behaviour and on the role of self-discipline in the development of society-wide civility, much of his work is deeply prescriptive rather than analytical.

One could argue that Confucius makes a significant sociological contribution in a sense that he traces some specific social processes such as the moral capacities of social orders through time, or the way he identifies particular social types such as the sage or the gentlemen. However, as his focus is almost exclusively on moral guidance rather than on explanation, his contribution never reaches the level of a fully fledged sociological analysis. For example, when he explores the role of rituals in social life his focus is not on how ritualism contributes to social cohesion as such, but rather on what the performance of rituals does to one's own moral cultivation. These issues are clearly addressed in his statements that emphasise continuous ethical self-development: 'Ask yourself constantly, What is the right thing to do?'; 'those who are firm, enduring, simple and unpretentious are the nearest to virtue'; Or 'to practice five things under all circumstances constitutes perfect virtue: these five are gravity, generosity of soul, sincerity, earnestness, and kindness'. While these moral prescriptions have enduring moral value, they do not offer sociological tools to understand how the social world works.

Moreover, Confucius's overemphasis on the role of individual responsibility and the lack of engagement with the social structure has generated a great deal of criticism. Hence South Korean scholar Kyong-il has been particularly critical of the Confucian notion of filial piety. This concept, which stands for the virtue of respect for one's fathers, elders and ancestors, has been described as deeply conservative and hierarchical and in this sense poses an obstacle to social change (Sun Lim & Soriano, 2016; Riegel, 2013).

Although Ibn Khaldun provides a sociologically more robust conceptual apparatus, he too was not immune to critical assessments. There are three types of criticism levelled against his approach. Firstly, some scholars have focused on his epistemological and methodological contributions. Here the central issue is a deep tension between rationalism and mysticism that characterises his main work, *The Muqaddimah*, and is also present in his other publications. Ibn Khaldun's rationalism is notable in his approach to the social development of cities, his analyses of state formation, dynastic rises and falls, and the broader civilisational changes as well as his studies of group solidarity. However, this rationalist approach that centres on causal relationships is often countered by regular bouts of mysticism that fill many pages of his work. For example, in *The Muqaddimah* he criticises the hagiographic and myth-making-oriented historical scholarship by emphasising the centrality of 'the factual proofs and circumstantial evidence' (2005: 23) while denouncing logic as a mechanism to understand the origins of social relations: 'The philosophers say that happiness consists in coming to perceive existence as it is, by means of logical arguments. This is a fraudulent statement that must be rejected' (2005: 402). Some scholars argue that Ibn Khaldun cannot resolve the inherent tension between faith and reason, while others criticise his nominalism, which does not allow for an explanation of the particular from the general (Alatas, 2014: 161; Brett, 1972).

Secondly, Ibn Khaldun's cyclical theory of history has been challenged by much of post-Enlightenment social science that subscribes to more linear models of social change. The theories of social cycles in history have been popular over the centuries and have been recently revived with the development of new mathematical models of socio-demographic cycles (Turchin, 2010; Turchin & Hall 2003). Nevertheless, most pre-Enlightenment cyclical models do not make room for the theory of evolution and as such cannot account for a substantial degree of biological linearity that underpins more recent cyclical models of history.

Thirdly, and sociologically most importantly, Ibn Khaldun's theories of social change have been criticised as insufficient to explain the complexity of social relations outside of the Maghreb and the pre-modern Islamic world. For example, Gellner (1981: 88–9) argues that Khaldunian theoretical models are excellent but only applicable to a specific time and place: Ibn Khaldun 'was the sociologist of Islam; notably of Islam as manifested in the arid zone, an environment which encourages tribalism by favouring nomadic or semi-nomadic pastorialism and which hinders centralising political tendencies'. In this context his theory of group solidarity is perceived to be valid for what Durkheim called 'mechanical solidarity' of small pre-modern groups but not adequate to account for the multifaceted nature of 'organic solidarity' that develops in the industrialised era. Some have also questioned the psychological postulates of Khaldunian arguments (Ritter, 1948). However other scholars have argued that although Ibn Khaldun could not envisage the emergence of modernity, his micro-sociology is still relevant and helps us understand micro-group dynamics in the modern world (Malešević, 2015; Alatas, 2014).

Conclusion

Together with most other social sciences, sociology has often been labelled as being deeply Eurocentric (Connell, 2007; Bhambra, 2007). In some respects this is true as the conventional sociological canon consists solely of European scholars (Marx, Durkheim, Weber or Simmel) and much of the sociological theorising over the past two centuries was produced by Europeans (or their descendants), for Europeans, and espousing a particular preoccupation with very European concerns. Moreover, sociological research has often benefited from the legacies of colonialism and imperialism and some non-European intellectual contributions have been deliberately ignored. However, as Hall (2001) and McLennan (2015) rightly argue, some of the post-colonial and de-colonial critiques also romanticise indigenous intellectual traditions and offer a rather static view of the contingent and contradictory historical processes. In this context one should not focus on recovering the non-European intellectual traditions just for the sake of some kind of quasi-equal representation or as a lazy form of political correctness. Instead sociological contributions should be analysed and judged on their intellectual merits. Both Ibn Khaldun and Confucius qualify easily on this account: while Confucius's social philosophy has established a foundation for the analysis of complex social relations between the state and society and as such has influenced millions of individuals throughout Asia, Ibn Khaldun is the true pioneer of comparative historical sociology.

Note

1 This section draws in part on Malešević (2015).

References

Abir, M. (1987) The Consolidation of the Ruling Class and the New Elites in Saudi Arabia. *Middle Eastern Studies*, 23(2), pp. 150–71.
Alatas, S. F. (1990) Ibn Khaldun and the Ottoman Modes of Production. *Arab Historical Review for Ottoman Studies*, 1–2, pp. 45–63.
Alatas, S. F. (1993) A Khaldunian Perspective on the Dynamics of Asiatic Societies. *Comparative Civilizations Review*, 29, pp. 29–51.
Alatas, S. F. (2007) The Historical Sociology of Muslim Societies: Khaldunian Applications. *International Sociology*, 22(3), pp. 267–88.
Alatas, S. F. (2014) *Applying Ibn Khaldun: The Recovery of a Lost Tradition in Sociology*. New York: Routledge.
Al-Azmeh, A. (1997) *Muslim Kingship: Power and the Sacred in Muslim, Christian, and Pagan Polities*. London: I. B. Tauris.
Arnason, J. P. and Stauth, G. (2004) Civilization and State Formation in the Islamic Context: Re-Reading Ibn Khaldun. *Thesis Eleven*, 76(1), pp. 29–48.
Brett, M. (1972) Ibn Khaldun and the Dynastic Approach to Local History: The Case of Biskra. *Al-Qantara*, 12, pp. 157–80.
Bhambra, G. K. (2007) *Rethinking Modernity: Postcolonialism and the Sociological Imagination*. Basingstoke: Palgrave Macmillan.
Cho, H. (1996) The Confucian Tradition of Civil Society as a Rich Terrain for Sociological Discourse. In: S. Lee (ed.) *Sociology in East Asia and its Struggle for Creativity*. Seoul: ISA, pp. 54–68.
Collins, R. (1998) *The Sociology of Philosophies: A Global Theory of Intellectual Change*. Cambridge, MA: Harvard University Press.
Confucius (1979) *The Analects*. London: Penguin.
Connell, R. (2007) *Southern Social Theory: The Global Dynamics of Knowledge in Social Science*. Cambridge: Polity.
Cory, S. (2008) Breaking the Khaldunian cycle? The rise of sharifianism as the basis for political legitimacy in early modern Morocco. *Journal of North African Studies*, 13(3), pp. 377–94.
Elkeddi, O. (2015) The fragility of the Libyan entity. *Lybia Prospect*. https://libyaprospect.com/2015/12/the-fragility-of-the-libyan-entity
Gellner, E. (1969) *Saints of the Atlas*. London: Weidenfeld & Nicolson.

Gellner, E. (1981) *Muslim Society*. Cambridge: Cambridge University Press.
Hall, J. A. (2001) Confessions of a Eurocentric. *International Sociology*, 16(3), pp. 488–97.
Ibn Khaldun (2005 [1377]) *The Muqaddimah: An Introduction to History*. Princeton, NJ: Princeton University Press.
Lacoste, Y. (1984) *Ibn Khaldun: The Birth of History and the Past of the Third World*. London: Verso.
Sun Lim, S. and Soriano, C. (2016) *Asian Perspectives on Digital Culture*. London: Routledge.
Malešević, S. (2015) Where Does Group Solidarity Come From? Gellner and Ibn Khaldun Revisited. *Thesis Eleven*, 128(1), pp. 85–99.
McLennan, G. (2015) Is Secularism History? *Thesis Eleven*, 128(1), pp. 126–40.
Mozi (2003) *Mozi: Basic Writings*. B. Watson, trans. Columbia, CO: Columbia University Press.
Newby, G. D. (1983) Ibn Khaldun and Frederick Jackson Turner: Islam and the Frontier Experience. *Journal of Asian and African Studies*, 18(3–4), pp. 274–85.
Ortega, Y. and Gasset, J. (1994 [1976]) *The Revolt of the Masses*. New York: W. W. Norton & Company.
Riegel, J. (2013) Confucius. *The Stanford Encyclopedia of Philosophy*. Summer edition. E. N. Zalta, ed. [online]. Available at: https://plato.stanford.edu/entries/confucius/ (Accessed 20 June 2019).
Ritter, H. (1948) Irrational Solidarity Groups: A Socio-Psychological Study in Connection with Ibn Khaldun. *Oriens*, 1(1), pp. 1–44.
Schmidt, N. (1967) *Ibn Khaldun: Historian, Sociologist and Philosopher*. New York: AMS Press.
Seok-Choon,L. Woo-Young, C. and Hye Suk, W. (2011) Confucian Ethics and the Spirit of Capitalism in Korea: The Significance of Filial Piety. *Journal of East Asian Studies*, 11(2) (May–August), pp. 171–96.
Stanford Encyclopedia of Philosophy (2010) https://plato.stanford.edu/ (Accessed 20 June 2019).
Tabib, R. (2014) *Stealing the Revolution: Violence and Predation in Libya*. NOREF Report [online]. The Norwegian Peacebuilding Resource Centre. Available at: https://www.clingendael.org/publication/stealing-revolution-violence-and-predation-libya (Accessed 20 June 2019).
Tinbor-Hui, V. (2005) *War and State Formation in Ancient China and Early Modern Europe*. Cambridge: Cambridge University Press.
Turchin, P. (2010) *Secular Cycles*. Princeton, NJ: Princeton University Press.
Turchin, P. and Hall, T. D. (2003) Spatial Synchrony Among and Within World-Systems: Insights from Theoretical Ecology. *Journal of World-Systems Research*, 9(1), pp. 37–64.
Wylie, D. (2008) Decadence? The Khaldunian cycle in Algeria and South Africa. *Journal of North African Studies*, 13(3), pp. 395–408.
Yung, Confucius Chung (1991) 'The Doctrine of the Mean'. Available at: http://www.acmuller.net/con-dao/docofmean.html.

III

TOCQUEVILLE AND MARTINEAU

Introduction

Sociology emerged as a fully fledged academic discipline at the end of the nineteenth and beginning of the twentieth century. However, a number of influential and creative thinkers provided sociological analyses of social reality long before the official birth of sociology as a discipline. Among these rare early analytical contributions two stand out – Alexis de Tocqueville and Harriet Martineau. Unlike many of their contemporaries, who were preoccupied with normative concerns and were still deeply imbued with the traditional understanding of social order, Tocqueville and Martineau opened new vistas for the sociological analysis of the world they inhabited. They were the pioneers of comparative historical sociology and also initiated the new methodological tools ranging from participant observation and ethnography to archival and documentary research techniques. In this chapter we trace the wider social context in which their work developed and we look at their biographies, historical and intellectual environment of their time. We also analyse their key contributions to sociological theory and then look briefly at the contemporary relevance and criticisms of their work.

Life and Intellectual Context

Tocqueville

Alexis Charles Henri Clérel, Viscount de Tocqueville, was born in Paris in 1805. His aristocratic family descended from Norman nobility and were loyal to the pre-revolutionary *Ancien Régime*. His parents were imprisoned after the French Revolution and were scheduled to be guillotined but narrowly escaped death by Thermidor. However, most of Tocqueville's close relatives had been killed during the Reign of Terror. This family tragedy had a profound impact on the young Alexis and probably influenced his perception of revolutions and popular rule.

Before the French Revolution Tocqueville's father was an officer in the Constitutional Guard of King Louis XVI and during the Bourbon Restoration (1814–30) was made a prefect and a noble peer. Since nearly all of their close family members were killed, the Tocquevilles inherited substantial properties and were a very wealthy family. However, as former nobility the family was largely isolated and excluded from the social and political life of the new regime. Furthermore, the chronic instability of post-revolutionary France was also reflected in the ever-present fear among the former aristocrats that they could be imprisoned and killed at any moment, so the possession of wealth also contributed to anxiety (Siedentop, 1994: 2). Young Alexis grew up in this environment of isolation and distrust. This was particularly pronounced during his school years when he experienced the pervasive hatred of aristocracy among fellow middle-class pupils. Initially he and his two older brothers were educated at home by the family friend and priest Abbe Lesuer, who encouraged Alexis's literary interests and provided him with Jansenist-inspired Catholic books. He attended the Lycée Fabert in Metz between 1817 and 1823 and during this period was keen on befriending middle-class pupils in order to integrate better into the new social order. At the school he also lost his religious faith and became a highly sceptical individual.

In 1823 young Alexis went to study law in Paris and after graduation became *juge auditeur* in the courts at Versailles. In 1831 his lifelong friend Gustave de Beaumont and Tocqueville were sent on a mission by the government to examine prisons in the United States. During this nine-month trip the two ex-noblemen travelled throughout the United States and Canada with Tocqueville taking extensive notes and recording his observations that would later serve as research material for his first book *Democracy in America* published in two volumes in 1835 and 1840. Upon his return from the United States Tocqueville resigned his magistrate post and decided to become a professional writer. The first volume of *Democracy in America* was a bestseller and attracted attention and recognition throughout Europe and the United States. The consequence of this literary success was Tocqueville's election to the highly prestigious Academie des Sciences Morales et Politiques at the young age of 30. Throughout the second half of the 1830s and the 1840s Tocqueville embarked on several exploratory trips including Ireland and England in 1835 and Algeria in 1841 and 1846. These research trips provided a wealth of information for his subsequent writings.

Tocqueville entered political life in 1839 and was elected a member of the Chamber of Deputies for the Manche department (Normandy). He represented this region until 1851 and as a parliamentarian was disliked by the left and the right-wing deputies as he advocated political positions that crossed the conventional left–right spectrum. For example, he was in favour of abolitionism and free trade while also supporting King Louis Philippe I's colonisation of Algeria. In 1849

Tocqueville briefly entered Odilon Barrot's government as Minister of Foreign Affairs. In this role Tocqueville found himself acting contrary to the views he professed in his books. Hence he approved laws restricting political freedoms including the free press and the rights of association as well as the activities of social and political clubs. He also supported the arrest of demonstrators and advocated the introduction of emergency measures during the June 1849 insurrection of Paris workers. Tocqueville was briefly arrested for protesting against Louis Napoléon Bonaparte's 1851 coup and after this episode retreated from political life. For the rest of his life he was opposed to the imperial rule of Napoleon III and was hoping that the Bourbon dynasty would eventually be restored to power. Tocqueville contracted tuberculosis and died in 1859 aged only 53.

Harriet Martineau

Harriet Martineau was born in Gurney Court, Norwich, England in 1802. She grew up in an affluent household of eight siblings with a textile manufacturer father and a mother whose parents were sugar refining industrialists and grocers. Martineau's father was also Deacon of the Octagon Chapel. The family was descended from French Huguenots and all were devoted Unitarians. In her biography Martineau emphasises that she did not have a close relationship with her mother, who was a traditionalist and disliked her daughter's intellectual pursuits. However, both of her parents were committed to the view that their children required good education. Initially the children were educated by private tutors and after that Martineau went to Bristol for further education.

For much of her life Martineau was hampered by ill health. As a child she lost the sense of smell and taste and as a young women she largely became deaf and had to rely on the help of an ear trumpet. Her brother Thomas, who encouraged Harriet to write and who was very close to her, died in 1824. Two years later her father died and by 1829 the family's textile business collapsed. With the loss of the family business there was no continuous source of income and Martineau decided to combine needlework with writing to support her family. She started writing early and by 1821 published anonymously several religious-themed articles in the Unitarian periodical, the *Monthly Repository*. Her articles were well received and she was paid to write regularly for this periodical. The members of the Unitarian Association were so impressed by her work that she received three essay prizes and soon became an established freelance writer. Her editor at the *Monthly Repository* commissioned her to write a series of popular short books aimed at illustrating and making accessible the ideas of economics and other social sciences to a wider audience. The first book in this series, *Illustrations of Political Economy* (1832) was a fictional narrative that summarised and explained the ideas of Adam Smith. This book quickly became a bestseller and outsold well-established authors such as Charles Dickens (Postlethwaite, 1989). With the unprecedented success of this book Harriet agreed to write a series of shorter stories on a similar theme.

By this time Harriet had settled in London and had also written other publications including 'Poor Laws and Paupers Illustrated'. In 1834 she travelled to the United States and lived in New York until 1836. There she supported the abolitionist movement and experienced hostility from the anti-abolitionists. In 1837 she published a book *Society in America*, which is now regarded as one of the pioneering sociological studies that utilises analytical methods. Over the next few years she became highly prolific and published a variety of books – novels, travelogues, biographies, children's stories, and sociological and historical treaties. Among the most successful were the best-selling novel *Deerbrook, The Hour and the Man*, the biography of Haitian leader Toussaint L'Ouverture, *Forest and Game Law Tales* and *The Playfellow*. In 1846 she toured the Middle East visiting Syria, Egypt and Palestine. The result of this trip was a travelogue published in 1848, which received a great deal of attention. Martineau argues in this book that religion was destined to evolve towards universal atheism. The book was followed by another critique of religion, 'Letters on the Laws of Man's Nature and Development', where she challenges and ultimately rejects religious beliefs. In 1853 Martineau published a highly influential sociological contribution, 'The Positive Philosophy of Auguste Comte', that includes a translation and creative explanation of Comte's work. At the end of her life she became more involved in political activities, supporting various feminist groups and petitions of universal suffrage. Harriet Martineau died of bronchitis in 1876 aged 74.

Historical, Social and Political Context

Both Tocqueville and Martineau lived in the same historical period – the first half of the nineteenth century. Although Martineau lived much longer, her intellectual activity was shaped by very similar early to mid-nineteenth-century social changes that took place in Europe. For one thing, this was a highly unusual moment in European history as with the exception of the Franco-Prussian War of 1870–1, there were no major wars fought in Western and Central Europe between 1815 and 1914. The mass slaughters and destruction of the Napoleonic Wars (1803–15) gave way to more sporadic and short-term conflicts involving either imperial 'policing' interventions or intermittent conflicts between smaller European states. However, this is not to say that the coercive powers of states were in decline as all major European countries were involved in the conquest and colonisation of Asia, Africa and the remaining territories in other parts of the world.

Furthermore, the Great Powers were also involved in several large-scale conflicts that took place on the periphery of Europe, such as the Greek War of Independence (1821–9) and the Crimean War (1853–6). Nevertheless the absence of protracted violent conflicts in Europe created fertile ground for economic and social development.

Hence this period is now associated with the rapid scientific and technological innovation that sparked the First Industrial Revolution. The early nineteenth century witnessed an unprecedented number of new inventions, including the Jacquard loom, the battery, gas lighting, the steam engine, the tin can, the balloon, matches, Portland cement, the electromagnet, the typewriter, the sewing machine, the telegraph, the revolver and the vulcanisation of rubber. These new discoveries revolutionised the nature of manufacturing, trade and industry. Thus by the 1820s many European industries had shifted from hand production to machine production and were able to utilise steam power and new machine tools to dramatically increase their outputs. These new technologies were especially deployed in the textile industry, which soon became the main sector for capital investments, employment opportunities and profit maximisation.

The early to mid-nineteenth century was also characterised by growing urbanisation. In the leading industrialist countries such as England and Holland, industrialists were in need of and had ultimately acquired large grazing fields for sheep whose wool was used in textile production. In this process of enforced 'enclosure' many small farmers became landless and as a consequence moved to newly industrialised cities such as Liverpool, Manchester, Amsterdam or Antwerp. As the textile industries expanded they were in need of and could absorb a large-scale labour force. However, the deeply exploitative nature of these early capitalist enterprises generated sharp class polarisation and ultimately gave birth to trade unions and labour movements. This was a period of pronounced class conflict characterised by periodic mass strikes, demonstrations and unrest throughout Continental Europe.

Social Changes

Urbanisation and industrialisation changed the character of social relations. The traditional, aristocratic and highly hierarchical social order was being challenged by new ideas and new social movements. France and the United States experienced a revolutionary change of government driven by the Enlightenment-inspired social movements that advocated moral equality of all human beings. However, since both the French and American Revolutions were led by middle-class representatives, once in power, these groups were reluctant to extend various social and political rights to other groups – women, manual workers, peasants or ethnic and religious minorities. Although the UK did not have a political revolution, it too was under pressure to change its traditional structure of governance. Hence the early to mid-nineteenth century was a highly turbulent period with various social groups advocating and fighting for the extension of citizenship rights – from universal suffrage to religious liberties, freedom of expression and political organisation, a free press and free assembly, to the abolition of slavery and improved rights of women and children among many others.

Tocqueville and Martineau were both deeply influenced by these unprecedented social upheavals. Although they both originally belonged to the privileged social strata, the political and economic changes of this period affected their own personal fortunes, thus making them aware of the new social realities. Furthermore, the views of these two scholars were also shaped by the geopolitical and economic currents of the early nineteenth century. Hence Tocqueville was affected by and reflected on the political changes that took place in post-revolutionary France and America, while Martineau focused on the social and political transformations taking place in the UK and United States. Tocqueville grew up during the conservative Bourbon restoration under Louis XVIII and Charles X (1814–30), was a young man during the liberal constitutional monarchy of Louis Phillippe I and was politically active during the Second Republic (1848–52). He also experienced the 1848 revolutions which toppled authoritarian governments throughout Europe. These revolutionary upheavals, rooted in part in the protracted economic recession and food shortages linked to several years of bad harvests, mobilised public discontent against the monarchies. Hence, in France, Louise Phillippe I was forced to abdicate and the revolutionaries proclaimed the Second Republic. However, the revolutionaries had very little in common as the middle-class representatives were concerned with electoral reform, while socialists such as Proudhon and Blanqui, advocated the establishment of a socialist republic that would introduce social welfare reform and also abandon its imperialist ambitions. These inherent political tensions escalated in the Paris working-class insurrection in June 1848, which was ultimately crushed resulting in 1,500 dead workers. The Second Republic was proclaimed in September 1848 when the new constitution was ratified, introducing universal suffrage and the separation of powers. Nevertheless, the new republic proved fragile as its newly elected president, Charles Louis Napoleon Bonaparte, staged a *coup d'état* in 1851 and established a Second Empire. Early nineteenth-century France experienced rather uneven modernisation with Paris developing as a world centre of commerce and luxury goods while the rest of France slowly caught up.

Industrialisation

Martineau experienced a rather different social environment as England was the pioneer of industrialisation, urbanisation and economic development. As industrialisation expanded it contributed to unprecedented population expansion: while in 1801 the UK had around 9 million inhabitants, by the end of the century there were over 40 million people including the large waves of migration from Ireland and abroad. The ever-increasing urbanisation changed the residential structure and by 1851 more than half of the British population lived in urban areas.

In 1830 the reformist Whigs gained power and introduced a number of social and political reforms including bills on eliminating inequalities in parliamentary representation, and extending voting rights, developing child labour laws, improving conditions for women workers, and the abolition of slavery in all British land possessions in 1834. The new government also attempted to tackle the pervasive poverty generated by rapid industrialisation and the 'enclosure' of farms; that is, the displacement of the peasantry and their migration to the cities. Thus the Poor Law (1834) established workhouses for 'able-bodied paupers' thus reducing the costs of poor relief and removing many poor individuals from the streets. However, such policies also stigmatised impoverished groups and fostered greater class resentment. While the rising trade unions and the labour movement attempted to negotiate better working and living conditions for the urban proletariat, their focus was more on men than women. Not only that, women had no right to vote or be elected in the early nineteenth century and also had little or no representation within the unions. Working-class women tended to be employed as servants (i.e. maids, cooks, cleaners, etc.) and as such received little political visibility.

Martineau was dedicated to the cause of abolitionism and has written extensively about this issue during her life, particularly during her two-year stay in the United States. She saw slavery as both immoral and economically irrational, a waste of labour and capital. She took an active part in the abolitionist movements both in the UK and United States. Furthermore, Martineau was also deeply affected by the gender inequalities of early to mid-nineteenth-century Europe. She wrote extensively about the unequal position of women in education, the workforce, political rights and personal dignity.

Arguments and Ideas

Democracy and Civil Society

Tocqueville is rarely listed among the founders of sociological thought, yet his concepts, ideas and in-depth social commentary indicate the presence of a highly developed sociological type of analysis. In some respects, just like Ibn Khaldun, Tocqueville was a sociologist before sociology was established as an academic discipline. This is apparent in his most influential book, *Democracy in America*, which challenges the traditional political analyses which focused on the government through the prism of law and state authority. Instead Tocqueville shifts his analytical gaze towards society and attempts to explain the American mode of governance through the changed character of its society. The book opens with a bold proclamation: 'A new political science is needed for a world itself quite new.' By this he meant that the American Revolution fostered the development of a novel mode of social order where the equalising of social conditions entailed the emergence of a different type of state and society – both of which derive their legitimacy from the idea of popular rule.

For Tocqueville, in the United States, the balance of power was shaped by the balance of property. In his view this was a society where the dominant ethic was built around the highly individualist notions of hard work and financial success. He saw US society as exceptional in having no legacy of aristocratic rule, which created an egalitarian social universe where ordinary people do not acquiesce to the political elites: 'Among a democratic people, where there is no hereditary wealth, every man works to earn a living... Labor is held in honor; the prejudice is not against but in its favour' (Tocqueville, 1998: 247). In his understanding, democratisation fosters a degree of societal homogeneity where the majority of the population subscribes to similar 'middling' values of hard work and economic success. For Tocqueville, these different structural conditions generate different forms of social order in Europe and the United States. While in the latter most people developed an aspiration to climb the social ladder and in this context were focused on making more money, which would allow them upward social mobility, this was not possible in Europe. As Tocqueville explains, in the traditional aristocratic orders chasing financial success was not a recipe for social advancement as the lower social classes had no access to money-making jobs and the upper classes inherited wealth and despised the 'new rich' as vulgar individuals lacking class and refinement.

Tocqueville was impressed by the resilience of US civil society. He was puzzled by the absence of centralised authority and the lack of a strong state apparatus in the United States. He noted that decentralised power can operate successfully in a democratic society as long as there is no pronounced class polarisation. In his view, unlike Europe, which is hindered by the deep legacies of class conflict, the United States lacks class consciousness. For example, whereas in France social distinctions are visible not just in the economic or political domain but also in terms of cultural tastes and status hierarchies, in the United States most (white) citizens do not feel very different from each other. In this context everybody, except for racial minorities, becomes a member of the middle class. This unusual class structure fosters a greater degree of social cohesion and contributes towards the development of civil society networks.

Although Tocqueville finds the US system more effective in balancing power and preventing tyrannical rule, he also identifies organisational weaknesses of the democratic model of rule including the questionable quality of the rulers and the possible tyranny of the majority. Simply put, for Tocqueville democratic rule often fosters populist politics that rewards mediocrity over knowledge and skill. In a democracy politicians compete for votes and public support and in order to maximise their chances of election they appeal to the lowest common denominators to attract the widest possible audience. Hence, those elected to the highest political offices often lack expertise and wisdom. For Tocqueville this situation curbs the development of new ideas and free thinking. Furthermore, since democracy is based on majority rule it can also oppress minorities. Once public opinion becomes an omnipotent force it can tyrannise all those who do not subscribe to the majority view. A democratic social order can also breed conformism where citizens prefer to centre on 'a relaxed love of present enjoyments' and constant 'circling for petty pleasures' instead of focusing on long-term projects and the future of their society.

Democracy in the United States combines sociological insights with normative evaluations. Tocqueville's sociological eye focuses on identifying what makes US society different from others. Thus he explores several causal links including the civic political structure, distinct religious tradition, environmental conditions and other social factors. He also zooms in on the character of everyday life in US towns and villages and analyses the role that education, market relations and the mass media play in influencing the social behaviour of Americans.

In particular Tocqueville identifies three key factors that have made American democracy possible: (1) the unique environmental conditions of North America; (2) the cultural traditions of the original settlers; and (3) the role of positive laws. Firstly, the geographical location of the North American continent with its boundless fertile 'empty' land provided the initial impetus for the European migrations and made many migrants substantial landowners. The presence of an almost unrestricted frontier where new settlers could push the boundaries of the new state in the search for land, contributed to the perception of the United States as a land of unlimited possibilities.

Secondly, the cultural habits and mores of the first settler communities have shaped the character of a new American polity. Tocqueville emphasises the significance of Protestant religious tradition and the middle-class background of the early English settlers who valued egalitarian principles of organisation. Moreover, strong Protestant religious commitments stimulated belief in the moral equality of all human beings, which in turn contributed towards popular recognition that freedom is one's birthright. In his view there was a 'wonderful alliance' between religion and liberty among the settler communities in New England. Finally, the early establishment of laws that regulate inheritance shaped the organisational stability of the new democratic polity. For Tocqueville the legal system was central in establishing property relationships and also shaping family structures. While formal equality before the law was crucial in maintaining a stable social order, the inheritance regulations prevented the development of large-scale landed property ownership commonly found in Europe.

The Social Origins of Revolution

While democracy in the United States charts the post-revolutionary experience of a new social order, Tocqueville's other influential book, *The Old Regime and the Revolution* (1856), explores the social conditions of pre-revolutionary France. Although the French Revolution is often depicted in terms of a complete break with the past, Tocqueville argues that this is not the case. Instead, despite the post-revolutionary rhetoric of democratisation and decentralisation of power, post-revolutionary France retained a centralised power structure that in some central respects resembles the *ancien régime*. In other words, Tocqueville identifies strong similarities between the patterns of governance exhibited in in pre-revolutionary royal absolutism and the revolutionary Jacobinism and post-revolutionary imperial politics.

To explain this continuity, he points to the social origins of centralised power in France. For Tocqueville, unlike the United States where people 'were born equal rather than having to become it', in France the traditional social order rested on the established feudal hierarchies of masters and servants, united through the social mechanisms of reciprocal interdependence. Even though the leaders of the French Revolution emphasised the egalitarian character of this event and framed the revolution as a movement for political transformation and social reform, the long-term outcome was rather different – the further centralisation of power. In his interpretation the revolution destroyed not only the ancient regime's mode of governance, but also the social networks that underpinned that order – the provincial assemblies, religious institutions, corporations, village communities and variety of intermediate groupings. This destruction of the social order generated cross-class discontent and many individuals lost their social role. In his view this individualism breeds atomisation thus making despotism possible.

For Tocqueville a simple equality which is not built on the virtue of liberty and active participation in communal affairs is likely to lead to autocratic rule. In this context the revolution was not a catalyst of unprecedented social and political change but rather a mechanism to speed up the already initiated centralisation of power. Although both France and the United States developed republican forms of government, their organisational structures remained very different: while in the United States the basis of economic and political life resides in private individuals who are actively and democratically involved in communal affairs, in France economic and political activities are initiated and co-ordinated by the central authorities. Hence, whereas the United States has a bottom-up system of governance, both pre-revolutionary and revolutionary France operate a top-down system of rule. The revolution changed the dominant ideology and the ruling elite but it did not change the top-down system of state and society organisation. In his own words, 'all the Revolution did would have been done without it; it was only a violent and hasty process with whose help the political state was adapted to the social state, the deeds to the ideas, and the laws to the customs' (Tocqueville, 1856: 129).

Tocqueville argues that the French Revolution was not caused by rampant poverty but, instead, came about following a protracted period of relative prosperity followed by a brief period of economic recession. More specifically he emphasises not the economic factors but the changing perceptions of social reality. Although eighteenth-century France experienced the ever-increasing centralisation of power, the *ancien régime* also attempted to reform and provide better economic conditions for its citizens. This situation contributed to increased expectations among many groups. Hence it was the unmet rising expectations of different social strata that triggered the social uprisings leading to the revolutionary outcome. The modest reforms centred on improving economic conditions fostered a greater demand for political reforms too. While the peasantry were focused on achieving social equality the bourgeoisie centred on attaining liberty too.

Although *Democracy in America* and *The Old Regime and the Revolution* have been his most influential books, Tocqueville's comparative sociological analyses are also discernible in his other writings including the *Report on Algeria* (1847), *Journeys to England and Ireland* (1835) and the *Memoir on Pauperism* (1835). His observations on Algeria reveal his understanding of imperialism. While he was a firm supporter of the French imperial project, his writings also indicate a more nuanced view of imperial rule. For example, on the one hand, he advocated the conquest of Algeria, while on the other hand, he was opposed to complete colonisation and the use of indiscriminate violence. He argues that the control of Algeria is necessary to restore French national pride after several military defeats and in this way raise its international standing. However, the conflict in Algeria is also understood by Tocqueville as a way out of the rampant individualism and obsession with the 'material pleasures' that beset post-revolutionary France. He saw external colonisation as a mechanism of internal social integration that would spur national solidarity and a shift from materialist individualism towards collective altruistic deeds. Nevertheless, the *Report on Algeria* is also critical of the traditional imperial strategies as employed in the European conquest of the American continent. He argues that one can avoid violent responses and protracted wars by treating the indigenous populations differently to what was done before.

However, this benevolent attitude towards the natives was not based on some higher ethical considerations, but largely on the view that the use of indiscriminate violence is counterproductive. In this context he differentiates between colonisation and dominance where the focus of the former is on securing control of the passageways and roads that allow the exploitation and transport of resources, while the latter is about direct control of the entire colony. In Tocqueville's view colonisation has the upper hand over dominance and hence the imperial policy is meant to prioritise the Strait of Gibraltar and the Port of Algiers over the rest of Algerian territory. In his writings on Ireland he is much more critical of colonialism. He visited the Irish countryside during the Great Famine and witnessed its devastating consequences.

Tocqueville's most controversial publication is *Memoir on Pauperism* (1835), which reflects on his experience of visiting English working-class areas. In this work he argues that the introduction of middle-class suffrage together with the enactment of the Poor Laws, both of which were aimed to make English society more equitable, had, in fact, the opposite effect. He contends that the Poor Laws did not end poverty but have actually created an underclass of paupers. The book focuses on the unintended consequences of legal charities and insists that any attempt to legalise the welfare protection of vulnerable groups will inevitably increase the numbers of such individuals and create social discontent among those who contribute to their financial support.

Political Economy and Capitalism

Just like Tocqueville, Harriet Martineau was a sociologist before sociology became an established academic discipline. Furthermore, she too shared Tocqueville's interest in comparative historical analysis, and also in making social analysis accessible and relevant to everyday social and political life. In this context she regularly combined scholarship with literary works, thus making her publications comprehensible to a wider audience. At the start of her career Martineau produced a series of short and highly accessible illustrated books that summarised and assessed the most influential economic and political theories of her time. These *Illustrations of Political Economy* proved very popular as they offered a succinct description and analysis of the work produced by Adam Smith, David Ricardo, James Mill and Thomas Robert Malthus among others.

Her early contributions were pioneering in several ways – she was not only highly knowledgeable, but also capable of communicating up-to-date scholarship to a wider audience. She was the first women to establish herself as a leading commentator on economic and political theories, and she was also a forerunner in successfully and creatively merging fiction with social science in order to influence and shape public opinion. These early publications also had a significant influence in linking political economy with household economy and making her readers, including other women, aware of the general social and economic patterns that shape everyday life. In addition to these popular illustrative works, Martineau has also written several other contributions that focus on explaining the social dynamics of laissez-faire capitalism, which dominated the nineteenth-century Victorian world.

Nevertheless, Martineau's main sociological contributions include two books published in the 1830s: *Society in America* (1837) and *How to Observe Morals and Manners* (1838). The first book tackles a similar problem to the one that Tocqueville attempted to address – how are US social norms and political institutions different from their European counterparts? However, while Tocqueville focuses on the legacies of different revolutionary experiences in France and the United States, Martineau explores whether US society has 'fulfilled the promise of its historic constitution'. She is adamant that the US democratic order has realised many of its stated ambitions but was not successful in addressing the status of slaves and women. *Society in America* provides a comparative analysis which is rooted in ethnographic research and participant observation that Martineau undertook during her two-year stay there. She travelled throughout the country and also visited southern states including Alabama, Georgia and Virginia. In these journeys she observed race and gender dynamics, and argued that slavery was not only immoral but also an economically irrational form of enterprise: 'The vicious fundamental principle of morals in a slave country, that labour is disgraceful, taints the infant mind with a stain which is as fatal in the world of sprits as the negro tinge is at present in the world of society' (Martineau, 1837: 217). The book also explores gender relations and points out that in many US states married women find themselves in a position which is not much better than slavery as they have no political or property rights. Here again Martineau emphasises the functional irrationality of this situation, indicating that the full participation of all citizens is economically beneficial for the society as a whole.

Morals and Manners

Martineau's focus on the economic rationality of social progress and the universal patterns of social behaviour is also visible in her 1838 book *How to Observe Morals and Manners*. In this study she challenges the popular Victorian handbooks centred on providing prescriptions for good manners and polite behaviour. Instead, her aim is to offer a sociological analysis which moves away from the question of how societies ought to behave, towards the question of how populations actually behave in everyday life. She insists that one has to observe and study individuals and groups on their own terms in order to understand fully how societies operate. In contrast to Mary Wollstonecraft, another influential feminist of her time, who pointed out that manners should be the 'natural reflection' of morals, Martineau (1838: 47) argues that 'manners have not been treated of separately from morals in any of the preceding divisions of the objects of the traveller's observation, the reason is that manners are inseparable from morals, or, at least, cease to have meaning when separated'. However, while the topic addressed in this book is highly relevant, what really stands out is the methodological approach that Martineau develops. Her starting position is that research entails a degree of training in objective observation. Hence the principal function of the research process is not to judge different social practices but to compare and contrast them with the already known cultural patterns of behaviour. In other words, Martineau shifts the focus from normative questions towards the analytical and explanatory ambitions of a researcher keen to understand the object of her study. However, this emphasis on generalisation does not preclude one maintaining activist dispositions. On the contrary Martineau was also a committed activist and championed many different causes during her life – from abolitionism to feminism to liberalism and atheism. The point is that she distinguishes between one's role as a dispassionate and open-minded observer guided by curiosity and scholarly interests and the committed activist who might rely on the results of such research to make a rational case for social reform. In this context Martineau encourages participant observation and interactive research practices: instead of reading or listening to what individuals say about morals one has to observe how values and norms are enacted, maintained and reinforced in practice. She argues that social interaction is the key to understanding the dynamics of the social world: to find out how morals operate it is necessary to engage with different social strata and gain access not only to the public but also to the private sphere. As a precursor to symbolic interactionism and ethnomethodology, Martineau sees a research practice as a continuous encounter with everyday life. In this sense she argues that one can glean more from the study of collective representations of groups, including their daily practices, than from official proclamations about their values. For example, she was the first sociologist who identified graveyards as sites for social research: 'He will find no better place of study than the Cemetery – no more instructive teaching than Monumental Inscriptions. The brief language of the dead will teach him more than the longest discourses of the living' (Martineau, 1995 [1838]: 113). In her view social artefacts such as gravestones or monument inscriptions represent a more accurate reflection of the dominant social norms of one's time than what individuals think and say about their morals.

Although Martineau was a pioneer of interactionist research she was also a child of the Enlightenment who passionately believed in developing social science in order to use it as a guide for social reform. In this context she understood social change as an evolutionary process developing according to the linear logic of progress. Thus, she was keen to identify the general social laws that shape social orders and saw science as the most advanced tool to explain and fashion the world. The publication of Auguste Comte's *Cours de Philosophie Positive* in 1853 proved to be an important moment in Martineau's intellectual development as she was highly impressed by Comte's positivism. Consequently she translated a condensed, yet two-volume, version which was published in 1853. As stated on the cover page this was 'freely translated', meaning that Martineau offered a creative articulation with substantial interventions that built on Comte's original ideas. The translation was a major success and even Comte advised wider audiences, and his own students, to read this translation instead of his own version.

Martineau has also contributed to comparative historical sociology. She wrote *The History of the Thirty Year's Peace, A.D. 1816–1846* focusing on England in times of industrial and scientific revolution. In this book she also emphasises the role of women's experiences and evaluates various social achievements in the context of the Enlightenment-driven narrative of progress (Easley, 2011). The relevance of comparative historical analysis is also visible in her writings and travelogues from the trip to the Middle East (1846) where she explores and compares the rise of religious traditions. Although she started off as a Unitarian Christian, she gradually became sceptical of all religious beliefs, and by the early 1850s became an atheist. Her co-authored work with H. G. Atkinson, *Letters on the Laws of Man's Nature and Development*, made an eloquent case for atheism and as such caused uproar when it was published in 1851. Martineau also wrote an autobiography in 1855, which was highly unusual for a woman of her time. However, she made sure that the book was published posthumously in 1877.

Contemporary Relevance and Applications

Although both Martineau's and Tocqueville's work did not receive much attention until the second half of the twentieth century, they are now regarded as the leading social thinkers of the early to mid-nineteenth century (Boudon, 2006; Hunter, 1995; Welch, 2001). Moreover, their work has influenced several strands of contemporary thinking and has been developed and applied outside of the social sciences.

AMERICAN EXCEPTIONALISM

In his early sociological analysis of democracy, Tocqueville focused on those aspects of US society that were especially suited to this form of organisation by comparison with the European societies from which he had travelled. First outlined in *Democracy in America*, the concept of American exceptionalism continues today to allude to the unique social, cultural, historical and even geographical aspects of the society that contribute to its particular affinity with democracy. American exceptionalism suggests that these aspects shape the practical mindedness and individualism that are definitive of the American character, while also binding this character with fidelity to the civic mores of the American people.

Several influential scholars including Raymond Boudon, Jon Elster and Robert Putnam have all developed a neo-Tocquevillian approach to the study of social phenomena. Boudon (2005) emphasises the contemporary relevance of Tocqueville's methodology. He sees Tocqueville as the pioneer of methodological individualism who dispenses with the subjectivism and collectivist epistemologies that characterised most of his predecessors. In particular Boudon argues that Tocqueville develops a comparative historical analysis that aims to identify and explain specific social facts by exploring the variety of conditional rules that make these social outcomes possible. In addition Boudon praises Tocqueville's focus on the meaningful individual and collective decision making of agents. Elster (2009) pushes this line of argument further and interprets Tocqueville's work not only as methodologically individual but as one of the earliest examples of game theory and rational choice analysis. By pinpointing various passages from *Democracy in America* and other works Elster shows how Tocqueville articulates a distinct explanatory model which looks for causal mechanisms such as individual rationality, the dilemmas of collective action and the role of social beliefs in one's behaviour. Both Boudon and Elster insist that Tocqueville's work is highly relevant in understanding contemporary social realities.

While Boudon and Elster emphasise the individualist and rationalist side of Tocquevillian analysis, Putnam zooms in on the role of emotions, collective attachments and their interplay in voluntary associations. More specifically

Putnam develops a neo-Tocquevillian theory of civil society that highlights the function of social capital in the workings of civil society. Drawing on Tocqueville, Putnam argues that strong democracies entail the presence of vibrant civil societies. The presence of non-governmental organisations contributes to the development of particular attitudes, knowledge and skills that make active and informed participation in the democratic process possible. In *Democracy in America* Tocqueville emphasised that the strength of US democracy is rooted in active and participatory citizenship. As Putnam points out, active and knowledgeable participation entails a relatively high literacy rate, increased educational standards, good access to information and socio-economic development. However, while the United States has experienced a substantial increase in all of these dimensions, this in itself has not stimulated greater public participation. On the contrary, Putnam argues that the opposite happened – US citizens have become disengaged and alienated from political life and also tend not to participate in traditional social activities, ranging from church support groups, women's clubs, Boy Scouts, the PTA to bowling leagues. In his highly influential neo-Tocquevillian study, *Bowling Alone* (2000: 35), he states:

> declining electoral participation is merely the most visible symptom of a broader disengagement from community life. Like a fever, electoral abstention is even more important as a sign of deeper trouble in the body politic than as a malady itself. It is not just from the voting booth that Americans are increasingly AWOL.

For Putnam this alienation stems from weakening social capital; that is, established networks, relations and connections between people rooted in reciprocal obligations. While these networks have been increasing for much of the twentieth century, the rise of technology (i.e. television, the internet), urban sprawl and increasing workloads that put pressure on time, have undermined existing social capital.

In contrast to the contemporary revival of Tocqueville, the reception of Martineau's work was much more sporadic and uneven. While she is now hailed as one of the forerunners of sociology as a discipline and a pioneering methodologist and ethnographer, there is still little sustained engagement with her work or serious attempts to develop a neo-Martineaunian sociological perspective. Nevertheless, it is clear that Martineau's work is highly relevant for contemporary times. In particular her writings on gender and race relations as well as her methodological contributions have indirectly influenced contemporary sociology and her work has still more to offer in bringing feminism and sociological research together. For example, feminist perspectives are sometimes criticised for lacking better methodological grounding and for privileging activism over explanation. Martineau's work could address this criticism as her epistemology successfully blends explanatory ambitions with committed ethical concerns centred on the equality of different social groups. More specifically, Martineau argues that it is possible to be an ethical researcher who remains deeply committed to changing unequal social conditions while also maintaining professional distances from the objects of one's research. In other words, she insists that there is no inherent conflict between pursuing gender, ethnic or racial equality while also conducting methodologically neutral research. Martineau insists that since human beings aspire towards happiness it is this aspiration that shapes social morals and manners. Hence, one can analyse objectively existing manners and morals while also maintaining a subjective commitment towards replacing patriarchal and racist social structures with a more equitable social environment. As Lengermann and Niebrugge-Brantley (2001: 92) point out, these issues remain vital for contemporary feminist thinkers and Martineau's work anticipated these concerns, including:

> resistance to domination, moral agency, material equity and inclusivity. She focuses throughout her analysis on indicators that address this cluster of concerns; for example, she is consistently interested in the class system of a society, the relative freedom of opinion and expression, the status of women, the relation between metropolis and province, and the practice of charity.

Leading sociologists have also recognised the relevance of her methodological work. For example, Lipset (1968: 2) described Martineau's *How to Observe Manners and Morals* as 'the first book on the methodology of social research in the then still unborn disciplines of sociology and anthropology'. However, there is much more in Martineau's work that needs to be rediscovered and developed further.

Criticism

While both Tocqueville and Martineau have regularly been praised for their exceptional observational skills and insightful social analyses, their work has invited criticism from different quarters. For example, although Tocqueville's comparative sociology is sensitive towards the differences among and within France, the United States or the UK, he expresses less analytical or ethical subtlety when dealing with the non-European populations. In fact, some of his statements are deeply Eurocentric and outright racist, such as 'the Turks will always outdo us because they are Muslim barbarians'. Although Tocqueville opposed slavery and racism in the United States he supported the French imperial project and the violent conquest of Algeria. In his writings on the Algerian conflict he is explicit in the view that the natives have to be violently subjugated:

> I think that all the means available to wreck tribes must be used, barring those that the human kind and the right of nations condemn. I personally

> believe that the laws of war enable us to ravage the country and that we must do so either by destroying the crops at harvest time or any time by making fast forays also known as raids the aim of which it to get hold of men or flocks. (de Tocqueville 1847, from Richter 1963: 372)

He was also a supporter of racial segregation in Algeria, advocating for the introduction of two legislations – one for the European colonists and the other for the local Arab population. It seems some of his earlier liberal views changed over the years, and especially once he entered political life and became a Foreign Minister of France, after which he advocated a more imperialist-oriented foreign policy.

Tocqueville's greatest work *Democracy in America* has also been the subject of intense criticism. For example, Damrosch (2011), Mansfield (2010) and Wills (2004) among others have identified glaring omissions in Tocqueville's analysis of US society. They argue that much of his study is not based on his direct observations but on his own understanding of how the United States developed in the aftermath of the revolution. Hence, the book does not deal with Andrew Jackson's United States that he visited, but rather with the United States (and France) in the age of revolution. Some critics point out that in praising New England town meetings without actually attending any such meetings he accepted the federalist critiques of President Jackson without even talking to him, although Tocqueville was offered a private audience. Tocqueville also made his judgement about the dominance of religion in the United States without engaging with church leaders or visiting religious institutions or talking to any American academics. Wills (2004) points out that *Democracy in America* has very little or anything to say about the key industries of the early to mid-nineteenth-century United States – namely, manufacturing, commerce and banking. Tocqueville is also coy about the unprecedented infrastructural developments that took place in the United States at that time – the building of railroads, canals, steamships and numerous factories. During his stay he visited no factory or university.

Both Tocqueville and Martineau have also been criticised for their lack of engagement with the issue of class in the United States. They saw US society as much more egalitarian than its European counterparts. Moreover, they shared the view that the non-existence of landed, inherited aristocracy allowed for greater social mobility in the United States. However, one of their early critics, Francis J. Grund, in his satirical book *Aristocracy in America* (1839), challenges Tocqueville's and Martineau's interpretations. Grund agrees that the United States had no European-style traditional nobility but he insists that US society has created its own aristocracy that has monopolised the economic, political and cultural power of the United States. Grund (1839: 120) was adamant that this social aristocracy had more power and economic influence than European commentators acknowledged, and for this they were 'characterised by a spirit of exclusiveness and persecution unknown in any other country'. In a proto-Bourdieusian analysis Grund finds American aristocrats – represented by wealthy industrialists and manufacturers, owners of big banks, railroad tycoons, merchants and traders – to be not only economically powerful but also able to influence politics and culture. He argues that they attain influence through regular social interaction (i.e. shared social circles) with politicians at the national and state level. They also shape status hierarchies as their wealth allows them to set the tastes and fashions for US society as a whole. In Grund's view, Tocqueville's and Martineau's overemphasis of egalitarian social values prevented them from realising how important the class dimension really is in the United States. He argues that precisely because American aristocracy is not so obvious as in Europe it is more dangerous because it possesses economic, political and cultural means to dominate the entire social order.

Some critiques have also questioned Martineau's treatment of other feminist scholars such as Mary Wollstonecraft. Although she appreciated Wollstonecraft's intellectual contributions, Martineau was critical of what she saw to be the radical and romantically excessive Wollstonecraft lifestyle (describing Wollstonecraft as 'a poor victim of her passions'). While Martineau was a stern critique of gender and racial inequalities she was also a reformer rather than a radical advocate of revolutionary social change. Although she challenged many taboos of her time, some critiques see her as still being shackled by the Victorian moral world that she was a part of. In this context some contemporary feminist scholars judge Martineau to be too conservative and as such operating within a masculinist tradition: 'conceiving of her life as a model for human development, she imagined herself as a representative "man". Despite her confidence, despite her certitude, however, this representative "man" remained keenly aware of her precarious position as unrepresentative "woman"' (Smith, 1987: 126).

Conclusion

Martineau and Tocqueville were sociologists before sociology emerged as an academic discipline. They both pioneered a new mode of social analysis which did not exist before. To understand comprehensively the different historical trajectories of the United States, France and the UK these scholars had to devise new methodological and conceptual tools of analysis. Tocqueville recognised this explicitly in *Democracy in America* – 'A new political science is needed for a world itself quite new.' What he could not know is that this 'new political science' that he was proposing and developing eventually became sociology. With their subtle comparative historical analyses of different social orders Tocqueville and Martineau provided a significant stepping stone towards the development of comparative historical sociology and also were central figures in the establishment of political sociology as an independent field of study.

References

Boudon, R. (2005) *Tocqueville aujourd'hui*. Paris: O. Jacob.
Boudon, R. (2006) *Tocqueville for Today*. Oxford: The Bardwell Press.
Damrosch, L. (2011) *Tocqueville's Discovery of America*. New York: Farrar, Straus & Giroux.
Easley, A. (2011) Harriet Martineau: Gender, National Identity, and the Contemporary Historian. *Women's History Review*, 20(5), pp. 765–84.
Elster, J. (2009) *Alexis de Tocqueville: The First Social Scientist*. Cambridge: Cambridge University Press.
Grund, F. J. (1839) *Aristocracy in America*. London: Richard Bentley.
Hunter, S. (1995) *Harriet Martineau: The Poetics of Moralism*. Aldershot: Scholar Press.
Lengermann, P. M. and Niebrugge-Brantley, J. (2001) The Meaning of 'Things': Theory and Method in Harriet Martineau's *How to Observe Morals and Manners* (1838) and Émile Durkheim's *The Rules of Sociological Method* (1895). In: M. R. Hill and S. Hoecker-Drysdale (eds) *Harriet Martineau: Theoretical and Methodological Perspectives*. New York: Routledge, pp. 75–97.
Lipset, S. M. (1968) Harriet Martineau's America. In: S. M. Lipset (ed.) *Society in America, by Harriet Martineau*. Gloucester: Peter Smith, pp. 4-42.
Mansfield, H. C. (2010) *Tocqueville: A Very Short Introduction*. Oxford: Oxford University Press.
Martineau, H. (1837) *Society in America*. London: Saunders and Otley.
Martineau, H. (1995 [1838]) *How to Observe Morals and Manners*. London: Charles Knight.
Postlethwaite, D. (1989) Mothering and Mesmerism in the Life of Harriet Martineau. *Signs*, 14(3), pp. 583–609.
Putnam, R. D. (2000) *Bowling Alone: The Collapse and Revival of American Community*. New York: Simon & Schuster.
Richter, M. (1963) Tocqueville on Algeria. *Review of Politics*, 25 (1), pp. 362–98.
Siedentop, L. (1994) *Tocqueville*. Oxford: Oxford University Press.
Smith, D. E. (1987) *The Everyday World as Problematic: A Feminist Sociology*. Boston, MA: Northeastern University Press.
Tocqueville, A. de. (1856) *The Old Regime and the Revolution*. J. Bonner, trans. New York: Harper & Brothers.
Tocqueville, A. de. (1998 [1935]) *Democracy in America*. London: Wordsworth.
Welch, C. (2001) *De Tocqueville*. New York: Oxford University Press.
Wills, G. (2004) Did Tocqueville 'Get' America? *The New York Review of Books*, 29 April [online]. Available at: https://www.nybooks.com/articles/2004/04/29/did-tocqueville-get-america/ (Accessed 18 June 2019).

IV

HEGEL

It is of course unusual to include a philosopher in a sociological theory book, and, moreover, one who is not only a philosopher but also writes extensively on metaphysics. Hegel is included here for two reasons. Firstly, because his thinking had a profound influence on various sociologists including Marx, the neo-Marxists and the Frankfurt School as well as Mead, Elias and Bourdieu. Secondly, however, because his thinking in many ways is proto-sociological, straining to break out of its philosophical standpoint towards a sociological understanding of the world. As Kilminster notes: 'in Hegel one can glimpse the furthest point that it is possible to reach within philosophy before the whole framework of concepts and argument founders on the rock of the social' (1998: xii). Hegel's work contains a strong historical and processual dimension, as well as an equally rigorous emphasis on the social and relational nature of social reality and human beings. His early writings examine the social reasons for the rise of Christianity; his later work, how states are connected to society and the unfolding of freedom.

Life and Intellectual Context

Georg Wilhelm Friedrich Hegel was born in Stuttgart in 1770 into a moderately well-to-do family. Hegel's father worked as a civil servant in the Duchy of Württemberg, a small Protestant state surrounded by Catholic territories. Many generations of Hegels had been Ministers in the Protestant church and Hegel was initially seen to be following in their footsteps. Though he was to have an idiosyncratic relationship with Christianity, Protestant thinking was to have a profound influence in shaping his thought. Having acquired Latin between the ages of 5 and 7, for the next 11 years he attended the Gymnasium Illustre in Stuttgart. Here he became steeped in the values of the French and German Enlightenment (*Aufklärung*) and with the Greek and Roman classics whose civilisations were seen to represent the pinnacle of social life.

Following his studies at the Gymnasium, he attended the Tübinger Stift, which served as a preparatory institution for future Protestant clerics who would serve in the Duchy of Württemberg. At the Stift he came into contact with two formative influences: the poet Friedrich Hölderlin and the prodigy philosopher Friedrich Schelling, three years his junior. In addition to reading philosophy – Plato, Rousseau, Voltaire, Kant, Schiller, Lessing and Jacobi – he studied theology, which at that time was not regarded as a distinct discipline from philosophy. After leaving the Stift Hegel became employed as a private tutor to the children of an affluent family in Berne in 1793. Most accounts report his having strained relations with his employer and experiencing feelings of isolation in a context where Berne's aristocracy thrived on nepotism.

During this period, he envisaged himself as becoming a *Volkslehrer* or *Popular philosopher*, a teacher of Enlightenment values to the people in the hope of facilitating the emergence of a republic based on reason. Here he composed the *Life of Jesus* in 1795 and *The Positivity of the Christian Religion* (1795). With the aid of Hölderlin, Hegel secured an improved post as a *Hofmeister*, this time for the family of a rich wine merchant in Frankfurt. Earlier biting criticisms he made of religion became more muted during this period. This is reflected in his essay 'Sketches on Religion and Love' written in 1797, which engaged with the writings of the romantics and foregrounded the notion of love as a means to move beyond a subject–object dichotomy in the world; and in 'Christianity and its Fate' (1798), which introduced a number of core concepts to feature in his later philosophy: an organic conception of the world, spirit, dialectic and reconciliation especially, with regard to romanticist mysticism and reason.

Move to Jena

In 1801 Hegel moved to Jena to join his friend Schelling. Jena had been the centre of philosophy but was now losing its intellectual stature, especially following the departure of the influential idealist philosopher, Fichte. Hegel secured a post as an unpaid lecturer – a *privatdozent* – while also living off an inheritance that he received from his father. Following the publication of a dissertation on the orbit of the planets, he completed his first major work in 1802, *The Difference Between Fichte's and Schelling's Systems of Philosophy*, in which he developed his concept of 'objective idealism'. He also became a co-editor with Schelling of *The Critical Journal of Philosophy*, which they jointly founded and in which both regularly published. Following Schelling's departure from Jena to Würzburg in 1803, Hegel began to develop his own philosophical position in his major work, *The Phenomenology of Spirit* (1807), a description of the journey of ordinary consciousness to the viewpoint of science. The work was being completed just as Napoleon entered Jena in 1806, following the Battle of Jena.

Unable to acquire a salaried position, Hegel was offered the job of a newspaper editor – the *Bamberger Zeitung*, in 1808. The paper largely supported Napoleon's reforms, especially as they affected Bavaria. With the aid of his close friend Niethammer, Hegel then secured a job at a Gymnasium (secondary school) where he remained for eight years between 1808 and 1816. During this period he completed three volumes of his *Science of Logic* (1812, 1813 and 1816) as well as getting married to Marie von Tucher in 1811, at the age of 41. In 1816 Hegel became Professor of Philosophy at the University of Heidelberg where he published a summary of his work, *The Encyclopedia of the Philosophical Sciences* (1816). In 1818, following an invitation by the Prussian Minister of Education, Altenstein, he accepted the post of Professor of Philosophy in Berlin, replacing Fichte. However, the reformist political movement to which he adhered came under attack from Friedrich Wilhelm III, who introduced the Karlsbad Decrees, which entailed a policy of censorship and police surveillance. It was partly in relation to this that Hegel wrote the *Philosophy of Right* (1821), where he defended his unique conception of freedom. In 1830 he became Rector of the University of Berlin. During this period, he published some of his most important works, including his *Lectures on the Philosophy of History* and two new editions of the *Encyclopedia*. He died in Berlin 1831 following an outbreak of cholera.

Intellectual Context

Hegel's intellectual work draws upon and synthesises a wide range of influences stretching from pre-Socratic Greek philosophy and history to the work of the German idealist tradition, of which he considered himself a part. It also borrows from the German romanticist or 'expressivist' tradition of Herder, also manifest in the *Sturm and Drang* literary movement led by Goethe, that emphasised subjectivity, art and feeling. Hegel draws on Plato's view that the self should ideally be a balance between reason and passion. He also drew on Aristotle's belief that the highest goal contained both a principle of finality – it was an end, not a means – and that it was complete in itself requiring no other good to improve it. The Aristotelian idea of entities in process moving from actuality to potentiality, not in a pre-formed way, but according to circumstances, also plays a central role in Hegel's social thought. In contrast to Plato and Aristotle, Hegel had a very positive view of Greek democracy. The Athenian demos reflected the balanced state of the relations as well as the unfragmented and unalienated nature of Greek citizens, in relation to both their state and society: Athenians were both radically free and subjectively undivided.

As Lukács notes, the education that Hegel received in the Tübingen seminary consisted of 'an Enlightenment adapted to aristocratic, courtly needs' (1975: 4). This included writers of the French Enlightenment such as Voltaire, Diderot, Rousseau, Holbach, Montesquieu, as well as the German Enlightenment, especially in the work of the German idealists, Kant and later Fichte. However, Hegel reacted against some of these writers and especially the individualistic, austere, materialist, and utilitarian aspects of Enlightenment thinking as found in Bacon, Hobbes, Descartes and Locke and reinforced in the science of Galileo and Newton. Kant's philosophy had seen itself as part of the age of reason in which criticism of existing knowledge and extant authority constituted a core feature. In the German idealist tradition, the modern subject became a 'self-defining' and free individual. In his *Critique of Pure Reason* (1781) Kant sought to show how experience is possible through the faculty of the mind. The mind played a central role in shaping experience by applying categories upon it. These categories constituted the 'transcendental conditions of possibility' of all knowledge and experience. Because our mind applies these a priori (pre-given) categories to our experiences or phenomena, to form and structure them, it is, according to Kant, impossible to ever know the world as it really is, as *nouema*, that is as a 'thing-in-itself' (*dich-in-sich*). In his second critique, *Critique of Practical Reason* (1788), and in *Groundwork for the Metaphysics of Morals* (1785), Kant extended some of these arguments by examining morality. In the *Groundwork* he argues that the individual and perceiving subject are separate from the perceived world, and therefore not subject to natural causality. Rather, the individual, as subject or transcendental idea, constituted a free, undetermined being. Free individuals had the capacity to follow a rational moral law in opposition to the pull of their natural desires from within, and an action could be deemed rational if, and only if, it complied with the standards of universality and consistency or the 'categorical imperative'. This entailed to: 'act only in accordance with that maxim through which you can at the same time will that it become a universal law' (Kant, 1785: 73).

Hegel draws on, but heavily criticises, Kant's individualistic and static account. For Hegel, Kant's view of moral life was both excessively formal and overly rigorous, and his conception of freedom came at the price of positing an enduring dualism between duty and inclination, volition and nature, reason and sensibility, as an enduring and marked division within the individual. Rather than seeing a dichotomy between the two, Hegel argued for the possibility of their expressive unity through the notion of spirit, human community and ethical life. In addition, Kant focused too narrowly and abstractly on the instruments of knowledge, and what we can know, imposing a number of boundaries on knowledge. Hegel challenges these preconceived epistemological restrictions, 'but to seek to know before we know is as incoherent as the Scholastic's wise resolution not to venture into the water until he had learned how to swim' (Hegel, 2010 [1892]: 38). Hegel argues instead that we need to examine humans as actors in the world and how knowledge as a phenemonon appears – phenomenology. He not only argues that the categories applied by the mind are social, developed within a community, but also that Kant's ideas of the 'thing-in-itself', of not being able to know the world as it is, and that only finite appearances were knowable, were questionable assertions. The infinite, Hegel believed, could be known since it was manifest in the finite, that is in the 'concrete universal' – in the here and now particularities of the concrete historical world (Kilminster, 1998: 28). Moreover, the knowing subject and the known object were dialectically interconnected and their relation shifted historically as the subject's point of view and frame of perception became burdened by contradictions, generating a new framework for perception, and so on, until eventually recognising that the subject no longer saw the object as alien or externalised other, but as a product of itself. The result was an expanded version of self-consciousness (Sperber, 2013: 50).

Hegel also drew on Spinoza's concept of substance, a term ultimately deriving from Aristotle, which referred to that which is sempiternal, without beginning or end, the aspect of an object that remains even though it has changed. It also referred to that which underlay appearances. For Spinoza, substance was that which could be understood by knowing its nature alone, as opposed to in terms of its relations with other things. Everything was part of this one substance – substance monism – mind, matter, etc. This could be either God or nature. This was referred to as pantheism.

Finally, Hegel drew on German romanticism which in some respects arose as a response to Kantian idealism and rationalism, and which tended to see matter as an active, self-directive force. Instead of focusing on the individual attributes of the social world it placed an emphasis on the whole being prior to and greater than the sum of the parts, and viewed both the social and the natural world organically, so that for example, the parts of the whole body were intrinsically organically interrelated, as in all biological organisms.

Historical, Social and Political Context

It has often been assumed that Hegel's life was uneventful. However, as Kaufmann points out, this is a gross misconception: 'In fact one cannot understand Hegel's philosophy at all adequately if one ignores his life and times, and there have been few periods on history when so much happened' (1978: 1). In *The Philosophy of Right* Hegel himself recognised this when he asserted that 'philosophy is its age comprehended in thought'.

The Situation in Germany and the French Revolution

Germany at the time of Hegel was composed of a hotchpotch of more than 300 duchies, states and free cities under the overarching umbrella of the Holy Roman Empire, led by Francis I of Austria. It did not become unified into a singular nation-state until 1871. 'Hegel', as Pinkard notes, 'grew up in a time when kings were secure on their thrones' (2001: ix). The King of Prussia, Frederick the Great (1712–86), looked to French architecture at Versailles and to the French language as a model, regarding German as half-barbarian. Moreover, the Prussian state was dominated by a traditional aristocratic Junker caste lacking substantial finances, but passionately militaristic. In addition, the German middle classes, which embodied the ideals of the Enlightenment, individualism, progress and reason, and could therefore theoretically constitute a counter-balance to the Junkers, in reality remained a weak social stratum. As a result a powerful, reactionary aristocracy promulgated and championed the retention of feudal privileges, hierarchy and traditional authority. It was within this hierarchical and socially divided context of a 'society of orders', where rights and duties were stratified and applied to groups, rather than individuals, that many German intellectuals welcomed the French Revolution of 1789. The revolution sent shock waves throughout Europe and was interpreted as the spread of Enlightenment values and the Rights of Man. The American and French Revolutions had both drawn on the ideas of the Enlightenment, of rational government in place of clerical hierarchy, and Rousseau's notion of men born with inalienable rights and a general will – where under a social contract, the state acted for the interests of all not just a few.

The French Revolution constituted for Hegel a 'glorious dawn'. It is difficult to overstate its importance for instilling in him a republican worldview even though he was only 19 years of age at the time. An apocryphal story from his first biographer, Rosencranz, relates how Hegel, Hölderlin and Schelling planted a liberty tree in a meadow in Tübingen following the revolution. Together with the American and French Revolutions, other unprecedented and rapid social, political and economic changes probably meant that 'no generation lived through such a wrenching transformation of ways of life as did Hegel's' (Pinkard, 2001: x).

However, just three years after the revolution, and anticipating attacks from neighbouring European powers following the Declaration of Pillnitz by the Holy Roman Emperor Leopold II, France was compelled to enter into a war against Prussia and Austria, some of which resulted in defeat. The resultant chaos, civil war and counter-revolutionary threat in France facilitated the rise of the Jacobins, who, in order to establish national unity, began to impose what became known as a 'reign of terror'. Violence and terror became an instrument of government. Based on what was conceived as fundamentally rational principles of government, in opposition, to clerical orthodoxy, a new republican calendar was instituted, while just under 17,000 death sentences were passed between June 1793 and July 1794. The Terror culminated in Robespierre's execution as part of the Thermidorian reaction of 1794 and led to the disillusionment of many German intellectuals (the *Bildungsbürgertum*), including Hegel. Hegel discusses the terror in the *Phenomenology of Spirit* in a section entitled 'Absolute Freedom and Terror', which rues the operation of an abstract, disembodied rationality. Nevertheless, he remained committed to the principles of the French Revolution throughout his life.

The Rise of Napoleon

Subsequent French victories against the Austrians and Spanish saw the emergence of General Napoleon Bonaparte, who began a major rout of Italian and Austrian forces in 1796, culminating in the Treaty of Campo Formio. In 1799 Napoleon had become First Consul of France and instituted a strong centralised bureaucratic state in France. Following his victory over the Russian–Austrian

Army in the Battle of Austerlitz in 1805 as part of the Fourth Coalition War, he went on to defeat the Prussians in Jena on 14 October 1806, trouncing the whole Prussian Army within 19 days and bringing an end to the Austrian-led Holy Roman Empire: an empire which had lasted over a thousand years. Hegel remained a lifelong admirer of Napoleon. Following Napoleon's entry in Jena, he wrote to his friend Niethammer:

> I saw the Emperor – the world spirit – riding out of the city on reconnaissance. It is indeed a wonderful sensation to see such an individual, who, concentrated here at a single point, astride a horse, reaches out over the world and masters it ... this extraordinary man, whom it is impossible not to admire. (1984: 114)

Napoleon's modernising reforms in Germany between 1806 and 1814 were to transform the country, challenging medieval privileges by establishing republican constitutions, promoting the freedom of religion, agricultural reform and opening a French-style centralised bureaucracy to all talented individuals. These social reforms, based on the idea of meritocracy and the talented individual, were welcomed by many German intellectuals. Though Frederick William III remained as king of Prussia till 1840, the Napoleonic reforms, by challenging medieval privileges and empowering the middle classes, facilitated the subsequent rapid industrialisation and urbanisation of Prussia, and demographic growth within Germany as a whole. It also saw the partial burgeoning of an educated middle class and the emergence of many liberal regional newspapers, though censorship of the press remained present. After the Napoleonic defeat at Waterloo to Wellington and Blücher, the map of Europe was again redrawn in the 1815 settlement that aimed to prevent further war and the possibility of another French Revolution. During the Restoration period (1815–30) European powers sought to turn the clock back to the time before the French Revolution. Moreover, Prussia became the dominant hegemonic state after it succeeded in acquiring large swathes of land. As Hobsbawm notes: 'In territorial and economic terms Prussia gained relatively more from the 1815 settlement than any other power, and in fact became for the first time a European great power in terms of real resources' (1996: 102).

Over time Frederick William III began to renege on his earlier promises of introducing a constitution, ushering in instead a period of marked political reaction. During this period of stultifying and oppressive political and bureaucratic quasi-aristocratic rule, the relatively disempowered German middle class responded by foregrounding a cult of inwardness (*Innerlichkeit*) and cultural and educational development (*Bildung*) and advocating abstract notions of duty, freedom and belonging as expressed by the philosopher Fichte.

By the 1820s the Industrial Revolution began to take off, and steam-powered engines, and train travel became widespread driving forces. Like many other European countries the political system in Prussia and Germany remained inadequate for the major social changes taking place, including the emergence of a labouring poor, increasingly pauperised, industrial working class and the unemployed. Hegel often made reference to the threats to the social order that the latter *Pöbel*, or rabble posed. The huge displacement of peasantry and the contradictions of these early industrial processes created a charged atmosphere with mass discontent reaching its climax with the re-emergence of a revolutionary fervour throughout Europe in the 1830s (Hobsbawm, 1996: 117–24).

The political rivalry between Prussia and Austria after 1815, which together with Russia formed the 'Holy Alliance', was offset by their shared reaction against an emerging progressive German nationalism promulgating self-rule. The *Carlsbad Decrees* of 1819, for example, followed the murder of the conservative writer August von Kotzebue by Karl Sand, a member of a liberal student fraternity (*Burschenschaft*), as well as an attempt on the life of Nassau President Karl von Ibell on 1 July 1819. Driven by the Austrian Minister of State, Klemens Metternich, the Prussian state sought to clamp down on the increasing sympathy towards German nationalism expressed in universities and liberal newspapers, by making the expression of liberal and nationalist sentiments illegal, removing liberal university professors, and censoring and clamping down on the press. In the context of the existence of a militarised and repressive Prussian state, Hegel responded in his discussion of the state as a rational institution in the *Philosophy of Right*, and especially in his aphorism claiming that 'what is actual is rational and what is rational is actual'. This has often been criticised for rationalising the extant Prussian state. However, as Wood argues:

> It is simply false to say that Hegel's philosophy aims at justifying the social and political status quo. On the contrary Hegel insists that every existing state, standing as it does in the sphere of transitoriness and contingency, is disfigured to some extent by error and wickedness, and fails to be wholly rational, because it fails to be wholly actual. *The Philosophy of Right* clearly leaves room for rational criticism of what exists, and also for practical efforts to improve the existing state by actualizing it, bringing it more into harmony with its own rational essence or concept. (1995: 9)

Nevertheless, Hegel's political views do exhibit a shift from the radical and republican ideas optimistically expressed in his early writings (Lukács, 1975) reaching a climax in the *Phenomenology of Spirit*, to *The Philosophy of Right*, the latter tempered by many political developments, including his further ruminations on the 'reign of terror' and Prussian social and political policies. *The Phenomenology*, though ostensibly concerned with 'What do we know?', emphatically emphasises the centrality of freedom:

> The core of Hegel's argument is that freedom is the identity of the personal goals of individual citizens and the public ends of the polity as a whole. This is a dynamic process in which the laws are created by

> each and all, and are in turn expressed and realized in the minds and actions of every member of society. Such was Periclean Athens in which a naïve trust bound the citizens to their city. The restless demands of reason were bound to break this spontaneous state of confidence and to assert the destructive force of individual autonomy... The demands of independence outrun reason itself... Politically they culminate in the French Revolution. (Shklar, 2010: xiv)
>
> [Republished with permission of Cambridge University Press, from *Freedom and Independence: A Study of the Political Ideas of Hegel's Phenomenology of Mind,* J. Shklar, 2010. Reproduced with permission of The Licensor through PLSclear]

Moreover, Hegel in his later writings, cannot be seen simply as a liberal thinker in our modern sense. He was against the universal right to vote and popular representation, even arguing against the English Reform Bill, which when passed after his death in 1832, aimed to reduce inequalities in membership in the House of Commons. His political legacy therefore remained ambiguous and contradictory.

Arguments and Ideas

Hegel is a difficult thinker, perhaps the most difficult thinker in philosophy and the social sciences. It is rumoured by the poet Heine that, on his death bed, Hegel remarked, 'only one man ever understood me, and even he didn't understand me'.

In his writings Hegel attempted to draw upon diverse theoretical traditions by synthesising their most important aspects and bring humans back into a harmonious relation to their world, within the context of a series of divisions that existed during his time. As Plant notes, Hegel was preoccupied with resolving the divisions and bifurcations 'between man and God, between man and society, between man and nature, and indeed the division within the individual's own personality between reason, imagination and feeling' (1997: 11). It was Hegel's ambition to develop an organic model of society in which individuals were able ultimately to achieve self-realisation, freedom, harmony, and reconciliation with the world, and ultimately to 'find themselves at home in the other'. As Beiser notes:

> We can formulate the highest good of Hegel and the young romantic generation in a single phrase ... unity of life. The highest good, the end of life, consists in achieving unity, wholeness or harmony in all aspects of our being. This unity holds on three levels. With oneself, with others and with nature. The main threat to such unity consists in division or alienation (*Entfremdung*). Though the self should live in unity with itself, others and nature, it finds itself divided from itself and from them. Its goal is to overcome these divisions and achieve unity, so that it is again 'at home in the world' (*in die Welt zu Hause*). (2007: 37)

Hegel's early work attempted this reconciliation through the development of a civic republican religion, followed by the promotion of love as a form of connection between individuals. But he came in time to see the latter as based on emotion rather than rationality. His later writings attempted this reconciliation through the development of an extensive philosophical system foregrounding the notion of reason as embodied in an ethical community, where each person acquires freedom and mutual recognition from one another, and duty and inclination become an expressive unity in a world which they have conjointly created.

Speculative Hermeneutics

Philosophy for Hegel is for the most part a backward-looking and reflective reconstruction of what has happened, that analyses how culture and values have meaning for humans, as he remarks: 'The owl of Minerva spreads its wings at dusk.' As Matarrese (2010) argues, Hegel's philosophy also contains a speculative hermeneutics: one that seeks to reconstruct the essential structure of the thing being interpreted. The essential structure that is being revealed is what Hegel calls its 'reason' or 'rationality', and it is to be distinguished from all that is contingent, accidental or merely possible. Speculative hermeneutics, then, attempts to reveal 'the rational in the real', which is a shorthand reference to Hegel's assertion that 'what is rational is actual'.

Such a hermeneutics is both descriptive and critical. It does not abolish the distinction between what a thing has in it to become, and what a thing currently happens to be; that is, in Aristotelian's terms between its actuality and potentiality.

> Whether Hegel focuses on thing or a state or a person he looks at its 'rationality' – the structure or basic organizing principle of the thing. He aims to indicate the goal or telos of the thing or object. Does the object or thing fall short of its rationality? Criticism is rarely from an external point of view but rather always internal: the typical internal argument tries to show that a particular point of view or practice cannot accomplish what it is after, that it cannot succeed on its own terms. (Materrese, 2010: 17)

Hegel is also profoundly historical in his approach: everything, he believes, needs to be understood in its historical context. By understanding things or the world we come to reconcile ourselves with them and the world. As he notes in *The Philosophy of Right*: 'to understand reason as the rose in the cross of the present and thereby to delight in the present – this rational insight is the reconciliation with actuality which philosophy grants to those who have received the inner call to comprehend' (2002 [1821]: 22).

Theory of the Absolute/God/Spirit

At the heart of Hegel's philosophy is a metaphysical monism that foregrounds an all-inclusive creative spirit whose movement is manifested in the unfolding of history. In German, the term *Geist* translates both as spirit or ghost and as mind or thought. Hegel deliberately plays on both of these meanings. As a result some commentators have read Spirit to mean 'God' while others can interpret it to mean the spirit of the times of a community, a *zeitgeist*. This is the basis for either a transcendent reading or an immanent reading of his work. Hegel's use permits both meanings simultaneously. Thus, Hegel refers to Spirit as the Absolute, as God, though importantly a non-transcendent Christian type of God. Rather, Hegel's God is immanent in the world. In such a perspective God is more than the Universe but not distinct from it. Following Whittemore (1960) this is often referred to as a 'panentheist' position.

In Hegel's understanding an *infinite* rational God needs to manifest itself through the *finite* world in order to come to know itself, and to realise its own nature, and that this world is its own product. In this educative journey or *Bildungsroman*, Spirit goes outside itself through differentiation and externalisation and then returns to itself, through an internalisation of the externalisation, but at a higher and more developed level. God or Spirit comes to reveal itself initially through the natural, and then through the social world. Nature is a revelation of God/Spirit and God's/Spirit's thinking, yet it remains an unconscious manifestation. Human life, by contrast, is a conscious manifestation; that is, an expression of subjective Spirit which reaches its highest level in human self-consciousness. These are stages in Spirit's self-knowledge. Society, culture and the state are not fundamentally different from nature, but are rather more complete, complex, organised and developed indicators of the organic powers of nature. Both are expressions of the unfolding of Absolute Spirit. According to Hegel, the creativity of subjective Spirit, of human culture and consciousness, is expressed and articulated through the hierarchical order of art, religion and, finally, philosophy. The sovereignty of creative Spirit finds its self-expression through people and through history. It ultimately comes to realise itself as freedom. Equally, humans, as vehicles of Spirit, eventually come to realise that they are free, self-determining beings, and rationally thinking beings, because Spirit comes to realise this through them. Hegel attempted to demonstrate that the history of the world was nothing other than the realisation of this freedom.

As in the rest of his philosophy, Hegel's understanding of the Absolute, as a rational subject coming to realise himself through individuals, contains three moments of organic development – unity, difference and difference-in-unity. Spirit moves through the world rationally in terms of three logical unfolding, yet contradictory, stages. In this sense spirit is *Logos*. This constitutes a central part of his dialectical view of development. Dialectic is the logic that traces this unfolding, spiralling, circular processes. Wood describes Hegel as 'the most methodologically self-conscious of all philosophers in the Western tradition' (1990: 1) and describes the dialectic thus:

> Neither in Hegel nor in Marx is dialectical thinking really a set of procedures for inquiry, still less a set of rules for generating or justifying results... Instead, dialectic is best viewed as a general conception of

> the sort of intelligible structure the world has to offer, and consequently a programme for the sort of theoretical structure which would best capture it. (2004: 198)

The usual way to talk about method or Hegelian dialectics is through the imposition of a triadic formula – thesis, anti-thesis and synthesis. Strictly speaking, however, the dialectic is not a method as normally understood involving pre-given rules and procedures that one applies to an object or processes to understand or investigate them. Rather dialectics is a process that attempts to capture the unfolding of truth, the dynamic of Being.

The term Hegel uses to describe the movement of one stage to another is *Aufhebung*, often translated as 'sublation', which means to negate, preserve and simultaneously to 'lift up'. This synthesis then becomes the basis of a new thesis and so on until we reach the level of self-conscious Absolute spirit. This is tied to Hegel's organicism and holism. Hegel examines social processes in terms of the totality or whole, as he asserts: 'the true is the whole'. For Hegel abstract thought is incomplete thought: As it becomes concrete or more determinate, the closer it corresponds to the truth, the whole. Such a standpoint contrasts with a Cartesian notion of mechanical causality, which conceives the world in terms of singular causes, for example A effects B, rather than in terms of a complex multidimensional, organic whole entailing reciprocal and multidimensional causality. Moreover, reason progresses through negation, by thought wrestling with its opposite – what he terms the labour of the negative. Hegel frequently uses the term mediation (*Vermittlung*) and immediate (*Unmittelbarkeit)* to refer to the dynamic relationships between entities and processes. As Inwood (1992: 184) notes:

> Thus in Hegel *Vermittlung* often refers to the uniting of two terms by a third term, e.g. the uniting of the Universal and the Individual in an inference by the Particular. But *Vermittlung* and *Unmittelbarkeit* are often used more widely. The immediate is unrelated to other things; simple; given; elementary; and/or initial. The mediated, by contrast, is related to other things; complex; explained; developed; and/or resultant.

The Phenomenology of Spirit, the Social Self and Recognition

Perhaps Hegel's most ambitious and difficult work, *The Phenomenology of Spirit*, captures the fluidity of this dialectical movement in the most detail. Written on the eve of Napoleon's entry into Jena following the Battle of Jena, the book attempts to analyse the journey of ordinary consciousness to the level of scientific understanding, not from an objective or impartial perspective, but from the standpoint of ordinary consciousness itself. As Norman notes:

> This idea, that consciousness tests itself and that we have only to look on, is an odd-sounding one, but Hegel takes it seriously... The work is written as a sort of 'biography' of consciousness, a narrative account of the various experiences which Consciousness undergoes... Hegel talks of what consciousness experiences, or recognizes or discovers. (1981: 21)

The German word for experience, *Erfahrung*, contains the verb *fahrung*, to journey. The journey ends when consciousness reaches the terminus of absolute knowledge: each form of consciousness emerges through a determinate negation of the previous, which it sublates (*aufheben*). As Norman notes: 'In knowing reality, the intellect knows itself, because it knows what it has itself put there' (1981: 17). Hegel's description of the journey of consciousness is both at the level of individual experience – discussed under the terms of consciousness, self-consciousness and reason – and at the level of social experience – discussed under spirit, religion and absolute knowledge.

The book also discusses the social experience of consciousness. Here Hegel points to the importance of the experience of desire in making individuals conscious of their own existence. Moreover, he argues, one cannot be fully conscious of oneself, have self-certainty, independently of other selves. We need others to recognise ourselves as independent, self-conscious beings. This process of highlighting the social nature of humans is discussed at a highly metaphysical level. In describing the process of how two individuals reach self-consciousness Hegel uses the metaphor of master and bondsmen (sometimes translated as slave) (*Herrschaft* and *Knechtschaft*). Self-consciousness he argues, cannot exist alone in one individual, but requires an external object that remains outside of itself and against which it can oppose itself. Moreover, self-consciousness does not need just an object, but another self-consciousness in order to contrast itself from other objects, and to constitute a mirror to see itself; that is, it requires recognition. However, this striving for recognition from another is fraught with difficulties including a dramatic life and death struggle:

> Each self-consciousness aims to be recognized by, and to find itself in, the other. However, insofar as its identity resides in an other, it is outside its own control; it must therefore also aim to destroy the other. And the conflict between them must be a struggle for life and death, since it is only by risking one's life that one is aware of oneself as a free, autonomous individual. (Hegel, 1977: 222–3)

By engaging in such a struggle, each person demonstrates that they really are a person. However, the death of one person suits neither of the protagonists since the defeated would be dead, and the victor would consequently not be able to experience recognition from the other. By sparing their life the victor transforms a situation in which two equal independent individual self-consciousnesses existed into an unstable unequal relationship between a master and a slave. But recognition in terms of personhood remains absent for both. For the master, the slave is a thing and therefore cannot give full recognition to the master. The slave also knows that he or she is only recognised as a thing. The slave views the world, and himself or herself, from the master's perspective, that is from an alienated point of view. Yet, a dialectic reversal takes place. By working for the master and producing things for him or her, the slave shapes the material world and thereby externalises his or her internal consciousness into permanent objects. Through their labour, and the objectification of their consciousness, slaves come to recognise the products of their own mind and acquire an independence through this educative process. The slave, therefore, achieves initial, but partial, self-realisation. By contrast, the master remains in a state of dependence on the slave.

For Hegel, if self-consciousness is to be fully and truly realised, there needs to exist a free society where everyone is recognised as a person and works on behalf of the community, so that mutual recognition pertains. Societies in which domination and oppression exist mean that self-consciousness remains partial and incomplete. As Smith (1987) notes, this is the basis of Hegel's notion of critique, which differs from Kant's, which only examines the conditions and limits of rationality:

> Firstly, whereas Kant meant by critique an enquiry into the nature and limits of rationality as such, for Hegel it took the form of an internal or immanent examination of the various sources of deception, illusion and distortion that the mind undergoes in its journey to Absolute Knowledge. Such an activity is critical, or in Hegel's term 'negative', precisely because it entails a conception of liberation from those historical sources of domination and coercion. Like Marx, Nietzsche and, later, Freud, Hegel sought to free human agents not only from the coercive illusions that inhibit their capacities for free thought and action, but also from the forms of social life within which those coercive illusions thrive and find expression. Philosophical critique necessarily spills over into social theory. Secondly, underlying the Hegelian conception of critique is the belief that human history expresses an immanent telos, the aim of which is the liberation of both the individual and the species from a system of constraints that are at least partially imposed by the minds of the agents to whom the theory is addressed. Hegel's argument depends upon the assumption that human agents are driven by a powerful common interest in freedom that persists through the interplay of their passions and actions. (Smith, 1987: 99–100)

The Philosophy of History

For Hegel consciousness proceeds on a dialectical journey, until it reaches absolute knowledge, yet the other side of this absolute knowledge is freedom. Reason and freedom are seen as identical. In his *Lectures on the Philosophy of History* (2009 [1837]), Hegel talks of history as the progress of the consciousness of freedom. For Hegel history is not a collection of chaotic random and contingent events, but rather, as is the case with Christianity, has a meaning, significance and pattern underlying it. Beneath the chaos, wars, suffering and injustices in history is the rational progression of Spirit marching towards human freedom. History produces a mass of individuals who come to understand eventually that the fundamental principle underlying their life is freedom. According to Hegel, this may strike us as an odd assertion when we survey world history, given the history of war and violence, barbarities, destruction, mindless pillaging, usurpation, colonialism, slavery, domination and inequality which have constituted the 'slaughterbench' of history. But for Hegel, behind these blind negative and chaotic processes, there is the operation of a positive process, of reason revealing itself incrementally and historically, what he calls 'the cunning of reason'.

The Philosophy of Right

Hegel, like Kant, believes freedom begins when individuals liberate themselves from their desires and act on a rational basis. This becomes possible not in civil society, where we follow our egoistic desires, but only in the ethical life of the state. Half of the *Philosophy of Right* discusses the concept of *Sittlichkeit.* This translates from the Greek concept of 'ethos', which refers to manners or a way of life of a people. In the German context *Sittlichkeit* also refers to what is customary and traditional. For Hegel, it contains three moments or stages and represents three modes of human relationships expressing a progressively more complex stage of mentality: (1) family – particular altruism and immediate unity; (2) civil society – universal egoism, divisive individualism and difference; and (3) the state – universal altruism and unity in difference. The first two moments are abstract expressions of *Sittlichkeit*, the last, a concrete expression of freedom as universal and objective.

Within the family individuals are bonded together through emotions of love and altruism. By contrast, civil society as *bürgerliche Gesellschaft* (bourgeois society) sublates the micro family as the central productive unit. The social life of civil society differs from the ethical life of the family, and the state. It deals with relationships that exclude mutual bonds and love but instead foreground self-interested atomistic needs and desires of individuals. Individuals use others as means (and not as Kantian ends) and follow the belief that when one pursues one's self-interest, one also satisfies the interests of others (e.g. by producing goods to be sold at a profit). Despite this competitive individualism, Hegel believes civil society constitutes a necessary stepping stone in the development of freedom through foregrounding notions such as the equality of opportunity, and the freedom to buy and sell.

Work is a fundamental way of meeting needs. However, given the nature of the market, Hegel recognised that extremes of wealth and poverty may emerge which challenge the very nature of ethical life. Sharp fluctuations in supply and in demand could eradicate whole industries and create a destitute mass as well as a rabble bent on challenging the social order. Lacking recognition and self-respect can lead or dispose this rabble towards rebellion and challenge the state and its values. Hegel sees no solution to their condition. Since a major value in modern society is self-reliance and upkeep, charity would only offend their sensibilities. He does, however, argue that some of the problems caused by the market, over-production and unemployment can be remedied by colonisation and emigration.

Continuing his view of the importance of totality, for Hegel, the state not only includes the government but is defined expansively to include all social life: it refers to the community as a whole. Because the state is based on rational principles, on the rule of law, it represents objective freedom: it is a rational state. These principles are embodied in the concrete institutions of the state. The state represents a higher form of consciousness than that found within civil society, where as we noted, competition and selfish actions predominate. Hegel therefore sees the state as a unique synthesis of individual freedom with community, both allowing subjective freedom and providing institutions that allow individuals to externalise their wills without contradicting one another. The state exists as an Idea in the minds of citizens.

Contemporary Relevance and Applications

Hegel's influence on Marx is of course well known, but he was also influential on a number of other European thinkers including Gramsci, Lukács, Marcuse, Adorno, Bourdieu, Elias, Horkheimer and Habermas, as well as the work of G. H. Mead. The second and third wave of Frankfurt School thinkers, including Jürgen Habermas and Axel Honneth, have tried to show the parallels in the writings of Hegel and Mead on the development of the self, intersubjectivity and recognition (Habermas, 1984; 1987; Honneth, 1995). In Gramsci's work Hegel's influence was mediated through the work of Bennodetto Croce, while in Lukács's writings the notion of totality and the Hegelian distinction between dialectical and ordinary understanding becomes a central feature of his analysis. For Marcuse, Hegel provides the foundation for a dialectical and critical view of society, while for Adorno, who is more ambiguous in his relation to Hegel's 'closed system', the concept of non-identity is nevertheless, crucial. By contrast to the German situation, Hegel's influence into social theory in France came through a radical interpretation of his work by the Russian-born French philosopher Alexander Kojeve, and to a lesser extent Jean Hyppolite. Kojève (1969) read Hegel's *Phenomenology of Spirit* through the lens of both Marx and Heidegger, in a reading that foregrounded the concept of desire and the projection of consciousness towards death, through work relationships, and recognition. His reading not only influenced Lacan, Foucault, Althusser, Derrida, Sartre, de Beauvoir, Žižek and Bourdieu – where for the latter the notion of recognition and misrecognition as well as of the state as acting on behalf of the universal, constitute core ideas in his sociology – but also Frantz Fanon (1925–61).

LEFT AND RIGHT HEGELIANS

After Hegel's death in 1831, divergent perspectives that had developed within the Hegelian School became more acute, ultimately leading to a schism into opposing factions. These are most accurately described along ideological lines as the 'Left' and 'Right' Hegelians. The focus of the division centred on the interpretation of Hegel's identification of reason and reality, with particular consideration for the existing political and religious reality of the Prussian state. The Left revolutionaries saw reason as a future goal not yet achieved. Its actualisation required a radical negation of those institutions restricting it, namely religion and the Prussian political system, as well as a transformative revision of Hegelian theory itself. The Right conservatives saw the historical process of the realisation of reason as completed. This provided the basis to affirm establishment politics and orthodox religion. Left Hegelianism found its most prominent representative in Karl Marx, with a line of development from here continuing to this day in Frankfurt School critical theory.

As well as being a trained doctor and member of the National Liberation Front, Fanon applied Hegel's discussion of the master–slave dialectic to the French treatment of Algerian and Martinique subjects. The psycho-pathological conditions characterising patients in his hospital included profound feelings of inadequacy and self-doubt. This, Fanon argued, in *Black Skin, White Masks* (1967 [1952]), was a direct result not of individual psychological impediments and blockages, but of French political, social and cultural colonial domination and especially from the linguistic imposition it entailed. Algerians were marked and rendered 'visible', as 'black' in an anti-black world. Through this 'epidermalization of inferiority', their colonised, marginalised and subordinated position was internalised, not just into individuals' consciousness, but into their whole-body schema. Inequality, racism and marginalisation through power differentials created an inferiority complex, a sense of shame and despair towards one's own skin, body and culture. It prevented black men and women from becoming truly human. As Fanon notes, drawing on Hegel's master–slave dialectic:

> Man (sic) is human only to the extent to which he tries to impose his existence on another man in order to be recognized by him. As long as he has not been effectively recognized by the other, that other will remain the theme of his actions. It is on that other being, on recognition of that other being, that his own human worth and reality depended. It is on that other being in whom the meaning of his life is condensed. (1967: 216–17)

Remedies to such colonial oppression could not, however, be achieved merely through a change of consciousness but, instead, required liberation through the cathartic use of violence, which Fanon discusses in *The Wretched of the Earth* (1962).

Fanon, however, modifies Hegel's view of the master–slave relationship and the struggle for recognition: the master seeks not only recognition, but also work, while the slave wants to be like the master (Macey, 2012: 161).

Criticisms

As we noted Hegel's work entails a great synthesis between the image of an integrated life drawn from ancient Greece, in which individuals are at one with themselves and others, an Enlightenment view positing individual freedom and self-direction, and aspects of the Christian religion. As Taylor (1975: 51) notes 'These three reference points were potentially in deep conflict and Hegel's mature thought is a heroic attempt to reconcile them'. Although heavily criticised by Schopenhauer and Kierkegaard, the most famous and well-known criticism of Hegel comes from Marx. Marx criticised Hegel in three major respects relating to what he construed as his idealism, his politics, his prioritisation of the state or for taking the standpoint of political economy. As Pelczynski notes:

> First, Marx questioned the philosophical context of the concept, the validity of the Hegelian form of the dialectic, and its mystifying treatment of real human, social, historical facts and processes as elements in the development of a mystical entity, the Spirit or the Idea. Second, while retaining the state/civil society distinction, Marx rejected the view that the state was an all-inclusive political community with a distinct ethical character, and denied it primacy in social and historical life. He reversed the Hegelian relation of the two and made civil (or rather bourgeois) society the ground of political life and the source of political change. Third, Marx decomposed the Hegelian civil society, which was a highly complex, structured concept, and reduced civil society virtually to the economic sphere of labour, production and exchange. (1984: 1–2)

[Republished with permission of Cambridge University Press, from *The State and Civil Society: Studies in Hegel's Political Philosophy*, Z. A. Pelczynski, 1984. Reproduced with permission of The Licensor through PLSclear]

Drawing on Feuerbach's 'transformative criticism', Marx argued that Hegel in his analysis of the state inverts subjects and predicates: 'i.e. that he had understood and presented an independent entity as an attribute, whereas something occurring only as an attribute of an independently existing object was presented as being itself an independent entity' (Ilting, 1984: 93). As Ilting expands:

> Hegel sought to comprehend the state as an object which existed independently of the individuals living in a state community and credited these individuals themselves with only a dependent existence... Hegel had thereby reduced the state itself to no more than an embodiment of an abstract 'Idea'. (1984: 93)

This criticism of reified concepts treated as self-moving personifications, for example the State or the Idea, instead of analysing real human individuals and their activity, was bound up with Marx's critique of Hegel's speculative idealism. Here history is seen as the logical unfolding of categories, which although recognising the material world, foreground Absolute Spirit. As Lukács noted in a 1926 essay:

> Hegel's tremendous intellectual contribution consisted in the fact that he made theory and history dialectically relative to each other, grasped them in dialectical reciprocal penetration. Ultimately, however, his attempt was a failure. He could never get as far as the genuine unity of theory and practice; all that he could do was either to fill the logical sequence of the categories with rich historical material, or rationalize history, in the shape of a succession of forms, structural changes, epochs, etc., which raised them to the level of categories by sublimating and abstracting them. (Cited and translated in Mészáros, 1971: 17)
>
> [Republished with permission of Merlin Press from *Marx's Theory of Alienation*, I. Mészáros, 1971]

Human social activity and social relations play an underdetermined role in Hegel's analysis; they are an effect of the logical unfolding of conceptual categories as Spirit comes to know itself.

Conclusion

Hegel was a profound and broad thinker. His arguments, though couched in a dense and difficult vocabulary, nevertheless contain some important social and historical insights on human history and human development as a process, especially the interconnectedness of the social world, the interdependence of individuals, the need of individuals for recognition as social beings and the importance of political economy. Different insights from his work were taken up by different subsequent theorists and sociologists (Bartonek and Burman, 2018) and reapplied to their understanding of the social world, especially by Marxists, thinkers from within the Frankfurt School, as well as Bourdieu, Mead, de Beauvoir and Elias.

References

Anderson, P. (2002) *A Zone of Engagement*. London: Verso.
Bartonek, A. and Burman, A. (2018) *Hegelian Marxism*. Stockholm: Elanders.
Beiser, F. (2007) *Hegel*. London: Taylor & Francis.
Fanon, F. (1962) *The Wretched of the Earth*. London: Penguin Books.
Fanon, F. (1967 [1952]) *Black Skin, White Masks*. C. M. Markmann, trans. New York: Grove Press.

Habermas, J. (1984; 1987) *The Theory of Communicative Action, 2 vols.* T. McCarthy, trans. Cambridge: Polity.
Hegel, G. W. F. (1977 [1802]) *The Difference Between Fichte's and Schelling's System of Philosophy*. Albany, NY: State University of New York Press.
Hegel, G. W. F. (1977 [1807]) *The Phenomenology of Spirit*. Cambridge: Cambridge University Press.
Hegel, G. W. F. (1984) *Hegel: The Letters*. C. Butler and C. Seiler, trans. C. Butler, commentary. Bloomington, IN: Indiana University Press.
Hegel, G. W. F. (2002 [1821]) *The Philosophy of Right*. A. White, trans. Indianapolis, IN: Focus Publishing.
Hegel, G. W. F. (2009) *Lectures on the History of Philosophy, 1825-6*. Revised edition. Oxford: Clarendon Press.
Hegel, G. W. F. (2010) *Encyclopedia of the Philosophical Sciences in Basic Outline: The Science of Logic*. Cambridge: Cambridge University Press.
Hobsbawm, E. (1996) *The Age of Revolution: Europe 1789-1848*. London: Weidenfeld & Nicolson.
Honneth, A. (1995) *The Struggle for Recognition: The Moral Grammar of Social Conflicts*. Cambridge: Polity.
Inwood, M (1992) *A Hegel Dictionary*. Blackwell: Oxford
Ilting, K. H. (1984) Hegel's Concept of the State and Marx's Early Critique. In: Z. A. Pelczynski (ed.) *The State and Civil Society: Studies in Hegel's Political Philosophy*. Cambridge: Cambridge University Press, pp. 114-36.
Kant, I. (1855 [1781]) *Critique of Pure Reason*. J. M. D. Meiklejohn, trans. London: Henry G. Bohn.
Kant, I. (2002 [1785]) *Groundwork for the Metaphysics of Morals*. A. W. Wood, ed. and trans. New Haven, CT: Yale University Press.
Kant, I. (2008 [1788]) *Critique of Practical Reason*. T. Kingsmill Abbott, trans. New York: Cosimo Classics.
Kaufmann, W. A. (1978) *Hegel: A Reinterpretation*. Notre Dame, IN: University of Notre Dame Press.
Kilminster, R. (1998) *The Sociological Revolution*. London: Routledge.
Kojève, A. (1969) *Introduction to the Reading of Hegel: Lectures on the Phenomenology of Spirit*. R. Queneau, assembly. A. Bloom (ed.) J. H. Nichols, Jr trans. Ithaca, NY: Cornell University Press.
Lukács, G. (1975) *The Young Hegel*. London: Merlin Press.
Macey, D. (2012) *Frantz Fanon: A Biography*. London: Verso.
Matarrese, C. B. (2010) *Starting with Hegel*. London: Continuum.
Mészáros, I. (1971) *Marx's Theory of Alienation*. London: Merlin Press.
Norman, R. (1981) *Hegel's 'Phenomenology': A Philosophical Introduction*. Brighton: Harvester Press.
Pelczynski, Z. A., ed. (1984) *The State and Civil Society: Studies in Hegel's Political Philosophy*. Cambridge: Cambridge University Press.
Pinkard, T. (2001) *Hegel: A Biography*. Cambridge: Cambridge University Press.

Plant, R. (1997) *Hegel*. New York: Routledge.
Shklar, J. N. (2010) *Freedom and Independence: A Study of the Political Ideas of Hegel's Phenomenology of Mind*. Cambridge: Cambridge University Press.
Smith, S. B. (1987) Hegel's Idea of a Critical Theory. *Political Theory*, 15(1), pp. 99–126.
Sperber, J. (2013) *Karl Marx: A Nineteenth-Century Life*. New York: Liveright Publishing.
Taylor, C. (1975) *Hegel*. Cambridge: Cambridge University Press.
Whittemore, R. C. (1960) Hegel as Panentheist. In: *Studies in Hegel. Tulane Studies in Philosophy*, 9. Dordrecht: Springer, pp. 134–64.
Wood, A. W. (1990) *Hegel's Ethical Thought*. Cambridge: Cambridge University Press.
Wood, A. W. (1995) *Hegel Elements of the Philosophy of Right*. Cambridge: Cambridge University Press.
Wood, A. W. (2004) *Kant*. Oxford: Blackwell.

V

MARX

Introduction

Karl Marx is one of the central figures in the sociological canon, together with Weber and Durkheim. However, this was not always the case but rather emerged from the 1960s onwards. Moreover, Marx would have probably eschewed the label of sociologist, given its association with the work of Comte, whom he heavily criticised. Besides, he saw his writings as simultaneously scientific and political. The fact that Marxism was a political practice, ultimately adopting the standpoint of the proletariat, had a profound influence not only in shaping his thought, but also in providing the context within which his analysis has been received, interpreted and applied. The term 'Marxism' itself arose in the 1870s, initially carrying stigmatising connotations and referring to his supporters (Rubel, 1977: 45). Furthermore, Marx only published three sole-authored books during his lifetime, and his reputation, for the most part, developed towards the end of his life and especially following his death (Kilminster, 2018). Much of the interpretation of his work, including the publication of his unpublished writings, was filtered through the arguments of his lifelong collaborator and friend, Friedrich Engels, as well as the political interests of the Second International, which attempted to establish a Marxist orthodoxy commensurate with its unfolding policies.

Although Marx's work underwent significant development and transformation, at its centre stands a 'materialist' and historical analysis of social relations that foregrounds the key role of productive activity, political economy and class struggle in shaping the possibility for human freedom and self-realisation.

Life and Intellectual Context

Born 5 May 1818 in Trier, in South-West Germany, Marx was the eldest son of Heinrich and Henrietta Marx. Both parents were from relatively prosperous Jewish, middle-class backgrounds. Following Napoleon's defeat, Trier came under the rule of Prussia, which re-instituted Jewish discrimination restricting access to delimited occupations, as well as conferring Jews with inferior civil rights. To practise as a lawyer, Marx's father converted from Judaism to a more liberal Lutheran Protestantism. Against the conservative Prussian state, Heinrich Marx remained sympathetic to the principles of the Enlightenment throughout his life.

In contrast to his father with whom he remained close, Marx retained a difficult relationship with his mother, Henriette Pressburg, who was descended from a Dutch Jewish family, a tense relationship later exacerbated by conflicts concerning his inheritance. The young Marx was not only influenced by his father but perhaps more so by his neighbour, a friend of his father, Ludwig von Westphalen, the father of his future wife, Jenny. After completing his schooling at the Trier Gymnasium at the age of 17, where he also came under the influence of the Gymnasium director, Johann Heinrich Wyttenbach, a radical Kantian, Marx enrolled at the University of Bonn to study law. As a member of the Trier drinking club, Marx, like many other middle-class German students of his and later generations, including Weber, participated in duelling, undertaking conflicts of honour with aristocrats from Prussia's eastern provinces. After a year in Bonn, and partly because of his father's concern at his increasingly wild lifestyle, Marx transferred his study to Berlin, where he became involved with a group of students, professors and Bohemians known as the 'Young Hegelians'. Under their influence, he switched from studying law to philosophy, submitting a doctorate to the University of Jena influenced profoundly by Hegel's philosophy, and entitled 'On the Difference between the Natural Philosophy of Democritus and Epicurus', in 1841. As Prussian bureaucrats became increasingly hostile to the ideas of the Young Hegelians, career opportunities in academia became restricted. After a brief foray into becoming a poet, Marx was asked by Moses Hess to become a journalist for the *Rheinisch Zeitung* (*Rhineland News*) in Cologne, and within a year rose to editor-in-chief of the paper. During this period, he published several articles on the social, economic and living conditions of the wine-growing Moselle peasantry as well as the experiences of the poor who took 'dead' wood from the forests.

As a writer for a liberally oriented newspaper, he engaged in constant battles with the authorities over censorship. Following the publication of a caustic analysis of Russia, the paper was banned by the Prussian authorities, forcing Marx 'to withdraw from the public stage into the study' (Marx, 1971 [1859]: 210).

In April 1843, after a prolonged engagement, he married Jenny von Westphalen. In the same year, they left for Paris where they lived for two years. In a relatively more open and tolerant context, Marx met many European radicals and revolutionaries, including Michael Bakunin, Heinrich Heine and Arnold Ruge. Always a voracious reader, he read not only the work of British political economists such as Smith and Ricardo as well as their critics (e.g. Sismondi), but also socialists including Cabet, Fourier and Saint-Simon as well as radicals such as Babeuf, Blanqui and Proudhon. In Paris, he also began to move increasingly away from the ideas of the Young Hegelians, publishing several articles in a journal he began to edit with Arnold Ruge, the *Deutsche-Franzosische Jahrbucher.*

Marx as a Communist

Although initially a radical democrat, his politics increasingly became associated with communism and the need for social revolution, especially under the influence of Moses Hess. In addition to many radical intellectuals and workers, he met his lifelong intellectual and political companion and friend – Friedrich Engels in 1843.

Their first joint publication, *The Economic and Philosophical Manuscripts*, written in 1844, remained unpublished during their lifetime (only published later in 1932). Marx continued his break from the Young Left Hegelians by writing another work with Engels, this time criticising the work of the Bauer brothers and Max Stirner, in a pamphlet entitled 'The Holy Family' (1845) (see Marx, 1975). In 1845 Marx was expelled from Paris at the behest of the Prussian government, following the publication of critical comments in the socialist paper *Vorwaerts.* He subsequently moved to Brussels, where he fostered contacts with German, French and Belgian revolutionaries. Of particular significance was the German Educational Workers Association, which had strong links with the Communist League based in London. With Engels, Marx published yet another critique of the Young Hegelians – the *German Ideology* written in 1846 (but again remaining unpublished until 1932) – in which they set out what was later dubbed their distinctive 'materialist conception of history'. In 1848 Marx and Engels were commissioned by the German Workers Educational Association to write a document adumbrating its principles shortly before a wave of revolutionary activity swept through Europe. Subsequently published as the *Communist Manifesto*, it remained largely ignored at the time. Amid a profoundly tumultuous period – the 1848 revolutions – Marx returned to Germany to edit the *Neue Rheinische Zeitung.* Having earlier renounced his Prussian citizenship, which effectively rendered him stateless for the rest of his life, his politically radical articles meant that he could at any time be expelled as an unwanted alien. Following another brief period living in France, he was again forced into exile, this time moving to London in 1849, where he would remain here for the rest of his life. Here he encountered a number of other German political refugees, who considered it as providing a more liberal atmosphere for exiles. After his arrival in London, he remained in relative poverty, under a burden of debt and increasing political isolation, living in one and a half rooms with his family. To add to his economic misery, two of his young children died within the space of 14 months, with the death of his two-year-old son Edgar especially throwing him into a deep depression lasting a few years. A Prussian spy depicted his living conditions:

> He occupies two rooms. The one looking out on the street is the living room, and the bedroom is at the back. In the whole apartment there is not one clean and solid piece of furniture. Everything is broken down, tattered and torn, with a half-inch of dust over everything and the greatest disorder everywhere. In the middle of the living room there is a large old-fashioned table covered with an oilcloth, and on it there lie his manuscripts, books and newspapers, as well as the children's toys, and rags and tatters of his wife's sewing basket, several cups with broken rims, knives, forks, lamps, an inkpot, tumblers, Dutch day pipes, tobacco ash – in a word, everything topsy-turvy, and all on the same table. A seller of second-hand goods would be ashamed to give away such a remarkable collection of odds and ends. (McLelland, 1981: 35)
>
> [Republished with permission of Macmillan from *Karl Marx: Interviews and Recollections,* D. McLelland, 1991]

Nevertheless, Marx helped form the Social Democratic Refugees Committee as well as joining the Communist League, with whose leading members – August Willich and Karl Schapper – he remained embroiled in ongoing acrimonious political disputes. Hoping for a rekindling of the revolutionary fervour pervading Europe during the late 1840s, Marx produced two important pieces of work: *The Class Struggles in France* (1850), a collection of essays examining the context for the February uprising in France and arguably one of his best socio-historical analyses; and *The Eighteenth Brumaire of Louis Bonaparte* (1852). The latter discussed the class context that facilitated Louis Napoleon-Bonaparte – Napoleon's nephew – in securing a dictatorial coup in France in 1851. Some of the harshest aspects of poverty afflicting him, and his family, were partially ameliorated with articles commissioned by the *New York Tribune* in the mid-1850s. These writings eventually constituted the most substantial part of his published work.

With the passing of the revolutionary ferment and the consolidation of counter-revolutionary policies in Europe, Marx partially retreated from political activity to the Reading Room in the British Library. With no job, and even rejected as a clerk for a railway office because of his illegible handwriting, he read extensively on the UK and British political economists.

Focusing increasingly on political economy, Marx wrote an outline for his major study of capital, the *Grundrisse*, in 1857–8 (published in 1973), and an outline of his materialist analysis of political economy, *A Contribution to the Critique of Political Economy*, in 1859. Following a further lull in revolutionary activity throughout Europe, he helped found the First International in 1863, consisting of groups of ideologically diverse workers from across Europe. Assuming its leadership, Marx wrote its Inaugural Address in 1864. As well as facing continual financial problems, he became embroiled in a number of factional struggles with liberals, anarchists, Proudhonians and Lassalleans. In 1867 he published *Capital* (1976 [1867]), which despite its dense prose gained him significant recognition in Continental Europe, becoming translated into numerous languages within a decade. It was followed a few years later by *The Civil War in France* (1871). In his later years, Marx wrote relatively little except a critical analysis of the draft programme of the United Workers Party of Germany, *Critique of the Gotha Programme* (1875). This pamphlet, among other things, discussed the transition from a dictatorship of the proletariat to communism, the withering away of the state, the distribution of social goods and working-class internationalism. Marx was often plagued by a debilitating illness which began in the 1860s – now diagnosed as Hidradenitis suppurativa, an auto-immune disorder producing painful, fist-sized growths and carbuncles on his skin. After receiving a regular annuity from Engels following the latter's inheritance of his father's cotton business, Marx began to live a more comfortable life while residing in Maitland Park, North London. Following the death of his wife Jenny in 1881, and his daughter Eleanor in 1882, Marx passed away on 14 March 1883. Only a handful of individuals attended his funeral.

Intellectual Influences

Lenin has famously argued that Marxist thought drew on three major intellectual lineaments: the German idealism of Hegel; the French socialism of Saint-Simon and Fourier; and the British political economy of Smith and Ricardo. This is undoubtedly true, though it downplays the major impact that the Enlightenment, and especially its idea of human and social progress and the rational power of humans to reason, and reflect, had on his work.

Often considered 'the Father of Socialism', in his ideology of industrialism, Saint-Simon divided the nation in terms of producers (which included the working class, but also what we would refer to as artisans and the bourgeoisie – manufacturers, merchants and bankers), and idlers, a superfluous class destined to disappear. He argued for collective rather than private ownership of property, minimising the role of the state to a few necessary functions, and envisaged its substitution by an industrial form of government. However, Saint-Simon remained a somewhat elitist writer with regard to the masses.

Marx shared Hegel's Enlightenment and progressive view that philosophy was the highest form of knowledge whose methods and conclusions were reproduced and evident in other forms of knowledge or *Wissenschaft*. Hegel's discussion of the dialectic, of history proceeding through contradictions rising to a higher level, and of the goal of history as man's realisation of freedom, also had a major impact on his thinking. In addition, Hegel's emphasis on the world as a product of human activity was fundamentally important. As Marx notes with regard to the *Phenomenology of Spirit*:

> The great thing in Hegel's *Phenomenology* and its final result – the dialectic of negativity as the moving and producing principle – is that Hegel conceives the self-creation of man as a process, objectification

> as a loss of object as alienation and as sublation of this alienation; that he therefore grasps the nature of labour and conceives objective man ... as the result of his own labour. (1975: 332–3)

After Hegel's death in 1831, the latter's ideas were carried forward by the 'Young Hegelians'. This group, which included writers such as Bruno Bauer, Edgar Bauer, Max Stirner, Arnold Ruge, David Strauss and Ludwig Feuerbach, was diverse in outlook. One core argument the group shared was that Hegel's later work – *The Philosophy of Right*, which had provided a justification for a constitutional monarchism in Germany – marked a sharp retreat from his earlier more radical republican work. This idea was most fully elaborated by Ludwig Feuerbach. Describing himself as 'a natural philosopher in the domain of mind' (Feuerbach, 1881: ix), he argued that philosophy's starting point should not be God, or the Idea, as in Hegelian idealism, but actual humans beings as a *species*, and their material world. Ideas reflected material practices and it was man who actively created the world (as well as the idea of God). Man was really the Subject but as a result of his alienation created God and had become a predicate of God. According the Feuerbach Man needed to correct this through a 'reinversion', by reinstating humans as the active creators and subjects of the world who needed to realise their innate species powers. Although Marx accepted Feuerbach's argument, he considered his approach as unhistorical, especially in his analysis of man as a fixed species-being.

Marx also drew on the work of political economists including Adam Smith (1723–90) and his student, David Ricardo (1772–1823). Ricardo's theory of rent, wages and profits, as well as his labour theory of value as developed in *The Principles of Political Economy and Taxation* (1951 [1817]), served as an even more important starting point for Marx's own economics, especially his theory of value. In his theory of value Ricardo argued that:

> The value of a commodity, or the quantity of any other commodity for which it will exchange, depends on the relative quantity of labour which is necessary for its production, and not on the greater or less compensation which is paid for that labour. (1951: 11)

Historical, Social and Political Context

As George Mosse argues, Marx 'was riveted to his age' (1977: 4). Marx was a figure whose 'systems of thought, his political strivings and aspirations, belonged primarily to the nineteenth century' (Sperber, 2013: xviii). Writing at a crucial juncture in history following the two major revolutions of the eighteenth century – the Industrial Revolution and the French Revolution – Marx was discussing emerging processes in terms of the conflicts and tensions they unleashed. These included the 1848 revolutions and the major convulsions in Europe around 1870. Marx, moreover, stood at the threshold of two modes of production – feudalism and capitalism – in which an organised proletariat and powerful bourgeoisie began to emerge; and two forms of political system – monarchy and democracy – in which consent of the masses for rule and universal civil rights became an increasingly accepted theme.

The profound economic changes unleashed by these revolutions differed according to different countries. Germany, as a unified state, did not emerge until 1871. Rather it signified a geographical expression denoting states that possessed a shared language and which had been part of the Holy Roman Empire. The country remained divided into 39 states, pursuing their own self-interest and ruled on the basis of various fixed estates. Although socialists only constituted a small component of the political horizon, French utopian socialist ideas began to be recognised in Germany from the 1830s onwards (Butler, 1926). Slow industrialisation saw a country characterised largely by agricultural peasantry – with three-quarters of the population living off the land (McLelland, 1970: 11). The breakdown of serfdom caused the emergence of large numbers of landless tenants, who either became day labourers, or moved into the towns to become part of the burgeoning proletariat. Moreover, as feudal estates became increasingly run on economic lines, land became concentrated, with 1 million hectares passing to large landowners between 1815 and 1846 (McLelland, 1970: 12). More specifically, eighteenth- and nineteenth-century Catholic Trier, where Marx grew up, had no industry and remained fundamentally rural and agricultural. Like all German states, it was organised based on a medieval 'society of orders' characterised by hierarchical rights and privileges. Here, 'rights and privileges, as well as obligations and restrictions, pertained not to individuals but to groups whose membership came from status derived at birth, or from membership of a religious confession. Members of different groups possessed very different rights and privileges, generally set down in legally binding charters' (Sperber, 2013: 4–5). However, this changed fundamentally with the invasion of Trier by France in 1794. In the name of a powerful republicanism, the latter implemented revolutionary and wide-scale social, political, administrative and legal reforms. The society of orders of differential rights, including minimal rights pertaining to Jews, became replaced by a system in which all individuals were equal before the law and in which sovereignty was associated with the will of the people rather than a hereditary sovereign. Though initially opposed, following Napoleon's reconciliation with the Catholic Church, these reforms began to receive more widespread support. This included support from Heinrich Marx, a strong advocate of Enlightenment thinking based on rationalist thinking, human equality and basic rights. However, the defeat of Napoleon in 1813, followed by the Congress of Vienna in 1815, reorganised Europe and granted large swathes of Germany west of the Rhine, which for the most part had adhered to Catholicism, to a dominating and monarchical Protestant Prussia within the context of the creation of a Confederation of German States. Politically, it was a period marked by acute repression, increased taxes and strict censorship. Promises of liberal reform disappeared under the reign of Frederick William III and his son, Frederick William IV. During the 1830s censorship was redoubled and surveillance of political agitators increased, with control over universities tightened. With no constitution, the institutionalisation of any of the fundamental rights of man – including parliament, trial by jury or rights to free speech – remained absent. Instead a powerful and reactionary self-interested Junker agricultural class, adhering to Protestantism, dominated German politics in Prussia.

Although industrial development remained both slow and uneven, the transformation of industry had huge demographic effects, with increases in the population of about 50% between 1815 and 1855 and large numbers moving from the countryside to the city, engendering a growing working class whose numbers increased seven-fold between 1800 and 1848 (McLelland, 1970: 17). Not only was the working day lengthened but women and children also became part of the industrial army. With falling wages, many lived well below subsistence level characterised by peculiarly high levels of squalor, immiseration and poverty. This socio-economic context created acute social tensions. Germany lacked a strong, self-conscious bourgeoisie which was fragmented between intellectuals and industrialists. Though economically lagging behind when compared with England, France and Belgium, it remained at the forefront of intellectual production – with philosophers including Kant, Fichte, Goethe, Hegel and Schiller. If Germany was intellectually a frontrunner in thinking, France was characterised by the most advanced political thinking and at the forefront of workers' revolutionary politics, while England remained the leading country economically. For much of his life Marx pinned his hopes of a socialist revolution on the French proletariat.

Marx therefore wrote at a time of profound social and economic turmoil not only in Germany, but throughout Western Europe generally, including France, Belgium and England. For example, uprisings took place in the 1820s and 1830s throughout Europe against reactionary despotisms, monarchies, but also in response to the profoundly unjust social and economic conditions that were developing. During the early 1840s, when Marx's political position was that of a radical democrat, his writings were aimed at the authoritarian Prussian rule and the lack of a democratic constitution, including many early articles on press freedom and censorship. When he moved to England in the late 1840s the country, unlike Germany, was at the forefront of industrial production propelled forward by mechanical and steam power. However, like Germany, the social transformations engendered by industrialisation and the economic wealth produced had profound socio-economic and dehumanising implications, creating an urban proletariat of factory workers, but also politically flourishing socialist groupings including Owenites and Chartists. In his powerful descriptions of the southern Lancashire cotton and textile industries containing poor labourers, Engels, in *The Condition of the English Working Class* (1845), noted how many displaced hand-loom weavers, artisans or agricultural labourers had been reduced to slum living conditions, dire poverty and experienced steep mortality rates.

Marx and Engels wrote the Communist Manifesto in 1848 on the eve of a whole series of revolutions which swept throughout Europe including in France, Belgium, Switzerland and Germany. In challenging the ancient regime, authoritarian monarchies and their fundamental beliefs, many saw Paris as the centre of these struggles, believing that if it toppled this would spark and lend military strength to other insurgencies. Moreover, the democratic revolution would, for Marx, constitute the prelude to a second workers' revolution. However, the failure of these revolutions led instead to a period of counter-revolution in Europe, exemplified by the assumption of power by Louis Napoleon in 1849. Nevertheless, after a lull, confrontations with the existing social order continued throughout the subsequent decades as social and political aspirations of the European working class endured. The years between 1866 and 1871 were again characterised by profound upheaval. Prussia's war with Austria in 1866, and with France in 1870, led to a surge in nationalism. In England struggles over expanding the democratic franchise saw the emergence of the Second Reform Act while opposition to English rule in Ireland grew. In France pro-republican struggles emerged against Louis Napoleon's rule, while a coup took place in Romania, and a revolution in Spain. Struggles and uprisings also took place in Italy as nationalist struggles in the Austrian Empire proliferated (Sperber, 2013: 365). All of these processes led to widespread strikes across Europe. Following the defeat of Napoleon III in France in 1870, a socialist revolutionary government led by the working class took charge for three months between March and May 1871. This was the first time that the proletariat had held political power. Despite its short existence Marx saw the French Commune as providing a future blueprint of future working-class rule or a 'dictatorship of the proletariat', which he discussed in his *The Civil War in France* (1871). However, various factional disputes that emerged after the collapse of the French Commune eventually led to the dissolution of the International.

As political and social processes unfolded Marx's politics also evolved. Although often painted as a intransigent revolutionary, his conception of the relationship between reformist and revolutionary politics was complex, non-dogmatic and many-sided.

Arguments and Ideas

Early Critique of Hegel

Marx's early works centre on his critique of monarchy, religion, Hegel and the Young Hegelians. Using the term 'critique' in both its Kantian and Hegelian sense, he sought to show the social and historical conditions of possibility of religion and how it could be transcended. Although ordinarily read simply as a materialist inversion of Hegel's idealism, Marx's critique saw materialism and idealism as interconnected moments incorporated in social practice. Drawing on Feuerbach's discussion of the problematic nature of abstraction in Hegel's work in which subjects and predicates are inverted, he criticised Hegel on several grounds: from his theory of law to his economics and his politics. For Marx, Hegel, despite his revolutionary thinking, ultimately adhered to the standpoint of political economy. Moreover, according to Marx, a resolution to the contradictions characterising the modern world could not come through philosophy or a critique of religion and consciousness, as many of the Young Hegelians believed, but only be realised in practice, through practical activity geared to changing the world. It was only on this basis that it was possible to create a society in which human self-realisation could flourish. This entailed both the abolition of the existing form of repressive state, and the increasingly pervasiveness of money, markets, capital, and commodities.

A Theory of Human Nature

Rejecting the idea that human beings were unchanging or that they had a fixed human nature, Marx argued that as society changes so do the beliefs, desires and conceptions of individuals. Human characteristics depended on the ensemble of the social relationships within which they were embedded. Nevertheless, humans possessed certain natural needs and desires. These include the need:

> for other human beings, for sexual relations, for food, water, clothing, shelter, rest and, more generally, for circumstances that are conducive to physical health rather than disease ... the need of people for a breadth and diversity of pursuit and hence of personal development, as Marx himself expresses these, 'all-round activity', 'all-round development of individuals', 'free development of individuals', 'the means of cultivating [one's] gifts in all directions', and so on. (Geras, 1983: 88–9)

Although they could be characterised by certain shared biological needs, humans differed from animals since they possessed the power of reflection: they were conscious or self-conscious beings. Through the power of reflection, and their ability to produce tools, providing them with a dialectical relation to nature, humans could reflect upon how they would produce and so meet their needs in different ways undetermined by their natural instincts. Human history for Marx, was about the different and shifting ways through which humans organised themselves to meet their needs through 'objectifying' themselves – a term derived from Hegel.

Furthermore, consciousness was, for Marx, inseparable from the productive activity in which humans engaged. In both his *Theses on Feuerbach* (1845) and, with Engels, in *The German Ideology* (1846), Marx reiterated the view that thought could not be isolated from social practice. Rather, it could only be understood as part of social life.

Productive Activity and Alienation

In his understanding of the social world, productive activity remained fundamental. Its importance was initially outlined in the *Economic and Philosophical Manuscripts*. As Arthur notes:

> In 1844 a turning point occurs in Marx's philosophical development. For the first time he attributes fundamental ontological significance to productive activity. Through material production humanity comes to be what it is. Through the process of production the worker realizes his potential and becomes objective to himself in his product. He develops his productive powers and knows himself in and through his activity and its result. (1986: 5)
>
> [Republished with permission of Basil Blackwell, from *Dialectics of Labour: Marx and his Relation to Hegel,* C. J. Arthur, 1986. Reproduced with permission of The Licensor through PLSclear]

Productive activity referred to more than 'economic practices' pointing to the externalisation of human capacities and powers. In addition, it bound humans to nature, so that as they transformed the latter by objectifying themselves through their labour power, they also transformed themselves. Through this process they expressed and realised themselves as a species-being.

The relation between humans and nature and between themselves was a dynamic one, in which both humans and nature were continually transformed. As a two-fold activity production was simultaneously a natural (biologically endowed) and a social activity involving the co-operation of several individuals. Humans, for Marx, were fundamentally social beings. As he notes: 'The human being is in the most literal sense a *zoon politikon* [social animal], not merely a gregarious animal, but an animal which can individuate itself only in the midst of society' (1973 [1858]: 84).

Changes in the organisation of production brought about changes in society, and therefore in people's ways of conceiving the world – their beliefs, desires, aims, etc. As a material interchange with nature, productive activity entailed the combination and transformation of raw materials into goods for human consumption.

A further fundamental concept Marx develops in his *Economic and Philosophical Manuscripts* (1844) is the concept of alienation. In a context where humans come to know themselves through a process of objectification, productive activity 'mediates' the relation between humans and nature. On the one hand they develop 'objective' productive powers allowing them to use natural materials with decreasing effort. On the other hand they cultivate a 'subjective' 'wealth of human needs' and human sensibilities (e.g. 'a musical ear, an eye for beauty') (Arthur, 1986: 7). However, within class societies, increasing control over nature becomes correlated with increasing alienation, so that humans begin to come under the sway of alien social forces that they themselves had created. Although alienation characterises all spheres of life, in modern capitalist societies it is rooted in the mode of work and how individuals produce. Productive activity itself becomes mediated through the development of what Mészáros (1971) calls 'second-order mediations' including the division of labour, exchange, wages and private property. Under capitalism waged work becomes a means rather than an end in itself, and the created product, and capital, begin to hold sway over humans. The labourer's productive activity becomes a commodity to be brought and sold like any other. It becomes 'estranged labour'.

Marx depicts four interrelated aspects or manifestations of alienation. A human is alienated as follows:

- from nature she or he is alienated from the products of his or her labour;
- from himself or herself (from his or her own activity and the act of production) 'his work activity does not belong to him';
- from his or her species being – 'Estranged labour turns man's [sic] species being ... into a being alien to him, into a means for his individual existence';
- from other humans.

One of the foremost expressions of alienation in modern life for Marx is money, a quasi-magical power which makes 'contradictions embrace'.

The Materialist Theory of History

In contradistinction to Hegel and the Young Hegelians, Marx develops what was referred to after his death as 'the materialist theory of history', though this later designation tended to downplay the role of consciousness in his work. This stated that:

> The premises from which we begin are not arbitrary ones, not dogmas, but real premises from which abstraction can only be made in the imagination. They are real individuals, their activity and the material conditions of their life, both those which they find already existing and those produced by their activity. These premises can thus be verified in a purely empirical way. (Marx and Engels, 1970 [1846]: 42)

In the two-fold nature of production noted above, the material aspect refers to the *forces of production* – the possession of tools, raw materials, machinery, computers, etc. – available in a society. Their development is both shaped by and in turn shapes the social aspect of production – *the relations of production* which concern the co-operation of individuals in producing the things they need. As he asserts: 'The first historical act is thus ... the production of material life itself. An indeed this is an historical act, a fundamental condition of all history' (1970 [1846]: 39).

For Marx, one cannot understand the nature of society without knowing who controls the means of production. Classes arise when the direct producers have been separated from the means of production which become taken up by a minority. This minority exploits the majority by appropriating their surplus labour. The historically specific combination and correspondence of forces of production and relations of production constitutes a *mode of production*. Marx identifies five (sometimes four) major modes of production that have heretofore existed: the Primitive; the Asiatic; the Ancient; the Feudal; and the Capitalist. He also posits a future mode of production, one that he believes will come into being, Communism. Of these the first and last are classless societies. Importantly, for Marx, relations of production in capitalism are not abstract relationships between individual and individual but social relations – between worker and capitalist, serf and landlord, etc.:

> Society does not consist of individuals but expresses the sum of interrelations, the relations within which these individuals stand. As if someone were to say: Seen from the perspective of society, there are no slaves and no citizens; both are human beings. Rather they are that outside society. To be a slave, to be a citizen, are social characteristics, relations between human beings A and B. Human being A as such, is not a slave he is a slave in and through society. (Marx, 1973 [1858]: 265)

For Marx the notion of an individual as an isolated subject independent of socio-historical context is equally as problematical as the concept of society as an entity existing over and above individuals. Both are problematical 'abstractions' generated in determinate social and historical conditions – specifically where alienated bourgeois social relationships predominate (Frisby and Sayer, 1986: 91). In such a context society appears erroneously as a second nature.

The dynamic which underlies the movement from one mode of production to another is to be found in the contradictions inherent in each mode, especially the contradiction between the forces and relations of production. Marx famously described such a process in the *Contribution to the Critique of Political Economy*:

> At a certain stage of their development, the material productive forces of society come into conflict with the existing relations of production, or – what is but a legal expression of the same thing – with the property relations within which they have been at work hitherto. From forms of development of these productive forces, these relations turn

> into their fetters. Then begins an epoch of social evolution. (Marx, 1971 [1859]: Preface)

The relation between the productive forces and the relations of production is a complex issue, though largely undeveloped in his writings. Although a dialectical, two-way relationship exists between them, for the most part Marx regards the relations of production as setting as limits or 'corresponding' to the forces of production (Cohen, 1978).

Class Struggle

According to Marx, explanations for understanding specific social formations hinge on the unequal access to the means of production and the class struggles that ensue. In the ancient mode of production slaves were owned by slave owners and were instruments of production. In feudalism, serfs have some access to the means of production in terms of owning tools and instruments, though they do not own the land in the formal sense. In such a context they are compelled to provide part of their labour either in produce or in terms of labour to the lord in lieu of 'renting' the land. In both contexts those who own the means of production use force or violence to extract surplus labour. By contrast, in capitalism, the worker is legally or formally free and, crucially, exploitation becomes hidden. However, because workers have no access to the means of production, which are owned by the bourgeoisie, they are compelled to sell their labour power. Marx sometimes dissolves this dichotomy between freedom and compulsion in capitalism by referring to this as a form of 'wage slavery'.

By occupying similar social positions vis-à-vis the means of production and their access to it, groups develop class interests and participate in class struggles to improve their collective fate. This process whereby a class becomes transformed from a 'class-in-itself' to a 'class-for-itself' is by no means automatic. The separate individuals 'form a class only insofar as they have to carry out a common battle against another class; otherwise they are on hostile terms with each other as competitors' (Marx and Engels, (1970 [1846]: 82). Nevertheless, through shared conditions of existence and struggle, and increasing communication facilitated in Marx's day by the factory system of mass production, workers can become a united and collective force.

The Role of Ideas and the State

Marx attempted to develop a deep connection between ideas, thinking and thought and the concrete social relationships within which these emerged. For Marx, the types of ideas held by individuals and groups correspond to the social and class positions of those who held them. That is, many philosophies and ideologies were the direct or indirect expressions of class interests and served functions for these groups, rather than expressing objective or neutral standpoints on the world. This was not to assert a reductive position in which all individual representatives of a class held the same moral, political, economic and social viewpoint, rather individuals generally and collectively express the class groupings' overall cast of mind.

Although Marx recognised the state as generally expressing class conflict, a coherent and systematic theory of the state remained elusive in his writings. Instead, his *oeuvre* is characterised by alternating emphases and discussions pitched at different levels of abstraction – sometimes contradictory and discontinuous – about the nature of the state. These, *inter alia*, see the state variously as acting as an instrument of bourgeois rule; distinguishing its ideological appearance as serving the general interests of society as a whole from its particular interest in serving capital; as constituting a relation of production; as acting as a guarantor of capital accumulation; as expressing the space within which class struggles unfold; and as maintaining the social order and protecting private property. In more empirical and less philosophical works such as *The Eighteenth Brumaire of Louis Bonaparte* (1852), Marx sees the state as having acquired a level of autonomy within the context of a temporary equilibrium in class struggles, emphasising the importance of the state's role in maintaining social order in facilitating bourgeois domination.

These more nuanced discussions of class can be contrasted with more simplistic comments and aphorisms in *The Communist Manifesto*, where the state in shorthand is 'a committee for managing the affairs of the bourgeoisie' (Marx and Engels, 1968 [1848]: 33), and in Marx's famous 1859 Preface to *A Contribution to the Critique of Political Economy* where the state is reduced to what he terms a 'superstructure'. In this famous base–superstructure model, Marx argued that the ideological, political and legal superstructures existing within a social formation were determined by an economic or material base:

> In the social production of their life, men enter into definite relations that are indispensable and independent of their will, relations of production which correspond to a definite stage of development of their material productive forces. The sum total of these relations of production constitutes the economic structure of society, the real foundation, on which rises a legal and political superstructure and to which correspond definite forms of social consciousness. The mode of production of material life conditions the social, political and intellectual life process in general. It is not the consciousness of men that determines their being, but, on the contrary, their social being that determines their consciousness... With the change in the economic foundation, the entire immense superstructure is more or less rapidly transformed. (1971 [1859]: Preface)

Political Economy

Capital (1976 [1867]) is often seen as Marx's magnum opus. Central to his whole analysis is the belief that capitalism is profoundly a revolutionary social form, and that it differs markedly from all previous modes of production. The complexity of the book is partly an effect of the Hegelian method he deploys which he describes in some detail in an earlier work that served as an outline to *Capital*, the *Grundrisse* (1973 [1858]). In the *Grundrisse* (1973 [1858]: 100–8) he talks of 'rising from the abstract to the concrete'. Such a method is necessary, he believes, since science would be superfluous if outward appearances and essences coincided. It is therefore his aim to penetrate beneath the surface appearances of capitalism and the semblances and illusory forms its produces, for example in terms of foregrounding supply and demand or focusing on individuals. Instead he attempts to reveal its underlying essence and inner logic and connections or in focusing on individuals rather than historically evolving social relationships. Supply and demand and the individual are both equally misleading phenomenal forms through which social relations appear, as akin to a mirage. To grasp this entails moving from the sphere of consumption to the 'hidden abode of production'. Rather than beginning with the population, which Marx regards as an abstraction, a 'chaotic conception' (1973 [1858]: 100), he begins with the simple world of commodities as they appear to us and moves with ever greater complexity as each step follows from the inadequacies and contradictions inherent in earlier ones.

Marx understood *Capital* as a 'critique' of political economy aimed to supplant the partial insights of political economists including Smith, Ricardo, Say, James and Malthus, not only by criticising capitalism's historical specificity, reflecting a given form of society, but also in terms of using a dialectical approach to criticise the limited and time-bound nature of the categories and abstractions that political economists used. In addition, although *Capital* contains historical discussions within it, it is not strictly speaking a work about the concrete history of capitalism, but rather a theory of capital. Although aimed at helping to explain capitalism, it is not about actually existing capitalism but about the the more general production process of capital. It has been argued that capital predates capitalism – as generalised commodity production – and could, therefore, also remain after it as in the Soviet Union (Mészáros, 2000). Furthermore, for Marx capital was not a thing, but a social relation, assuming the form of a relation between things. In pre-capitalist societies such as ancient Greece, where limited forms of commodity production existed, a commodity, C, was exchanged for money, M, to buy another commodity, C: this simple exchange could be expressed in the formula C–M–C. In capitalism, by contrast, the circulation of commodities takes the form of M–C–M. Money is invested to produce commodities which are then exchanged for more money, which was greater than the original investment. The use of money to increase value, converts it into capital. Moreover, capital only really came into existence when the commodity bought and sold was of a special type, namely labour power, since only this allowed the 'self-expansion of value'.

As Sperber notes, Marx's discussion of political economy is 'framed by five conceptual distinctions':

> Between use value and exchange value; between the use of money to exchange commodities and the use of money to accumulate capital; between labour and labour power; between constant and variable capital; and between the rate of surplus value and the rate of profit. (2013: 427).

Capital expands the discussion of the labour theory of value initially developed by Adam Smith and Ricardo. In previous modes of production, production was aimed solely at producing objects with use-values to be used and consumed by the producer. However, in capitalism they also acquired an exchange-value – they were produced in order to be exchanged rather than used directly. If use-value was concrete and qualitative, referring to the quality an object had, and its ability to meet a specific need, exchange value by contrast was abstract and quantitative, reflecting what commodities had in common. It was *value*, Marx argued, that commodities shared, and which made incommensurable objects such as wheat or linen commensurable, facilitating their exchange. Value itself was a reflection of the cost to society of producing that commodity in terms of the amount of labour power expended to produce it, its socially necessary labour time. The exchange value of labour power was the labour time required to produce that labour power and keep it in subsistence. A central feature of Marx's analysis is the domination of the qualitative differences of objects, as expressed in their use-value, by quantitative differences as denoted by the abstraction of value and expressed through money.

In pre-capitalist social formations the distribution of labour was for the most part known, controlled and collectively regulated as producers knew what to produce to meet their needs, as well as those of the exploiting class. Capitalism, however, entails private individuals working independently. Yet, even though producers become increasingly interdependent on one another, production becomes blind and unplanned, since there is no necessary connection between the useful labour of private individuals and the needs of society as a whole. If private useful labour only becomes social when its products are sold, the only means for realising how much socially necessary labour each product contained was through money – a commodity that constituted a universal equivalent. In capitalism producers compete with other producers to make goods as cheaply as possible to sell on the market. This entails increasing the productivity of labour by adopting state-of-the-art production techniques used by rivals.

In his analysis of exploitation, Marx argues that the labourer creates more value during a working day than the wages he or she receives in renumeration from the capitalist. If a worker works for 10 hours, he or she may only be paid for 5 hours; the excess of 5 hours constitutes the level of surplus value. The rate of surplus value – the ratio of the profit the capitalist acquired in relation to costs and expenditure – could be increased either in absolute terms, by making the worker work longer during the day, or in relative terms by increasing the intensity and efficiency of the work and/or the productivity of labour. Although both forms of surplus value existed, as capitalism develops relative surplus value becomes increasingly important. As capitalists push to increase profits and productivity, so workers resist such increasing exploitation, for example by campaigning for shorter hours and a reduced working day or lower productivity targets through unions.

Marx also made a fundamental distinction between constant and variable capital: the former includes production facilities, raw materials and machinery, while the latter referred primarily to the cost of workers' wages. Only the latter, variable capital, increases value. It was the relation between dead and living labour – the organic composition of capital – that determined the rate of profit.

In addition, as capitalism develops, a shift from 'manufacture' to 'machinofacture' takes place wherein the 'broad foundation of the town handicrafts and the domestic industries of the countryside' (1976 [1867]: 490) becomes replaced by machines, and the labour process relentlessly modified by technological innovations.

According to Marx, economic crises were inherent in the commodity form. The effect of constant innovation and the introduction of new technologies to increase productivity and surplus value tended to reduce the general rate of profit, so there existed a tendency for the rate of profit to fall in capitalism. As Callinicos notes: 'The greater productivity of labour, which reflects humanity's growing power over nature, takes the form, within capitalist relations of production, of a rising organic composition of capital, and hence a falling rate of profit. It is this process which underlies economic crises' (1983: 132). As more workers are replaced by machines as a result of intensified competition between capitalists, there is a shift in the organic composition of capital, so that less labour is available to produce value, and less money becomes available for workers to buy goods and commodities, which in turn creates a vicious cycle leading to a further decline in the rate of profit.

In *Capital*, Marx also pointed to the increasing centralisation and concentration of capital. The latter took place when various capital, as a result of competition and the expanded use of machinery to increase productivity, grew through the accumulation of greater amounts of surplus value. Centralisation entailed the absorption of smaller firms, which could not compete with larger ones. As well as the displacement of smaller firms, competition and mechanisation led to the increasing immerisation of the proletariat as less labour became required and wages reduced, creating both emigration and the formation of an unemployed 'industrial reserve army' which could be drawn upon in times of boom. It also produced a potentially volatile contradiction between the enormous creation of wealth for the bourgeoisie and the acute poverty and misery experienced by the workers through exploitation. Volume 1 of *Capital* focused on production and distribution, while Volumes 2 and 3, compiled by Engels from Marx's various manuscripts after Marx's death and published in 1885 and 1894, respectively, focused on distribution and the transformation of value through sale into price as well as the falling rate of profit, while Volume 3 focused on both production and circulation, examining credit and finance, currency and forms of agricultural production.

Contemporary Relevance and Applications

Marx's work has had an enormous impact on subsequent writers, perhaps more so than any other sociological thinker. Given that he himself wrote on philosophy, history, politics and sociology, his work has expanded into numerous areas.

THE CRITIQUE OF CAPITALISM TODAY

The 2007–8 global financial crisis paved the way for a renewed interest in Marx, having been relatively marginalised in the era following the collapse of the Soviet Union. Though there are many aspects to his thought, Marx's main contribution to social theory is to initiate the critique of capitalism, which he understands as a social system congenitally restricted by the necessity of capital accumulation. While capitalism harbours great emancipatory potential in its technological and organisational capacities, these are operationalised through social relations of domination. This central contradiction is structurally anchored in the economic imperatives at root of the societal design. Capitalism is a deeply irrational social system that, unbridled, will always invert its immanent potential. Today, as well as various societal crises evidencing system-internal contradictions, we also have various ecological crises evidencing system-external contradictions in our relation to the environment. This leads us to reconsider seriously two of Marx's central questions: whether capitalism has real and determinable limits; and whether enlightened, self-conscious and radical social transformation is possible from within.

Robert Brenner has made significant contributions to Marxist analysis in both economics and history. In history, he forwarded what became known as the 'Brenner thesis' with his paper 'Agrarian Class Structure and Economic Development in Pre-industrial Europe' (1976). In this paper he challenged Henri Pirenne's thesis argument concerning the development of capitalism in England as opposed to other countries including France. More generally, Brenner re-examined the transition from feudalism to capitalism. Looking at the demographic impact of the Black Death from around 1350 on the fief system, and in a context of a weak extant peasantry, Brenner argued the decrease in population meant that many powerful landlords took over fiefs – gaining almost three-quarters of the land. These landlords then leased these to capitalist tenants, introducing rents, as well as employing rural peasants as wage labourers, while improving and investing in production techniques to sell produce on the market. Class struggle and the balance of forces between the classes constituted the engine driving these processes. This initiated an agricultural revolution in fifteenth-century England in which capitalist farming subsequently spread into the development of capitalist industry.

By contrast, in France, a strong peasantry and peasant revolts resulted in consolidated small and medium-sized peasant holdings and customs, and laws preventing the introduction of rising rents and the alienability of land. The paradoxical result was stagnant forms of agricultural development and protracted rural poverty. As well as challenging developmental economists including Andre Gunder Frank and Paul Sweezy for their belief that economies in developed countries entailed underdevelopment in poorer peripheral countries as a form of 'neo-Smithian Marxism' (Brenner, 1977), Brenner examined the development of the current global economic crises in *The Economics of Global Turbulence* (2006). The long-term crisis in profitability since the Second World War, he argued was the result of competition between capitalists rather than an outcome of the ongoing class struggle between labour and capital.

The American Marxist Erik Olin Wright has made a significant contribution in extending Marx's analysis of class to understand contemporary society. Wright (1978) attempts to theorise the development of problematic middle-class groupings – managers, small employers and semi-autonomous wage earners which challenge the simple two-class binary model ordinarily associated with Marxism. According to Wright, managers occupy a contradictory class location between the bourgeoisie and proletariat, while semi-autonomous workers occupy a position between the petty bourgeoisie and proletariat, and small employers between the bourgeoisie and petty bourgeoisie. Moreover, classes can be distinguished not only according to their ownership of the means of production, but also in terms of their control over investment and accumulation, control over the means of production and control over labour power. The bourgeoisie have control over all three of these dimensions, while classes such as the petty bourgeoisie do not control labour power. This can be seen in Figure 1.

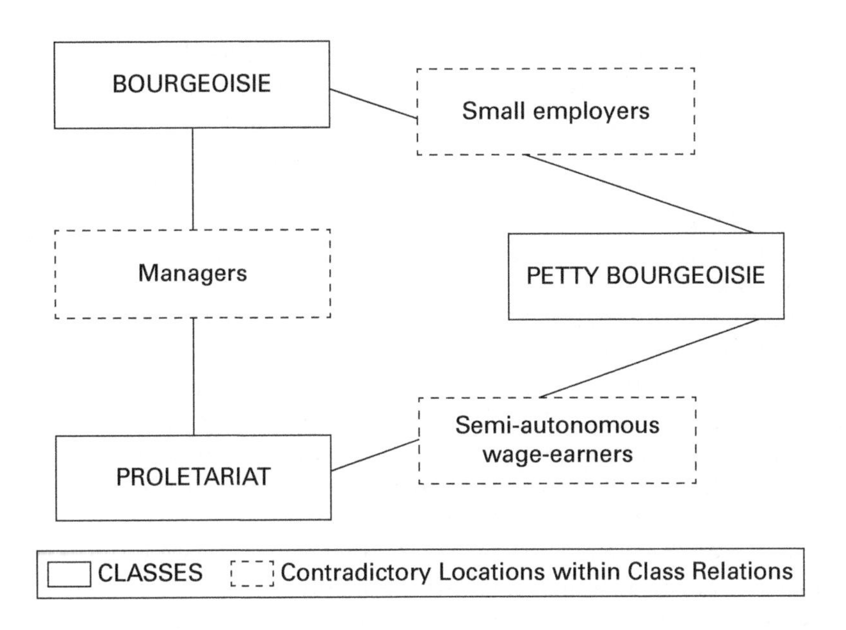

Criticisms

Given that Marxism was a political practice, it followed that as political conditions changed so too did the reception and interpretation of Marxist theory and thinking. The most influential interpreter of Marx's thought after his death was undoubtedly Engels, who became heavily influenced by Darwinism and evolutionary theory, which became popular after Marx's death. However, the biggest single factor shaping the reception of Marx's writings after his death was the Russian Revolution and the political leaders and thinkers through which many of Marx's complex ideas were simplified. Consequently, one of the major criticisms of Marxism has been for its economic reductionism manifested most significantly in the metaphor of a base–superstructure. During his lifetime Engels in a letter to J. Bloch had already responded to such reductive 'economistic' readings by seeing the 'material' element as the ultimately determining force:

> According to the materialist conception of history, the ultimately determining element in history is the production and reproduction of real life... Hence if somebody twists this into saying that the economic element is the only determining one, he [*sic*] transforms that proposition into a meaningless, abstract, and senseless phrase. The economic situation is the basis, but the various elements of the superstructure ... also exercise their influence upon the cause of the class struggle and in many cases are preponderant in determining their form. (Engels to Bloch 21 September 1890, cited in Sayer, 1987: 6)

Nevertheless, although the base–superstructure model has been reinterpreted and defended (MacIntyre, 1953; Sayer, 1987; Thompson, 1978; Williams, 1977) other sociologists have preferred to adopt what they see as Weber's more flexible multi-causal model, which allows social, ideological and political factors, including the state, more explanatory autonomy than permitted by Marx's understanding. But conversely, the Weberian approach, with its focus on contingency, lacks the developmental historical framework underpinning Marx's work.

The second major sets of criticism directed at Marx centre on the difference between capitalism in Marx's day and capitalism today. Writers including Elias (2012) and Dahrendorf (1959), for example, have argued that the structure of capitalism has changed profoundly since Marx's day. These changes are evident in the ownership structure of capital, with the rise of shareholders. But there are also fundamental changes in the modern class structure with the development of white-collar workers and the services sector at the expense of manual and factory workers of nineteenth-century capitalism as well as the institutionalisation of trade unions, which act as a buffer in the antagonistic relation between capital and labour. Others in the Frankfurt School have argued that capitalism has shifted from its liberal, unregulated form in Marx's day to a monopoly type of state capitalism (Pollack, 1990).

Finally, Marx's economics have been criticised by, among others, the Austrian economist, Eugene Böhm-Bawerk (Böhm-Bawerk et al., 1984 [1896]), who through his theory of time preferences argues that Marx's theory of value and exploitation is highly questionable for ignoring the fact that the same amount of labour should receive different rewards according to when it takes place.

Conclusion

Marx's distinction between feudalism and capitalism, and the profoundly distinct and revolutionary character of the latter, shares family resemblances with other sociological binaries such as Tönnies' *Gemeinschaft* (community) and *Gesellschaft* (society), Maine's status and contract, Weber's traditional and rational societies, and Spencer's military and industrial societies. Yet, his narrowing in on capital, a social relation, as the hidden explanatory force, together with the role of the working class in shaping the totality of modern social life, differs from their foci.

When theorists move beyond simple reductionist understandings of Marx's work, it is difficult to overstate his importance in helping to understand the shifting nature of social relations, processes of exploitation and domination, and the central roles that capital and capitalism play in structuring and shaping society within a social and historical framework. However, it is important to recognise that he was writing at a time in history very different from the current conjuncture where capitalism was only beginning to develop and monarchy, not political democracy, was the norm. If for Hegel private property and recognition was central for human freedom, for Marx it was the abolition of private property and the mutual recognition by humans of one another as people with needs. This formed the basis not of a monetary form of equality, but of an equality of self-realisation and the basis for human social freedom.

References

Arthur, C. J. (1986) *Dialectics of Labour: Marx and his Relation to Hegel*. Oxford: Basil Blackwell.

Böhm-Bawerk, E., Sweezy, P. and Hilferding, R. (1984) *Karl Marx and the Close of His System & Böhm-Bawerk's Criticism of Marx*. New York: Orion Editions.

Brenner, R. (1976) Agrarian Class Structure and Economic Development in Pre-Industrial Europe. *Past & Present*, 70, pp. 30–75.

Brenner, R. (1977) The Origins of Capitalist Development: A Critique of Neo-Smithian Marxism. *New Left Review*, 104, pp. 25–92.

Brenner, R. (2006) *The Economics of Global Turbulence: The Advanced Capitalist Economies from Long Boom to Long Downturn, 1945–2005*. London: Verso.

Butler, E. M. (1926) *The Saint-Simonian Religion in Germany: A Study of the Young German Movement*. Cambridge: Cambridge University Press.

Callinicos, A. (1983) *The Revolutionary Ideas of Karl Marx*. London: Bookmarks.

Chitty, A. (2013) Recognition and Property in Hegel and the Early Marx. *Ethical Theory and Moral Practice*, 16 (4), pp. 685–97.

Cohen, G (1978) *Karl Marx's Theory of History: A Defence*. Oxford: Oxford University Press.

Dahrendorf, R. (1959) *Class Conflict in Industrial Society*. Revised edition. London: Routledge & Kegan Paul.

Elias (2012) 'Karl Marx as Sociologist and Political Ideologist', in *What is Sociology*. Dublin: UCD Press, pp. 173–200.

Engels, F. (1845) *Condition of the Working Class in England* [online]. Available at: https://www.marxists.org/archive/marx/works/download/pdf/condition-working-class-england.pdf (Accessed 22 July 2019).

Feuerbach, L. (1881) *The Essence of Christianity*. London: Trubner.

Frisby, D and Sayer, D. (1986) *Society*. London: Tavistock.

Geras, N. (1983) *Marx and Human Nature: Refutation of a Legend*. London: Verso.

Kilminster, R (2018) Karl Marx: New Perspectives'. In: J. E. Castro et al. (eds) *Time, Science and the Critique of Technological Reason: Essays in Honour of Herminio Martins*. London: Palgrave, pp. 231–61.

MacIntyre, A. (1953) *Marxism: An Interpretation*. London: SCM Press.

Marx, K. (1845) *Theses on Feuerbach* [online]. Available at: https://www.marxists.org/archive/marx/works/1845/theses/theses.htm (Accessed 22 July 2019).
Marx, K. (1850) *The Class Struggles in France, 1848-1850* [online]. Available at: https://www.marxists.org/archive/marx/works/download/pdf/Class_Struggles_in_France.pdf (Accessed 22 July 2019).
Marx, K. (1852) *The Eighteenth Brumaire of Louis Bonaparte* [online]. Available at: https://www.marxists.org/archive/marx/works/1852/18th-brumaire/ (Accessed 22 July 2019).
Marx, K. (1871) *The Civil War in France* [online]. Available at: https://www.marxists.org/archive/marx/works/1871/civil-war-france/ (Accessed 22 July 2019).
Marx, K. (1875) *Critique of the Gotha Programme* [online]. Available at: https://www.marxists.org/archive/marx/works/1875/gotha/ (Accessed 22 July 2019).
Marx, K. (1971 [1859]) *A Contribution to the Critique of Political Economy*. London: Lawrence and Wishart.
Marx, K. (1975 [1844]) *Economic and Philosophical Manuscripts of 1844*. New edition. London: Lawrence & Wishart.
Marx, K. (1970 [1843]) *Critique of Hegel's Philosophy of Right*. Oxford: Oxford University Press [online]. Available at: https://www.marxists.org/archive/marx/works/download/Marx_Critique_of_Hegels_Philosophy_of_Right.pdf (Accessed 22 July 2019).
Marx, K. (1973 [1858]) *Grundrisse: Foundations for the Critique of Political Economy*. Harmondsworth: Penguin.
Marx, K. (1975) *Early Writings*. London: Harmondsworth.
Marx, K. (1976 [1867]) *Capital: A Critique of Political Economy*, Vol. 1. Harmondsworth: Penguin.
Marx, K. and Engels, F. (1970 [1846]) *The German Ideology: Selections*: London: Lawrence and Wishart.
Marx, K and Engels, F. (1968 [1848]) *The Communist Manifesto*. Peking: Foreign Languages Press.
McLelland, D. (1970) *Marx Before Marxism*. London: Macmillan.
McLelland, D. (1981) *Karl Marx: Interviews and Recollections*. London: Macmillan.
Mészáros, I. (1971) *Marx's Theory of Alienation*. London: Merlin Press.
Mészáros, I. (2000) *Beyond Capital: Toward a Theory of Transition*. New York: Monthly Review Press.
Mosse, G. L. (1977) 'George Lichtheim: Sketch for an Intellectual Portrait'. In: Shlomo Avineri (ed.) *Varieties of Marxism*. The Hague: MartinusNijhoff, pp. 1–6.
Pollack, F (1990 [1941]) 'State Capitalism: Its Possibilities and Limits'. In: P. Piccone (ed.) *The Frankfurt School Reader*. New York: Continuum. pp. 71–93.
Ricardo, D. (1951 [1817]) *On the Principles of Political Economy and Taxation*. Cambridge: Cambridge University Press.

Rubel, Maximilien (1977) Friedrich Engels - Marxism's Founding Father: Nine Premises to a Theme'. In: Shlomo Avineri (ed.) *Varieties of Marxism*. The Hague: MartinusNijhoff, pp. 43-52.
Sayer, D. (1987) *The Violence of Abstraction: The Analytic Foundations of Historical Materialism*. Oxford: Basil Blackwell.
Sperber, J. (2013) *Karl Marx: A Nineteenth Century Life*. New York: Liveright Publishing.
Thompson, E.P. (1978) *The Poverty of Theory and Other Essays*. London: Merlin Press.
Williams, R. (1977) *Marxism and Literature*. Oxford: Oxford University Press.
Wright, E. O. (1978) *Class, Crisis, and the State*. London: New Left Books.

VI

WEBER

Introduction

Durkheim, Simmel and Marx all had enormous influence on the development of sociological theory in the twentieth and twenty-first centuries. However, looking at the number of citations and publications devoted to his work it seems that Max Weber has been the dominant figure among the classics of sociology over the past 30 years. While other classical sociologists remain central to their respective schools of thought (i.e. neo-Durkhemian or neo-Marxist approaches) Weber had great impact across different intellectual traditions. In many respects Weber's legacy is claimed today by very diverse theoretical positions from rational choice theory, structural functionalism, conflict theory, symbolic interactionism to critical theory and comparative historical sociology to name a few. In order to understand fully Weber's continuous influence, it is necessary to situate his main ideas and concepts within broader historical and biographical contexts. Hence this chapter aims to outline and assess Weber's central contributions to sociological thought as well as to analyse briefly the contemporary relevance of his work.

Life and Intellectual Context

Karl Emil Maximilian 'Max' Weber was born in 1864 in the Prussian town of Erfurt as the oldest of eight children. His parents were members of the professional German Protestant elite who moved to Berlin shortly after Max's birth. In Berlin Weber's household became a site for regular visits and exchange of views from prominent academics, artists, lawyers, politicians and businessmen, and from early on Weber was exposed to the intellectual debates of his time. His father was a wealthy and well-known civil servant, and, at times, a Prussian parliamentarian and the Berlin city councillor for the centrist National Liberal Party.

Unlike his father, Max senior, who was not particularly religious, Weber's mother, Helene Fallenstein, was a devoted Calvinist who espoused strong moral principles. His father was a strict authoritarian and his mother an extremely demanding person who was a selfless and strong woman but also somebody who 'always applied absolute standards ... and was never satisfied with herself and always felt inadequate before God' (Radkau, 2009: 16). Weber's younger brother Alfred, who was later to become another prominent sociologist, also played a significant role in his life: they shared intellectual, political and personal interests, and their relationship was strong albeit full of tension and rivalry.

Weber attended a private school in Charlottenburg, Berlin, and after taking his *Abitur* became a student of jurisprudence (with history, economics and philosophy) at Heidelberg University in 1882. A year later Weber began his military service in Strasbourg and by 1884 he was back in Berlin and Göttingen attending lectures by leading German academics of his day, including von Treitschke, Mommsen, Gneist and Goldschmidt. During the 1880s Weber interrupted his studies on several occasions to complete his military training and by 1887 he was promoted to first lieutenant. In 1889 he received a doctoral degree on medieval trading companies. Only two years later he completed his *Habilitation* (a second doctorate) on Roman agrarian history, which qualified him to take up a post as a lecturer in law in Berlin. In 1893 Weber was appointed professor of economics at the University of Freiburg and married his distant cousin, Marianne Schnitger. Two years later the Webers moved to Heidelberg where Max took up a chair in economics. In 1898 he experienced two nervous breakdowns that made him incapable of holding a regular teaching job. It took a number of years before he was capable of returning to academic activities and writing.

In 1904 Weber visited the United States where he was mesmerised by the urban sprawls, democratic institutions and meritocratic ethos of US society. This visit gave him a new impetus to work, the direct outcome being now-famous essays collected in the book *The Protestant Ethic and the Spirit of Capitalism* (1904–5). A year later he was enthralled by the events in Russia and in order to understand the 1905 Revolution he taught himself Russian and wrote extensive essays on social and political developments in Russia. In this period his research interests widened substantially and he embarked on producing a series of comparative historical manuscripts on world religions which were later published as *The Religion of China: Confucianism and Taoism; The Religion of India: The Sociology of Hinduism and Buddhism*; and *Ancient Judaism*. In 1909 together with Georg Simmel and Werner Sombart he founded the German Sociological Association. As Weber did not hold a permanent job it was Marianne's inheritance from the Oerlinghausen firm that provided for a relatively comfortable lifestyle.

The Legacy of War

The outbreak of the First World War saw Weber volunteering for military service but because of his age and ill health he was not involved in military activities. In the last two years of the war Weber was also preoccupied with a series of conceptual essays that were posthumously published as *Economy and Society*. Although many German academics were hostile towards the Weimar Republic, Weber supported the new state and took part in the debates about its new constitution. In addition he also participated in the negotiations of the Peace Treaty at Versailles and opposed the Allies' demand for war reparations. In the immediate post-war period he co-founded the centrist German Democratic Party but was unsuccessful in his attempt to secure a party nomination as a candidate in the national elections. In 1918, after two decades away, Weber briefly returned to teaching as he accepted a chair at the University of Vienna. A year later he moved to the University of Munich where he combined his teaching activities, delivering his famous 'Science as a Vocation' and 'Politics as a Vocation' lectures, with an intense research and publication schedule. In the summer of 1920 Weber contracted Spanish flu, which caused severe pneumonia, and he died on 14 June of that year.

There is no doubt that Max Weber was a uniquely talented individual who also had an extraordinary capacity for work. He was a highly energetic person capable of remembering nuanced historical details and producing subtle theoretical analyses on the spot – while giving lectures or engaging in debates with his colleagues and students (Radkau, 2009). However, his ideas were also the product of a collective endeavour. From early on in his education, both at home and in various schools and universities, he inhabited a world of leading German intellectuals with whom he had the opportunity to learn and to exchange ideas. In addition, similarly to his parent's home, his and Marianne's household was renowned for hosting regular social gatherings for intellectuals and students who would engage in extensive debates on a variety of academic and political subjects (Radkau, 2009). Some commentators refer to these gatherings as the 'Weber Circle', which included many prominent social scientists of the time who would regularly visit the home of Webers: Jellinek, Troeltsch, Sombart, Bloch, Michels and Lukács among others.

Furthermore, Weber lived at a time when Germany had by far the best system of higher education in the world (Collins, 1998; Poggi, 2006). German academics had national and international visibility and a high reputation among the wider public. Many intellectual debates took place in the leading newspapers and at political meetings and civil society events. In this context Weber's key theoretical and comparative historical contributions were built on, and in dialogue with, the leading ideas of his time.

For example, Weber's novel arguments about methodology including the concept of *verstehen*, value neutrality (*Wertfreiheit*) and ideal types all developed in the context of pervasive intellectual debates about methods in Wilhelmine Germany. Rather than constructing a new methodological position from scratch, Weber's ideas originated in reflection on the fierce dispute between positivists, who aimed to mould the study of social and cultural phenomena on the blueprint of natural sciences and the so-called historical school that emphasised the uniqueness of every social event. His originality often stems from unusual and unorthodox syncretic developments whereby he manages to bridge fruitfully very different epistemological traditions. For example, he combines neo-Kantian idealism with the materialist conflict tradition.

Furthermore, he articulated his position as a 'methodological individualist' while most of his published work focuses on long-term historical structural transformations. Although socially a bit of a loner who was tormented by 'inner demons', Weber was fully in tune with the latest developments in social science, history, religion and philosophy and was in regular contact with most of the leading German, and some international, intellectuals of his time. He also directly influenced a generation of some leading academics such as Sombart, Michels, Lukács and Parsons who were all his students and many more who embraced his key concepts and ideas. When Weber died his close friend, a world-leading existentialist philosopher, Karl Jaspers, declared Weber to be 'the greatest German of our era'.

Historical, Social and Political Context

Although Max Weber was a product of Wilhelmine Germany and many of his ideas originated there, in its specific social and historical context, he was also a highly atypical late nineteenth- and early twentieth-century German intellectual. For example, in contrast to the majority of German academics, who eschewed the 'materialist' world of public life, politics and business, Weber valued these spheres of social life and often acted as a passionate public intellectual. It is true that for most of his life he shared the dominant perspective of the German intelligentsia of his time, which was supportive of the imperial project and German nationalism (Parkin, 2002; Allen, 2004). Nevertheless, he profoundly disliked social conservatism and authoritarianism, which were the backbone of the Wilhelmine world. Weber developed many of his views in opposition to an older generation of conservatives who valorised the Prussian bureaucracy and celebrated the paternalism of state and society (Beetham, 1974: 20). Late nineteenth-century Germany was an unusual social creation that, on the one hand, was characterised by a highly advanced industrial economy, unmatched educational system, intellectual creativity, effective civil service and the developed welfare provisions, but on the other hand, German society was also deeply conservative, militarist, rigidly hierarchical and authoritarian.

Weber was born and spent most of his life in a world where the middle class was for the most part economically prosperous, but politically stifled, as the state was controlled by the courts, top civil servants and military officers mostly composed of the landed nobility, Junkers. The Prussian military and administrative core of the Wilhelmine state was crucial for the development of a paternalist system, which combined formal legalism with authoritarian rule and a degree of social protection (Coser, 1971: 254). The state introduced the most advanced welfare protection system which included medical care, old age pensions, accident and unemployment insurance, but the main reason behind this unusually progressive policy was the attempt to suffocate the emergence of organised labour, trade unions and more radical social movements. In this context the militarist ideas of duty and loyalty were highly praised, and reformism and radicalism were not only discouraged but also intensely policed.

Reform and Empire

In his role as a public intellectual Weber often stood against such a status quo, advocating liberal reform and social progressivism while still envisaging Germany as a major world power. In this sense his early writings on the agricultural issues in East Elbia reflect the concern, that in the long term, the lack of reform is likely to have devastating effects for the German state. More specifically he argues that the traditional Junker dominance in the East is bound to create economic dissipation which ultimately will enhance the influence of the non-German population (Poles) and thus weaken the German state in the East. As a sociologist Weber understood the social significance of political and economic liberties with the disenchanted and disenfranchised middle classes and proletariat seen as destined to revolt and produce internal instability. Furthermore, as German industrial output was on the rise, the size of the population was continuously increasing and the state's educational system was generating high-quality graduates, many of whom were unlikely to find employment in the already massive civil service, the public sphere became preoccupied with solutions to these problems. Most intellectuals and politicians favoured one of two options – substantial reform of the political and social system or large-scale imperial expansion.

The conservative sections of society including the military, the aristocracy and the top civil servants were supportive of the recent colonial acquisitions in Africa and the Pacific, and advocated the redistribution of colonial possessions throughout the world. In contrast, the liberals focused on the internal radical changes in Germany's political, economic and social system. This is not to say that some liberals, including Weber, were opposed to the imperial project. On the contrary many of those who supported reforms were convinced that greater social inclusion and political freedoms were preconditions for effective imperial dominance in Europe and the world. It is for this reason that Mann has referred to Weber as a 'liberal imperialist' (Mann, 2018: 39).

Wilhelmine Germany was a prosperous, powerful and expanding state whose leaders were obsessed with what they perceived to be their country's subordinate position in world politics. This view was shared by many intellectuals who linked British imperial supremacy to the strength of its navy. Hence there was strong support for further militarisation and the building of a powerful German Navy. Young Weber was an enthusiastic member of the German Navy League and was often referred to as 'the Fleet Professor' (Hall, 2002). Although young Weber started his political life on the conservative right, which was reflected in his Freiburg inaugural lecture 'the National State and Economic Policy' and in his brief membership of the nationalist *Alldeutscher Verband*, he gradually moved to the liberal left. At the onset of the First World War Weber was a proponent of liberal nationalism and German imperial power but the experience of war made him much more reflective so that he became close to the radical opponents of war. As his political views evolved, he focused on social and political reforms and was highly sympathetic to many ideas advocated by the Social Democrats.

In addition to the political debates of his time Weber was also sensitive to the dramatic social changes brought about by modernisation and industrial warfare. Throughout his life he regarded capitalism as 'the most fateful force' (cited in Beetham, 1974: 20). The belated but very intensive economic development of the German state, including rapid industrialisation and national unification, had deep consequences for German society. Weber was well aware of the complex social stratification developing in the Wilhelmine world with the economic class polarisation and new political movements emerging in the midst of deeply entrenched traditional status-oriented hierarchies. In contrast to many of his romanticist contemporaries who focused on the so-called moral shortcomings of modern lifestyles and who glorified the supposed innocence of the traditional world, Weber was a sociological realist who was more interested in the structural implications of social change. In this context he was more worried about the organisational monopolies of modern bureaucratic institutions and less about the imaginary visions of the harmonious past.

Cultural Values

Weber was also interested in the role cultural values play in the transformation of social orders. In this context he was reflecting on the dominant debates about religious differences and their impact on social development. In the German context this was still a sensitive issue as Bismarck's early attempts to make Protestantism the leading religion and curtail the influence of the Catholic Church in the new German state through the *Kulturkampf* of 1871–80 largely backfired. Thus, instead of pacifying Catholics, Bismarck's coercive policies helped politicise and mobilise Roman Catholic groupings throughout Germany. Despite the political difficulties associated with the issue of religious denominations Weber was determined to deploy his sociological tools to explore the relationship between specific religious belief systems and the direction of social development.

Furthermore, the rulers of the new German state were also preoccupied with the idea of forging a single and unified German nation. Since Germany's unification was belated and contested as it was not completely clear whether the German polity and German culture should overlap, the new state authorities embarked on an extensive Germanisation of the population. This included restricting the cultural and political rights of minorities, including Poles and Jews, but it also targeted non-Prussian German speakers, some of whom were not enthusiastic about the Prussian dominance of the new German Empire. These policies gave impetus to the debates about the so-called national question where Weber regularly stood apart from the majority position that tended to perceive nationhood in restricted ethnic terms. Instead, for Weber, both ethnicity and nation are not primordial static givens but are conceptualised as dynamic processes defined by social action and individual self-determination (Weber, 1968; Malešević, 2004).

Many of Weber's principal ideas originated in the vigorous intellectual conflict with the academics, politicians and activists of his time. He lived in a profoundly turbulent historical period that generated fierce intellectual and existential social conflicts, and his rich theoretical opus reflects this only too well.

Arguments and Ideas

Methodology

For Weber sociology is 'a science concerning itself with the interpretative understanding of social action and thereby with a causal explanation of its course and consequences' (1968: 4). This definition is unusual in the sense that it attempts to sidestep the traditional divide between those who sharply differentiate between the natural and social sciences (anti-positivists) and those for whom sociology should apply the same methodological principles as the natural sciences (positivists). Thus, in contrast to the positivists, Weber perceives sociology as an interpretative discipline focused on understanding the complex meanings and values behind social actions. In other words, for Weber the relationships between human beings cannot be analysed in the same way as those between bricks and the gravitational poles: human beings create, search for, manipulate, utilise and are shaped by complex and changing meanings and as such their behaviour is often contingent and arbitrary. However, Weber also rejects the anti-positivist view which holds that since human actions are complex and non-uniform this automatically implies that all explanations are subjective and relative. Instead he attempts to go beyond both positions, arguing that objective sociological analysis is possible but that this objectivity cannot be generated from the simple mechanical causality as observed in the natural world. Rather, as human behaviour is often motivated by a combination of interests, passions and beliefs, the focus of a sociologist's analysis should be the social action itself. Weber emphasises that in order to fathom individual and collective action it is necessary to engage in an interpretative process of understanding (*verstehen*). Although a researcher's own interests, passions and beliefs may influence the research process itself, Weber insists that this risk can be minimised by openly declaring one's own value judgements before the research takes place, by striving to keep separate factual knowledge from one's own judgement and by testing the validity of the research process and results with researchers who share very different value judgements.

Although Weber was well aware that complete value freedom was not possible, his position was that interpretative analysis rooted in intellectual honesty was more likely to generate profound sociological analyses than either narrow positivist absolutism or extreme subjectivism.

To demonstrate the analytical advantage of his qualified objectivist methodology Weber developed the notion of an ideal type (or pure type). In his understanding the ideal type stands for a hypothetical abstract concept which is used as a kind of a benchmark against which one could measure and assess concrete empirical cases. In this sense an ideal type is a theoretical, generalising construct developed to identify the conceptual and actual variety of social phenomena in order to create an analytical terrain for causal explanations. Ideal types are rarely if ever found in real life, but are 'one-sided accentuations' which help emphasise the distinctive qualities of social processes. Simply put, an ideal type is a mental construct derived from observable reality but rather than conforming to this reality in specific details it represents a deliberate exaggeration or simplification. As Weber points out. 'Whatever the content of the ideal-type ... it has only one function in an empirical investigation. Its function is the comparison with empirical reality in order to establish its divergences or similarities ... and to understand and explain them casually' (1949: 43). In this context Weber identifies many ideal types such as bureaucracy, the Protestant ethic, charismatic authority, the messianic sect, social stratification, etc. For example, the ideal type of bureaucracy would include such features as a consistent and uniform system of abstract rules, impersonal order, transparent hierarchies, professional relationships between employees regulated by written technical rules, a meritocratic system of promotion and a clearly defined division of labour. Although it is unlikely that any actual bureaucratic organisation complies fully and consistently with all these principles, it is the dominance of such organisational norms that differentiates bureaucracy from patrimonial and other forms of social organisation (Weber, 1968).

Historical Sociology

Weber's attempt to surpass the positivist vs. anti-positivist methodological disputes was also reflected in his socio-historical analyses. Whereas most historians subscribe to the anti-positivist interpretations of historical processes by emphasising the unique quality of specific events in the past, much of social science is concerned with establishing trans-historical and law-like generalisations about social phenomena. In contrast to both positions, Weber employs his interpretative analytical framework to provide wide-ranging but historically specific generalisations: the fact that history is full of random and contingent events does not rule out the possibility that some events and processes are more patterned than others.

Although Weber's analyses start from the individual, meaningful, action of human beings, much of his empirical work is focused on collective action.

As Poggi (2006: 38) emphasises, for Weber 'groups develop when a plurality of individuals, each oriented in conduct by subjective processes of his/her own, is, as it were, traversed by commonalities existing between the respective processes'. In other words, it is organised social action that is at the heart of historical transformations. For Weber social groups are rarely fixed and unchanging entities: instead it is shared collective action that makes groups into durable and meaningful organisations. In this context the long-term historical processes help forge social structures, which ultimately arise from, and remain part of, the interlocking patterns of social interaction. Protracted and co-ordinated social action generates relatively stable organisational forms which in turn shape the individual actions of other individuals. In Weber's historical analyses collective action is understood through the prism of what he refers to as 'material and ideal interests'. Simply put, social action can originate in a variety of individual and collective motives including instrumental rationality, value rationality, emotional and habitual objectives.

Whereas instrumental rationality is governed by principles of materialist self-interest, value rationality refers to a strong commitment to a particular set of beliefs and values as actors believe 'in the value for its own sake of some ethical, aesthetic, religious, or other form of behaviour, independently of its prospects of success' (Weber, 1968: 25). Nevertheless, Weber also acknowledged that emotions play an important part in social action as well as that a substantial proportion of everyday acts consist of routine, habitual, practices.

The full complexity of 'material and ideal interests' is also reflected in Weber's understanding of social power and stratification. He distinguishes between the possession and exercise of different forms of social power. While to possess power means to control directly specific social resources such as capital, land, expert knowledge, physical strength or social respect, all of which can be used to enhance further one's position of dominance, the exercise of power refers to an ability to impose one's will despite resistance. In this context the control of specific social resources such as capital or expert knowledge is likely to increase one's capacity to exercise more power than those who lack such resources.

For Weber, social power and stratification are deeply linked as complex social orders inevitably rely on hierarchical systems of domination. Although social mechanisms of domination change through time and place and shift from traditional towards more bureaucratic systems of rule, the key principles of social hierarchy tend to remain in place. In other words, the historical dynamics of social stratification tend to develop around three central stratifying dimensions – the political, the economic and the cultural. In contrast to Marx, who emphasises the economic foundations of social divisions, Weber argues that social stratification generally involves three distinct but often mutually interdependent phenomena that he termed, class, party, and status (Weber, 1968).

Firstly, Weber accepts Marx's point about the enormous significance of social classes throughout history. The unequal access to material resources tends to establish sharp hierarchical relationships. However, unlike Marx, for whom the ownership of the means of production was a key factor of the class divide, for Weber, class is first and foremost an economic situation: it is an individual's position in the market that determines one's class position. Hence as market conditions change so too can one's class position. For example, if the market price of shoes suddenly plummets the former shoe factory owner or that company's principal shareholders are likely to change their market situation – from being wealthy owners of the means of production to being bankrupt and unemployed.

In addition to the economic power of class position, social stratification also includes political power. By political power (i.e. party) Weber understood one's ability to use organisational might to control the actions of others. For example, the leaders of political parties, trade unions or influential civil society organisations can influence the drafting and implementation of particular laws that are likely to privilege some groups over others. Simply put, political power is a capacity to influence decision-making processes without necessarily possessing formal political or economic authority. Although political and economic power can be deeply interrelated, with the same individuals possessing economic resources and political control at the same time, this is not always the case in modern societies and has been even less of the case throughout history. For example, the members of the Central Committees of the Communist Party in the Soviet Union had enormous political power without having the right to hold any significant economic possessions.

Nevertheless, for Weber it is the cultural/ideological aspect of social stratification that has most often been decisive in determining one's life chances – social status. In contrast to political and economic power which are regularly reflected in specific material advantages ranging from tangible assets and possessions to the concrete instruments of control, social status operates through shared belief systems. Status hierarchies relate to the different levels of prestige and different lifestyles of specific social groups. In Weber's view social status includes a specific 'social estimation of honour' which is created and reinforced through the different lifestyles of groups.

For example, the historical record is full of different status groups who maintained their distinct position through endogamy and other marriage and contact restrictions, through the sharing of specific dietary practices or through the strict reinforcement of cultural and religious traditions. An ethnic collectivity would be a typical status group. Although Weber recognised that ethnicity is a dynamic, amorphous social relation, he argued that historically ethnic group action fostered endogamy and preservation of distinct cultural practices, all of which were legitimised through the idea of shared common descent (Malešević, 2004: 25). In this context the members of the group would invoke the notion of 'ethnic honour' defined by Weber (1968: 391) as 'the conviction of the excellence of one's own customs and the inferiority of alien ones'. In much of his empirical opus status groups assume a central role in the historical processes. For Weber status membership is often more exclusive and exclusionary than either class or party as it is rooted in a strong 'sense of dignity' and different, sometimes mutually exclusive, lifestyles.

A direct consequence of status exclusivity is the tendency towards monopolistic social closure. Weber differentiates between open and closed social relationships and sees status membership as the crucial mechanism for the institutionalisation of social hierarchies. Unlike open social relationships, which allow 'outsiders' to participate, closed relationships prevent non-members from taking part in any or most social activities associated with a specific group. Throughout history social status was regularly a potent social device used to control access to group resources and symbolic benefits. This process of monopolistic social closure was generally utilised to maintain the group's political or economic dominance but also to foster in-group solidarity and homogeneity. Hence the dominant groups would emphasise particular cultural, religious, dietary, linguistic or physical features to close access to non-members. For example, the medieval European aristocracy relied on the idea of the divine origins of monarchs to secure access to ruling positions to fellow aristocrats while prohibiting others from even contemplating the possibility of participating in the political or economic power structures. Similarly the Indian caste system (varna) was the perfect example of monopolistic social closure in practice as one's social status was rigidly determined by membership of the endogamous hereditary groups, castes (yati), which developed highly complex systems of exclusion focused on dietary and clothing requirements, cultural practices and the established monopolies on specific professions. Moreover, the caste system was especially strict in relation to the so-called untouchables, the members of the Dalit ethnic group, who were prohibited from eating with members of other castes, from entering village temples, from wearing sandals, riding bicycles or using public restaurants. Although social status has historically been the most visible device for monopolistic social closure, other forms of social division such as the class, estate or political party have also played a similar role.

Religion and Capitalism

Despite the fact that Weber's general sociology tends to give equal explanatory weight to the political, economic and cultural factors in the interpretation of social processes, his studies of religion are more focused on the role of cultural variables. Much of Weber's early fame rested on the essays collected in *The Protestant Ethic and the Spirit of Capitalism* (1904–5). The main topic of these essays was the relationship between Protestant Christianity and the expansion of the social and economic principles of capitalism. More specifically Weber attempted to demonstrate that early forms of Protestantism such as Calvinism were highly compatible with the spirit of modern, rationalist, capitalism.

To understand this link fully it is necessary to review briefly Weber's typology of capitalisms. In contrast to Marx, Weber does not see capitalism as a solely modern phenomenon. Instead he distinguishes between several forms of capitalist historical experience. For example, traditional capitalism was present in all early civilisations and was defined by trade and the temporary gathering of wealth for very specific and limited ends, unlike the continuous accumulation of profit that characterises modern-day capitalists. Booty capitalism was also widespread throughout history as wealth was generated through wars of conquest, plunder and robbery-centred expeditions. Weber also identifies something he called pariah capitalism, associated with specialised commercial activities such as money-lending.

According to Weber, pariah capitalism was usually practised by religious or ethnic minorities while the members of the majority society were excluded from such practices (i.e. with religious prohibitions on money-lending with interest in Islam and early Christianity, religious 'pariah' groups such as Jews, the Chinese, Armenians, etc., tended to carry out such financial transactions). Although all these forms of early capitalism were instrumental in fostering market relations and a degree of capitalist spirit, Weber (1930) argues that modern, rational, capitalism is different in the sense that it operates according to specific rules, including regulated book-keeping with precise calculability, employment of formally free labour, the legalised and systematic pursuit of profit, and the existence of a regular market. For Weber it is only this rational-type capitalism that underpins modern economic relations and as such its origins are to be found in Europe. In his view the development of rational capitalism entails the presence of specific institutional ('substance') and normative ('spirit') preconditions. Whereas the previous forms of capitalism generally lacked either the institutional or the normative preconditions (i.e. tribal societies had neither of the two while most pre-modern orders developed one or the other), it is only in early modern Europe that the two factors coincidentally coalesced and helped generate a unique symbiosis of capitalist 'spirit' and religious 'substance'. For Weber the gradual dominance of Protestantism, particularly its early Calvinist version, was instrumental in creating particular institutional conditions which ultimately have proved beneficial for modern capitalism.

The Calvinist belief system was centred on the afterlife and was rooted in the doctrine of predestination (i.e. the idea that only God decides who will be saved and who is destined for eternal damnation). Since no one is guaranteed the heavenly afterlife the one way to please the divinity is to lead an extremely pious and moral earthly life. Furthermore, Calvinism preaches the pursuit of an ascetic lifestyle while also advocating strict discipline, hard work and the rejection of material pleasures. In this context and paradoxically the early Protestant ethic appears to be highly compatible with the contemporary capitalist environment. Since modern capitalism entails the disciplined pursuit of profit with the accumulation of wealth, savings and reinvestment at the heart of capitalist enterprise, the ideal Calvinist believer appears to be someone best suited for maintaining the spirit of capitalism. In other words, despite nominally very different ethical principles there is a strong 'elective affinity' between the early Protestant sects and capitalist entrepreneurship. Even though Weber was explicit that this relationship is not causal, that is Calvinism is not the cause of capitalism as capitalism is a complex historical phenomenon emerging in different forms and in different parts of the world, his analyses do emphasise the significance of particular belief systems as necessary if not sufficient for the development and expansion of capitalist economies.

Power, Legitimacy and Bureaucracy

Although Weber has traditionally been misinterpreted as a representative of an epistemologically idealist sociology (Parsons, 1951), much of his opus is in fact focused on the political and economic foundations of social action. This is particularly visible in his political sociology, which emphasises domination and power politics as the key constituents of social life: 'Domination in the most general sense is one of the most important elements of social action... Without exception every sphere of social action is profoundly influenced by structures of dominancy' (Weber, 1968: 941). In Weber's view political power, by which he meant the probability that an individual in a social relationship can impose his or her own will against the resistance of others, was a defining feature of both the micro and macro social world. On the macro level, the most influential container and wielder of power is the state. For Weber, the state is first and foremost a coercive institution, an entity that controls the use of force. In his own words the state is a 'human community that successfully claims the monopoly of the legitimate use of physical force within a given territory' (Weber, 2004 [1919]). State power operates both externally and internally. At the external level the world outside the state is characterised by violent anarchy as international relations are largely shaped by geopolitical power struggles between the states. In this context the states grapple over prestige, territory, material resources or geopolitical domination.

Internally, the state's dominance rests on its ability to control fully the military, police and courts. In both instances the state rulers regularly rely on nationalism to justify their internal monopolisation of force and external conflicts including wars. On the micro level, Weber also emphasises the coercive underpinning of social relations. He conceives power relations in terms of the capacity of some individuals 'to awaken fear in others, putting at stake their survival and physical integrity' (Poggi, 2006: 90). Since in his account the relationships between human beings involve a substantial degree of power, and status struggle, Weber was interested in the processes through which individuals and groups acquire power, and how such power is transformed into legitimate and durable domination.

One of the key social mechanisms in this process is the rise of disciplined social action. As Weber explains, discipline is at the heart of social development and disciplinary action is firmly rooted in coercive control. As he emphasises:

> military discipline gives birth to all discipline ... the sober and rational Puritan discipline made Cromwell's victories possible ... gunpowder and all the war techniques ... became significant only with the existence of discipline ... the varying impact of discipline on the conduct of war has had even greater effects upon the political and social order. (Weber, 1968: 1155, 1152)

Nevertheless coercive power rarely operates on its own. Rather most social orders combine coercion with different forms of political legitimacy.

Weber identified three dominant ideal types of legitimate authority: legal–rational, traditional and charismatic. The legal rational form of legitimacy is largely based on the bureaucratic model of organisation, which generates its authority from 'a consistent system of abstract rules'. For Weber the legal–rational system of order implies 'domination through knowledge' and as such it operates as a meritocratic impersonal order with the clearly defined and transparent rule of the law (Weber, 1968: 225). In this model of authority there is a hierarchy based on competence with all personnel having already completed specialised training for their respective roles. The professional relationships between individuals are regulated by written technical rules and the employees are separated from ownership of the means of production. For Weber this was the most efficient and economic system of legitimacy.

In sharp contrast the traditional models of legitimacy (such as patrimonialism or sultanism) are based on 'an established belief in the sanctity of immemorial traditions and the legitimacy of those exercising authority under them' (Weber, 1968: 215). In this type of order personal loyalty and the authority of traditional form of conduct trump instrumental rationality or economic efficiency. The traditional modes of domination involve patrimonial forms of recruitment whereby commanding roles were given to one's own clan or family members. In this system, knowledge and expertise are subservient to one's traditional status and the rulers often have the right to interpret the traditional codes as they see fit.

While profoundly different the legal–rational and traditional models of legitimacy are both tied to the specific organisational structure. This is not the case with Weber's third ideal type of legitimacy: charismatic authority. This form of legitimate rule stems from an individual's exceptional qualities or more precisely from the fact that some individuals are perceived by a large number of people as possessing such charismatic features. Hence when a leader is associated with supernatural heroism, magical powers, prophetic vision or exceptional management skills, one can encounter the emergence of the charismatic form of legitimacy. As Weber explains, this type of order is rooted in the belief that the charismatic personality can perform miracles or some other superhuman feats. The charismatic mode of domination often possesses regularly strong revolutionary aspirations and as such dismisses previous social orders. However, as this type of authority, ordinarily built around strongly emotional connections between the charismatic individual and his or her community of followers, is unstable and inefficient, it usually does not last for long periods of time. Hence most models of charismatic authority become routinised over time and transform into either the traditional or legal–rational form of legitimacy.

Contemporary Relevance and Applications

Max Weber's work has had an enormous impact on the social sciences over the past 60 years and continues to be highly influential in the twenty-first century. Not only is he regarded as one of the founders of sociology but his huge intellectual output has also had a profound impact on the development of many contemporary sociological schools of thought: from neo-Weberian conflict theory and Parsonian structural functionalism, to the Frankfurt School critical theory, and further afield. In addition, Weber's central ideas and concepts have been applied to many contemporary social contexts. For example, his theories of rationalisation and bureaucratisation have inspired managers and civil servants throughout the world. In particular, his notion of legal–rational authority was utilised by business corporations and early post-colonial administrators who aimed, with more or less success, to realise the elements of this ideal type in their post-colonial realities (Brooks and Dunn, 2009).

RATIONALISATION, VALUE FRAGMENTATION AND THE LOSS OF MEANING

Rationalisation is the central process that Weber identifies with the historical development of modern capitalism. At the cultural level this involves a fragmentation of values from a previously holistic worldview. This is driven by specialisation and expertise, especially in modern science, which deconstructs and de-legitimates other sources of value creation in its own self-development. Weber anticipated a paradox whereby the success of cultural rationalisation would result in a new form of polytheism. The scientific deconstruction of sources of value ultimately undermines any objective basis to reconcile value differences. The result is a proliferation of incompatible subjective values, all contesting like warring deities. How appropriate is this thesis to the contemporary world of fake news, flat-earthers and conspiracy theorists?

More recently sociologists influenced by Weber have analysed how his predictions about the ever-increasing rationalisation have largely materialised in many areas. Hence, Ritzer (1996, 2000, 2002) has applied Weber's key ideas to explain how many spheres of contemporary life have become hyper-rationalised in an instrumental sense. Ritzer writes about 'the McDonaldisation of society' and traces how these standardised models of food management and organisation are applied to many other areas of social life. He identifies four central organising principles at work in most modern organisations:

1. Efficiency, involving a quick, cheap and easy system of product delivery with a standardised system of pre-designing and pre-packaging of products. This model applies to diverse areas such as weight-loss programmes, online utility bill payments to internet banking, dating services or online gambling, to name but a few.
2. Predictability, which relates to the fact that as rationalisation expands the focus shifts towards greater standardisation of goods and services. In this context the expectation is that all products and the customer experiences generated by the same company will be almost identical: from the restaurant food eaten in the same chain in different countries (i.e. Burger King, Pizza Hut, Subway) to the clothes, cars or entertainment that one purchases in different places (i.e. Pennies, Toyota or Hollywood blockbuster sequels).
3. Calculability, which fosters the popular perception of 'value for money'. In other words the standardised products and services all acquire numerical value: from the standardised meal sizes in McDonald's restaurants to quantified test results, citation indexes in academia, statistical breakdowns of the individual achievements of players in various sports. etc.
4. Control, which underpins the dynamic of success in such organisations. More specifically all large-scale corporations now employ similar work practices focused on maximum efficiency, calculability and predictability that range from the hiring and treatment of employees to the preparation and delivery of products and services. Such systems involve long-term planning, complex division of labour, diverse types of expertise, management control and a hierarchical chain of command. Hence many modern corporations look very similar as they operate, applying the Weberian logic of organisational management.

Bryman (2004, 2001) has developed the concept of disneyisation in order to analyse how consumption practices become homogenised and standardised. Drawing on the image of the Disney theme parks Bryman extends the Weberian understanding of rationalisation to different fields of social life. He argues that the key principles of the Disney theme parks have been utilised widely in the merchandising and sale of goods, services and entertainment. This usually involves an attempt to remove the authentic features of places, events and people and repackage them in a highly sanitised format. Hence disneyisation prioritises positive images and pleasant experiences, and eliminates any references to the events and practices that might invoke negative feelings. In this context the tourist destinations become themed with recognisable and friendly ideas that reinforce stereotypical images of places and nation-states:

from Oktoberfest drinking Germans to Kenyan safari trips to Australian barbeques to Brazilian samba dancers. The disneyisation also spreads to hotels, restaurants, shopping malls and many outlets that tend to resemble each other – from the worldwide spread of the Hard Rock Cafés and Starbucks to the almost identical shopping malls and hotel chains.

This broad Weberian theme of ever-increasing rationalisation is also applied to the political and cultural sphere. For example, Meyer and his collaborators (Meyer, 1996; Meyer and Jepperson, 2000, Drori et al., 2006) have identified how state institutions throughout the world have become more similar over the last 50 years or so. This process, which Meyer calls structural isomorphism, involves the gradual adoption of similar bureaucratic and rationalised systems of the state organisation worldview: from standardised educational systems with fixed curricula, universal constitutional arrangements, similar demographic record-keeping practices and census data collections, to population control policies, welfare provision, economic policies and greater equalisation of citizens' rights.

Scholars have also identified the darker side of rationalisation as similar organising principles have been applied in the systematic, industrialised slaughter of animals for food consumption. Thus Cudworth (2015) and Pachirat (2011) demonstrate how the mass production of meat for human consumption has led to routine, institutionalised and normalised mass-scale killings of billions of animals. With the development of new technologies and better systems of rational organisation the scale of mass killings has dramatically increased. The same principle has also been applied to the mass murder of humans. As both Bauman (1989) and Mann (2005) show, the Holocaust and other twentieth- and twenty-first-century genocides owe a great deal to the effective systems of rationalised bureaucratic control.

Criticisms

There is no doubt that Weber is one of the most influential sociologists of all time and that his work is still highly regarded within and outside of sociology. Nevertheless, he has also generated a great deal of criticism over the years. Some critiques focus on his political and ethical stands such as his early enthusiasm for the German imperial project, his stringent nationalist views, his moral elitism and a degree of support for militarism (Allen, 2004; Mommsen, 1974; MacRea, 1974; Aron, 1964). It is true that at the beginning of his career Weber was sympathetic to some of these ideas and this was clearly pronounced in his early publications such as his inaugural lecture at Freiburg University (1895) and his writings on the Polish question in Eastern Germany (1892) where he espouses strong support for economic nationalist policies and ruminates on the displacement of German workers by Polish immigrants who represent a 'less developed cultural type' (cited in Beetham, 1974: 37). However, these youthful episodes gave way to a much more sober and mature scholar who became less supportive of such ideas and who at the end of his life was rather hostile towards nationalism and the imperial projects (Palonen, 2001).

Nevertheless, more significant are the sociological criticisms that centre on his methodology, epistemology and his theories of religion, capitalism, social stratification and legitimacy. Thus, some commentators have questioned his methodological approach. Although Weber defined his position as both interpretative and methodologically individualist, much of his empirical work focuses on long-term structural changes where he also emphasises the role material factors play in these processes. This has led some scholars to judge his methodology as being too inconsistent and too syncretic. Others have been critical of Weber's nominal rejection of nomothetic causality in favour of the interpretative analysis that centres on understanding (*verstehen*). This was seen as being too subjectivist and ultimately too relativist a method, which could not generate replicable and trustworthy scientific findings. In particular, his model of the ideal type has been criticised as attempting to merge descriptive and explanatory features when in fact, these two processes are for the most part mutually exclusive (Grafstein, 1981). For example, when Weber distinguishes between the legal–rational and traditional modes of legitimacy he identifies the key descriptive characteristics of an ideal-type bureaucracy. However, as Grafstein correctly notes, there is an inherent tension between the explanatory and the descriptive understanding of the bureaucratic model: 'Validation requires the descriptive dimension of the ideal type and that, in turn, eliminates the very multiplicity being validated' (1981: 466).

These methodological criticisms are often tied with critiques of Weber's epistemological position. His highly influential Protestant ethic thesis has been particularly scrutinised. Some analysts have focused on the epistemological idealism of Weber's argument while others have questioned his historical evidence. For example, one of the early critics, the Marxist Henryk Grossman (1934), has challenged Weber's argument by downplaying the role of ideas and beliefs and by emphasising the material and coercive mechanisms that were decisive in the birth of modern capitalism. More specifically Grossman demonstrates how the enclosure of commons in England generated major population shifts that led to the dramatic increase of the urban poor in English cities. To manage this sudden overpopulation the state introduced rigid penalty systems for 'idleness' and 'vagabondage'.

The state-enacted coercive policies fostered a transition from serfdom towards a cheap wage labour system that ultimately produced the capitalist model of economic relations. Other critics have questioned Weber's dating and locating of early capitalism as well as his assumption that Protestantism and social development are regularly linked. Hence Schumpeter (1954) identified fourteenth-century Italian city-states rather than eighteenth- and nineteenth-century England as the true beginning of capitalism. Dickson and McLachlan (1983) and Stokes (1975) have demonstrated how Calvinism in Scotland and South Africa did not generate economic growth as predicted by Weber's thesis.

In contrast Stokes (1975) shows how Afrikaner Calvinism has in fact reinforced conservatism and prevented economic development. Furthermore, the Catholic parts of Belgium had undergone industrialisation much earlier than the Calvinist Netherlands. More recently scholars have pointed out how capitalist expansion has proceeded much faster outside of the Protestant centres in the Asian economic successes from Singapore, Malaysia, Taiwan, South Korea to China and further afield.

The neo-Marxist and the neo-Durkhemian critics have also slated Weber's individualist rationalism, which underpins his theories of social stratification and social organisation. For Marxists the tripartite model of power is inadequate to explain the historical dominance of economic relations. While agreeing that social status and political power contributed to economic relations they strongly disagree with Weber over his view that no form of social stratification has the ultimate priority. A more sympathetic critique acknowledges the relevance of the three forms of power but insists that in addition to economic, political and cultural power one also has to analyse the autonomy of military power (Mann, 1986, 1993, 2013). The Durkhemian critics highlight Weber's neglect of collective emotions and the role group morality plays in social action. While Weber does acknowledge emotional action as one of the four central types of action, he does not devote much attention to the study of emotions and collective ethics in his empirical work. They argue that Weber's theory of rationalisation with its focus on disenchantment and the lack of meaning cannot account for the persistence of group rituals, collective effervescence and the new social movements that often achieve popularity through the collective generation of meanings. While Weber sees individual humans as meaning-oriented creatures he has less to say about the strength of the collective narratives and institutions that sustain such meanings.

Conclusion

Among the classics of sociological thought Max Weber remains a unique figure. There is no doubt that Marx's ideas had much more impact on the shaping of the late nineteenth and early twentieth century as his work has influenced numerous revolutionaries, social movements and governments throughout the world. In some respects Durkheim also had greater impact in this period as some of his ideas were utilised not only by the French establishment but also by many governments of the newly recognised states from Turkey's ideological founders such as Ziya Gökalp (Nefes, 2013) to the Brazilian state-sponsored social science (de Oliveira, 2013) to the Japanese educators (Kurauchi, 1960), to many post-colonial rulers and administrators in Africa and Asia. Nevertheless while Marx and Durkheim still remain highly influential outside sociology, Weber's work has had more impact on the formation of sociological thought as such. Moreover, the past 30 years or so have witnessed the continuous rise of Weber's influence worldwide and his central ideas have been used as a springboard for the development of highly diverse contemporary sociological approaches. More than any other classic of sociology, Weber remains a constant source of fresh and creative ideas which can be deployed, adapted and continuously rearticulated to make sociological sense of the contemporary world.

References

Allen, K. (2004) *Max Weber: A Critical Introduction*. London: Pluto Press.
Aron, R. (1964) Old Nations, New Europe. *Daedalus*, 93(1), pp. 43–66.
Bauman, Z. (1989) *Modernity and the Holocaust*. Cambridge: Polity.
Beetham, D. (1974) *Max Weber and the Theory of Modern Politics*. London: George Allen and Unwin Ltd.
Brooks, L. J. and Dunn, P. (2009) *Business & Professional Ethics for Directors, Executives & Accountants*. Boston, MA: Cengage Learning.
Bryman, A. (2001) The Disneyization of Society. *The Sociological Review*, 47(1), pp. 25–47.
Bryman, A. (2004) *The Disneyization of Society*. London: Sage.
Collins, R. (1998) The Four M's of Religion: Magic, Membership, Morality and Mysticism. *Review of Religious Research*, 50(1), pp. 5–15.
Coser, L. A. (1971) *Masters of Sociological Thought: Ideas in Historical and Social Context*. New York: Harcourt Brace and Jovanovich.
Cudworth, E. (2015) Killing Animals: Sociology, Species Relations and Institutionalized Violence. *Sociological Review*, 63(1), pp. 1–18.
de Oliveira, M. (2013) The Career of Émile Durkheim in Brazilian Sociology, 1899–2012. *Durkheimian Studies*, 19, pp. 81–100.
Dickson, T. and McLachlan, H. (1983) Scottish Capitalism and Weber's Protestant Ethic Theses. *Sociology*, 17(4), pp. 560–8.
Drori, G. S., Meyer, J. W. and Hwang, H. (2006) *Globalization and Organization*. Oxford: Oxford University Press.
Grafstein, R. (1981) The Failure of Weber's Conception of Legitimacy: Its Causes and Implications. *Journal of Politics*, 43, pp. 456–72.
Hall, C. (2002) *Civilising Subjects: Metropole and Colony in English Imagination, 1830–1867*. Cambridge: Polity.
Kurauchi, K. (1960) Durkheim's Influence on Japanese Sociology. In: K. H. Wolff (ed.) *Émile Durkheim, 1858–1917*. Columbus, OH: Ohio State University Press, pp. 52–64.
MacRae, D. G. (1974) *Weber*. London: Fontana.
Malešević, S. (2004) *The Sociology of Ethnicity*. London: Sage.
Mann, M. (1986) *The Sources of Social Power 1*. Cambridge: Cambridge University Press.
Mann, M. (1993) *The Sources of Social Power 2*. Cambridge: Cambridge University Press.

Mann, M. (2005) *The Dark Side of Democracy*. Cambridge: Cambridge University Press.
Mann, M. (2013) *The Sources of Social Power 3*. Cambridge: Cambridge University Press.
Mann, M. (2018) Have Wars and Violence Declined? *Theory and Society*, (47), pp. 37–60.
Meyer, J. W. (1996) 'Otherhood: The Promulgation and Transmission of Ideas in the Modern Organizational Environment'. In: B. Czarniawska and G. Sevón (eds) *Translating Organizational Change*, Berlin: de Gruyter, pp. 241–52.
Meyer, J. W. and Jepperson, R. L. (2000) The 'Actors' of Modern Society: The Cultural Construction of Social Agency. *Sociological Theory*, 18(1), pp. 100–20.
Mommsen, W. J. (1974) *The Age of Bureaucracy: Perspectives on the Political Sociology of Max Weber*. Oxford: Blackwell.
Nefes, T. S. (2013) Ziya Gökalp's Adaptation of Émile Durkheim's Sociology in his Formulation of the Modern Turkish Nation. *International Sociology*, 28(3), pp. 335–50.
Pachirat, T. (2011) *Every Twelve Seconds: Industrialized Slaughter and the Politics of Sight*. New Haven, CT: Yale University Press.
Palonen, K. (2001) Was Max Weber a 'Nationalist'? A Study in the Rhetoric of Conceptual Change. *Max Weber Studies*, 1(2), pp. 196–214.
Parkin, F. (2002) *Max Weber*. Revised Edition. London: Routledge.
Parsons, T. (1951) *The Social System*. Glencoe, IL: Free Press.
Poggi, G. (2006) *Weber: A Short Introduction*. London: Polity.
Radkau, J. (2009) *Max Weber: A Biography*. London: Polity.
Ritzer, G. (1996) *The McDonaldization of Society: An Investigation Into the Changing Character of Contemporary Social Life*. Thousand Oaks, CA: Pine Forge Press.
Ritzer, G. (2000) *The McDonaldization of Society*: New Century Edition. London: Sage.
Ritzer, G., ed. (2002) *McDonaldization: The Reader*. Newbury Park, CA: Pine Forge Press.
Schumpeter, J. (1954) *History of Economic Analysis*. London: Allen & Unwin.
Stokes, R. G. (1975) Afrikaner Calvinism and Economic Action: The Weberian Thesis in South Africa. *The American Journal of Sociology*, 81(1), pp. 62–81.
Weber, M. (1930) *The Protestant Ethic and the Spirit of Capitalism*. T. Parsons, trans. New York: G. Allen & Unwin.
Weber, M. (1949) *Max Weber on the Methodology of the Social Sciences*. Glencoe, IL: The Free Press.
Weber, M. (1968) *Economy and Society: An Outline of Interpretive Sociology*. New York: Bedminster Press.
Weber, M. (2004 [1919]) *The Vocation Lectures*. Indianapolis, IN: Hacket Publishing.

VII

DURKHEIM

Introduction

Durkheim is now regularly listed as one of the one of the classical sociological theorists often together with Marx and Weber and possibly a few other names. However, at the end of nineteenth and beginning of the twentieth century, Marx, Weber and other big names were not regarded as sociological thinkers and it was only Durkheim from this 'holy trinity' who stood out as the leading sociologist of his time. Hence Durkheim was already recognised during his lifetime as an original and influential social thinker and his ideas have had a lasting impact over the past hundred years or so. Nevertheless, unlike other classics of sociology, who focused mostly on developing new theories and conducting novel empirical research, Durkheim was also focused on the institutionalisation of sociology as an academic discipline and on its recognition within French society. In this context he was the driving force behind the projects aimed at introducing sociology and other social science subjects into the French educational system. These institutional developments led by Durkheim proved later to be crucial for the development of sociological thinking throughout the world as many educational ministries followed the French example and introduced sociology into their educational programmes. In this chapter we explore Durkheim's contribution to sociological thought. The first part looks at his life and the wider historical, political and social context. The second part dissects Durkheim's key ideas and theories, while the final section zooms in on the contemporary relevance of his work and the critical appraisals of his legacy.

Life and Intellectual Context

Émile Durkheim was born in Épinal, in the province of Lorraine in France in 1858. He grew up in a highly religious family, both of his parents coming from a long line of devout French Jews. Moreover, on his father's side three generations of his ancestors were all rabbis. Initially young Émile intended to follow the family tradition and enrolled in a rabbinical school where he studied Hebrew, the Talmud and the Jewish bible. However, soon after his Bar Mitzvah at the age of 13 Durkheim became detached from Judaism and, influenced by one of his teachers, showed some interest in Catholicism and decided to enrol in a mainstream school. Soon after he embraced a more agnostic attitude but retained a strong analytical interest in religion for the rest of his life. He was an excellent student at a secondary school in Épinal where he won many prizes. Realising that he would need to move to Paris to increase his chances of getting into a top university, Durkheim switched schools and completed his secondary education at one of the most prestigious Parisian schools, the Lycée Louis-le-Grand. In 1879 he gained a place in the leading academic institution, the École Normale Supérieure.

During his time at the École Normale Durkheim was mentored by the leading French classical historian Numa Denis Fustel de Coulanges, and also read extensively, including the sociological contributions of Comte, Spencer and others. He was also influenced by his other teacher, the philosopher Émile Boutroux, who was a fierce critic of individualist approaches that tended to reduce social life to psychology or biology. Some of Durkheim's fellow students would later become highly influential French thinkers, including Henri Bergson, the philosopher of vitalism, and Jean Jaurès, a leading socialist. However, Durkheim was dissatisfied with the academic traditionalism that underpinned the École Normale where the focus was on mastering the literary classics instead of studying contemporary phenomena. He graduated in 1882 and for the next five years was employed as a philosophy teacher at several secondary schools outside of Paris. During this period, he also spent two years in Germany where he studied moral philosophy and social science in Berlin, Leipzig and Marburg. In Leipzig he was particularly influenced by the empiricist approach developed in Wilhelm Wundt's Psychological Laboratory.

This experience shaped the young Durkheim's admiration for explanatory precision and scientific objectivity. His studies in Germany played a crucial role in his academic career: he published a series of articles on German academia which were well received among the French academic audience. These publications helped a 29-year-old Durkheim to secure his first academic appointment at the University of Bordeaux in 1887 where he taught the first ever sociology course in France. He also lectured on pedagogy and was influential in helping reform the French school system by making social science a significant part of the educational programme. In the same year Durkheim and Louise Dreyfus were married and soon had two children. In 1893 he completed and defended his PhD thesis, which included his study of Montesquieu (in Latin) and the Division of Labour (in French), the latter forming the core of his highly influential first book. Both Montesquieu and Rousseau remained strong influences in Durkheim's life and work. While studying Montesquieu, Durkheim articulated his holistic view of social order with an emphasis on the interconnectedness of social processes; Rousseau was the main influence in identifying group solidarity as a key sociological phenomenon.

The Durkheimian School

Two years later he published another path-breaking study, *The Rules of Sociological Method* (1895), which was followed by another key text, *Suicide*, published in 1897. In 1898 Durkheim and his collaborators established the first social science journal in France: *L'Année Sociologique*. This journal attracted creative young scholars who were deeply influenced by Durkheim and as such were instrumental in developing a distinct, Durkheimian school of thought. The two leading representatives of this school were Marcel Mauss and Maurice Halbwachs, both of whom would later go on to establish their own sociological approaches that were influenced by Durkheim. The journal published a variety of contributions ranging from sociology, geography, education, history and criminal law to philosophy and anthropology.

Durkheim published several of his key articles in the journal, including the programmatic piece of the Durkheimian School, *Individual and Collective Representations* (1898). During this period his main intellectual opponent was Gabriel Tarde (1843–1904), another prominent social thinker who challenged Durkheim's approach. In *The Laws of Imitation* (1890) Tarde develops a social theory centred on the idea that imitation underpins much of human social activity. He argues that new inventions and discoveries are regularly initiated in face-to-face interactions, but their influence remains dependent on mass-scale imitation in the sense that individuals at the lower end of the social hierarchy tend to imitate those at the top. Hence most innovations involve a top-down communication whereby elites shape the behaviours of the masses. For Tarde society is no more than a collection of hierarchically placed individuals where some imitated others. In contrast, Durkheim insisted that society was a reality in itself where individuals often behave differently as individuals and as members of specific groups. Thus, Durkheim rejected Tarde's psychological view, arguing in favour of the sociological and structural understanding of human relationships. Outside of France the most significant contemporary intellectual influence for Durkheim was Herbert Spencer. Although he admired Spencer's contributions, he profoundly disagreed with Spencer's individualist epistemology. He challenged Spencer's view that self-interest alone could uphold social order. Instead Durkheim was adamant that the idea of self-interest and the attainment of individual happiness are themselves products of specific social conditions that are unique to a particular time and place.

Educational Reforms and War

By the beginning of the new century Durkheim was universally regarded as the leading French social scientist and consequently was appointed to the chair of education at the Sorbonne in 1902. Four years later he became a full professor of the science of education, which in 1913 was renamed 'Chair in education and sociology'. Being recognised as the leading authority in education Durkheim also acted as an adviser to the Ministry of Education where he was able to enact several reforms of the French educational system. Most significantly his influence was decisive in introducing sociology into the French school curricula. He was also a public intellectual involved in the social and political debates of his time and was regarded as a scholar who was sympathetic to a variety of centre–left political causes.

In addition to his public activities he remained committed to sociological research and in 1912 his magnum opus, *The Elementary Forms of the Religious Life*, was published to great acclaim. Nevertheless, the outbreak of the First World War had a profoundly negative effect on Durkheim. The war acted as a shock to this Enlightenment-oriented scholar, who until then harboured rather optimistic views of social development. He perceived the war as a temporary pathological state that is bound to stop eventually and give way to a normal state of affairs. The intensity of the war experience involving mass-scale destruction and killings affected Durkheim significantly and his scholarly analyses were replaced by propagandistic pamphlets that defended France's role in the war and fiercely attacked Germany as an adversary. Durkheim was appointed secretary of the Committee for the Publication of Studies and Documents on the War and in this capacity published several nationalist pamphlets.

In these pamphlets Durkheim (1915: 45) was highly critical of the 'German war mentality' that was rooted in the long history of militarism and 'hypertrophy of the will'. He blamed German intellectuals such as Heinrich von Treitschke for being directly responsible for the militarist ethos that paved the way for war. He also witnessed many of his young students being recruited for war and perishing on the battlefields of Europe. The series of personal tragedies including the death of his son André, a promising young scholar in his own right, on the frontline at the Dardanelles in December 1915 reinforced his one-sided view of the Great War and also led to chronic depression. Devastated by grief Durkheim experienced a stroke and died in Paris less than two years later on 15 November 1917.

Historical, Social and Political Context

Although Durkheim was born and spent much of his childhood during the second French Empire under Napoleon III (1852–70) his adult life took place under the French Third Republic (1870–1940). In the wake of the humiliating defeat that the French military experienced in the Franco-Prussian War (1870–1) where it lost the key provinces of Alsace and Lorraine, the new republican government also faced a tremendous financial burden including the excessive war reparations it had to pay to Prussia. The aftermath of war was followed by social unrest and political instability. The largest unrest took place in the Paris Commune when radical revolutionary groups established a temporary government that ruled Paris for two months in 1871.

After the French government's military defeat, which was sealed with the surrender of Paris to Prussian troops at the end of January 1871, radical members of the French National Guard refused to relinquish their weapons and rejected the authority of the existing government, which moved from Paris to Bordeaux. Instead the members of the National Guard elected their own Central Committee as an alternative government. The leader of the Paris Commune aimed to implement substantial reforms including the separation of church and state, abolition of interest on debts, pension rights for children and unmarried women, better working conditions, the introduction of the right for employees to run their enterprises if deserted by the owners, and so on. However, after prolonged violent conflicts the Commune was crushed by French Army troops in May 1871 and during the 'Bloody Week' thousands of communards were killed. The experience of the Paris Commune showed how polarised French society was.

Political Divisions

Initially the new republican order was set up as a temporary arrangement until a new monarch was selected, but as there was no agreement on who would replace Napoleon III, the republican order was maintained by default. The 1875 constitution created a rather weak political system that generated constant tension between the president and the parliament. After the conservative president Patrice de MacMahon's attempt to consolidate his power by dissolving parliament, the left-leaning republican candidate, Jules Grévy, won the presidential election in 1879. During this period the political elite were split between the conservatives and left-wing republicans. The leading conservatives were keen to restore the Bourbon dynasty to power and were generally supported by the higher echelons of the Catholic Church, big landowners, the military establishment and wealthy industrialists. In contrast the republicans, whose main support base included the lower middle strata, urban workers and many intellectuals, were opposed to any form of monarchy, were eager to enact social reforms and were hostile towards the Church. This was a pivotal moment in maintaining and reinforcing the republican mode of governance. Nevertheless, the subsequent left-leaning republican governments remained weak and incapable of implementing substantive social, political and economic reforms. One of the few areas where the republican government was able to enact reforms was the education system. The Jules Ferry Laws passed through parliament in 1882 thus making public education compulsory, free and secular. At the same time the third-level Catholic institutions, which often arbitrarily referred to themselves as universities, lost this title and the state authorities were made the only legitimate body for issuing university diplomas. The government also introduced new educational opportunities for women and other disadvantaged groups by funding the building of new schools, universities and training colleges. The educational reforms intensified by the end of the century and Durkheim played a key role in making the social sciences a part of the school curriculum throughout France.

In the 1880s and 1890s the French political establishment was marred by several scandals that had a profound impact on French society. In 1889 a highly popular general, Georges Boulanger, won several electoral victories and was contemplating establishing a dictatorship through a *coup d'état*. He built up wide public support ranging from traditionalist Catholics and royalists in the countryside to impoverished workers in the cities, and his aggressive attitude towards Germany was also very popular. However, facing a series of scandals the general fled to Belgium where he committed suicide. The death of Boulanger undermined the conservative forces and strengthened the republican left.

The Dreyfus Affair

Nevertheless, the most politically significant moment in modern French political history was the Dreyfus affair. In 1894 Alfred Dreyfus, an army captain of Jewish origin, was charged with treason for selling secret documents to the German military. Although the counterintelligence was not certain who was responsible for this act, the anti-Semitic media, headed by the right-wing journalist Edouard Drumond, put a great deal of pressure on the military to convict Dreyfus. Hence, after a short and closed trial Dreyfus was sentenced to life imprisonment for treason and was deported to Devil's Island in French Guiana. However, his family were determined to contest this ruling and focused on collecting evidence that would prove Dreyfus's innocence. Soon the new head of the secret service, Colonel Georges Picquart, found credible proof that the real culprit of treason was Major Ferdinand Esterhazy, but the General Staff refused to consider the new evidence.

The Dreyfus family sought support among politicians and intellectuals and the Dreyfus affair polarised the French political and intellectual establishment. The conservatives, the religious authorities, the nationalist right-wing groups and the military elite were almost unanimous in their negative view of Dreyfus as an unfaithful and perfidious traitor of the French nation, emphasising his Jewish background. In contrast, leading intellectuals and left-wing republicans supported Dreyfus and demanded a new trial. Durkheim also expressed his strong support for Dreyfus. In 1898 Esterhazy was acquitted of treason and fled the country while several anti-Semitic groups organised riots in many French cities. In this environment the leading French writer Émile Zola published his declaration 'J'accuse...!', which soon gained wide support among intellectuals. Under this public pressure the military were forced to organise a new trial in 1899. However, despite the wealth of evidence the court martial confirmed the original decision and only reduced Dreyfus's sentence to 10 years. This judgment provoked an outcry among left republican groups and consequently the president of the French Republic, Émile Loubet, issued a pardon that would release Dreyfus from prison. It took another seven years for the legal rehabilitation of Dreyfus, who in 1906 was reinstated into the army with the rank of major and later became an active participant in the

First World War. This affair had a long-term impact on French social and political life, which remained ideologically split for much of the twentieth century. The anti-Semitic discourse that the Dreyfus affair unleashed directly affected Durkheim too as he was periodically attacked by the right-wing media, who questioned his loyalty to the French nation-state.

At the turn of the century France was not just politically divided, as the Dreyfus affair revealed, it was also a deeply class-divided society. Although agriculture was still the main source of economic production it was rapidly giving way to industry. For example, while in 1870 less than 23% of the population worked in industry, by the beginning of the First World War it was close to 40% of industrial workers and artisans in France (Wright, 1960). However, while industrial workers and farmers constituted an overwhelming majority of French society the key economic and political positions were occupied by wealthy industrialists, large landowners and other members of the Parisian establishment. In addition, the Third Republic expanded its colonial possessions throughout the world – from West Africa and Madagascar to Indochina and Polynesia. This rapidly changing and highly unequal social environment offered a natural social laboratory for a sociologist interested in social change, and although Durkheim was interested in developing universalist explanations there is no doubt that the turbulent experience of French society had a decisive impact on his sociological theories.

Durkheim's political outlook developed as a mid-way position between a reactionary Catholicism and a revolutionary Marxism. He advocated a scientific and rationally grounded form of republican-socialism led by Jaures (Lukes, 1973: 332). Durkheim believed in a future society based on the scientific and rational prognosis of its counterpart sociology, drawing on its comparative and statistical findings. A future republican society would come about through evolution rather than revolution, it required a powerful and active state which operated as a 'social brain' regulating the collective consciousness and representations pervading society.

Arguments and Ideas

Durkheim's social thought was deeply influenced by the continental philosophical traditions. However, his sociology was rather unusual as it drew upon two very different if not incompatible analytical positions – positivism and neo-Kantianism. The positivists, such as Auguste Comte, aspired to develop social science on the blueprint of the natural sciences. In this context they focus on the identification of empirical facts aiming to build cumulative knowledge which would ultimately help to identify a small number of general and universal laws about social relations. In contrast, neo-Kantians, such as Wilhelm Windelband, insist that the sheer complexity and unique nature of human experiences makes it impossible to capture social interactions using the means of the natural sciences.

Hence, Windelband differentiates between the nomothetic approach centred on identifying regularities and generalisable laws and the ideographic approach focused on the uniqueness and meanings that lie behind individual and contingent experiences, arguing that social science and humanities can only develop using ideographic methods. Durkheim attempted to reconcile these two positions by recognising that the social world differs substantially from the natural world but also arguing that this in itself is no reason to give up developing the scientific method for social science and sociology in particular.

The Science of Sociology

In one of his early publications, *The Rules of Sociological Method* (1895), Durkheim offers a programmatic agenda for sociology. More specifically he attempts to position sociology as a science capable of explaining variety of social phenomena. In this he privileges direct observation of social reality over generalised speculative approaches that dominated in his time. In his view, for:

> science to be objective, it must take its departure not from concepts whose formation has preceded it, but from sense data; from these must be directly drawn the components of its initial definitions ... it needs concepts which convey adequately things they are, not as it is convenient to conceive of them for practical purposes. (Durkheim, 1997: 81)

For Durkheim sociology can exist as an independent academic discipline only if it has its own distinct object of study and if it develops and utilises objective scientific methods of analysis. In his view this distinct object of study is social facts. He defines a social fact as 'every way of acting, fixed or not, capable of exercising on the individual an external constraint; or again, every way of acting which is general throughout a given society, while at the same time existing in its own right independent of its individual manifestations' (Durkheim, 1964: 13). What distinguishes social facts from individual facts is their independent quality. In other words, a social fact is not just a simple amalgamation of individual actions but something that acquires a distinct existence of its own. For instance, if an individual takes part in a collective event the individual brings his or her attributes to that collective event.

However, if the event is protracted and emotionally intense the collective experience that arises from this event generates a new social reality. For example, when individuals are involved in violent collective events such as lynch mobs, they often regret such experiences later. These individuals tend to describe their participation in terms of the collective euphoria under which they could not control their individual actions. Such sudden events can change individual behaviours and turn ordinary peaceful human beings into violent brutes. It is these autonomous collective experiences that Durkheim identified as social facts, arguing that the complexity of the social world can only be explained through specific social facts.

Durkheim is committed to establishing sociology as a science that possesses the requisite methodological tools to study social facts. However, he recognises that social life is multifaceted and unpredictable and as such operates according to a different logic to those that one could see in nature. The social world is full of formal and informal rules and norms and as such it is difficult to discern human motivations and their behaviour. Hence one can never study human social relations in the same way that physicists study gravity or thermodynamics. In this context, Durkheim distinguishes between the facts of nature, the primary focus of natural science, and social facts, which require sociological analysis. Unlike natural facts, which can be observed as they appear in nature, the causes of social facts are to be determined not by analysing the consciousness of individuals but by identifying the 'antecedent social facts'. Nevertheless, despite these differences, for Durkheim sociology is conceptualised as an empirical, objective and observation-grounded comparative discipline and as such it is a study of objective social facts. Hence to capture a social fact fully it is crucial to treat it as a thing: 'social phenomena are things and should be treated as things' (Durkheim, 1997: 69). This does not mean that all social facts appear in a material form. Obviously most social phenomena such as language or religion are symbolic forms of social relationships. Instead, being a thing implies that social phenomena have a life of their own. They have a *sui generis* quality – they operate as external reality to individuals and also have enormous influence on how individuals behave. In his own words: 'far from being the product of our own will, social facts determine it from outside; they are something like a mould into which we are obliged to pour our actions' (Durkheim, 1997: 70).

However, this potency of social facts does not stem from biology or psychology but is grounded in social relations. It is society that shapes many of our actions by imposing itself on individuals. For example, even when individuals believe that they have a great deal of freedom to choose, such as what they wear or where they live, 'we cannot choose the form of our houses any more than we can that of our clothes; at any rate one is obligatory to the same extent as the other' (Durkheim, 1997: 58). Precisely because societies are so embedded in our daily activities their power is often overlooked or ignored. Hence to capture fully this social embeddedness at work it is paramount to move away from simple biological, psychological or philosophical interpretations and develop the science of sociology.

Social Change

There is no doubt that Durkheim was deeply influenced by the evolutionary theory of social change. His first book, *The Division of Labor in Society* (1893), draws in part on the work of Auguste Comte and Herbert Spencer, both of whom articulated social change through the prism of clearly defined evolutionary stages. However, by focusing on the different sources of social integration Durkheim offers a subtler sociological model. Instead of taking social order as a given, and inevitable, he aims to explain what makes social integration possible. In other words, since human beings have different interests, ambitions, values and perceptions, it is not clear why humans live in societies. For Durkheim social order is rooted in different forms of solidarity. In his view complex orders could be held together only through one of two modes of organisation: either they are based on shared homogeneity or they result from functional heterogeneity.

Simply put, Durkheim distinguishes between two forms of solidarity – mechanical and organic solidarity. The key features of mechanical solidarity are cultural resemblance of its members and shared collective conscience. In his own words, this form of group integration dominates where 'ideas and tendencies common to all members of the society are greater in number and intensity than those which pertain personally to each member. This solidarity can grow only in inverse ratio to personality' (Durkheim, 1956: 129). In contrast, organic solidarity involves highly diverse individuals where social cohesion is not built on similarity but on functional interdependence. This is a solidarity that stems from the complex division of labour where every individual performs a unique role and as such contributes to the functioning of the entire social system. Such social orders are:

> constituted, not by repetition of similar and homogenous segments, but by a system of different organs each of which has a special role, and which are in turn formed by different parts. The social elements are not either juxtaposed to one another like the rings of an earthworm, nor enclosed within one another, but coordinated and subordinated vis-à-vis one another around a central organ which performs a moderating action towards the rest of the organism. (Durkheim, 1997: 132)

This model presupposes an evolutionary social change whereby the traditional world is associated with mechanical solidarity and modernity is tied to networks of organic solidarity. For Durkheim tribal communities are characterised by shared moral attitudes and beliefs – collective conscience (*conscience collective*) – and as such members of the group tend to act and think in a similar way. It is this value-based similarity that preserves the social order and makes society possible. Where mechanical solidarity dominates, an attack on an individual is perceived as an attack on the entire group. Similarly, committing a crime such as blasphemy is understood as an offence against the collective conscience. Hence, to prevent such acts the laws in traditional societies tend to be punitive and strict. In contrast, modern societies involve complex relationships between individuals and groups and as such require different forms of social glue to keep them together. Since they are rooted in the elaborate systems of a division of labour, they operate as composite systems where individuals perform different roles according to their skills and individual capacities.

Modern social organisations are shaped around merit-based systems of job allocation and rewards involving educational credentials and professionalisation. In this type of society shared values and shared moral principles stem from a functional interdependence, which is also reflected in dominant normative and legal regulations. Hence, unlike traditional societies where the focus is on disciplinary measures and retributive punishments against offenders, in modern societies the emphasis is on restitutive justice and the quick re-establishment of functional relationships in society. Although Durkheim subscribed to the evolutionary view of social change where the ties of organic solidarity were bound to gradually replace the mechanical solidarities of the traditional world, he was critical of other evolutionary perspectives that understood this transition as unidirectional and inevitable. Instead he perceived this transition as wrought with tension and discords often resulting in deep crises and disorder.

For Durkheim such transitional situations periodically generate the state of anomie – a situation where social orders transition from one to another moral universe and as a result many individuals find themselves in moral limbo lacking a clear set of ethical principles to uphold. Such anomic conditions contribute to the rupture of social bonds between people where some individuals lose the capacity for integration within the existing norms. In other words, anomie stands for the lack of shared norms (a normless environment) that transpires when there is a disparity between the collective norms and individual values. However, Durkheim argues that once the state of anomie is addressed and rectified, society is in position to establish new normative frameworks. Once these new value systems are firmly entrenched throughout the social order, they provide stronger ethical guidelines which make modern societies better integrated than their pre-modern counterparts.

The Sociology of Deviance

When studying social facts, Durkheim differentiated between the normal and the pathological forms. He defined normal social facts as those that occur in everyday life, and are regarded by society as conventional events that facilitate social integration. In contrast, pathological social facts are perceived as an aberration that undermines social cohesion. For example, whereas a marriage would be an example of a normal social fact, divorce would represent a pathological social fact. Durkheim made it clear that all social facts are context dependent and vary from time and place. However he was also adamant that all societies deploy this normal vs. pathological parameter to distinguish a socially desirable behaviour from socially undesirable actions. In this context, he analysed various forms of social deviance, arguing that 'crime is normal' in a sense that the breaking of established norms and laws reinforces their relevance in any given society. The fact that all modern societies possess legislation on criminal behaviour indicates that there is an expectation that these laws and corresponding norms will be broken by some individuals at some point in time.

Furthermore, such periodic norm infringements actually help reassert the existing norms as the members of society express outrage at those who break the norms and, in this process, reaffirm these norms, thus fostering and enhancing the social integration of their society. Much of Durkheim's work was focused on how individual and social violations of norms help ultimately to reinforce these very norms. This is particularly visible in his pioneering sociology of suicide. Whereas previous studies conceptualised suicide as a psychological response of individuals, Durkheim analyses suicide as a social fact which is shaped by the wider structural context. In *Suicide* (1897) Durkheim offers a sociological analysis of a unique form of deviance. Utilising the available statistical data on suicide rates across selected European countries he shows how the scale of this phenomenon varies in terms of class, gender, religious affiliation, age, education and residential location. Even though every instance of suicide is a product of unique individual experience Durkheim shows that there is a stable social pattern of how suicides happen across the population.

Hence, his study demonstrated that higher educated individuals were more likely to commit suicide than the rest of population. His research also indicated that suicide rates were higher among men than women, and among Protestants than Jews and Catholics. He also identified higher rates of suicide among soldiers compared with civilians, and a substantial decrease of suicide during wartime. His study also found that single individuals were more likely to commit suicide than those in relationships, while those who have children were the least likely to commit suicide. Although Durkheim provided insightful and comprehensive empirical analyses of suicide, rates it was his theoretical contribution that was truly original and pioneering. For one thing, he rejected the conventional explanations of suicide, which overemphasised the pathological character of individuals. He also was critical of theories that identified geographical and economic causes (i.e. poverty, inequality or climatic differences) or psychological motivations. Instead, he argues that suicide is a social phenomenon resulting from the lack of social integration and mismatches in the patterns of social solidarity. For another thing, he articulated a highly influential typology of suicides which can be used to explain the sociological difference between the types of suicide.

Thus, Durkheim differentiates between egoistic, altruistic, anomic and fatalistic suicides. Egoistic suicide is triggered by the sense of despair that individuals experience when they are not integrated into a specific community. Such individuals are usually affected by depression, apathy and a sense of meaninglessness that stem from social isolation and lack of deeper bonds with other human beings. For Durkheim these individuals, who are often defined by 'excessive individuation', experience a sense of detachment and commit suicide from individualist motivations. In other words, suicide happens as an act of a conscious decision that arises from a self-centred view of the world. Durkheim's statistical data indicated that egoistic suicide was more prevalent in modern societies, and among men who were not in a relationship and had no children.

In direct contrast, altruistic suicide transpires in situations where individuals are deeply integrated in their communities. This type of suicide characterises traditional communities (i.e. tribal organisations) or contemporary secret societies (i.e. revolutionary fraternities, terrorist networks, etc.) where group bonds are very deep and intimate. Altruistic suicide arises when individuals feel that they have to sacrifice themselves for the good of the entire group. Hence, unlike egoistic suicide, which is a result of the lack of social integration, altruistic suicide stems from too much integration. Typical examples would include the Hindu tradition of Sati in which a widow is willingly immolated with her deceased husband.

The dramatic social change followed by the breakdown of established social norms often results in what Durkheim calls anomic suicide. This type of self-harm is generated by moral disorder in the wake of sudden social transformations. In these situations individuals lack moral guidance and are often incapable of dealing with radical change. For example, winning the lottery or experiencing unexpected bankruptcy can ultimately trigger ultimately anomic suicide as a particular individual has no moral parameters within which to understand the new situation.

The final type of suicide Durkheim identifies is fatalistic suicide, which is a product of overregulated societies. In such social orders where there are severe constraints on individuals, people have little choice and could commit suicide as a form of an escape from the oppressive environment. Typical examples would include slaves or prisoners who choose death over enslavement.

For Durkheim suicide types are determined by social change and are dependent on the levels of moral regulation and social integration of individuals. Thus, the pace of social change can generate different forms of suicide.

The Sociology of Religion

Durkheim's last sociological book, *The Elementary Forms of Religious Life* (1912), was his most ambitious and most successful undertaking. Although he emphasised the role of religion in his previous writings, this book develops a comprehensive and highly original sociological understanding of religion. Durkheim (1954: 47) defines religion in the following terms: 'a unified system of beliefs and practices relative to sacred things, that is to say, things set apart and forbidden – beliefs and practices which unite in one single moral community called a Church, all those who adhere to them'. The key focus here, just as in his other contributions, is the view of religious experience as a social rather than individual phenomenon.

He conceptualised religion as a non-material social fact and shifted his focus from the belief in a supernatural deity, which he saw as a relatively novel development, towards the more 'elementary forms' of communal beliefs.

Durkheim argues that religion is one of the pristine social institutions that has influenced the development on many other social organisations. To understand fully these social dynamics, Durkheim aimed to dissect what he considered to be the simplest form of religious life – totemism. By exploring the ritualistic practices of the Arunta and other native Australian populations Durkheim identified what he believed to be the universal features of all religions – the sharp distinction between the sacred and the profane and the totemic principle of collective self-worship. For Durkheim religious experience depends on the separation between the profane world, characterised by everyday, routine and practical activities, and the realm of the sacred, defined by extraordinary, transcendental and spiritual acts.

However, such a distinction is not predetermined: an object such as a sacrificial knife, amulet or a grail becomes sacred only when removed from everyday use and purified through specific ritual practices. The point is that sacred-ness is defined in direct opposition to the profane; the two spheres can never overlap, they are absolute – that which is holy cannot be profaned and holiness is established through its distinction from the profane: 'the sacred and profane have always been conceived as separate kinds, as two worlds which have nothing in common' (Durkheim, 1995: 36). In Durkheim's view this universal distinction makes religion possible and as such also defines the key moral parameters of a particular religious group. Shared religious experience provides emotional security as it binds members of the religious community together. In his understanding the realm of the sacred reflects these emotional ties and through shared belief in a sacred 'thing' the group establishes the boundaries of belonging. Moreover, the totemic principle is a manifestation of group consciousness through which the group worships itself. In other words, through the totemic principle a clan/tribe expresses reverence for a particular totem which in itself represents that very clan/tribe.

Hence by worshiping a sacred kangaroo a tribe worships their own community:

> So if [the totem] is at same time, the symbol of the god and of the society, could it not be the case that god and society are one and the same thing?... The god of the clan, the totemic principle, cannot be other than the clan itself, though personified and represented to the imagination under the material appearances of the vegetable or the animal that serves as totem. (Durkheim, 1995: 208)

This principle that 'god is society' has its origins in totemism but it is equally visible in other, more complex, religious practices. Durkheim argues that the monotheistic religious traditions operate through very similar social processes: the ritual sacraments, shared prayers and the use of sacred objects are all deployed as a vehicle for the self-worship of one's community. Religious practice is not only a mirror of a particular society but also a source of group identity. Although he recognises that modernity has brought about intense secularisation in some parts of the world, he is adamant that religion remains a powerful force of social integration and as such is unlikely to disappear in the future: 'There is something eternal in religion that is destined to outlive the succession of particular symbols in which religious thought has clothed itself' (Durkheim, 1995: 429). While traditional religious practices might lose their support base, the totemic principle and the sacred/profane dichotomy are bound to remain as they underpin the social cohesion of any community. Hence Durkheim believed that belief in science, the 'cult of the individual' and nationalism often emerge as the modern equivalents of the totemic principle through which contemporary societies continue to worship themselves.

Contemporary Relevance and Applications

Durkheim's work had enormous influence on the development of sociological thinking and it still serves as an inspiration for many contemporary sociologists. Initially his ideas were utilised by influential French sociologists such as Maurice Halbwachs and Marcel Mauss, who articulated novel approaches in the study of collective memory and the sociology of gift exchange, respectively.

ANOMIE

Durkheim's concept of anomie today remains one of the cornerstone critical concepts in sociology. Key to Durkheim's critique is that modern society is not inherently problematic; it can be harmoniously integrated. This provides the normative basis to consider conditions of insufficient regulation of social relations, or those where regulations are not consistent with the degree of societal development, as conditions of an anomic division of labour. Both Talcott Parsons and Robert Merton took up this concept in the 1950s, the former aligning closely with Durkheim and the latter entwining it with a sociological theory of deviant behaviour in which deviance was conceived as the normal outcome of anomic social conditions. After waning in popularity, the concept is experiencing resurgence again today, finding new relevance in societal conditions marked by neoliberal economic de-regulation.

In his book *On Collective Memory* (1950) Halbwachs draws on Durkheim's key concepts to argue that in addition to individual acts of remembrance societies also generate collective memories which are determined in part by the group's location within a particular society. Hence, our understanding of the past is always shaped by collective consciousness and collective representations. Mauss's key publication, *The Gift* (1950), echoes Durkheim's emphasis on the role of morality in social relations. The book explores how traditional social orders treat gift exchange as a mechanism for building social relationships. Thus, rather than treating gift giving as a simple economic transaction, Mauss's analysis centres on the moral obligations that frame the dynamics of gift exchange: the social reciprocity in giving and receiving. The moral principles that underpin the informal rules of gift exchange do not concern individual relationships only, but are grounded in social relationships between groups. For Mauss there are no genuinely free gifts as they necessarily involve an obligation to reciprocate in some way. Gift giving creates a social bond and the inability to reciprocate impacts on one's status and honour, thus creating an asymmetrical social relationship between the gift giver and gift receiver. Drawing on Durkheim, Mauss describes the practice of gift exchange as a 'total social fact'; that is an activity which has monumental implications for society as a whole.

Durkheim's work also had substantial impact outside of France. In the UK Mary Douglas was one of the first scholars who utilised Durkhemian framework to analyse complex social processes. Her book *Purity and Danger* (1966) explores how the ideas of ritual purity and pollution operate in different social and historical contexts. Drawing on Durkheim's distinction between the sacred and the profane Douglas identifies how the notions of purity and pollution are not tied to fixed things, places or people, but are shaped by contextual logic and the rituals associated with that logic. For example, the conventional explanations tend to see the religious prohibitions on food (such as kosher or halal) as the tests of one's faith or as traditional forms of health regulation. In contrast, Douglas interprets such strict regulations, including the bans on eating specific animals (pigs in Islam and Judaism or cows in Hinduism), as social facts that establish and maintain symbolic boundaries between groups. She identifies a strong link between ritual pollution and social danger where eating forbidden food symbolically undermines the boundaries of one's group.

In the United States several cultural sociologists adopted and further developed Durkheim's key ideas. Robert Bellah articulated the concept of civil religion to explain the dynamic of social cohesion in the United States. Bellah (1967, 1975) argues that most Americans share a common civil religion that binds society together and that these shared beliefs are maintained and reinforced through regularised ritualistic practices and established institutions. This civil religion co-exists with, and also infuses, specific religious denominations of individuals and groups that inhabit and identify with the American polity. Such a widely shared belief system is grounded in shared sacred texts and symbols such as The Declaration of Independence, The Constitution, the national flag, and is enacted through common rituals such as 4 July parades, presidential inaugurations, the school-organised pledge of allegiance ceremonies and the singing of the national anthem at major sporting events. Bellah singles out US presidents as having a key role in performing and maintaining the civil religion, with assassinated presidents such as Abraham Lincoln or John F. Kennedy acting as martyrs for the sacred nation.

Durkheim's work has also influenced the Yale School of cultural sociology represented by Jeffrey Alexander, Philip Smith and Philip Gorski. In his recent work Gorski (2017) revisits the civil religion thesis and argues that the United States was established as a polity built on Judaeo-Christian religious ethics and the political legacy of Western civil republicanism. However, unlike Bellah, who emphasises the stability and social cohesion of American civil religion, Gorski focuses on the deep social, ideological and political tensions that undermine this 'American covenant'. He argues that the US public sphere is deeply polarised between the two mutually exclusive ideological forces: the religious nationalists, who envisage the United States as a God-given polity bent on acting as a battleground for the ultimate war between good and evil, and the radical secularists, centred on completely extinguishing religion from the public arena. To counter these two trends and to rectify civil religion Gorski emphasises the interdependence of the religious, republican, nationalist and secular traditions in American history.

Criticisms

Conventional critics of Durkheim tend to zoom in on the social and political implications of his work, which has often been negatively contrasted with that of Marx and Weber (Allen and O'Boyle, 2017; Bottomore, 1981). Hence Durkheim's overemphasis on social cohesion and order has contributed to his being characterised as a conservative sociologist. For example, Allen and O' Boyle (2017) argue that unlike Marx, who was interested not only in diagnosing the structural sources of social inequalities but also in offering a lasting remedy for these problems, Durkheim was a conservative scholar who ultimately supported the republican status quo. Nevertheless, much of the recent scholarship has questioned these traditional interpretations of Durkheim by pointing out the complexity of his social and political allegiances and by reinterpreting his work (Poggi, 2000; Collins, 2004, 2008). For example, Collins has attempted to disentangle Durkheim's work from the hard grip of American structural–functionalists such as Parsons and Merton. For Collins (2004) Durkheim's micro-sociological analyses of solidarity bring him much closer to Goffman and the symbolic interactionists than the macro-structural approaches of Parsons.

However, despite these various recent attempts to recast Durkheim as a more nuanced social thinker, there is no doubt that his approach has generated a number of criticisms. Firstly, Durkheim's view of sociology as an objective, rational and causality-driven science that is in many ways similar to the natural sciences has been judged by some critics as a form of narrow positivism which is inadequate to capture the complexity of social action (Allen and O'Boyle, 2017; Bottomore, 1981; Lukes, 1973). Although Durkheim was critical of Comte's positivist philosophy, he still argued that sociologists' 'main goal is to extend scientific rationalism to human conduct ... what has been called our positivism is but a consequence of this rationalism' (Durkheim, 1895). This positivist ambition was underpinned by functionalist reasoning that characterises much of Durkheim's work. For example, he aims to explain the crime rates in terms of the functions they perform in specific societies, but he does not tell us much about the social origins of deviance. One is informed that crime is functional as it reaffirms shared moral values of what is right and what is wrong, and in this way it enhances social cohesion. However, by stating that something is functional one does not offer a coherent explanation as why, when and how criminal activity transpires. Despite his nominal positivism Durkheim's explanations are often too functionalist and as such lack causal direction. Needs are not causes. Instead they are only consequences of a particular action that requires proper explanation. The same problem is discernible in his theory of suicide – the functionality of altruistic suicide in the traditional world and egoistic suicide in the modern world are not deduced through the causal patterns of social action but are simply taken at face value on the basis of different modes of group solidarity. Durkheim's functionalism is also pronounced in his understanding of social discords as a form of pathology. Thus, rather than recognising that societies consist of diverse individuals and groups who have different economic, political or ideological interests and as such are bound to find themselves in the state of mild or severe conflicts, Durkheim treats all forms of dispute and struggle as pathological action that undermines the normality of social cohesion.

Secondly, critics have identified Durkheim's general approach as epistemologically idealist in a sense that it leaves little or no room for the material forms of social action (Malešević, 2006; Lukes, 1973). Durkheim perceives human beings primarily as norm-driven creatures who act based on ideas, values and moral preconceptions that underpin the social order they inhabit. For example, his view of religion as a form of self-worship leaves no space for the role of political or economic factors. Obviously, religious beliefs cannot proliferate by themselves. Instead, the success of any religion is in part determined by its organisational capacity, material incentives, its relationship with political power and many other non-ideational factors (Mann, 1993). Furthermore, Durkheim's firm distinction between the sacred and the profane has been challenged on empirical grounds. Many anthropologists have demonstrated that traditional, just as modern, societies rarely divide strictly between the sacred and the profane. In everyday life people might use ritual knives to peel potatoes and the religious temples could be used for worship on one day and for children's playgroups on another day (Lukes, 1973). In addition, Durkheim's identification of the social with the sacred is also untenable as many forms of social action have very different sources – instrumental, value-rational, habitual or emotional (Malešević, 2006). Critics have also questioned the Durkhemian understanding of social order – how can collective self-worship generate group solidarity when the worshipping group has already to be there in the first place? As Hamnett (2001: 55) puts it, does this religious experience express 'the pregiven solidarity of the group, or bring it about?'.

Thirdly, Durkheim's theory has often been characterised as a form of social determinism (Lehmann, 2013; Giddens, 1978; Malešević, 2006). In this approach there is no distinct role for human agency and all social processes are perceived always to have social causes. In Durkheim's view of society individual autonomy is largely invisible and there is no space for the subjective interpretations of social reality. As Lehmann (2013: 45) puts it: 'in a cause/effect schema, it is society that has precedence. It is the whole that determines the nature and behaviour of the parts.' This determinism is particularly pronounced in his depiction of traditional societies where all individuals look and act in the same way. The concept of mechanical solidarity is built on the highly problematic idea that tribal and village-based traditional cultures are closed systems of meaning where there is no individual autonomy or independent agency. In Durkheim's (1893) own words: 'the individual personality is absorbed into the collective personality'. This model of 'total socialisation' (Lehmann, 2013: 46) is empirically inaccurate as even in the most collectivist societies individuals retain a degree of autonomy. Moreover, this approach tends to reify and psychologise groups by attributing individual psychological qualities to entire groups. However, as Brubaker (2004) rightly argues, this form of epistemological groupism represents a flawed explanatory strategy as it treats heterogeneous and complex groups as if they are homogeneous and bounded actors. Groupism is a 'tendency to take discrete, sharply differentiated, internally homogeneous and externally bounded groups as basic constituents of social life, chief protagonists of social conflicts, and fundamental units of social analysis' (Brubaker, 2004: 8).

Conclusion

Durkheim has left a rich and lasting intellectual legacy. For one thing he was pivotal in establishing sociology as an academic discipline and a teaching subject in France. He also was a public intellectual who made sociological analysis visible and relevant for a wider audience. For another thing Durkheim created a unique sociological perspective which influenced and is still influencing generations of sociologists. His novel ideas, including the notion of social fact, anomie, altruistic suicide, organic solidarity, the sacred vs. profane distinction and many other concepts, still shape contemporary debates within and also outside sociology. There is no doubt that Durkheim was, is and will remain a towering intellectual figure in sociological theory.

References

Allen, K. and O'Boyle, B. (2017) *Durkheim: A Critical Introduction*. London: Pluto Press.

Bellah, R. N. (1967) Civil religion in America. *Daedalus*, 96, pp. 1000–21.

Bellah, R. N. (1975) *The Broken Covenant: American Civil Religion in Time of Trial*. New York: Seabury Press.

Bottomore, T. (1981) A Marxist Consideration of Durkheim. *Social Forces*, 59(4), pp. 902–17.
Brubaker, R. (2004) *Ethnicity without Groups*. Cambridge, MA: Harvard University Press.
Collins, R. (2004) *Interaction Ritual Chains*. Princeton, NJ: Princeton University Press.
Collins, R. (2008) *Violence: A Micro-Sociological Theory*. Princeton, NJ: Princeton University Press.
Douglas, M. (1966) *Purity and Danger: An Analysis of Concepts of Pollution and Taboo*. London: Routledge & Kegan Paul.
Durkheim, E. (1915) *'Germany Above All': The German Mental Attitude and the War*. Paris: Librairie Armand Colin.
Durkheim, E. (1954 [1912]) *The Elementary Forms of Religious Life*. London: Allen & Unwin.
Durkheim, E. (1956 [1893]) *The Division of Labor in Society*. New York: Free Press.
Durkheim, E. (1964 [1895]) *The Rules of Sociological Method*. New York: Free Press.
Durkheim, E. (1995 [1912]) *The Elementary Forms of Religious Life*. K. E. Fields, trans. New York: Free Press.
Durkheim, E. (1997 [1893]) *The Division of Labor in Society*. W. D. Halls, trans. New York: Free Press.
Durkheim, E. (2002 [1897]) *Suicide: A Study in Sociology*, 2nd edition. J. A. Spaulding and G. Simpson, trans. London: Routledge.
Giddens, A. (1978) *Durkheim*. London: Fontana Modern Masters.
Gorski, P. (2017) *American Covenant: A History of Civil Religion from the Puritans to the Present*. Princeton, NJ: Princeton University Press.
Halbwachs, M. (1992 [1950]) *On Collective Memory*. L. A. Coser (ed.) and trans. Chicago, IL: University of Chicago Press.
Hamnet, I. (2001) Durkheim and the Study of Religion. In: W. S. F. Pickering (ed.) *Émile Durkheim: Critical Assessments of Leading Sociologists*. London: Routledge, pp. 50–73.
Lehmann, J. (2013) *Deconstructing Durkheim: A Post-Post Structuralist Critique*. London: Routledge.
Lukes, S. (1973) *Émile Durkheim, His Life and Work: A Historical and Critical Study*. London: Allen Lane.
Malešević, S. (2006) *Identity as Ideology*. New York: Palgrave.
Mann, M. (1993) *The Sources of Social Power: The Rise of Classes and Nation-states, 1760–1914*. Cambridge: Cambridge University Press.
Mauss, M. (1966 [1950]) *The Gift: Forms and Functions of Exchange in Archaic Societies*. London: Routledge & Kegan Paul.
Poggi, G. (2000) *Durkheim*. Oxford: Oxford University Press.
Wright (1960) *France in Modern Times*. Chicago, IL: Rand McNally.

VIII

SIMMEL

Introduction

Simmel is now justifiably regarded as one of the 'founding fathers' of sociology. However, this was not always the case. During his lifetime he was well known and highly respected. He was universally regarded as a brilliant lecturer and astute cultural analyst. His work was influential throughout Europe and North America and some of his key publications were also translated and published in the United States, France and further afield. Nevertheless, after his death much of his work was marginalised, misinterpreted and forgotten. Throughout the twentieth century Simmel was generally perceived as no more than a representative of the passé formalist school of thought. It is only in the late 1980s and early 1990s that Simmel was 'rediscovered' as a major social theorist and also as somebody whose work was able to speak to the social concerns of the late twentieth- and early twenty-first centuries. Over the past two decades Simmel's work has suddenly and dramatically gained recognition not only in sociology, but throughout the social sciences, humanities and art. In this chapter we briefly review and analyse Simmel's main contributions and link his work to the broader social and historical context of *fin de siècle* Europe and Germany. We also explore the biographical and intellectual currents that have shaped Simmel's thought.

Life and Intellectual Context

Georg Simmel was born on 1 March 1858 in Berlin, the city where he would spend most of his life. Both of his parents were originally Jews but later converted to Christianity. Georg too was baptised Lutheran, but this had little impact on popular perceptions in Prussia and Germany at that time, where he was, throughout his life, regarded as a Jew. It seems that his mother was a domineering person with whom Georg had a quite distant and cold relationship (Coser, 1977). His father, co-owner of a chocolate factory, died when Georg was 16 years old. Following his father's early death, a good family friend,

Julius Friedlander, a wealthy founder of the international music publishing house, was named young Simmel's guardian. Being brought up in an affluent environment, Simmel was in a position to enrol in the top Berlin primary and secondary schools. Following this, at the age of 18 he went to the University of Berlin where he initially studied history under the leading German historians including Mommsen, Droysen, Grimm and Treitschke.

Nevertheless, he gradually became more interested in philosophy and he switched his courses to study under Lazarus and Steinthal, the founders of *Volkerpsychologie*, as well as Harms, Zeller and Bastian. He also completed modules on medieval Italian and wrote a minor thesis on Petrarch. As was the standard at that time Simmel completed his studies with a doctorate in philosophy in 1881. His thesis centred on Kant's philosophy and was later published as *The Nature of Matter According to Kant's Physical Monadology*. Although his doctoral work was judged by the examination committee as of high quality, there was a debate on whether to award a degree or not on the grounds that the work was littered with spelling mistakes (a possible sign of dyslexia?) and many of his citations were provided in the original languages, which his examiners could not read.

The Unpaid Lecturer

By 1885 Simmel was appointed as an unpaid lecturer (Privatdozent) at the University of Berlin where in addition to philosophy, he offered a wide range of courses including logic, art, social psychology, ethics, history of philosophy and sociology. In 1887 he became the first person to offer a sociology module at a German university. This teaching position was not permanent, did not provide good career prospects and its financing was for the most part dependent on the number of students who opted to register for the Privatdozent's courses. Despite his numerous applications, often backed up by glowing references from the leading social scientists of his time, including Weber and Tönnies, he was unable to secure a permanent professorial position in Germany until very late in his career. Thus Simmel remained a temporary lecturer for 15 years and only in 1901 was he granted the rank of professor without a chair, which was more of an honorary title as it did not permit him to take part in everyday academic affairs and it did not include financial remuneration. After many failed attempts and following almost 30 years of temporary unpaid positions, Simmel was eventually appointed a full professor at the University of Strasbourg in 1914 at the age of 56.

In 1890 Simmel married Gertrud Kinel, a philosopher who published under the pseudonym Marie-Luise Enckendorf and later also under her married name. She produced influential studies on the philosophy of religion and sexuality. Having inherited a relatively large sum of money the Simmels were in a position to live affluent, protected bourgeois lives. Their Berlin household was famous as a venue for the leading German intellectuals of the time and they would regularly organise intellectual events and parties and host notable German intellectuals and artists.

Although Simmel could not secure a permanent academic position this did not mean that he remained an insignificant figure in the intellectual life of Germany. On the contrary his writings, both scholarly and journalistic, together with his lecturing have made him a recognisable name not only in Berlin and Germany but throughout Europe and North America. During this period, he authored many books and articles which attracted a great deal of attention and some of which were translated into English, French, Polish, Italian and Russian. One of the principal reasons why his writings had such a popular appeal was that his writing style was highly accessible and completely devoid of any academic jargon. Simmel favoured elegant dichotomies, lively metaphors and unsystematic expressions which were highly untypical for academic works at that time. As Wolff (1950: xix) points out: 'Simmel often appears as though in the midst of writing he were overwhelmed by an idea, by avalanche of ideas, and if he incorporated them without interrupting himself, digesting and assimilating only to the extent granted him by the onrush'. Nevertheless, some of his early publications were written in a more conventional way as attempts to emulate the dominant writing paradigm. For example, one of his earliest publications *On Social Differentiation* (1890) clearly lacks the flair of his later works such as *The Philosophy of Money* (1990), *The Philosophy of Fashion* (1905), *Sociology* (1908) or *The Metropolis and Mental Life* (1903).

While this type of writing won Simmel admirers outside of academia it also damaged his prospects of winning a permanent professorship as his playful and nonchalant style of expression was deemed to lack academic rigour. Another, more significant reason why Simmel was denied a permanent position reflecting his international eminence was the widespread anti-Semitism that permeated much of German, and European, academia.

In addition to being a prolific and widely read author Simmel was also an excellent public speaker. As Coser (1977 [1959]) emphasises, he was a 'virtuoso on the platform' who would mesmerise his audiences. He developed an unusual way of lecturing which combined clear expression with the 'abrupt gestures and stabs, dramatic halting, and then realising a torrent of dazzling ideas'. Simmel was well known as a speaker who was thinking creatively and developing new ideas in the process of lecturing. In this way most of his lectures were always new and fresh, thus attracting attention from not only students, but also fellow academics and the wider public, all of whom flocked to hear Simmel speak.

Public Intellectual

In many respects Simmel was a true public intellectual who would regularly reflect on the contemporary developments in Berlin, Germany and the world.

As he was extremely well versed in philosophy, sociology, the arts, religion and economics he often provided extensive commentaries for newspapers and other popular outlets. However, he generally lacked interest in the current political issues. While he provided commentary on some political questions including the position of women or the role of crime in society, his focus was much more on the cultural foundations of social processes. Most of his journalistic pieces were balanced, analytical and detached. Nevertheless, this changed dramatically with the onset of the First World War when he became passionately involved in the war propaganda effort. Although some of his popular publications from this period contain valuable sociological insights, most of his war-focused articles were one-dimensional nationalistic pamphlets defending Germany's position and virulently attacking French and British academics, and their respective societies. Simmel was also highly active in promoting the social relevance of social sciences, philosophy and art. Together with Weber and Tönnies he founded the German Society for Sociology. He also took a very active part in artistic circles and public debates with the leading novelists, poets and other artists of Germany.

Simmel's creativity thrived in the unique social environment of pre-war Berlin. He was fully in tune with the latest intellectual and artistic developments of the city that was in the midst of tremendous social change. As a polymath and a person of wide interests, Simmel was often the epicentre of several intellectual circles. He was a close friend of Germany's leading poets, namely Stefan George and Rainer Maria Rilke, and his house was frequently visited by Max Weber, Edmund Husserl and many influential German philosophers, journalists, historians and art critics. This highly diverse intellectual environment, underpinned by the persistent debates and disagreements, stimulated the proliferation of new ideas and unique concepts. Since Simmel was not a proponent of systematic theories and causal methods, these diverse influences have helped shape a distinct and highly original way of thinking. Although his work directly influenced a large number of scholars including a young Georgy Lukács, and later, Elias and Goffman, he left no disciples or recognisable school of thought. Despite his international fame Simmel was well aware of these issues concerning the legacy of his work. In his diary he notes that: 'I know that I shall die without intellectual heirs. My legacy will be, as it were in cash, distributed to many heirs, each transforming his part into use conformed to *his* nature' (Coser, 1977: 199). Simmel suffered from liver cancer and died on 28 September 1918.

Historical, Social and Political Context

Just like Weber, Simmel too grew up in Prussia and spent most of his mature life in Wilhelmine Germany. However, unlike Weber, who was preoccupied with the political, military and geo-strategic questions of Germany's role in the world, Simmel was first and foremost a sociologist and philosopher of culture. These different intellectual trajectories of the two leading German sociologists were in part a reflection on their different social backgrounds. Although both scholars had a privileged, upper middle-class upbringing, Weber also came from a family with a strong tradition of involvement in politics. In contrast Simmel's Jewish heritage and the lack of notable ancestors in a still deeply conservative, status-conscious, German society probably played a significant role in his general lack of interest in formal politics.

German Society and Cultural Change

Nevertheless, both men thrived intellectually in the new Germany, which was becoming an economic, cultural and political powerhouse of Europe. While Weber directly opposed the authoritarian and conservative ideas that dominated the Wilhelmine world, Simmel was more interested in how such ideas co-existed with the Enlightenment-inspired economic and cultural progress that German society was experiencing. More specifically, Simmel focused on how profound social changes impact on individual characters and personalities, and how changed environmental conditions shape new ways of living. It is no accident that he was keen to understand how big urban conglomerations influence mental life, and how industrial culture melts traditional social bonds, for this is something he could observe in his native Berlin, which was dramatically expanding and changing in front of his eyes. The economic prosperity and the growing confidence of the Wilhelmine state elite were also reflected in the material and social transformation of its capital city. Berlin was now the bedrock of new styles of architecture and visual arts, exemplified by the neo-Baroque buildings, the grandiose Siegesallee and the Wilhelmine Ring, all designed to project the grandeur of a new imperial power. The wide streets and extravagant boulevards were all built to indicate the ambitions of the new rising power.

In addition, as the new state attempted to maintain some of the old conservative traditions while also pursuing intense economic development, this in itself created social tensions and ambiguities which were directly reflected in Wilhelmine social and cultural life. The ever-increasing urban population, the expanding educational system and the rising middle class, all put an enormous strain on traditional culture. While externally the new state elite were preoccupied with the acquisition of new overseas colonies and the projection of imperial might, Simmel's focus was firmly on internal social changes and everyday social interactions.

In this sense Simmel was puzzled by different questions to Weber. Whereas Weber's interest was in macro-sociological issues including the role of the state, prestige, geopolitics, rationalisation and religious transformations, for Simmel, the main sociological concerns were those from the micro world: How are social groups formed and maintained? How do social dynamics change when group size increases? Why and how do individuals develop attachments to specific collectivities?

Nevertheless, to provide coherent sociological answers to these questions Simmel also had to understand the impact of structural transformations on German society as he was well aware that the changes in everyday social interactions owed a great deal to concrete material transformations. For example, the rise of Berlin as a world metropolis from which sprung new cultural movements and novel artistic developments was largely dependent on the economic boom that Wilhelmine Germany experienced in the late nineteenth century. The unification of Germany removed border tariffs, trade duties and other protectionist measures that were in place between the various small German states and principalities. This development, together with the intense railway construction and ever-expanding industrial production, created the conditions for economic and technological growth. Since the state elite were oriented towards geopolitical expansion, they fostered the development of heavy industry (metallurgy in particular), which enhanced the infrastructure but was also crucial for the production of armaments.

New Germany also sported a powerful banking system capable of providing credit and investment for private and public ventures. With the ever-increasing population (rising from 40 million in 1880 to almost 59 million in 1910) and sprawling new cities, the state also possessed a huge workforce able to meet the requirements of industrialisation and modernisation. The sheer intensity and speed of German industrialisation at the turn of the nineteenth and beginning of the twentieth century could be compared with similar developments in China today: a state-sponsored accelerated modernisation of a rising power that is catching up and gradually overtaking other world-leading economies. The fact that by the early twentieth century German steel production exceeded that of until then the dominant industrial European power, namely the UK, was a sign of the state's technological and industrial strength.

However, being a late (and speedy) moderniser meant that German society had to undergo dramatic social changes in a very short period of time. The transition from a predominantly agrarian economy and rural society towards being one of the world-leading industrial powerhouses was anything but smooth. The mass-scale industrialisation, urbanisation and modernisation had profound effects on the social structure of German society. Although the new Germany remained dominated by the old, semi-feudal, Prussian landed aristocracy (Junkers) its social and cultural life was now generated in the big cities by the newly emerging middle strata. This new creative environment gave birth to a variety of social and cultural movements from Werkbund to Bauhaus. Moreover, the inherent tension between the political domination of old aristocrats on the one hand, and the rising economic and cultural power of the new middle classes on the other hand, forged the emergence of unique social and cultural forces able to merge the instrumental with the aesthetic. As Trommler (1992: 39–40) argues in the context of German modernism:

> The central contribution of the German reform movement to development of what has been labelled Modernism or International Style was the break with the nineteenth-century juxtaposition of art and industry. It is characterised by the compromise with which artistic elites reclaimed important segments of society's material life for an aesthetic approach: the compromise with the pragmatics of capitalist production and consumption.

Interactions and Urban Life

Simmel zoomed in on these unprecedented social transformations. He wanted to capture analytically how a new social order changes human interactions and how new forms of sociality are created. In particular, he focused on how the changes in the economic sphere impact on cultural values. In this context Berlin was envisaged as a social laboratory of modernity where intensive urbanisation and industrialisation forged new types of personality: the blasé *flâneur*, the marginal stranger, the detached financier, the fashionable starlet, the adventurer, the renegade, and so on. The social consequences of large-scale structural changes are, for Simmel, seen most clearly in the social interactions that take place in the big cities. It is there that new forms of sociality emerge with human beings losing traditional kinship-based bonds and acquiring new types of conditional attachments towards others. For Simmel social distance becomes important in such a context as the inherent value of people and things is determined by the distance from each other.

Although he was an authentic Berliner who found comfort in the close friendships of his fellow intellectuals, Simmel was also able to observe and analyse the other side of urban expansion: the coldly detached interactions between neighbours living in a big city, the social transformation of immigrants from the countryside, or the upward and downward social mobility of different social strata. Nevertheless, in his analyses of metropolitan social life Simmel offers rather different accounts to most other sociologists of his time. While both Durkheim and Marx emphasise the dark sides of modernisation, for Simmel the shift from the traditional to the modern word is always multifaceted and full of ambiguous consequences. Hence, what Durkheim sees as a temporary break of fundamental norms (anomie), and Marx as the alienation of workers from themselves and their fellow workers, Simmel interprets as a new form of social life that contains both subjugating and liberating components. He recognises that modernity dispenses with the emotional attachments and moral values that characterise the communal life lived in proximity of one's village.

However, he also emphasises the empowering character of city life, which generates new forms of freedom and individuality that stimulate creativity and the establishment of new types of voluntary sociations. This is clearly spelled out in *The Metropolis and Mental Life* (1976 [1903]: 185) where Simmel says:

> The eighteenth century may have called for liberation from all the ties which grew up historically in politics, in religion, in morality and in economics in order to permit the original natural virtue of man, which is equal in everyone, to develop without inhibition; the nineteenth century may have sought to promote, in addition to man's freedom, his individuality ... and his achievements which make him unique and indispensable but which at the same time make him so much more dependent on the complementary activity of others.

In other words, life in a modern metropolis changes people but these changes do not necessarily mean the end of human sociality. On the contrary, cities like Berlin, Vienna, Paris, New York or London become hubs of new forms of complex and liberating human interactions.

As Pietila recognises (2011: 100) a central concern for Simmel throughout his work 'was how to reconcile individuals and the social whole to each other. His sociology advised human beings to meet each other in a reasoinable way in their exchanges and interactions.' In a democracy this included compromise. Nevertheless, like many other German intellectuals of the time, including Weber – whom Ringer (1983) refers to as part of a class of 'German Mandarins' – Simmel responded ambivalently towards the abrupt period of industrialization and the social and cultural strains and dislocation it engendered including the development of a bureaucratic state and commercial marketisation. In his view the creation of democratic mass civilisation and a soulless, mechanistic, modern age had profound implications for the freedom of the individual, and for intellectuals as 'bearers of culture' (Ringer, 1983: 3). It fostered a deep cultural pessimism in Simmel's work expressed in his initial support for the First World War, which he saw as providing the possibility of redemption and radical change. The war, he believes, would move individuals away from an excessive materialism by diffusing non-individual, non-instrumental values, which had become a pervasive characteristic of individuals in their interactions in a highly differentiated world.

Arguments and Ideas

Methodology

There is an interesting paradox that underpins Simmel's methodology. During his lifetime he was persistently accused, and on that basis denied promotion, for being a profoundly unsystematic writer and an analyst whose essays lacked academic rigour and a formal style of analysis and expression. The fact that his work was read and enjoyed by a wide, non-academic audience was taken as further proof of this accusation, thus putting a final nail in the coffin of his academic career. However, in deep contrast to this view the reception of Simmel's work after the Second World War emphasised his methodical and logical typologies, clearly defined concepts and dichotomies, and his meticulous arguments.

Moreover, for much this of period (the 1950s to 1980s) Simmel was universally regarded as a classical representative of sociological formalism. While one can find that both of these elements feature in his work, what really underpins much of his methodology is a particular form of dialectics. However, this is neither Hegelian nor Marxist dialectics, though Simmel was to some extent influenced by both of these thinkers. Just as in the traditional dialectical method Simmel's work focuses on the contradictions, conflicts and dualisms that are integral to human relationships and social interactions, he too emphasises the dynamic quality of social action and intrinsically changeable social relations through time and space.

The key notion here is that social relations are always multidirectional and that everything is in some way connected with everything else. However, Simmel's method differs from both Hegelian–Marxist and positivist alternatives. Unlike positivism, which is centred on the sharp differentiation between facts and values and aims to establish monocausal explanations, Simmel's dialectical method not only is interpretative and multicausal, but also rejects the simple distinction between values and facts. Instead Simmel was deeply influenced by neo-Kantian idealism where such hard distinctions were seen not to be analytically sustainable or epistemologically meaningful. Simmel's methodology also differs from Hegelian–Marxist dialects, in the sense that his focus is primarily on the contradictory and dualist relationships between individuals and society.

Whereas in certain readings of Hegel and Marx social structures ultimately trump individual action, for Simmel individuality always retains a substantial degree of autonomy. In this view individuality and sociality are often integrated through their contradictory positions, which allows for a particular dualist relationship with individuals being at the same time integrated in a society and standing against that particular society. In other words, an individual is simultaneously inside and outside of society. This means that our sociality is not a reflection on being partially individual and partially social. Instead, our existence as human beings is defined by a 'fundamental unity' achieved through the synthesis of 'two logically contradictory determinations: man, is both social link and being for himself, both product of society and life from an autonomous centre' (Simmel, 1908: 403). Hence Simmel's starting position is that human beings are always involved in dual, dialectical relationships which make them at the same time subjects and objects of social action. In many respects this is both a blessing and a curse as it is only through the institutional formations that humans can achieve true freedom, but these very same institutions are the ones that also stultify human action.

Simmel's dialectical method was largely focused on the micro world of face-to-face interactions. In such an environment most social action is considered by him to be ambivalent and ambiguous. In this reading, interactions between human beings regularly included contradictory behaviour: they are shaped by attraction and repulsion, love and hate, and conflict and harmony.

As a sociological realist Simmel was well aware that universal harmony is a sociologically impossible state of being. Hence, rather that attempting to remove conflicts from social relations one has to acknowledge that conflicts generate social life.

Although conflicts can have destructive consequences, they are also productive in a sense that they bring about development, transformation and social change. This dialectical dualism is for Simmel apparent in every form of social relationship – from family life to state diplomacy. For example, even the most intimate relationships are not free from tension, ambiguity and conflict. Two people in love are still defined by their individuality and their sociality and it is not easy to differentiate love and respect from the 'urge to dominate or the need for dependence'. But more importantly Simmel argues that 'what the observer of the participant himself thus divides into two intermingling trends may in reality be only one' (1971: 79).

In Simmel's dialectical approach all power relations exhibit a dualist character. Even in the most asymmetrical orders, subordination is never complete but depends on a degree of reciprocity. Simmel notes that the social relations which from the outside seem to represent a straightforward case of absolute power are often in fact more complex and to some extent deceptive of actual relations. In his words, power often 'conceals an interaction, an exchange ... which transforms the pure one-sidedness of superordination and subordination into a sociological from' (Simmel 1976: 186). Thus, to study power relationships it is crucial to explore both ends of social relationships as there is no domination without acceptance of subordination.

One of the key features of this dialectical model is the view that the social analyst should never take a particular social interaction at face value. Instead, Simmel differentiates between appearances and realities, arguing that no social relationship is devoid of conflict, tension and contradiction. Just as the most harmonious communities often hide deep divisions and conflicting interests so the most antagonistic social relationships conceal inherent reciprocities, empathies and unique forms of social bonds. For example, whereas deep ethnic group conflicts often involve complex relationships with the enemy side that might involve hatred but also mutual respect, idyllic egalitarian village communes often harbour profound internal discords.

Social Interactions

Simmel is to some extent unique among the classics of sociology in his prioritisation of the micro-social world. While Marx, Durkheim and even Weber were largely focused on the long-term macro-sociological processes, Simmel's work is primarily centred on face-to-face interactions. More specifically, Simmel understood sociology as a study of human sociations. Sociation (*Vergesellshaftung*) is a central concept in Simmel's analytical toolbox. He coined this term in order to distinguish it from the conventional idea of society.

For Simmel, the term 'society' is imprecise, vague and too general to describe the subtlety of human interactions: 'one should properly speak not of society but of sociation. Society merely is the name for number of individuals connected by interaction' (Simmel, 1950: 10). Instead, sociation is 'the form (realised in innumerably different ways) in which individuals grow together into a unity and within which their interests are realised' (Simmel, 1971: 24).

The concept of sociation is also linked with Simmel's other important distinction – the form and content of interactions. The content is defined as concrete individual biological or psychological qualities which by themselves do not generate social action but can contribute to that process. In contrast, the form represents a generalised pattern of interaction through which individuals become social beings in the sociological sense. Thus, for Simmel sociation is always a form, never a content. It is a dialectical process through which disparate individualities, interests and actions are transformed into socially meaningful activities, thus forming relatively integrated collectivities. Simply put, a form is a type of social interaction that is abstracted from the number of particular contents (Malešević, 2004: 22).

This emphasis on the significance of forms has led many commentators to label Simmel's work as representative of a sociological formalism. Nevertheless, Simmel's idea of form has very little to do with strict and conceptually rigorous formal models. Instead, his notion of 'the form' in some ways resembles what Weber had in mind when he adopted the concept of an 'ideal type'. So, for Simmel 'the form' is a theoretical abstraction intended to highlight the features of different social processes. He argues that there are no 'pure forms' in social life, they are all abstract creations representing overly emphasised social attributes.

As Simmel points out, 'pure forms' are constructs intended to exaggerate 'so as to bring out configurations and relations which underlie reality but are not factually actualised in it' (Wolff, 1959: 84). For example, describing certain marital relationships as traditional or patriarchal is an indication of a specific social form, not the description of particular content. While every concrete case of patriarchy or traditionalism is different, and no single case fits all criteria, they all do approximate a pure type of patriarchal or traditional marital relationships.

Although Simmel emphasises the significance of individuality his research project was not focused on individual consciousness but almost exclusively on social interactions. He understood human beings as intrinsically social creatures who possess an 'impulse for sociability'. For Simmel, sociability was 'the play-form of association' shaped by intense social interactions: 'amicability, breeding, cordiality and attractiveness of all kinds' (Ritzer, 2007: 158). In studying different types of interactions Simmel concludes that the size of the group regularly influences the character of social relations. In this context, he developed his social geometry, which articulates the complexity of interactions ranging from the smallest group (a dyad) to extremely large collectivities.

Hence for Simmel there is a substantial difference between the dyadic and triadic interactions.

The dyad is unlike any other group in a sense that each of its members is socially dependent on the other. While in larger groups there is a possibility to transfer power, responsibility, and duties, in a dyad both individuals are fully responsible for their actions as well as for the production of any collective actions. The dyads also lack a degree of 'super-personal' structure that characterises larger collective entities. The consequence of this is the possibility of a more intense relationship, but this relationship is always fragile as the departure/retreat of one person instantly destroys the entire relationship: 'A dyad depends on each of its two elements alone – in its death though not in its life: for its life it needs both for its death, only one' (Simmel, 1969: 61).

On the surface the transformation from the dyad to triad seems simple. However, Simmel argues that adding just one new person changes qualitatively the dynamic of social interaction. The intrinsic reciprocity that underpins dyadic relationships is lost when a third member is included, for triads are the simplest structures where the collective as a whole can attain dominance over the triad's constituent parts. Hence for Simmel the triad is the simplest form of sociological reality that permeates all larger groups than dyads: the issues of autonomy and dependence, freedom and constraint, power and powerlessness. The triadic model offers a great variety of relationships.

For example, the new member can establish dominance by playing off the other two against each other (a divide and rule strategy). Or the new member might assume the role of moderator between the other two members, thus enhancing the social cohesion of the entire group. Or the third member might side with one of the remaining two to create a dominant position vis-à-vis the remaining member, and so on. Simmel demonstrates that with triads numerous possibilities open up. Moreover, his analyses of microgroup dynamics indicate that the narrow psychological and biological models which treat human beings solely as genetically programmed species cannot account for the changes observed when dyads are transformed into triads.

This relationship between the size of the group and its internal dynamics is particularly pronounced when one compares small, face-to-face groups with huge collectivities such as ethnic or religious groups, nations and states. Whereas in small groups one can operate with tacit rules and can reach agreements on the spot, complex, large-scale groupings cannot operate without institutions that facilitate the patterning of social interactions. Thus, while small egalitarian hunter–gatherer bands could be more spontaneous and ad hoc in their everyday decision making, nation-states would disintegrate without formalised social hierarchies, complex divisions of labour, professional offices, delegation of tasks and duties, etc. This hierarchical complexity increases the functionality of large collectivities but this is achieved at the expense of internal social cohesion. For Simmel small, face-to-face interactions are more intense, more frequent and as such regularly stronger than those that occur in large-scale groups. The degree of homogeneity attained in huge collectivities entails structural pressure, which is less present among small groups. The consequence of this is greater social distance between individuals as well as between single individuals and the central authority. In his own words, a large entity 'gains its unity, which finds its expression in the group organs and political notions and ideals, only at the price of a great distance between all of these structures and the individual' (Simmel, 1976 [1903]).

Modernity

Simmel's work is firmly centred on the micro world of social interactions. Nevertheless, what also comes across from his analyses, and what distinguishes Simmel from many other interactionist sociologists, is awareness that all micro-level relations are rooted in macro-historical contexts. Hence the emergence of different social types such as the *flâneur*, the mediator or the renegade owes a great deal to the structural changes that brought about modernity. In line with most sociological classics Simmel differentiates between the traditional and modern character of group formation. In his view traditional social orders were characterised by the limited number of small-scale social circles – kinship groups, clans, lineages, guilds, villages, towns. In such entities an individual was largely invisible and submerged into the collective of which the individual was a member.

The pre-modern world was composed of groupings organised in linked concentric circles so that a person could join wider circles only by virtue of being already a member of a smaller circle, never by their own choice. Thus, a burgher is a citizen of a particular free town and his membership with the wider world is determined by whether that particular town is conquered by a neighbouring lord or is able to join the federation of free towns (i.e. Hanseatic League). In contrast modernity is built on the multiplicity of social circles to which one belongs. In the modern world no social entity can completely control one's social circle and the 'number of different circles in which individuals move, is one of the indices of cultural development' (Simmel, 1903). Therefore, a modern person's life is highly compartmentalised: family is separated from professional life, religious attachments are distinguished from citizenship, and so on. Simmel argues that such a multiplicity of roles in different social circles fosters the development of one's self-consciousness and stimulates individualist orientations.

However, this gradual structural shift from status-based to contract-based relationships also generates a particular tension and ambivalent relationships. For example, modern life includes ever-present reliance on science and technology with the increased proliferation of objects that constrain and dominate one's needs and wishes. For Simmel, despite its liberating features technology also produces surplus knowledge, a by-product of technological autonomy, which is often superfluous and sometimes directly harmful. In the traditional world the production of culture was limited to the socially necessary practices that helped maintain social cohesion (i.e. rituals of initiation, peace offerings, etc.). By contrast, in the modern world there is no limit to cultural production most of which contains little in a sense of providing social meanings to individuals and collectivities. Simmel views this as another dualism at the heart of modern life: the overproduction of culture becomes oppressive as modern individuals cannot assimilate huge quantities of such cultural products. Yet they cannot reject these cultural elements as they are also the principal ingredients of one's cultural development. In Simmel's (1903) words: 'the cultural objects become more and more linked to each other in a self-contained world which has increasingly fewer contacts with subjective psyche and its desires and sensibilities'.

This inherent ambiguity of modern life is visible in the social impact of large cities on one's socio-psychological development. In *Metropolis and Mental Life* (1903) Simmel argues that since in the large urban congregations, social interactions are short and temporary, such life stimulates instrumental relationships between individuals. The big cities differ from traditional communal living in two senses: (1) they cannot provide the emotional attachments that most small communities can; and (2) they generate an inflation of sensory stimulus that requires intense and permanent screening if one is to cope and prosper in such an environment. Both of these features foster rational and instrumental forms of social interactions. For example, life in the modern metropolis privileges the meaning of time in a quantitative sense. As everyone works on a fixed schedule, the measuring of time becomes of central importance. This further stimulates quantification of social relations, leading to the formation of blasé interactions shaped by superficiality, indifference and alienation. On the other hand, life in the metropolis is also liberating as it allows individuals to break free from the communal bonds of traditional social orders.

This line of argument is fully articulated in Simmel's masterpiece *The Philosophy of Money*. In this book, Simmel explores the social implications of financial transactions. Although money has traditionally been understood as a mere means of exchange and transaction, Simmel argues that monetary transactions are always much more than simple financial matters. Instead money, as a mechanism of economic exchange, is also a crucial form of social interaction. Simmel compares monetary transactions with their historical predecessors – systems of barter. While the two types of economic transactions largely perform similar roles (i.e. the exchange of goods that are considered to be mutually valuable by the two sides) the social implications of these two exchange models are profoundly different.

For one thing barter is a substantially less precise form of exchange – one could swap a cow for two or three sheep but not for 2.74 sheep. For another thing, barter might incorporate an element of empathy and emotions as the buyer might be willing to recognise that the seller is about to part with a beloved horse or precious tool that has been in the seller's family for many generations. In contrast, all monetary transactions are grounded in precise, exact division and measurement equivalence. The price of a car varies but one is likely to pay the exact sum with the recognised currency which one could also use for any other economic transaction.

Furthermore, there is no personalised attachment to money in a way that one might have with specific things or living beings. All monetary transactions are standardised and uniform. For Simmel the shift from barter to monetary transactions was a significant moment in human history as it had a profound impact on social relations. Since money involves exact measurements, quantifiable division, precision and equivalency, the transition to monetary exchange has gradually stimulated a change in social relations. With money there is little room for personal attachments as monetary transactions promote impersonal exchange and rational calculation. In this sense the increase in monetary transactions weakens traditional personal bonds with more impersonal relations limited to a specific, functional, purpose.

The constant use of money fosters abstract calculation and rationalisation of the social order where even kinship ties might gradually become invaded by financialisation. With the growing increase in financial transactions, traditional roles give way to one's ability to make things happen. For example, while in the traditional patriarchal world the father was a source of respect by virtue of his position in the household, in the modern world social respect is given to anybody who can generate financial well-being in other individuals. In addition to this structural change, Simmel also emphasises that greater financialisation tends to increase social differentiation and personal liberties as human beings move away from the traditional forms of group attachments towards more voluntary associations. In this sense the cash nexus often operates as a great leveller – it melts down the social differences between things and people.

Contemporary Relevance and Applications

Unlike Marx, Durkheim or Weber, whose work gained in influence after their deaths, Simmel was much more influential during his lifetime than in its immediate aftermath. Until the 1990s he was largely perceived as a marginal figure associated with the relatively inconsequential tradition of formal sociology. Although Lewis Coser, Reihard Bendix and Kurt Wolff translated and popularised some of his essays (such as 'The Conflict', 'The Web of Affiliations' and 'The Metropolis and Mental Life' among others) Simmel's work did not receive a great deal of attention outside of very narrow sociological circles. This all changed with the cultural turn in the social sciences in the late 1980s and early 1990s when Simmel was rediscovered as the major theorist of society and culture.

INDIVIDUALISM AND THE CULTURE OF THE CITY

While Marx, Durkheim and Weber each recognised the significance of individualism in modern society in their own respective ways, Simmel's approach to this theme aligns much more seamlessly with our experience of everyday life in contemporary society. Simmel's insights regarding the potential freedom of anonymous urban living over repressive aspects of community life remain pertinent in considering continuing and growing urbanisation. For many, the draw of the city is the possibility of individual identity formation and self-realisation unrestricted by tight bonds. This is reflected in a plethora of personality types and a great pluralisation of forms of life in the contemporary city.

With the rise of post-structuralist and post-modernist perspectives Simmel was often hailed as the pioneer of social constructivism and anti-essentialism. Moreover, he has been characterised as the post-modern thinker before post-modernism (Weinstein and Weinstein, 1993; Bergey, 2004) or somebody who anticipated the post-modern movement (Frisby, 2002). His general diagnoses of modernity, which emphasise its inherent ambiguity and ambivalence, have influenced many contemporary sociologists including Zygmunt Bauman, Harrison White, David Frisby and others. In a similar way his micro-level analyses have inspired generations of symbolic interactionists and ethnomethodologists to study the minute details of complex interpersonal dynamics. Unlike many other classical scholars, who emulated the discourse of science and adopted static categories of analysis, Simmel's relational and dynamic concepts were seen as offering something different and more applicable for the analysis of ever-changing social relations. In addition, his implicit critique of modernism, as articulated in 'The Crisis of Culture' (1917) and 'The Conflict of Modern Culture' (1918), were used to develop new analytical tools for the critique of science, technology and the Enlightenment project.

Simmel's work has also had a substantial impact on urban sociology with a focus on the relationships between the rise of metropolitan centres and changed social relations. Simmel's concepts of blasé personalities, *flâneur* or stranger have all found much use in the attempts to make sense of the complex and contradictory social relations in modern cities. For example, Simmel's essay on the stranger has a strong resonance in the contemporary sociology of ethnic relations focused on large urban congregations. The stranger is described as an ambiguous person, a 'potential wanderer' who is never a full member of a group but who also 'imports qualities into it which do not and cannot stem from the group itself' (Simmel, 1976 [1908]: 37–8). The urban ethnic immigrant experience mirrors these ambiguities whereby an individual who is 'is near and far at the same time' defines and also navigates group boundaries within the city (Malešević, 2004: 22).

His essays on fashion, flirtation, group cohesion and secrecy have all had an impact on such diverse contemporary fields as mimetic studies, the sociology of sexuality, network analysis and organisational theory. Simmel's view of fashion emphasises the inherent tensions of most forms of social behaviour. Although fashion stems from imitation it is also premised on the need to distinguish oneself from others. In this context both imitation (conformity with the latest fashion) and differentiation (rejection to conform) indicate a strong sense of sociality as for Simmel differentiation is actually an inverse form of imitation. In his view fashion is for the most part a product of class distinction. Since fashion operates through the dialectic of imitation and differentiation it can tell us a great deal about the changing social dynamics. Hence the scholars of mimetic processes have utilised Simmel's work to develop simulation models which would help identify under which social conditions individuals imitate others and aggregate together (Benvenuto, 2000).

Simmel's essay on flirtation has also influenced contemporary studies of sexuality. By analysing flirting not as a specific type of sexual innuendo but as a dialectical relationship Simmel emphasises the complexity of human interactions. For Simmel flirtation involves simultaneous accommodation and denial, which provokes a 'game of possibilities' and thus generates a sense of freedom and potentiality. In this sense a flirt represents the 'distances of desire' as the direction of the particular social relation always hangs in the balance. Furthermore, participation in flirtation generates a shared secret which enhances the sense of belonging. This idea has been developed further by symbolic interactionists such as Tavory (2009) and others who zoom in on the 'actualisation practices' that remain unrealised in the act of flirtation, and that such a phenomenon represents a form of the luminal act that is defined by its inherent, but never realised, potentiality.

Simmel's work has also influenced the sociology of organisations, including Burt's (2004) theory of structural holes and brokerage, Krackhardt and Kilduff's (2002) concept of 'the Simmelian tie' and Diani's (2000) analysis of networks in social movements. Building on Simmel's notion of conflicting group affiliations, Burt has demonstrated that by being further away from the centre of the group one is more likely to be open to new ideas. Since the opinions and behaviour are generally more homogeneous within rather than between groups, being near the holes in a social structure is often linked with greater openness to new ideas. Even more influential has been the idea of the 'Simmelian tie', which refers to the strong group ties of individuals who form a clique.

The Simmelian tie represents a basic form of connection between the small groups of individuals which helps strengthen the micro-group relationship through external restrictions and internal group norms (Krackhardt and Kilduff, 2002). One could argue that the entire research field of network analysis, which spans several academic disciplines, has been built on the basis of Simmel's contribution. From Granovetter's (1973) paper on the strength of weak ties to more recent analyses of computer-mediated communication (i.e. social media) scholars have found Simmel's theories of social space, group formation and sense of belonging as highly relevant to the digital age. For example, Feldman (2012) shows how sociality in cyberspace involves the ambivalent and paradoxical relationship centred on proximity and distance, mobility and stasis, and inclusion and exclusion, which all mirror Simmel's idea of a stranger.

Criticisms

Many of the criticisms levelled against Simmel during his life were centred on his style of expression and analysis: his avoidance of academic jargon, the use of playful metaphors and literary idioms, and the reliance on non-technical language. In the world of early twentieth-century (German) academia, where sociology and other social sciences were still trying to establish themselves as legitimate academic disciplines, the use of technical and professional language was highly valued. However, what was considered to be a major shortcoming a hundred years ago is generally deemed to be a strength today. Hence Simmel's playful expressions and inventive metaphors have now become an object of praise. In this sense his style of writing has been emulated by many analysts in the humanities and social sciences.

Another early criticism, already voiced during his lifetime, focused on his formalist approach: the study of the underlying forms of social relations. Simmel's ambition to analyse the geometry of social life was traditionally misunderstood as an obsession with form over content, function or social structure. Thus, he was regularly grouped with Leopold von Wiese and Alfred Vierkandt as representatives of the rather static and formulaic approach termed formalism. In this view formalism stands for the sharp distinction between content and form whereby form requires more analysis than the transient content. Nevertheless, much of this criticism is displaced as Simmel offers a nuanced and highly dynamic view of the social world. By differentiating form and content he does not intend to diminish the significance of the specific experience but instead aims to find commonalities between the different types of social experience. Hence, he identifies conflict and competition as the universal forms that appear in different contents (wars, family, work, politics, etc.). His main aim is to show how contents change, but forms remain largely stable over long periods of time.

The more taxing critiques have focused on Simmel's epistemology. For example, both Coser (1965: 5) and Ritzer (2008: 282) zoom in on the inherent tension between Simmel's micro and macro sociology. While on the one hand, he emphasises the centrality of agency and sees interactions as the primary source of social change, on the other hand in some of his more prominent analyses, structures seem to have the upper hand. Although he was deeply suspicious of static concepts and perceived society as a set of interactions, he also maintained the view that 'society transcends the individual and lives its own life which fallows its own laws. It, too, confronts the individual with a historical, imperative firmness' (Simmel, 1950: 258). This paradoxical stance is even more pronounced when one compares and contrasts Simmel's early and later works.

Thus in 'On Social Differentiation' he adopts the standard evolutionary account of social change and sees modern social orders as exhibiting a greater level of social differentiation than their pre-modern counterparts. In contrast his later essays on interactional dynamics and group boundaries, such as 'The Poor', 'Subordination under a Principle' or 'How is Society Possible?', make no room for the structural or biological sources of social action and place emphasis on the ambiguity of micro interactions. This issue is also linked with Simmel's later preference for epistemological idealism and a vitalist philosophy. For example, his magnum opus *The Philosophy of Money* has been criticised by his former student, Georg Lukács, as combining idealism with vitalism, which ultimately produces a deeply pessimist view of the future and has little to say about class inequalities. Even though Simmel's analysis is critical of the capitalist economy, and he utilises similar concepts to Marx (such as 'reification'), Simmel's theory remains grounded in an idealist metaphysics of culture which postulates no way out from the 'tragedy of culture'. As Lukács points out, Simmel's thesis aims to substitute Marxist analysis with a '*Lebensphilosophie* framework' with its 'insoluble opposition between subjectivity and cultural forms, between soul and mind. The opposition is, according to Simmel, the peculiar tragedy of culture' (Lukács in Frisby, 2002: 26).

Simmel's embrace of vitalist philosophy became even more visible during the last years of his life when he agitated passionately for the German cause during the First World War. Some of his last publications were nationalist pamphlets that exalted militarism and the ideas of voluntary sacrifice for the nation. Although these war writings are often dismissed as an aberration, they in fact fully reflect the vitalist notions that underpin Simmel's social philosophy. In line with other vitalist critiques of modernity he too rages against consumerism (in his terms 'mammonism' and 'chaos of the soul') and money worship and sees warfare as a 'unifying, simplifying and concentrating force' that liberates human potentials (Malešević, 2010: 45). This glorification of war has opened up Simmel to the fierce and justified criticisms of what is clearly a morally indefensible position.

The most common appraisals of Simmel's work have focused on the fragmentary character of his analyses. Unlike other classics of social thought such as Marx, Durkheim or Weber, who developed relatively coherent and systematic models of social enquiry, Simmel's work is largely disconnected and, as Frisby (2002) puts it, 'impressionistic'. While there is no doubt that Simmel offers a wealth of new ideas, perceptive and unusual insights, and novel concepts, these are rarely linked in a coherent whole. In part this is a product of his style and approach, which deliberately avoided systematic theory building. This haphazard mode of writing was also linked to Simmel's very wide interests that covered sociology, philosophy, art, economics, politics, history and many other areas, and his ambition to contribute to the debates in all of these areas. As a result of this fragmentary nature of his contribution there never was a Simmelian school of thought in the same way as one can identify the Weberian or Marxist Schools.

Conclusion

Georg Simmel was a true polymath who easily and successfully navigated very different disciplines – from the philosophy of history, literary criticism, history of art, urban studies, to sociology and psychology. He was also a uniquely gifted scholar who could think on his feet and provide subtle and instant analyses of contemporary events and processes. As such his mode of work was particularly well suited to capture the inherent ambiguities and ambivalence generated by the onset of modernity. Simmel's dialectical approach to social life, with its continuous search for the universal with the particular and the particular with the universal, has had a huge impact on contemporary social sciences and humanities. Perhaps more than any other classic of sociology, Simmel has provided potent analytical tools to understand how macro-level contexts shape the micro universe of social life.

References

Bergey, J. (2004) Georg Simmel's Metropolis: Anticipating the Postmodern. *Telos: Critical Theory of the Contemporary*, 129, pp. 139–50.

Benvenuto, S. (2000) Fashion: Georg Simmel. *Journal of Artificial Societies and Social Simulation*, 3(2) [online]. Available at: http://jasss.soc.surrey.ac.uk/3/2/forum/2.html (Accessed 7 March 2019).

Burt, R. (2004) Structural Holes and Good Ideas. *American Journal of Sociology*, (110), pp. 349–399

Coser, L. A. (1965) *Georg Simmel*. Englewood Cliffs, NJ: Prentice Hall.

Coser, L. A. (1977) *Masters of Sociological Thought: Ideas of Historical and Social Context*, 2nd edition. New York: Harcourt Brace Jovanovich.

Diani, M. (2000) Simmel to Rokkan and Beyond: Towards a Network Theory of (New) Social Movements. *European Journal of Social Theory*, 3(4), pp. 387–406.

Feldman, Z. (2012) Simmel in Cyberspace. *Information, Communication & Society*, 15(2), pp. 297–319.

Frisby, D. (2002) *Georg Simmel*. London: Routledge.

Granovetter, M. (1973) The Strength of Weak Ties. *American Journal of Sociology*, 78(6), pp. 1360–80.

Krackhardt, D. and Kilduff, M. (2002) Structure, Culture and Simmelian Ties in Entrepreneurial Firms. *Social Networks*, 24(3), pp. 279–90.

Malešević, S. (2004) *The Sociology of Ethnicity*. London: Sage.

Malešević, S. (2010) *The Sociology of War and Violence*. Cambridge: Cambridge University Press.

Pietila, K. (2011) *Reason of Sociology: George Simmel and Beyond*. London: Sage.
Ringer, F. (1983) *The Decline of the German Mandarins*. Lebanon, NH: University of New England Press.
Ritzer, G. (2007) *Classical Sociological Theory*, 5th edition. New York: McGraw-Hill.
Ritzer, G. (2008) *Sociological Theory*, 7th edition. Boston, MA: McGraw-Hill.
Simmel, G. (1950) The Abstract Character of Sociology. In: K. Wolff (ed.) *The Sociology of George Simmel*. New York: Free Press, pp. 11-13.
Simmel, G. (1969) *The Sociology of Georg Simmel*. In: K. H. Wolff (ed.) New York: Free Press.
Simmel, G. (1971) *On Individuality and Social Forms*. D. Levine (ed.). Chicago, IL: University of Chicago Press.
Simmel, G. (1976 [1903a]) The Metropolis and Mental Life. In: K. Wolff (ed.) *The Sociology of Georg Simmel*. New York: Free Press, pp. 409-26.
Simmel,G. (1976 [1903b]) The Triad. In: K. Wolff (ed.) *The Sociology of Georg Simmel*. New York: Free Press, pp. 145-69.
Simmel, G. (1976 [1908]) Stranger. In: K. Wolff (ed.) *The Sociology of Georg Simmel*. New York: Free Press, pp. 402-8.
Simmel, G. (1976) Leader and Led. In: K. Wolff (ed.) *The Sociology of Georg Simmel*. New York: Free Press, p. 185.
Simmel, G. (1990) *The Philosophy of Money*, 2nd edition. D. Frisby (ed.) London: Routledge.
Tavory, I. (2009) The Structure of Flirtation: On the Construction of Interactional Ambiguity. In: N. K. Denzin (ed.) *Studies in Symbolic Interaction (Studies in Symbolic Interaction, Volume 33)*. Bingley: Emerald Group, pp. 59-74.
Trommler, F. (1992) Rethinking Modernity in Germany. In: H. Lehmann (ed.) *Culture and Politics in 19th and 20th Century Germany*. Washington, DC: German Historical Institute.
Weinstein, D. and Weinstein, M. A. (1993) *Postmodern(ized) Simmel*. London: Routledge.
Wolff, K. H. (1950) *The Sociology of Georg Simmel*. Glencoe, IL: Free Press.
Wolff, K. H. (1959) (ed.) *Georg Simmel, 1858-1918: A Collection of Essays with Translations and a Bibliography*. Columbus, OH: Ohio State University Press.

IX

PARETO, MOSCA AND MICHELS

Introduction

Niccolo Machiavelli was generally considered to be one of the first theorists capable of distinguishing between normative ideals and empirical reality. As Kaplan (2005) highlights: 'he emancipated politics from theology and moral philosophy. He undertook to describe simply what rulers actually did and thus anticipated what was later called the scientific spirit in which questions of good and bad are ignored, and the observer attempts to discover only what really happens.' This analytical and realist model of enquiry has underpinned much of early Italian social and political thought (Femia, 1998). The Machiavellian heritage with its emphasis on the cyclical nature of social and political life and its cynicism about the power relationships has provided the foundations for the classical elite theory. Pareto, Mosca and Michels were all deeply influenced by Machiavelli's political realism and his essentially pessimist view of social change. Nevertheless, while Machiavelli remained focused on the questions of utility of particular types of social and political action the classical elite theorists were the first to develop elaborate models attempting to explain the nature of social and political life from this realist perspective. In particular this approach centres on the historical sociology of power relations and the role elites play in this process. In this chapter we review and analyse the key concepts and theoretical contributions of Pareto, Mosca and Michels. We also zoom in on the social and historical context of late nineteenth- and early twentieth-century Italy, which was central for the development of this approach.

Life and Intellectual Context

Vilfredo Pareto

What immediately comes across when examining the biographical details of the three leading representatives of the classical elite theory in sociology are the striking similarities in their social background. All three scholars, Pareto, Mosca and Michels, grew up in privileged, upper middle-class families. Vilfredo Pareto (1848–1923) was a son of an exiled noble Genoese family who settled in Paris where Pareto was born. His father, a Ligurian marquis who worked as a civil engineer, was an Italian nationalist who was forced to leave Italy for France where he met Vilfredo's mother. Both of his parents shared the ideals of the 1848 liberal nationalist revolutions thus naming their son Fritz Wilfrid. This name was changed to Vilfredo Frederico once the family returned to Italy in 1858. The life of privilege allowed the young Pareto to attend the best schools in Italy and, following in the footsteps of his father, he was awarded a doctoral degree in 1869 in engineering from the University of Turin.

Initially Pareto worked as a civil engineer, soon becoming a general manager of Italian Works. During this period he gradually moved away from his parents' left-leaning republicanism towards a free trade liberalism. He was fiercely opposed to the protectionist policies of the new Italian government and wrote a series of newspaper articles attacking the government's economic policies. In 1882 he unsuccessfully ran as an opposition candidate for the Florence constituency. This experience had a significant impact on Pareto as he perceived elections to be rigged and that the entire political system was corrupt. Following this episode and his parents' deaths in the early 1880s, he decided to change his career. In 1883 he become a lecturer in economics at the University of Florence. Over the next few years Pareto was focused entirely on the study of economics and he also translated classical works from several European languages.

While lecturing in Florence he continued his newspaper contributions attacking the government's policies. As Coser (1977: 404–8) notes, he published 167 articles between 1889 and 1893 ranging from virulent journalistic pieces to more scholarly analyses of Italian economics. In 1893 he was appointed to a chair of political economy at the University of Lausanne, Switzerland. In the last period of his life Pareto became completely disillusioned with the parliamentary democracy, perceiving it to be just another form of minority rule. Due to health issues he retired in 1907 but continued to give occasional lectures on sociology, economics and politics. Upon Mussolini's ascent to power Pareto was proclaimed a senator of the Kingdom of Italy. While initially showing strong sympathy for Mussolini (who was a great admirer of his work) Pareto protested when the fascist regime abolished free speech and the autonomy of the universities. He died only a year into Mussolini's reign (1923) and did not see the consequence of fascist rule.

Gaetano Mosca

Mosca's life had a different trajectory but his social background was also one of relative privilege. He was born in 1858 in Palermo, Sicily, as the seventh child of an upper middle-class family. His father was a state administrator in the postal service. Young Mosca grew up in the new Kingdom of Italy, which incorporated Sicily in 1861. However, the new union proved a major disappointment for most Sicilians as the northern rulers tended to treat the south, including Sicily, as a colony. The consequences of such a policy were periodic rebellions, the imposition of martial law, fraudulent elections, rampant corruption and state violence. All of this had a significant impact on Mosca's early interest in social and political issues. In 1881 he graduated from the University of Palermo's law school.

As a part of his degree he wrote a dissertation on national identity, arguing that such an idea represents a political myth and that the real sources of social identification are usually much smaller – local or regional. Mosca largely maintained this sceptical attitude towards grand political projects for the rest of his life. In 1883 he moved to Rome to continue his studies and where he published several articles and a treatise on the theory of government which was well received. However, his hopes of securing a university position were dashed and he returned to Palermo to teach in a secondary school for a year. A year later he was successful in his application for a university position and he became a lecturer in constitutional law at the University of Palermo. Dissatisfied with the relatively poor career prospects after not being able to secure a full professorship Mosca decided to return to Rome. He took part in the national civil service examination where he won a position as an editor of the official publication of the Italian parliament's Chamber of Deputies. Although Mosca continued to research and publish during his time in Palermo the new position provided an excellent opportunity to examine the political system from the inside. This is reflected well in his publications.

Soon he completed his most significant book *The Ruling Class* (1896) and produced a number of other important works. Following the success of this book Mosca was appointed chair of constitutional law at the University of Turin in 1896. He remained in this role for 28 years before taking up his final academic position as a professor of public law at the University of Rome. Mosca was also active in the political and public life of Italy. He worked as a political journalist for the *Corriere della Sera of Milan* (1901–11) and the *Tribuna of Rome* (1911–21). From 1909 to 1919 he served as an MP in the Chamber of Deputies of Italy. He was also an under-secretary for the Colonies from 1914 to 1916 and in 1919 was nominated life senator of the Kingdom of Italy. Although several fascist intellectuals were admirers of his theories Mosca disliked and openly opposed fascist rule. In this context he resigned his senatorial position in 1926 and retired from public life. He died in Rome in 1941.

Robert Michels

Michels was born in Cologne in 1876 in a prosperous, patrician household. His family had a cosmopolitan background including German, French and Belgian heritage. The family wealth allowed Michels to pursue his studies at the best secondary and tertiary educational institutions. Thus he completed his studies in the Berlin Gymnasium, and after compulsory military service, went to study in London and at the Sorbonne. He returned to Germany to continue his studies at the University of Munich and at the University of Leipzig. He completed his studies with a dissertation in history at the University of Halle in 1900. Like Pareto and Mosca, Michels was also politically active for much of his life.

After taking up his first academic post at the University of Marburg he became involved in socialist and trade unionist activities. Initially he was a member of the German Social Democratic Party, belonging to its radical left wing. He stood unsuccessfully as a candidate for the SDP in the federal election in 1907. Following this disappointment he left the party soon after. His political radicalism had a negative impact on his academic career as German universities were reluctant to appoint a socialist to a prestigious chair. By this time Michels had already published a number of influential studies, some of which appeared in the highly regarded journal *Archiv für Sozialwissenschaft und Sozialpolitik*, edited by Max Weber.

Even though he was a protégé of Weber, who was very impressed by his young disciple, Michels could not achieve his academic ambitions in Germany. Hence he decided to move to Italy where he could pursue both his academic and political goals. With Weber's help he was appointed professor at the University of Turin where he lectured in sociology, political science and economics until 1914. During this period he completed and published many books and articles including his most influential study *Political Parties: A Sociological Study of the Oligarchical Tendencies of Modern Democracy* (1911). Michels was great admirer of Italian culture and quickly became immersed in Italian academic, cultural and political life. He already had strong links with Italian revolutionary syndicalism but was gradually moving to the right of the political spectrum.

In 1914 Michels became a professor of economics at the University of Basel, Switzerland, where he lived until 1926. After the war he became a member of the Italian fascist party, believing that the charismatic personality of Mussolini, together with the Italian working classes could be the only force capable of overcoming the oligarchic and bureaucratic tendencies of modern states. In addition to his political activism Michels continued his prolific academic output: he wrote 30 books and over 700 articles. The last decade of his life was largely spent in Italy: he was appointed professor at the University of Perugia and also lectured in Rome where he died in 1936.

Historical, Social and Political Context

It is no historical accident that all three leading classical elite theorists have lived and worked in Italy. Although late nineteenth- and early twentieth-century Italian society shared many similar problems with other late-developing societies, its size and geopolitical significance have fostered a relatively unique set of obstacles that were more pronounced here than anywhere else in Europe. On the one hand, Italy experienced many typical problems of a late-developing society: deep social polarisation, rampant corruption, weak institutional structure dominated by patrimonial relationships, lack of democratic traditions, deeply entrenched traditionalism and patriarchy, a low educational base and high levels of illiteracy. In this sense Italian society at the turn of the century resembled much of Southern and Eastern Europe.

On the other hand, unlike its eastern and southern neighbours, Italy was a large and influential state which from its belated unification in 1861 quickly developed a sense of geopolitical significance including pronounced imperial ambitions. However, since much of Italy remained underdeveloped and socially deeply polarised its imperial goals regularly proved to be overambitious and as such largely remained unfulfilled. While its size, historical legacies and geographical location have all contributed towards the imperial outlook of the Italian political and cultural elites, domestic politics proved often incapable of addressing some basic social problems. Hence late nineteenth- and early twentieth-century Italian politicians developed grand expansionist plans centred on the conquest of South-Eastern Europe (Albania, Montenegro, Croatia) and parts of Africa (Eritrea, Somalia and Libya). However, to finance such extravagant plans the rulers had to create a viable state and a relatively homogeneous society at home.

Social Divisions in Italy

One of the main obstacles to doing so was the profound divide between the relatively prosperous north and the underdeveloped rest of the new nation-state. This sharp economic division was also reinforced by strong regional identities and the general lack of cultural homogeneity. For example, when Italy was established as an independent state in 1861 only 2.5% of its population was fluent in the standardised Italian language. Not only was the majority of the essentially peasant population reliant on the strong local and regional dialects, but even the educated elites did not converse in Italian, but mostly in French, and to some extent German, as pertinently reflected in February 1861 when Victor Emmanuel assembled the deputies of the first Italian parliament in Turin where they communicated in French, not Italian (Malešević, 2013).

The new state was also characterised by a relative dearth of natural resources, feeble infrastructural capacities, and deep class divides, which were particularly pronounced between the relatively affluent urban centres and the mostly impoverished rural areas. In this type of social environment, even when parliamentary institutions were put in place, political power was often used in the most cynical way in order to maintain the status quo. Hence although the new Kingdom of Italy preserved the Piedmont's Albertine Statue that guaranteed basic freedoms, it also retained the electoral system which restricted the electorate to property-owning educated men. It was only in 1913 that Italy introduced universal suffrage for all men (but not women).

These legal provisions fostered deep class polarisations between the urban and rural population as well as between the industrialised north and non-industrialised south. While the northern elites were firmly focused on the geopolitical ambitions of the new would-be empire, the impoverished peasantry were forced to emigrate to the north or abroad. In this environment, where the political institutions were weak and where social divisions were deep, the only way one could get things done was through the established networks of patronage and clientelism. In most cases these networks were built around powerful men with aristocratic backgrounds. New Italy was created on noble ideals such as the unity, fraternity, equality and liberty of all Italians.

However, in most instances these ideals remained unrealised as the new society maintained very a similar social structure to its pre-modern counterparts. Although the kingdom experienced regular changes of government and top state administrators, they all pursued very similar strategies of rule which prioritised the northern elites over the rest. Hence, regardless of whether the moderate left or centre–right parties were in government, they behaved similarly when in power: irrespective of the position on the political spectrum they occupied, the politicians tended to utilise their governmental positions for self-interest and the pursuit of political and economic favours of their patrons.

War and Social Change

Italy's disastrous military adventures in Africa together with the huge losses during the First World War further intensified social and geographical polarisation between its citizens. The First Italo-Ethiopian War (1895–6) resulted in no less than 15,000 Italian casualties with as many as 10,000 killed at the Battle of Adwa. Such a staggering number of dead soldiers, fighting mostly against an enemy armed with spears and swords, was unprecedented and deemed to be greater defeat than any other major Italian battle in Europe of the nineteenth century (Vandervort, 1998: 164). This military disaster led to the collapse of the government and riots in Italian cities. Although Italy joined the war only in 1915 its forces suffered heavy casualties – over a million deaths. Although the end of the war brought some territorial gains at the expense of the collapsed Austro-Hungarian Empire, the state was economically ruined, teetering on the brink of bankruptcy. All of this intensified social polarisation and further weakened the state thus contributing to the eventual rise of fascism.

Pareto's contempt for the existing political system was equally voiced by Mosca and Michels. In his role as the editor of the Chamber of Deputies of Italy and later as an elected MP Mosca had the opportunity to witness directly the hypocrisy of most politicians who tended to speak in the name of the collective good but were more likely to pursue their own self-interests. This discrepancy between state goals and the actual behaviour of political representatives made Mosca deeply sceptical of conventional parliamentary democracy.

Unlike Mosca, whose political experience was deeply linked to the Italian system, Michels had the opportunity to live and work throughout Europe. Nevertheless, it is precisely this wider geographical and social experience that made Michels disillusioned with parliamentary democracy. Starting off as an enthusiastic member of the German SPD, he soon realised that the party's proclaimed goals of transparency, openness and internal democracy did not match in any way its actual mode of operation, which remained hierarchical with the main decisions always made by a handful of leaders. Moving to Switzerland and later to Italy, where he had the opportunity to work and engage in political activities, only confirmed his previous suspicions, which ultimately led to his developing an extremely hostile attitude towards large-scale social organisations. As a result he perceived direct elite action as a mechanism that would prevent the corruptive potential of organisational power.

The obvious inadequacy of the Italian political system fostered deep scepticism towards political organisations, the state and parliamentary institutions. Hence it is no coincidence that the leading Italian social theorists developed similar approaches that centre on the role elites play in social and political life. The prominence of this Machiavellian tradition was equally visible on the left and the right of the political spectrum – from Pareto, Mosca and Michels to Gramsci.

Arguments and Ideas

Pareto and the Circulation of Elites

For Pareto sociology was a science which requires analytical tools similar to those used in physics or chemistry. Building on his knowledge of engineering and economics, he envisaged sociology as a science of social systems where individual action was to be analysed in a similar way to molecules studied in chemistry. More specifically he perceived human behaviour as comparable to 'the mixtures of chemical compounds found in nature'. His influential *The Mind and Society: The Treatise on General Sociology* (1942 [1918]) was written as an attempt to develop a sociological model capable of analysing social systems that fall outside of economic action. In other words, after devoting years of research to economics he was adamant that economic models can only deal with the rational/logical forms of action while sociology was seen as a science capable of explaining what he termed non-logical or non-rational action. In Pareto's view most types of social action belong to the non-logical category as they are not open to verification. Such actions are usually rooted in strong emotional commitments that he called residues.

Pareto distinguishes between residues and derivations: while the former represent manifestations of sentiments, the latter operate as rationalised justifications. In his view most human action is driven by residues, that is non-logical commitments, but in social interactions such residues are generally framed and communicated through intellectual rationalisations – derivations. For example, the CEOs of giant corporations often present the takeover of another company as a rational project to create more new jobs and bring social development to a particular region (derivation) while in fact their primary motivation is usually profit maximisation (residue). In a similar way politicians invoke the notion of group solidarity to justify self-interest:

> A politician is inspired to champion the theory of 'solidarity' by an ambition to obtain money, power, distinctions ... If the politician were to say, 'Believe in solidarity because if you do it means money for me,' they would get many laughs and few votes. He therefore has to take his stand on principles that are acceptable to his prospective constituents. (Pareto, 1942 [1918]: 502)

Nevertheless, Pareto recognises that self-interest might also have unintended consequences so that a politician's derivations might ultimately coincide with residues:

> Often the person who would persuade others begins by persuading himself; and even if he is moved in the beginning by thoughts of personal advantage, he comes eventually to believe that his real interest is the welfare of others. (Pareto, 1916: 114 in Adams and Sydie, 2002: 229)

By focusing on the irrationality of social action Pareto attempts to explain the way power relations operate in human history. He interprets historical change in cyclical terms and argues that much of social and political life is determined by the continuous struggle of elites. More to the point for Pareto, social change is rarely, if ever, driven by the masses but almost exclusively through the ongoing circulation of elites. Hence revolutions and other changes of regime do not transpire because of popular revolt but largely through the conflicts between distinct elites where the masses act only as followers of one or the other elite group.

For Pareto the concept of elite has no moral value but is used as a descriptive category that stands for 'a class of the people who have the highest indices in their branch of activity'. He also distinguishes between two primary types of elite: the governing elite who directly or indirectly hold the reins of political, economic, military and cultural power, and the non-governing elite, who aspire to replace the ruling elite.

Furthermore, drawing on Machiavelli's typology he differentiates between the two dominant personality types of elites: foxes and lions. Whereas foxes are seen to be individuals who deploy innovation, experimentation and creative action to attain power, lions rely more on force and coercion to achieve their political ambitions. While lions display a greater sense of group loyalty and solidarity they usually lack the organisational flexibility and intellectual subtlety to manipulate the masses. In contrast, foxes are less committed to shared principles, lack fidelity and coercive strength, but can utilise their creative potential to navigate power struggles.

For Pareto, all successful governments require a good balance of lions and foxes as the organisational dominance of one group is likely to create a situation where rulers rely too much on manipulation (foxes) or brute force (lions). This applies equally to the non-ruling elites, who also require a fine balance between the two groups. Looking at his own contemporaries, Pareto was of the view that in Europe as a whole, and particularly in Italy and France where he spent most of his life, foxes were outnumbering lions both in and outside of governments. He predicted that this will negatively impact social equilibrium and is likely to generate ultimately a system collapse which is destined to bring the lions to the fore. Nevertheless, as lions do not possess the requisite intellectual skills and knowledge to maintain social equilibrium they would eventually have to open up space for the gradual influx of foxes. Once back in the saddle, foxes would attempt to impose themselves on the lions and the power circle would continue.

Thus for Pareto history is nothing more than 'a graveyard of aristocracies': elites are continuously replaced by other elites. In his words:

> the governing elite is in a state of continuous and slow transformation. It flows like a river, and what it is today is different from what it was yesterday. Every so often, there are sudden and violent disturbances. The river floods and breaks its banks. Then afterwards, the new governing elite resume again and slow process of self-transformation. The river returns to its bed and once more flows freely on. (Pareto, 1966: 250)

While the social world changes and new institutions emerge, their form might change but, Pareto argues, their substance remains the same. While in medieval Europe the rulers invoked the divine origins of ruler theory to justify their right to rule, today's rulers deploy the notion of democracy for the same purpose. In Pareto's view both of these concepts are just a form of derivation utilised to mask the potent residues that govern the action of all rulers.

In this context, social change is possible and desirable, but for Pareto such change is rooted in the mechanisms of ubiquitous elite circulation which makes social equilibrium attainable. However, he is more sceptical of Enlightenment-induced ideas of progress, evolution and emancipation. Instead, for him, history is a continuous process of repetition. This is not to say that elite circulation is a closed system of power relations. On the contrary, Pareto sees this historical mechanism as a principal driver of social mobility as talented members of non-elites can and do assume the place of decadent and decaying members of the old elites. This shift from the non-elite to elite can happen either through violent uprisings and revolutions, or through gradual infiltration.

Mosca and the Political Class

Just like Pareto, Mosca too was puzzled by the inherent contradictions that characterised the Italian social and political system of his day. Moreover, being involved with the political institutions and representatives of the Italian state, Mosca was in a position to observe directly the behaviour of the political elites. In this context he developed a theory centred on similar themes to those that underpin Pareto's approach: the dominance of the elites over the masses, the cyclical nature of political power, the sharp discrepancy between the state objectives of politicians and industrialists and their actions in everyday life. Although Mosca prefers to write about the 'political class' rather than elites his general arguments are very similar to Pareto's. His main point is that regardless of the formal designation a state might have (i.e. a liberal democracy, theocracy, socialist republic, etc.), all governments operate in a similar way in the sense that an organised minority dominates a disorganised majority.

More specifically, Mosca argues that throughout history one can identify a stable pattern where political power is always wielded by a small group of individuals, which he terms a political class. What distinguishes a political class from the rest of the population is not some inherent genetic predisposition, but primarily their superior organisational capacity. What this means is that theoretically almost any individual could develop such organisational skills so as to become a member of the political class. For Mosca the nature of the social and political system of a particular state is largely determined by the character of its political class.

In this context he zooms in on the organisation and formation of the political class. In terms of formation he differentiates between two mutually exclusive processes: democratisation and aristocratisation. Whereas aristocratisation stands for the tendency to monopolise governing structures through the hereditary transmission of power, democratisation indicates a trend towards the opening up of ruling roles to organisationally talented individuals who grew up in the non-ruling classes. In terms of organisation, Mosca distinguishes between the centralised authority that imposes decisions in a top-down fashion (autocracy), and the political class that rules through negotiations with the wider society (liberalism). The combination of these categories provides a typology of political systems which Mosca labels: (1) aristocratic–autocratic; (2) aristocratic–liberal; (3) democratic–autocratic; and (4) democratic–liberal.

For Mosca, all governments face similar problem of trying to balance liberty and authority on the one hand, and stability and social change, on the other. Hence more radical forms of democratic–liberal rule may offer more liberty but this can have a negative impact on the government's authority and stability. In a similar way aristocratic–autocratic rule might generate stability and authority, but at the expense of liberty and social development. Thus Mosca was adamant that neither of these two models were effective in the long term and his view was that only mixed forms of government are capable of moderating these contradictory tendencies.

In this sense Mosca was sceptical of any possibility to establish a genuinely democratic political system. He perceived the democratic ideal both as an illusion and as an internal contradiction. In his view, if democracy is to be understood as a rule of the people by themselves then political decisions have to be made by all members of the respective polity. For Mosca this is not only impractical as one could not consult all the electorate on every important political decision, but also impossible because it would mean that the political class would, for the first time in history, incorporate the entire society. This ultimately leads to the contradictory character of such a proposition as the full application of this idea would negate the distinction between the popular will and one's right to make decisions. Since not all citizens are equally equipped to influence decision making, the elites would be in a position to utilise their organisational superiority to shape decisively the process of decision making, thus making the ideal of democratic deliberation obsolete.

In seeing the organisational dominance of elites as a universal and trans-historical phenomenon, Mosca was deeply sceptical of any radical attempts to transform social and political systems. For example, he argued that the Marxist idea of revolutionary change is flawed as it is premised on the utopian notion of power relations. In Mosca's view socialist revolution is unlikely to dispense with class inequality and the political dominance of a minority. Instead revolutions are bound only to replace one political class with another and would not result in a more democratic social order.

Also like Pareto, Mosca argues that the social asymmetry of political life does not rely on coercion and organisational capacities alone, but it also requires a degree of ideological legitimacy. In *The Ruling Class* (1939 [1896]) he provides a historical analysis of this process and argues that all ruling groups had to combine coercion with ideological justification in order to dominate their subjects. For Mosca, such justification is regularly achieved through what he calls a political formula. This term stands for the abstract principles and ideas that help justify political dominance. Although a political class may often invoke a specific set of principles that are seen as the key drivers of social action, Mosca stipulates that 'it is not the political formula that determines the way the political class is structured. On the contrary, it is the latter that always adopts the formula that suits it best.' (Mosca, p. 47).

Since political formulae only help to justify the right to rule, they can easily change as historical conditions change. Thus, in some historical contexts the political class can invoke religious foundations to justify rule. Typical examples here are the divine authority theory in Christendom, the caliphate tradition of Muhammed's successors in the Islamic world and the legacy of 'heavenly sovereigns' such as the emperors of Japan seen as the direct descendants of the sun-goddess Amaterasu, as formulated in the Shinto religious tradition. In many other instances a political class is likely to rely on very diverse sources of secular principles: from the notion of popular sovereignty ritualised in periodic elections of liberal democracies, to class equality and people's democracy of state socialism, to the libertarian principles of autonomy and freedom of choice or environmental concepts of sustainability and land ethic. For Mosca, all these ideas ultimately serve the same purpose: to justify the rule of minorities over majorities.

Michels and the Iron Law of Oligarchy

In many respects Robert Michels builds on Mosca's central proposition that organised minority always dominates disorganised majority. However, unlike Mosca who focuses on the agency ('political class'), Michels is more interested in the structural underpinnings of this historical process. Hence the focal point of his study are the organisations and the nature of political power in a rapidly bureaucratised world. As one of Max Weber's star students Michels was greatly influenced by his teacher's theory of bureaucracy. Nevertheless, while Weber identified both the effective and unproductive features of the modern bureaucratic order, Michels' empirical work was much more centred on the 'dark' sides of organisational power. His most influential book *Political Parties* (1911) was an empirical study of power relations within the German SPD.

Michels started this project with the assumption that unlike the conservative parties, which usually value authoritarian leadership or just devote less attention to internal democracy, the progressive parties would have a more democratic organisational structure. However, his in-depth analysis of the German SPD until then widely regarded as one of the most democratic associations, indicated that even this organisation was governed by a very small group of individuals. Building on his empirical material Michels developed a notion of the 'iron law of oligarchy'. This formulation was intended to capture the findings of his study, which emphasised that all social organisations have a tendency to be run by a small and organised elite – an oligarchy. In his own words: 'who says organization, says oligarchy' (Michels, 1966: 365).

For Michels all large-scale complex organisations inevitably succumb to oligarchic forms of rule. Although many such organisations might start off as genuinely democratic their sheer size and complexity lead towards centralised and hierarchical decision making. Since the principles of direct democracy simply cannot be implemented in huge and changing organisational contexts, the very existence of such entities is dependent on the centralisation of power. Even when power is delegated to individuals there is no mechanism to prevent one's monopolisation of decision making: 'It is organization which gives birth to the domination of the elected over electors, of the mandatanes over the mandators, of the delegates over delegators' (Michels, 1966: 365).

Michels argues that all organisations tend to resemble each other in the sense that they eventually end up governed by a 'leadership class' which consists of party leaders, executive committees, spokespeople, strategists, organisers, paid administrators, and so on. Unlike ordinary members who are generally less involved in the organisation's day-to-day activities and as such tend to be more passive or indifferent, the leadership class is often directly involved and well informed about the organisation. Hence by controlling access to information the leadership can successfully centralise the power structure without much accountability. Michels is adamant that any attempt to control the leadership class fully is unlikely to succeed as leaders are in a position to control the information and reward loyal members thus preventing any challenge to their rule. Moreover, with the professionalisation of leadership roles such individuals acquire technical specialisation and organisational skills that ordinary members lack and as such can detach themselves from the masses and pursue their self-interests. As he put it bluntly: 'Historical evolution mocks all the prophylactic measures that have been adopted for the prevention of oligarchy' (1966: 423). In this context he shares Pareto's and Mosca's scepticism about representative democracy. For Michels, since genuine direct democratic decision making can never be achieved in large-scale organisations the representative democratic model inevitably reproduces the oligarchical system of rule. In this understanding the nation-state is just another type of large-scale social organisation which cannot be governed successfully without centralisation, hierarchies, delegation of responsibility and decision making. Since all modern states inevitably rely on bureaucratic power, which by definition constrains individual liberties, they are nothing more than enormous oligarchical systems. In Michels' (1966: 188–91) view such gigantic oligarchies can be destroyed or dismantled but their replacements are just as likely to be as oligarchical. Thus, instead of one large oligarchical system one would end up with many smaller oligarchies.

Michels' concept of oligarchical rule differs from Pareto's. While Pareto sees history in terms of permanent circulation and the renewal of elites, Michels argues that the oligarchical nature of organisations tends towards entrenching elite power thus leaving little room for the genuine social mobility of elites. Michels recognises that different groups of elites compete over organisational resources but this conflict rarely ends in the full replacement of one elite groupings by another. Instead, Michels is adamant that established elites are more likely to assimilate segments of the new elite: 'old aristocracy does not disappear, does not become proletarian or impoverished (at least in absolute sense), does not make way for new group of rulers, but that always remains at the head of nations, which it led over the course of centuries' (1966: 75).

Furthermore, Michels distinguishes between two layers of dominant elite: nobility and the ruling class. Unlike Mosca, for whom all rulers constitute a political class, Michels contends that not all members of the ruling class have the same organisational power. For Michels, it is the nobility that constitutes a smaller but more influential part of the elite, capable of shaping agendas and making key decisions. Since oligarchical structure entails a very small number of decision makers and the ruling strata are generally much larger, there is always an elite within the elite which dominates the rest. It is this small group that 'pervades, conquers, and moulds, the high middle class according to its own moral and social essence' (Michels, 1966: 77). What is also distinct about the nobility is its relative homogeneity. Hence for Michels it is this social cohesion at the very top that sustains elite dominance and often prevents the substantive circulation of elites to happen.

In contrast to nobility the rest of the ruling class (which Michels terms 'aristocracy') is much more heterogeneous. Michels (1966: 76) differentiates between four principal types of aristocracy/ruling class: (1) hereditary aristocrats; (2) aristocratic government clerks; (3) moneyed aristocracy; and (4) aristocracy of knowledge. While all these unique skills help maintain organisational dominance of the elite as a whole, this heterogeneity of the ruling class/aristocracy also allows the nobility to establish and maintain oligarchical forms of domination over these groups and the rest of society.

Contemporary Relevance and Applications

The classical elite theory was quite popular and influential in Europe, the United States and Latin America in the 1920s, 1930s and early 1940s. This is well illustrated by the translations of key publications of Pareto, Mosca and Michels in multiple languages as well as in frequent citations of their work throughout the world. However, the military defeat of Mussolini's Italy, which was in part inspired by the works of elite theory, and Michels' work and to some extent Pareto's involvement with the fascist regime, had largely discredited these theorists. Hence the wider academic community tended to shun their contributions for years. Furthermore, with the expansion of Keynesian economics, the welfare state and universal suffrage the developmental trajectory of the world after World War Two seemed to favour more optimistic approaches centred on greater social egalitarianism and wider political participation where there was no room for theories focused on elite power.

ELITE THEORIES OF LEFT AND RIGHT

Though its roots are situated closer to the political right, the tense combination of left and right variations within the paradigm of elite theory makes it an especially interesting perspective. This tension plays out even within individual elite theorists themselves, as in the intellectual and biographical development of Robert Michels. The point of distinction, however, can be identified in relation to capitalism: elite theorists on the left interpret elite rule in modernity as the outcome of the elevation of economic and political elites by structural dynamics within the capitalist system itself; those on the right, by contrast, attach elements of universalism to elite rule, either via the inherent characteristics of superior individuals or through the inevitability of hierarchy in all societies for effective social co-ordination.

Nevertheless, with the crisis of the welfare state and the rising political and economic inequalities in the world from the 1970s onwards, scholars and the general public have become more interested in the development and application of classical elite theories. Hence throughout the 1970s and 1980s one could witness a revival of this approach under the umbrella term 'neo-elitism'.

The scholars who articulated this new approach attempted to situate classical elite theory within the existing framework of liberal democracies. More specifically they reformulated the theories of Mosca, Pareto and Michels so that they could accommodate democratic political systems. The early version of the neo-elite approach, as exemplified by the publications of Domhoff (1967) and Mills (1956), identified the central role played by corporate power in the US political system whereby a small number of well-interconnected elites, not parliamentary institutions, were found to be the key decision makers. Mills singled out the organisational dominance of the military–industrial complex involving big-business executives, military leaders and top politicians.

Field and Higley (1973) and Higley and Field (1980) focused on the role political elites play in the development and persistence of democratic institutions. Drawing on the classical elite theory, they maintain that elites remain the decisive factor in the political process. However, unlike Michels, Pareto or Mosca, they argue that elite power and democratic institutions can be fully compatible. For example, Higley and his collaborators (Dogan and Higley, 1998; Field and Higley, 1973; Field et al., 1976; Higley and Burton, 1989) have studied a variety of states that were involved in the democratisation processes in the 1970s, 1980s and 1990s, and have found that the degree of elite cohesion was one of the central variables for the success or failure of these processes.

In this context, Higley and Burton (2006) contrast the experience of post-2003 Iraq with post-apartheid South Africa, arguing that any attempt to democratise the state and society without securing the consent of elites is bound to fail. Thus, the US coercive dismantling of the Iraqi Ba'athist regime together with its organisational structure and elite networks has proved highly detrimental to the democratisation process, and ultimately has generated well-organised violent resistance led by these excluded elite groupings. In contrast, by pursuing the elite settlements between the leadership of the African National Congress and the white Afrikaner elites, South Africa underwent a more effective and less violent transition towards democratic social order. The neo-elite approaches zoom in on the capacity of elites to act cohesively and share interests and resources. In this context Higley and Burton (2006) differentiate between situations where elites are deeply polarised and disunited and situations where there is shared consensus or ideological unity between elite groupings. They argue that functioning democracy entails consensual elites while full ideological unity is only possible in the totalitarian orders. Hence, much of their focus is on the elite disunity that often characterises authoritarian regimes attempting to democratise. Their research indicates that democratisation is more likely through long-term negotiations leading towards elites settlements that would accommodate competing claims of diverse and disunited elites.

Other recent applications of elite models have explored the historical relationships between the rulers and the institutions of the modern nation-state. Hence, Mann (1987) has analysed the expansion of citizenship rights in

Europe and North America through the prism of different types of elite bargaining with the networks of civil society. For Mann the institutionalisation of class conflict in Europe was shaped by specific geopolitical events and different domestic political cleavages, which ultimately generated distinct strategies towards citizenship entitlements. Hence due to the early expansion of economic liberalism, early industrialisation and wider political participation in revolutionary upheavals, both the US and UK elites were forced to concede civil and political rights and develop a constitutional model of citizenship.

In contrast, the absolutist elites of Germany, Russia and Austria were able to deny universal citizenship rights and instead granted only limited civil and social rights. As these states were dominated by the agricultural nobilities and had a small number of industrial workers, they could block access to political and economic rights. In other parts of Europe such as Italy, Spain and France, citizenship developed through the violent conflicts between monarchists and the Church on the one hand, and secular liberals and socialists, on the other. The outcome of these protracted struggles was weaker social and political rights. In parts of Europe such as Scandinavia where this bargaining between elites and the civil society was less violent and more consensual, the outcome was much stronger welfare states. Therefore, in each case the expansion of citizenship rights was not an evolutionary development prompted by popular demand but mostly a distinct form of elite strategy to fend off the masses.

Other scholars have also deployed the tools of elite theory to analyse the origins of modern institutions. For example, Acemoglu and Robinson (2000) have empirically demonstrated that the emergence of social democratic regimes was largely the outcome of the perception of the threat of elites. The wider acceptance of welfare provisions and other social protection measures developed as a social mechanism to fend off the political threats posed by non-elites. It is no historical accident that one of the most authoritarian European states, Bismarck's Prussia, was the first to introduce elements of the welfare state. By expanding these social rights the elites were able to stifle the rise of trade unions and mass political parties.

Criticisms

Despite its early popularity in the 1920s and 1930s classical elite theory always had been contested within and outside of sociology. The fact that some of its most prominent proponents became sympathetic to or even directly involved with radical right-wing politics has often been invoked to delegitimise its use today. However, since no social theory is immune from politicisation and misuse it is important to differentiate between the normative and explanatory aspects of this approach. In other words, as we have argued elsewhere, one can disassociate oneself from the political recommendations and moral evaluations of a particular theory while still aiming to preserve its valuable conceptual and explanatory potential (Malešević, 2010). Hence the focus of this section will not be its normative implications but solely the sociological criticisms of elite theory. Among these, three types of critique stand out: the relationship between elitism and democracy; the asymmetrical position of the elites and masses; and the role ideological factors play in elite dominance.

The theorists of elites have often been dismissed as cynics who interpret all forms of power relationships as very similar and who do not differentiate between democratic and non-democratic forms of governance. Political sociologists see this as a type of epistemological relativism that is not well grounded in empirical research. While there is broad acceptance that all forms of governance entail a degree of elite dominance, scholars insist that the democratic models fully equipped with the institutionalised mechanisms of division of power with checks and balances are much better at constraining elite power than the authoritarian systems that lack such measures (Wintrop, 1992; Walker, 1966). In some respects this critique has been take on board by the neo-elitist approaches, which now argue that democracy and elite rule are not mutually exclusive but are in fact compatible. From Weber and Schumpeter to the more recent works of Higley and Etzioni-Halevy, scholars have attempted to show how and why democratic elitism differs from the authoritarian models of rule. The emphasis here is on the relatively arbitrary character of decision making in authoritarianism. In contrast democracies are defined by institutional arrangements which allow for the legitimised competitive struggle of elites for the popular vote.

One of the defining features of elite theory is its sharp differentiation between the elites and masses. In the works of Pareto, Mosca and Michels, elites are the primary subject of history and as such they receive a great deal of attention. At the same time other individuals who are not members of the elite groups are perceived to be passive and indistinguishable masses. Although there are important differences in how each theorist conceptualises who constitutes an elite, they are very similar in their underestimation and lack of analysis of the masses. While elites are seen to be heterogeneous, complex, driven by interests and passions, the non-elites are largely invisible. This is deeply problematic for a number of reasons. For one thing elites too are often constrained in their actions and cannot predict or control the (unintended) consequences of their actions (Malešević, 2004). For another thing non-elite agents are never simple puppets of elites, for if this were the case one could not explain how some elite actions are fiercely resisted by elites to the point of removing them from power (i.e. revolutions, rebellions, strikes, etc.) while others are accepted and supported. Furthermore this deeply asymmetrical view of the two groups cannot explain how marginal members of the masses can join elites or how disposed elites become part of the masses, which has happened throughout history.

This point is linked with the elite theorists' overemphasis on agency over structure. Some critics have described elite theory as lacking any interest in the study of structural change while focusing almost exclusively on the agents – elite individuals and groups. Hence Cammack (1990) and Collier (1999) argue that such an approach is built on the wrong, voluntaristic, assumption that elite behaviour is always causally linked with state policies, while in fact elite actions might only represent a small segment of the wider, structural, causes of such policies. Early Marxist critics such as Lukács, thought that this agency-centred theory was the product of relatively unique structural conditions in Italy, which did not have institutions of 'bourgeois democracy' and hence its theorists overemphasised the role of political leaders (Bottomore, 1964: 9–10). Nevertheless, one should distinguish between Pareto on the one hand, and Mosca and Michels on the other, as the former does not fully explore the role of organisational structures while the latter devote a lot of attention to organisations. In fact, one could argue that Michels in particular, sees elite action in modernity through the prism of the increased structural capacity of organisations.

Finally the classical elite models have been criticised for their lack of understanding of ideological power. While Mosca, Pareto and Michels have all identified the role of shared values as crucial in generating public support for the elites, they tend to see these values in extremely instrumentalist terms. In other words Pareto's derivations, Mosca's political formulae and Michels' suggestion all indicate that they see ideas and values only as mechanisms of elite manipulation: the elites create particular narratives to justify their hold on power and in this way they exploit the ignorance of the masses. In this sense elite theory resembles some forms of early Marxism as they all subscribe to the 'false consciousness' thesis. This thesis is built on the functionalist proposition that the masses internalise and hold on to distorted views of social reality and as such tend to act contrary to their own self-interest. However, many empirical studies have corroborated the fact that ideological commitments are rarely if ever built on ignorance and manipulation alone. Instead, most individuals are quite capable of identifying their own interests and values and whether or not they overlap with those of the ruling elites. Hence, if they perceive that such interests and values are not fulfilled or pursued by the respective elites, mass support is likely to dwindle. Although a degree of political manipulation might be involved in this relationship, the rulers that rely on fabrication of the truth alone cannot sustain public support for long. Therefore ideological power requires a kernel of truth and tacit consent from those that are ruled by the elites (Malešević, 2002).

Conclusion

In the aftermath of the Second World War, classical elite theory was largely marginalised and ignored. Being tainted by its association with Mussolini's fascism, this approach was deemed to be unsuitable for the post-war world. Furthermore, the relative dominance of Marxist and structural–functionalist theories of social change indicated that there was no need to draw upon the Machiavellian tradition to explain the new social processes. With the world-wide proliferation of Keynesian economic models of development, expansion of welfare provisions and the rise of the politics of peaceful co-existence, it seemed that social and political inequalities and belligerent politics are things of the past. Nevertheless, with the gradual exhaustion of these peaceful developmentalist strategies and the sharp rise of inequality and violence throughout the world, elite theories have become ever more relevant. The profound economic crises, wars and rise of extremist politics have all led towards what Habermas calls 'the loss of utopian energies'. In this context one could witness the expansion of populist politics and demagogic leaders willing to exploit fear to further their own self-interests. All of this indicates that the classical elite theory is still highly relevant and capable of explaining a variety of contemporary phenomena – from Brexit to Trump.

References

Acemoglu, D. and Robinson, J. (2000) Why Did the West Extend the Franchise? Democracy, Inequality, and Growth in Historical Perspective. *Quarterly Journal of Economics*, 115(4), pp. 1167–200.

Adams, B. and Sydie, R.A. (2002) *Classical Sociological Theory*. Thousand Oaks, CA: Pine Forge Press.

Bottomore, T. B. (1964) *Elites and Society*. New York: Basic Books.

Cammack, P. (1990) A Critical Assessment of the New Elite Paradigm. *American Journal of Sociology*, 55(3), pp. 415–420.

Collier, R. B. (1999) *Paths Toward Democracy: The Working Class and Elites in Western Europe and South America*. Cambridge: Cambridge University Press.

Coser, L. A. (1971) *Masters of Sociological Thought: Ideas in Historical and Social Context*. New York: Harcourt Brace Jovanovich.

Dogan, M. and Higley, J. (1998) (eds) *Elites, Crises, and the Origins of Regimes*. Boulder, CO: Rowman & Littlefield.

Domhoff, W. G. (1967) *Who Rules America?* Englewood Cliffs, NJ: Prentice Hall.

Femia, J. V. (1998) *The Machiavellian Legacy: Essays in Italian Political Thought*. London: Palgrave.

Femia, J. V. (2004) *Machiavelli Revisited*. Cardiff: University of Wales Press.

Field, G. L. and Higley, J. (1973) *Elites and Non-elites: The Possibilities and Their Side Effects*. Andover, MA: Warner Modular Publications.

Higley, J. and Burton, M. G. (1989) The Elite Variable in Democratic Transitions and Breakdowns. *American Sociological Review*, 54(1), pp. 7–32.

Higley, J. and Burton, M. G. (2006) *Elite Foundations of Liberal Democracy*. Oxford: Rowman & Littlefield.

Higley, J. and Field, G. L. (1980) *Elitism*. London: Routledge & Kegan Paul.

Higley, J., Field, G. L. and Knut, G. (1976) *Elite Structure and Ideology: A Theory with Applications to Norway*. Oslo: Universitetsforlaget.
Kaplan, J. (2005) *The Modern Scholar: Political Theory: The Classic Texts and Their Continuing Relevance*. [Audiobook]. Prince Frederick, MD: Recorded Books.
Malešević, S. (2004) *The Sociology of Ethnicity*. London: Sage.
Malešević, S. (2010) *The Sociology of War and Violence*. Cambridge: Cambridge University Press.
Malešević, S. (2002) *Ideology, Legitimacy and the New State*. London: Routledge.
Malešević, S. (2013) *Nation-States and Nationalisms: Organisation, Ideology and Solidarity*. Cambridge: Polity.
Mann, M. (1987) Ruling Class Strategies and Citizenship. *Sociology*, 21(3), pp. 339–54.
Michels, R. (1966 [1911]) *Political Parties: A Sociological Study of the Oligarchical Tendencies*. London: Free Press.
Mills, C. W. (2000 [1956]) *The Power Elite*. New edition. New York: Oxford University Press.
Mosca, G. (1939 [1896]) *The Ruling Class*. London: McGraw-Hill.
Pareto, V. (1942 [1918]) *The Mind and Society: The Treatise on general Sociology*. New York: Harcourt, Brace & Co.
Pareto, V. (1966) *Sociological Writings*. New York: Praeger.
Vandervort, B. (1998) *Warfare in Colonial Africa: Wars of Imperial Conquest in Africa, 1830–1914*. London: UCL Press.
Walker, J. L. (1966) A Critique of the Elitist Theory of Democracy. *American Political Science Review*, 60, pp. 285–95.
Wintrop, N. (1992) Elite Theory and Neo-Elite Theory Understandings of Democracy: An Analysis and Criticism. *Australian Journal of Political Science*, 27(3), pp. 462–77.

X

HINTZE, GUMPLOWICZ, RATZENHOFER, WARD AND SMALL

Introduction

The leading representatives of the classical bellicist tradition such as Otto Hintze, Ludwig Gumplowicz or Gustav Ratzenhofer are rarely mentioned in contemporary sociology textbooks. Even when there is a brief reference to Gumplowicz, the tendency is to mischaracterise his work as belonging to a dreaded form of social Darwinism. However, a brief glance at late nineteenth- and early twentieth-century periodicals and social science books indicates that these names featured prominently not only in Europe, but also in the Americas. For example, the earliest issues of the *American Journal of Sociology* bring out many articles that characterise Ratzenhofer and Gumplowicz, together with Simmel and Durkheim as the founding 'fathers' of sociology (Bentley, 1926). Similarly, Hintze was generally regarded as the leading scholar of the German Empire and the Weimar Republic (Daum, 2016). There are many reasons why the classics of the bellicist approach have been ignored by contemporaries including the dominance of the Enlightenment heritage following the Second World War that privileged theories centred on scientific progress, economic growth, rationality and peace (Malešević, 2010: 17). In this context these scholars, whose work was primarily focused on the causal role of war and violence that have played in state formation and the transformation of social relations through history, have largely been marginalised. Nevertheless, since the classical bellicist tradition was highly influential at a time when sociology was institutionalised and publicly recognised as an academic discipline it is important to review and analyse these contributions. This chapter looks at the historical and biographical context under which bellicist tradition emerges and develops. We also provide a critical analysis of their key ideas and explore their relevance for the contemporary world.

Life and Intellectual Context

Otto Hintze

Hintze (1861–1940) is now generally recognised as one of the first historical sociologists. He was born in Pyritz, Pomerania, into a middle-class family of civil servants. Initially he enrolled in 1878 to study history, philology and philosophy at the University of Greifswald. During his two-year stay in Greifswald he became influenced by the strong nationalist ethos of the place and joined the nationalist fraternity, Germania. In 1888 he moved to Berlin where he specialised in medieval history, studied under Dilthey and Droysen, and completed his PhD under the foremost German medieval historian, Julius Weizsäcker. During this period Hintze was already involved with several research projects including the Prussian Academy's multi-volume study on the economic and administrative organisation of Prussia. The director of this project, Gustav Schmoller, was a leading comparative historical economist who, together with Heinrich von Treitschke, a world-renowned German nationalist historian, became a supervisor for Hintze's second PhD.

Upon completion of this thesis in 1895, Hintze attained a Professorship in Political, Constitutional, Administrative and Economic History at the University of Berlin. By this time he was regarded as a conservative monarchist deeply influenced by Treitschke and Schmoller. However, his political persuasion gradually changed. Following his marriage to his former student Hedwig Guggenheimer, who was a liberal and an expert on *ancien régime* France, Hintze became less conservative (Ertman, 2017). In 1915 he published the *Hohenzollern and Their Legacy* which is now regarded as one of his major works. With the defeat of Germany in the First World War and the collapse of the Weimer Republic, Hintze lost much of the stringent nationalism that characterised his pre-war outlook. In this period he had a serious eye operation which ultimately forced him to retire in 1920. Until then he was extremely productive, publishing no less than 263 academic works, including several monographs (Ertman, 2017). Unfortunately, one of his most important books, a hefty comparative study of constitutions, was lost during the war. Hintze's most influential sociological publications include *Sociology and History* (1943) and *The State and Constitution* (1962). Nevertheless, with the Nazi's takeover of the German state in 1933, Hintze decided to stop publishing. He spoke against Einstein's expulsion from the Prussian Academy of Sciences and in 1938 resigned from the Academy in protest against rising authoritarianism and racism. His wife, who had a Jewish and leftist background, was forced to leave her academic post and eventually committed suicide in 1942, to avoid deportation to the death camps. Otto Hintze died in 1940.

Ludwig Gumplowicz

Gumplowicz (1838–1909) was one of the founders of sociology as an academic discipline. He was born in Kraków, Poland, in 1838 into a middle-class, Polish-speaking, Jewish family. His parents had strong intellectual and activist backgrounds that were centred on liberal causes, including Jewish emancipation, and resistance against the Austrian occupation. His father Abraham was strongly influenced by the Jewish Enlightenment movement, Haskalah and as an assimilated Jew attained citizenship rights, which was highly unusual for the Austrian-ruled Kraków of this period (Pocar, 2007). Hence his household was the epicentre of political activism, with Ludwig's older brothers taking part in insurgency against Austrian rule. Young Ludwig was deeply influenced by this social environment and early on focused on trying to understand the historical and social context of group relations. In order to emphasise his full assimilation as well as to avoid anti-Semitic discrimination, Gumplowicz embraced the Calvinist religion.

In 1857 Gumplowicz enrolled to study law at the Jagiellonian University in Kraków but he then moved to Vienna where he graduated in 1860. Upon graduation he returned to Kraków and enrolled as a PhD candidate. He also practised law and was elected to the city council. He completed his PhD in law in 1864 but his Habilitation thesis was rejected because of its pronounced anti-clericalism. Due to his hostility towards the clergy and the Catholic Church he could not find academic employment in Poland. Hence, he worked as a journalist, a notary public and the chief editor and owner of the Kraków liberal magazine *Kraj* [*Country*] (Konieczny, 2015). In 1874 he moved to Graz (Austria) where he successfully defended his thesis on Robert von Mohl and his philosophy of the state and was appointed docent (lecturer).

As a Jewish–Polish immigrant Gumplowicz's career advancement was very slow and it was only when he attained international fame that he was promoted to a full professorship in 1893 (Pocar, 2007). Gumplowicz was a highly productive writer and his books such as *Race and State* (1875), *Constitutional State and Socialism* (1881), *The Race Struggle* (1883) and the *Foundations of Sociology* (1885) achieved international recognition. He significantly influenced early American sociologists such as Lester Ward and Albion Small. During this period, he married Franciszka Goldman and they had three sons who all died prematurely. In 1909 Ludwig and Franciszka became severely ill (Ludwig having tongue cancer) and jointly committed suicide.

Gustav Ratzenhofer

Ratzenhofer (1842–1904) was one of the first European sociologists who together with Gumplowicz shaped the character of sociology as a discipline in

Europe and North America in the *fin de siècle* period. He was born in 1842 in Vienna into a middle-class family of watchmakers. Almost uniquely among leading sociologists Ratzenhofer was largely self-taught as his formal education ended in secondary school. He joined the Austrian Army in 1859 as a master watchmaker and then embarked on a highly successful military career: from ordinary cadet (1859) to second lieutenant (1864) to general and member of the General Staff (1872), to director of the Army Archives (1878) and finally attaining the rank of Field Marshal (Feldmarschall) and president of the Supreme Military Court (1898–1901).

During this period, he also wrote numerous sociological and historical treaties, some of which were translated into several languages and were highly influential in Europe and North America. Upon his retirement from the army in 1901 until his death in 1904 Ratzenhofer was completely dedicated to sociological and philosophical research and writing. As a Habsburg officer he was preoccupied with the question of the empire's survival, advocating the importance of the centralised state while also valuing the preservation of individual liberties. His sociological writings include *The Nature and Purpose of Politics* (three volumes, 1893), *Sociological Knowledge* (1898), *Critique of the Intellect* (1902) and *Sociology* (1907). Ratzenhofer died in 1904 on the ship that was taking him home from a conference in the United States.

Lester Ward and Albion Small

Ward (1841–1913) and Small (1854–1926) were pioneers of American sociology. They were instrumental in establishing sociology as an academic discipline in the United States. Hence Ward was the first president of the American Sociological Association while Small founded the first US department of sociology (in Chicago in 1892). In addition, he published the first sociological textbook (*An Introduction to the Study of Society*, 1894) and also established the *American Journal of Sociology* (1895). Lester Frank Ward was born in Joliet, Illinois, in a large farming family with 10 children. His mother was an educated women who enjoyed literature and who stimulated her children's interests in learning. However, soon after Lester's birth his father started running a sawmill business making railroad ties but died prematurely while Lester was still a teenager.

As their family business collapsed Lester worked as a farm labourer and later as a country schoolteacher to fund his studies at the Susquehanna Collegiate Institute. In 1862 Ward was mobilised to fight during the American Civil War where he was wounded three times. After the war he attended Columbian College where he graduated in 1869 with an AB, and in 1871 with an LLB and also received his AM degree in 1872. However, soon after, he shifted his interest towards geology and palaeontology, and in 1883 became an assistant geologist of the US Geological Survey (USGS). From 1892 to 1906 he was employed as palaeontologist of the USGS. During this period Ward combined his interests in palaeontology and geology with the emerging social sciences. Thus between

1883 and 1906 he published several books including *Dynamic Sociology* (1883), *Outlines of Sociology* (1898), *Pure Sociology* (1903) and *Applied Sociology* (1906). These publications cemented Ward's reputation as a pioneering sociologist, and he was appointed to the chair of sociology at Brown University in 1906. Ward was a liberal who supported gender, ethnic and class equality and saw universal education as a way to attain greater equality. He died in 1913.

Albion Woodbury Small was born in Buckfield, Maine, into a middle-class family. His father was a priest and religious ethos dominated the family household. Initially Albion pursued religious studies, graduating from Colby College in 1876 and working in the Baptist ministry at the Newton Theological Institution (1876–9). However, as he become more interested in social thought he decided to study history, economics and social policy in Europe (in Berlin, Leipzig, Weimar and London, 1879–81). Upon his return to the United States, he was employed as a part-time lecturer in history and political economy at Colby College, while simultaneously pursing his PhD studies at Johns Hopkins University where he graduated in 1889. Soon after he was appointed president of Colby College where he introduced sociology, thus making Colby College one of the first US academic institutions where sociology was taught. In 1892, Small was appointed to the first sociology chair in the United States – at the University of Chicago. It is here that he established the first US accredited department of sociology where uniquely in the world, sociology was taught at undergraduate and graduate levels. In 1905 Small published *General Sociology*, focusing on the role of conflict in social relations. He died in Chicago in 1926.

Historical, Social and Political Context

The Legacy of German Unification

Although *fin de siècle* Germany and Austro-Hungary were very different societies they were both beset by the deep structural problems stemming from uneven state organisation. The unification of 1871 established a large German state in place of numerous small kingdoms, grand duchies, duchies, principalities, free cities and territories. However, the new state lacked internal cohesion: its infrastructure was underdeveloped, its economy was not unified, and its political system was incoherent as it maintained different and at times mutually exclusive models of governance. Most of all, the new polity lacked legitimacy as large sections of the population were dissatisfied with the political and economic organisation of the state. Despite the proclaimed goals of national accord, many citizens of southern states such as Württemberg, Baden, Hesse and Bavaria perceived the new state more in terms of establishing Prussian occupation rather than German unification (Confino, 1997).

Furthermore, the new state organisation did not satisfy the interests of many groups. Nationalists were resentful of the fact that the new state did not incorporate all German-speaking lands but settled for a smaller Germany. Liberals, socialists, republicans and other social reformers were deeply dissatisfied with the authoritarian and monarchical structure of the state where the military and the large land-owning strata (i.e. Junkers) preserved their dominance. The conservatives were unhappy that new Germany lagged behind the UK in terms of its geopolitical influence in Europe and the world. In this context German academia reflected the ongoing debates with some intellectuals focusing on the questions of political representations, social rights and economic inequalities, while others emphasised the necessity of greater national homogenisation and state centralisation, and the need to expand military power.

The leading German intellectuals of this period, such as Otto Hintze's teachers Treitschke and Droysen, were preoccupied with the questions of state power and national identity. In this sense Hintze's early work reflects this concern with the origins and transformation of state power. However, despite his strong nationalism, Hintze's own biography reflects inherent contradictions of *fin de siècle* Germany: although he was in favour of German unification his intellectual and emotional commitment was deeply Prussian. In other words, his initial concept of Germany was very much in line with the Bismarckian notions of monarchist and aristocratic, Prussian-dominated German lands. Nevertheless, Hintze's political views changed significantly over the years. The defeat of Germany in the First World War had a profound impact on many intellectuals, including Hintze and Weber, whose political preferences shifted from nationalism and imperial grandeur towards democratic liberalism.

Cultural Difference and the Austro-Hungarian State

In contrast to many German intellectuals, who were advocating greater centralisation and national homogenisation as a long-term solution for the new German state, Austrian intellectuals were focused on the questions of cultural difference and decentralisation. Since Austro-Hungary developed as an empire that incorporated highly diverse ethnicities, the central issue for the state authorities was the question of ethnic politics. Initially the main tension was between the Hungarian and Austrian aristocracies, who were fighting over control of the Habsburg Empire. With the establishment of the constitutional union in 1867 that created the joint Austro-Hungarian state, the main bone of contention was the political representation of other ethnic groups within the empire: the Czechs, Slovaks, Croats, Slovenes, Poles, Ukrainians, Romanians, etc.

With the expansion of nationalism as a popular ideological discourse from the mid-nineteenth century onwards, Austro-Hungary witnessed the dramatic rise of social movements, associations and political parties advocating reorganisation of the state. To respond to these ever-increasing demands for greater cultural, political and economic rights left-wing intellectuals devised several models for state reorganisation including the Austro-Marxists (Victor Adler, Otto Bauer, Karl Renner and Max Adler), who later became well known for their theories of cultural autonomy that aimed to disjoin ethnicity from territory thus preventing possible secession. In contrast, the right-wing intelligentsia were more focused on the question of unification with Germany where conspiracy theories and anti-Semitism loomed large.

The liberals were less concerned with 'the national question' and more with the extension of individual rights and the constitutional transformation of the empire. In this environment of ever-expanding group polarisation Gumplowicz and Ratzenhofer attempted to understand and explain why group cohesion matters to individuals and why groups engage in conflict with each other. In Gumplowicz's case, these research interests were also in part driven by his biography: as an assimilated Polish Jew he faced discrimination for much of his life. In his native Kraków he was resented for his Jewish roots, his conversion to Protestantism and for his anti-clericalism despite his lifelong commitment to the Polish cause. In Graz, he faced discrimination for being a patriotic Pole of Jewish extraction. In this context it is quite understandable why Gumplowicz interpreted the world as being driven by group conflicts. Although Ratzenhofer did not share such personal experiences, as a military officer he was a direct witness to the continuous ethnic group polarisation that permeated Austro-Hungarian military forces for much of this period.

The United States and Social Change

The late nineteenth- and early twentieth-century United States was a quite different society when compared with its European counterparts. However, it too was going through unprecedented social change. On the one hand, after the Civil War the United States had become a more centralised state capable of projecting power throughout much of its territory while also gaining greater international influence and visibility. For much of this period the United States had experienced rapid economic expansion, making it the world leader in industrial production, agriculture and in general economic output. The abundance of natural resources and cheap energy extraction coupled with the proliferation of railroads stimulated the expansion of industry.

This period of unprecedented economic prosperity was well illustrated by massive increases in a worker's average annual income, which grew by 108% between 1865 and 1918. The United States was also the world leader in urbanisation with the main cities expanding dramatically in the period from 1850 to 1900: New York from 500,000 to 3.5 million, Philadelphia from 100,000 to 1.2 million and Chicago from 30,000 to 1.7 million, making it the fastest growing city in the world (Rees, 2013: 44). This staggering population rise and economic growth were largely generated and sustained by an enormous wave of immigration, with 27.5 million European migrants settling in the United States between 1865 and 1918 (United States Census Bureau, 1976).

On the other hand, US society was deeply polarised by various social conflicts: the Southern whites who lost the war and were lagging behind in economic prosperity resented the new social order; the African Americans continued to experience institutional racism throughout the country, which intensified with the Jim Crow system of segregation in the South and widespread prejudice in the rest of the country; the coercive assimilation and intensified violence against Native populations; the persistent exploitation of non-unionised, mostly immigrant, labour; and the ever-increasing economic divide between extremely wealthy 'robber barons' and the rest of the population. As the US state developed and strengthened its foreign policy became more assertive.

The outcomes of this change were several wars (i.e. with Spain and the Philippines) and military interventions (in Mexico, Nicaragua, Haiti, the Dominican Republic etc.). In this context the rising intellectual debates were centred on the questions of immigration, labour rights, race and ethnicity, religion and geopolitics. Albion Small and Lester Ward were very much involved in these debates focusing on the role that social conflict and violence play in the transformation of social order. Both Ward and Small were influenced by the Enlightenment paradigm believing that social science can contribute to progressive social change. For example, Ward understood sociology to be a science capable of identifying social laws that can be used to control and shape the future. In particular, he perceived universal education as a means to attain greater social equality including gender, ethnicity and race. Similarly Small valued progressive education and conceived of sociology not only as descriptive and analytical, but also as a proscriptive discipline centred on identifying group conflicts and then finding mechanisms to resolve these discords through innovative conflict resolution designs.

Arguments and Ideas

Otto Hintze and the Historical Sociology of Coercive Power

In sharp contrast to influential Marxist and other economic theories that emphasised class conflict as a driving force of history, Hintze argued that political power matters more. In his view states rather than classes were the principal generator of social change. More specifically, he was critical of the views that aimed to explain social phenomena by focusing almost exclusively on internal social dynamics. Instead, he accentuated the ever-changing geopolitical environment and the long-term historical context as being crucial for understanding social change. To capture the causes of large-scale social transformations, Hintze argues, one should not study a single state in isolation but look at the wider geopolitical and historical environment: one should not 'wrench each single state from the context in which it was formed ... exclusive in itself, without raising the question whether its particular character is co-determined by its relation to its surroundings' (1975: 159). For Hintze the history of state formation is the history of organised violence: 'all state organisation was originally military organisation, organisation for war'. Even the institutions that are today perceived to be the epitome of peaceful and institutional regulation of conflicting social interests such as the parliaments have their origins in violence. In several of his studies Hintze traces the development of parliamentary systems to assemblies of warriors whose membership in a specific political community was dependent on their willingness and ability to fight in various wars. By exploring the historical dynamics of ancient European institutions including the Greek and Roman assemblies, the medieval congregation of warriors, the polity of estates and other forms of social organisation, Hintze surmises that state formation has historically been shaped around two central processes: the external ordering of states and the structuring of social classes. In his view both of these processes are closely linked to war and are often mutually interdependent in the sense that external conflicts stifle internal animosities and vice versa.

In Hintze's view European state formation was shaped by the continuous threat of war which ultimately generated two principal types of states – the British model, characterised by a strong parliamentary system, self-government as well as a relatively weak state; and the continental model, exemplified by Prussia, which combined military absolutism with a highly bureaucratic administration. While the former could operate without a large military, the latter was dependent on the existence of powerful armies. For Hintze these two different types of state formation were rooted in different geopolitical contexts. The UK as an island-based power did not require large land force and could divert most of its finances towards building a potent navy that eventually dominated much of the world.

In contrast the geographical location of European continental states created an unstable geopolitical environment where the threat of war loomed large and as such these states had to build strong military forces. In order to finance and manage such large armies it was also necessary to create large and efficient bureaucratic apparatuses. Hence the origins of strong and bureaucratic European continental states are to be found in the war-prone geopolitical environment of Europe. According to Hintze (1975) this process of state formation was slow, uneven, and involved various setbacks and historical reversals. However the continental state system generally underwent the following three stages: (1) the emergence of the tribal and clan-based models where the military was the state and where social cohesion was rooted in kin- or clan-based solidarities; (2) the development of the feudal systems of military and state organisation with a loose central authority and a deeply hierarchical social order rooted in the military dominance of the horse-riding aristocracy (i.e. the ascendancy of well-armed and skilled cavalry over unskilled infantry); and (3) the militarist era where ever-expanding European warfare generated continuous fiscal crises that forced rulers to introduce military conscription and increase revenue collection by centralising states and building a large civil service.

This last period was crucial for state formation as it eventually involved planned institutionalisation of state development with the rulers acquiring loans from other states to fund large-scale projects – from transport and communication networks to the administration, military, police and other state sectors. For Hintze this period, associated with rapid political, military and economic growth, was also a period defined by the proliferation of warfare. In other words, Hintze's historical sociology identifies the Janus face model of modernity as intense social development going hand in hand with the increased destructive potential of modern social organisations.

Ludwig Gumplowicz and the Group Struggle

Most contemporary commentators tend to describe Gumplowicz as a typical representative of European social Darwinism (Joas and Knöbl, 2013; Hawkins, 1997). However, this characterisation does not square well with his main concepts and theories. For one thing Gumplowicz was dismissive of any attempts to deploy biological models to explain social phenomena (Malešević, 2010: 33). This was already recognised by sociologists close to Darwinism such as Stark (2013 [1962]: 6), who criticised Gumplowicz for invoking non-biological ideas to explain social change and for using the term 'race' in a non-hereditary sense.

For another thing Gumplowicz's insistence that groups, not individuals, are the primary agents of social action goes against biological interpretations that posit individual genes as the principal agents of all behaviour. In this sense Gumplowicz is a predecessor of Durkheim as he argues that social facts cannot be reduced to individual actions. They both belong to the classical positivist tradition that views social processes as being governed by similar laws to those of the natural world. In this context Gumplowicz sees social groups as the principal unit of social order and as such he believes that group action should be the primary focus of any social analysis. However, he differs substantially from Durkheim in his emphasis on the role conflict plays in social life. While Durkheim was essentially a sociologist of consensus, Gumplowicz's sociology was centred on the idea that group struggle defines human history.

One of his key theoretical concepts is syngenism, which stands for group feelings of solidarity that stem from joint action and shared cultural markers. For Gumplowicz syngenism develops over the long course of human history and its cohesive features generate ethnocentric feeling that ultimately foster animosities between different groups. In further contrast to Social Darwinism, which operates with a strictly evolutionary model of social change, Gumplowicz developed a cyclical view of history where social life was understood to be shaped by uneven patterns of group conflicts. In this view syngenic ethnocentrism stimulated the development of ever-larger groups – from 'hordes', clans and tribes to ethnic groups and nations that expanded or contracted through violent encounters. In his works he often uses the concept of 'race' to denote the syngenic qualities of these groups.

Nevertheless, it is important to emphasise that the term 'race' was not used by Gumplowicz in the biological or hierarchical sense. Instead 'race' here stands for what we would today describe as 'ethno-linguistic groups' (Konieczny, 2015: 2). In his most influential book, *Der Rassenkampf* (1883) [*The Race Struggle*], Gumplowicz articulates a pioneering theory of social conflict which is premised on an idea that most modern institutions including private property, law, the arts, economic systems, nuclear family and the state itself were all created through warfare and violence between different groups. More specifically he traces the origins of these institutions to the violent zero-sum conflicts between syngenic groups where the winners would appropriate the resources, land and weaponry while enslaving defeated warriors and capturing and assimilating women and children into their group. For Gumplowicz the origins of the state as a centralised coercive authority are also to be traced to violent conflicts.

Long before Charles Tilly (1985), Gumplowicz argued that war made the state and vice versa. In this account state formation was a by-product of one group subjugating its neighbours and, in this process, institutionalising serfdom and/or slavery upon which the state institutions developed. This process of state formation involved the gradual merger of different groupings into a larger, and strictly hierarchical, social structure that was legitimised by the emerging legal systems shaped in order to justify the deeply stratified division of labour in the new polity. For Gumplowicz (1883), this is not unique to the pre-modern world as social inequalities remain a backbone of most social orders. Just as states emerge and develop through violent conquests, so do culture, art and science. In Gumplowicz's theory cultural advancement was, and remains, dependent on previous conquests as war victories generate an aristocratic parasitic strata that build civilisation on the corpses of defeated groups.

Gustav Ratzenhofer and the Conflict of Group Interests

Ratzenhofer was deeply influenced by Gumplowicz's ideas and was also his collaborator. However, unlike Gumplowicz, who generally disliked biological interpretations of social phenomena, Ratzenhofer was very sympathetic to evolutionary models of social analysis. His general approach, which he called positive monism, was significantly influenced by Herbert Spencer and Adolf Bastian. Nevertheless, just like Spencer, Ratzenhofer's evolutionary theory was not Darwinian but much closer to Lamarck's model of evolution where one of the central propositions is that evolution progresses through the inheritance of acquired characteristics. In this context Ratzenhofer interpreted social change through the evolutionary prism where societies move up from primitive 'hordes' towards more complex and advanced social orders. At the heart of his theory is the idea that conflict is the driving force of social life.

Utilising the Hobbesian idea of conflict of all against all, Ratzenhofer postulates the 'law of absolute hostility' as a natural condition of all life. He argues that all social relations are driven by 'elemental forces' of self-preservation (*Brotneid*, i.e. inherent rivalry for food) and sex (*Blutliebe*, i.e. the blood bond). While these forces generate conflict, they can also be used to forge group cohesion. For example, Ratzenhofer sees the blood bond as a social mechanism deployed to tame individual conflicts within the 'primitive horde' and as an organisational tool to build military alliances against other groups. In this account the developmental stages of each social order are defined by a plethora of internal and external conflicts where violence and social progress constitute each other: 'Wars are consequence of social development' (Ratzenhofer, 1904: 186). He shares Gumplowicz's idea that sociological analysis should give priority to collective action over individual motivation and structural contexts, arguing that sociology is first and foremost 'the science of the reciprocal relationships of human beings' (Ratzenhofer, 1904: 177).

Nevertheless, he departs from Gumplowicz's understanding that groups are the key generators of social action. Instead, for Ratzenhofer, it is collective interests that underpin all social conflicts. In this view social interests mould individual and group action and as such we inhabit a world that comprises millions of mutually incompatible interest-driven actions. As Bentley (1926: 252–3) shows, for Ratzenhofer interests are highly dynamic entities that transcend physical individuals and as such are difficult to identify. Hence it is the sociologist's job to abstract such phenomena from real life. For Ratzenhofer the collective interests appear in a variety of guises and at different levels of abstraction ranging from the more abstract 'general interest', 'class interest' or 'national interest' to the interests that operate at a lower level of generality such as 'creedal interest', 'rank interest' or 'pecuniary interest' (Small, 1905: 252).

This multiplicity and dynamic quality of group interests combined with the fact that they are not inherent to any specific group indicate for Ratzenhofer that they can be negotiated, contained and harmonised in order to prevent violent conflicts. This rather optimistic conclusion differentiates Ratzenhofer's model from the much more pessimistic theory of Gumplowicz. Although the two scholars share the idea that state formation emerges and develops through violent conquests, Ratzenhofer argues that such a conquest state (*Erobererstaat*) that shaped much of human history is gradually becoming replaced by a more peaceful culture state (*Kulturestaat*). Hence what initially was created through numerous violent conquests, is gradually institutionalised and pacified through the expansion of civilisation.

Lester Ward and Social Synergy

Fin de siècle American sociology has largely developed in a dialogue with its European counterparts. While Robert Park was a student of Georg Simmel in Berlin, Lester Ward's and Albion Small's work developed in continuous interaction with Gumplowicz and Ratzenhofer. Ward was keen to disseminate the theories of the two European sociologists and in this context was responsible for translations and interpretations of their work in the United States. This intellectual compatibility with Gumplowicz and Ratzenhofer was well reflected in Ward's general theories of social change where conflict was understood to be a defining feature of nature. More specifically, Ward understood conflict as the creative force that underpins the physical and social world. He borrowed the Greek term synergy from physiology to explain the universal properties of nature as being shaped by the dynamic interplay of centrifugal and centripetal forces: 'the wholesome, constructive movement consists in the properly ordered combination and interaction of both these principles. This is *social synergy*, which is a form of cosmic synergy, the universal constructive principle of nature' (Ward, 1918: 358). In this context he interpreted the origins of state, stratification systems and gender inequalities as all being rooted in violent conflicts of the past eras.

Using a very similar argument and terminology to Gumplowicz, Ward insists that both class relations and state formation emerge through violence:

> The race [group] struggle has been universal, and everywhere it has produced the same effects. The first important institution to grow out of it is that of caste, and social classes even of the modern times and in the most advanced nations are all consequences, modified forms, and true survivals of the original system of caste. (1908: 622)

For Ward war and violence are the principal generators of human progress. He argues that violent conflict was the backbone of human development as it is through violence that humans established dominance over the animal world. Similarly he sees warfare as the key social vehicle for the advancement of civilisations. For Ward, war fosters self-discipline and enables organisational control over nature and in this sense stimulates civilisational advancement. Just like Gumplowicz and Ratzenhofer, Ward is a neo-Lamarckian who privileges environmental factors over genetics. In this sense Ward (1907) perceives warfare as evolutionary development which, just like other evolutionary processes, is slow, unplanned and painful.

Hence to maximise the progressive input of war experience while minimising its destructive outcomes Ward became preoccupied with identifying an alternative to war and violence. Believing strongly in the superiority of the artificial over the natural order, he was committed to developing telic models of social intervention (Telesis) that would direct the social evolution of humankind. In this context he saw science and universal education as the principal tools to accomplish planned and directed social progress which would minimise poverty, social inequality, gender and racial discrimination.

Albion Woodbury Small and the Sociology of Conflict

Ward drew extensively on Gumplowicz's ideas while Small's work has often been seen largely as no more than a commentary on Ratzenhofer. The fact that

Small devotes no less than 200 pages of his main book, *General Sociology* (1905), to the interpretation of and dialogue with Ratzenhofer's work might indicate that he was little more than an American follower of the Austrian scholar. Nevertheless, as Aho (1975) rightly insists, some of Small's key ideas were articulated well before he encountered Ratzenhofer's contributions. For example, in his early writings one can recognise that he understood conflict to be a dominant form of social interaction. In this context he conceptualised the state with its legislative and executive powers as 'the regulative system' that successfully mediates conflicting group interests (Aho, 1975: 164–7).

Furthermore, Small developed more dynamic models of social change that conceptualised social processes as continuously evolving, adjusting and developing. Thus for him the main subject matter of sociology was 'the process of human association' (Small, 1905: 3). In this he was syncretic in borrowing from Ratzenhofer, Marx and Schmoller among others. Although he certainly was a great admirer of Ratzenhofer's sociology he did not vehemently subscribe to all of Ratzenhofer's ideas. Hence in *General Sociology* (1905) he accepts Ratzenhofer's general diagnosis of the social world as being shaped by universal conflicts of interests, but he distances himself from Ratzenhofer's notion of 'absolute hostility'. For Small this concept should be qualified as such primeval hostility is not to be seen, as he emphasises, as 'literally absolute as a general relation between men' but as a variable and contextual phenomenon. In his view there is a universal conflict of interests, but he also notes that absolute hostility is not necessarily a universal phenomenon (Small, 1905: 204).

In addition, Small was sceptical of Ratzenhofer's ambition to provide a fully fledged theory of state formation, arguing that the scant archaeological records do not allow for testing such speculative models. Instead Small's focus was firmly on contemporary social conflicts where evidence is available. In this context he was more optimistic than either Ratzenhofer or Gumplowicz on the ability of modern institutions to tame violent conflicts. In Small's interpretation, contemporary nation-states possess organisational mechanisms that can temper different group interests. Since he conceptualised both society and the state as dynamic, evolving, entities, Small was adamant that one could control social change through social reform and the gradual introduction of ethical principles of governance.

Contemporary Relevance and Applications

Although the classical bellicist approaches dominated sociological thought at the end of the nineteenth and early twentieth century they have largely been forgotten. Hence contemporary sociological textbooks rarely if ever refer to Hintze, Gumplowicz and Ratzenhofer, while Ward and Small are only referred to in the context of the early institutional development of American sociology. This disciplinary amnesia is in part grounded in the legacy of the Second World War where bellicist thought became associated with social Darwinism, traditionally considered an intellectually repugnant paradigm. Although none of these scholars directly espoused Darwinist ideas, and many of them were clearly Lamarckian, the fact that they all emphasised the role that war and violence play in social development has negatively impacted on their visibility in post-war sociology.

In the wake of the most destructive war fought on this planet the general orientation of social science in the post-war period was towards social theories that focus more on the economic or cultural sources of social change. Hence not only were *fin de siècle* bellicists in part held responsible for the carnage of the Second World War, but also their theories were deemed to be irrelevant for explaining the social dynamics of the second half of the twentieth century (Malešević, 2010: 45–6). Consequently, from the 1950s till the 1980s sociological thought was dominated by the 'pacifist' social theories with their focus on the transformation of normative values (structural functionalism), bureaucratic rationality (neo-Weberian approaches) or economic inequalities (neo-Marxist approaches).

THE SOCIOLOGY OF WAR

Despite its status as a constant in human history, war has not been properly established as a domain of sociological enquiry and has only recently come into focus with the emergence of the sociology of war as a subfield. The sociology of war concerns the role of collective violence in societal development, considering war as a force for change or stability of state and society. Somewhat embedded in comparative historical sociology, the subfield has interesting overlaps with political sociology and international relations. For social theory, the sociology of war shifts the locus of social change from processes taking place within societies to those taking place between societies. This shift coincides with an altered perspective on the state, seeing it as an autonomous actor with geopolitical interests of its own. War is then a political phenomenon, using organised violence in the pursuit of interest. In Karl von Clausewitz's classical definition: 'War is the continuation of policy by other means.'

Nevertheless, from the mid-1980s onwards one can track a gradual renewed interest in the study of war and organised violence within sociology. Comparative historical sociologists such as Charles Tilly (1985), Michael Mann (1986, 1988), John A. Hall (1985, 1986), Martin Shaw (1988) and Anthony Giddens (1987) among others, have devoted a great deal of attention to the study of warfare and the role that military and coercive power plays in the formation of states. This reinvigorated interest was in part sparked by the intensification of proxy wars between the two twentieth-century superpowers (i.e. in Afghanistan, Lebanon, Mozambique, Salvador, Angola, etc.) as well as by the brief Falklands/Malvinas War of 1982. In this context the classical bellicist tradition has experienced a partial revival in the sense that some of the most prominent ideas have been 'rediscovered' and utilised to explain long-term social changes. However, it is only in rare instances that this new scholarship made direct reference to the works of classical bellicists such as Mann's and Giddens' occasional invoking of Otto Hintze's contribution (Giddens, 1987: 26–9; Mann, 1988).

In most other cases this link is more indirect or not acknowledged at all. For example, Tilly's now famous quip that 'wars make states and states make wars', first developed in his 1985 essay 'War Making and State Making as Organised Crime', does not make any reference to the classical bellicist scholars. Yet many of his central ideas owe a great deal to the previous work of Hintze, Gumplowicz and Ratzenhofer. For instance, Tilly's notion that state formation was historically for the most part a coercive process whereby the character of warfare shaped the structure of the state was very much a leitmotiv of Ranzenhofer's and Gumplowicz's contributions. Furthermore Tilly's focus on the impact that inter-state wars have had in the pacification and eventual democratisation of European societies is directly echoed in Hintze's idea that modern-day parliamentary systems were in part a product of the military/political independence of medieval warriors whose assemblies established the seeds of nineteenth- and twentieth-century parliamentarism. Similarly Mann's emphasis on the role geo-politics plays in state formation as well as his emphasis on the strong historical link between the mass participation in war and the gradual extension of citizenship rights is firmly rooted in Hintze's analytical apparatus. Hintze's influence is also visible in Giddens' critique of historical materialism where Giddens, just as his barely acknowledged predecessor, identifies political power as an autonomous force that has historically proved to be a more important generator of social change than the social class.

Recent work by Joas (2003), Joas and Knöbl (2013) and Bowden (2013) reaffirms the arguments made by Gumplowicz, Ratzenhofer and Ward that civilisational advancements emerge on the backbone of previous wars. In this context, Ratzenhofer's distinction between the conquest state and the culture state finds its contemporary rehabilitation in the analyses of Bowden and Joas, who both challenge the traditional, Enlightenment-inspired view that civilisations emerge outside of violence. Hence, in contrast to this modernist dream they demonstrate that the emergence of advanced division of labour, complex modes of organisation, sophisticated technology, literacy and many other features of civilisation has largely developed as a by-product of the war machine. Not only have new technologies and organisational advancements been regularly pioneered in the military sphere, and then gradually incorporated for civilian use, but also war conquests have established the long-term stratification patterns which allowed the descendants of victorious warriors to monopolise certain professions and use their free time to generate artistic, scientific and other achievements.

In addition to these more macro-sociological contributions, the classical bellicists have also influenced some recent micro-sociological developments. For example, Gumplowicz's concept of syngenism and the centrality of group action have clear resonance in contemporary military sociology, which grapples with the issues of what motivates soldiers to fight in wars. Thus the ongoing debates largely clash over the role that small group solidarities play in this process. Although the leading representatives of this debate, Anthony King (2013) and Guy Siebold (2007), sharply disagree over the primary sources of military cohesion, they both indirectly draw on Gumplowicz's ideas. Hence, Siebold (2007) argues that the social cohesion on the battlefield is rooted in the peer bonding of the 'primary groups' whereby military action is dependent on the level of unit cohesion. In contrast King argues that high group motivation does not equate with high performance so social cohesion stems from 'the collective action itself, and specifically [from the] successful collective performance, not to sentiments which encourage that performance' (2013: 37). Nevertheless, despite these contrasting interpretations both Siebold and King share Gumplowicz's view that violent social action (i.e. military action) is rooted not in individuals but in groups and that such groups share a sense of cultural solidarity.

Criticisms

Much of the criticism of the bellicist tradition has centred on the normative implications of these theories. In particular, Gumplowicz and Ratzenhofer have been criticised for advocating militarist, naturalist and social Darwinist interpretations of social life. The critics have emphasised that any attempt to place violence and coercive domination at the heart of social relations glorifies militarism and is likely to lead towards fatalistic conclusions on the future of human relations (Hawkins, 1997). For example, Gumplowicz (1885: 229) was adamant that the historical moral progress of the human race is nothing but an illusion: 'lying and deceit, breach of confidence and betrayal, is on every page of ... [human] history ... no ethical law or moral obligation, only the fear of the stronger, holds them in check'. In this understanding morality and progress are no more than a fig leaf used to camouflage the institutional dominance of the stronger groups who often utilise the discourse of rights and justice to pursue their own self-interests.

The problem with these types of critiques is that they blend the normative and explanatory elements. For example, saying that these theories are immoral, fatalist or militant does not necessarily make them epistemologically unsound. By identifying the crucial role that violent action and coercion play in social life one does not automatically imply that this is morally right or historically inevitable. Hence, rather than focusing on the moral implications of these theories it is more productive to dissect their epistemological standing. In other words, whereas ethical critiques operate on the normative level and as such cannot undermine the explanatory foundations of these approaches, epistemological criticisms can challenge the very foundations of this position. In this context, labels such as militarist, social Darwinist or immoral are not particularly helpful as they shift attention from epistemology towards normative judgements.

The more pertinent critiques would single out the naturalist and essentialist models of social development that underpin this paradigm. Although they were nominally critical of the organicist imagery borrowed from biology, both Gumplowicz and Ratzenhofer shared the naturalist and essentialist conceptions of history. In particular, their group-centric view of social change does not leave much room for free will or the individual autonomy of agents. The two Austrian scholars, just like Ward and Small, were explicit in their rejection of the role that individual action plays in historical development. In this view groups have transformed throughout the course of human history, evolving from 'primitive hordes' to complex nation-states, but the substance of group action and motivation is perceived by bellicists to be rather stable and determined by incessant conflict over mutually exclusive collective interests.

This type of analysis, which leaves no room for individual motivations, ongoing tensions and intra-group conflict, cannot adequately explain how, when and why, some groups disintegrate while others maintain internal coherence over long periods of time. Moreover, this rather static view of groups cannot account for the changing dynamics of group cohesion whereby some individuals might be at one point willing to sacrifice themselves for their group, while at other times the same individuals might express complete indifference towards their groups. In this context, the bellicist perspective is prone to conflate the form of the group with the social action often carried out in the name of the group.

However, as Weber (1968) made clear a long time ago, one cannot assume that individuals who share the same group designation (i.e. Germans, whites, workers, Muslims, etc.) automatically engage in shared collective action. Rather, this process of turning multifaceted and different individuals into collective actors entails the presence of durable social organisations or social movements involved in prolonged group mobilisation. Hence, it is only under specific social and historical circumstances that the group action materialises as such, while in most cases individuals manage to evade such social cages. Furthermore, the bellicist tradition is a typical representative of what Rogers Brubaker (2002: 2) calls groupism – a 'tendency to take bounded groups as fundamental units of analysis (and basic constituents of the social world)'. This groupist fallacy is deeply problematic as it ignores that group membership is not a fixed state of existence but a dynamic and variable process. Instead of analysing historical change through the prism of overly stable groups it is epistemologically much more fruitful to explore the specific social organisations that utilise group categories, cultural idioms or discursive frames to mobilise individuals around specific political projects.

The bellicist paradigm is also criticised for its lack of engagement with the economic factors of social change. Otto Hintze's work in particular has been put under scrutiny for its overemphasis on the geopolitics and the autonomy of state power while downplaying the role that capitalism has played in the transformation of the modern world. For example, Immanuel Wallerstein (2011: xxii) criticises the neo-Hintzean theories of state which insist on separate spheres for economic and political power, arguing that 'economic and political variables reside in a single area ... political institutions were simply one institutional structure alongside others within the modern world system'. Although Wallerstein contends that the neo-Hintzeans were more guilty of this separation between the economic and the political sphere than Hintze himself, most economic and political sociologists are highly critical of what they see as Hintze's neglect of the class dynamics, stratification patterns and capitalism throughout the course of human history (Mann, 1986, 1988).

Finally, bellicist scholars have also been criticised for their epistemological insensitivity to culture. Although Hintze, Ward and Small have all written about the significance of religion and cultural values, the tendency is to understand these ideational factors as largely dependent on the political and military mechanisms. For example, in his influential essay on Calvinism Hintze (1975), he identifies the affinity between religious reform and the development of the modern state in Prussia, but rather than highlighting the importance of Calvinist ideas in this process, his focus is firmly on the role political factors have played where religion is more of a supplementary variable (Oestereich, 2008). The recent cultural turn has been highly critical of the overly materialist models of social action developed by the bellicists. Hence Gorski (2001, 2003), Smith (2008) and Alexander (2011) have all insisted that the historical direction of modern state formation would be unthinkable and impossible without the presence of ideational factors such as religion and culture. For example, Gorski (2003) argues that the rise of state power in early modern Europe owes less to the military and geopolitics and much more to the disciplinary revolution initiated by the Reformation and especially Calvinist ideas and practices.

Conclusion

The classical bellicist approaches have unjustifiably been ignored, marginalised and misinterpreted in contemporary sociological debates. In this chapter we have tried to show why some concepts and ideas developed by Hintze, Gumplowicz, Ratzenhofer, Ward and Small remain relevant for the study of social life. Although much of the post-Enlightenment social theory was, and remains, oblivious to the impact that war and violence have on social relations, as bellicists demonstrate, it is impossible to understand long-term historical change without proper analytical engagement with the role that coercive power plays in society. The classical bellicist tradition offers alternative heuristic tools that can help us understand the long-term dynamics of organised violence and especially how this historical dynamic continues to shape contemporary social life.

References

Aho, J. A. (1975) *German Realpolitik and American Sociology: An Inquiry into the Sources and Political Significance of the Sociology of Conflict*. London: Associated University Presses.

Alexander, J. (2011) *Performance and Power*. Cambridge: Polity.

Bentley, A. (1926) Simmel, Durkheim and Ratzenhofer. *American Journal of Sociology*, 32, pp. 250–6.

Bowden, B. (2013) *Civilization and War*. Cheltenham: Edward Elgar.

Brubaker, R. (2002) Ethnicity without groups. *European Journal of Sociology*, 43(2), pp. 163–89.

Confino, A. (1997) *The Nation as a Local Metaphor: Württemberg, Imperial Germany, and National Memory, 1871-1918*. Chapel Hill, NC: University of North Carolina Press.

Daum, A. (2016) Refugees from Nazi Germany as Historians: Origins and Migrations, Interests and Identities. In: Andreas Daum et al. (ed.) *The Second Generation: Émigrés from Nazi Germany as Historians*. Oxford: Berghahn Books, pp. 1–52.

Ertman, T. (2017) Otto Hintze, Stein Rokkan and Charles Tilly's Theory of European State-building. In: L. Kaspersen and J. Strandsbjerg (eds) *Does War Makes States?* Cambridge: Cambridge University Press, pp. 52-70.

Giddens, A. (1987) *The Nation-State and Violence*. Cambridge: Polity.

Gorski, P. (2001) Beyond Marx and Hintze: The Third-Wave Theories of Early State Formation. *Comparative Studies in Society and History*, 43(4), pp. 851–61.

Gorski, P. (2003) *The Disciplinary Revolution: Calvinism and the Rise of the State in Early Modern Europe*. Chicago, IL: University of Chicago Press.

Gumplowicz, L. (1885) *Grundriss der Soziologie*. Vienna: Manz.

Gumplowicz, L. (2007 [1883]) *Der Rassenkampf: Soziologische Untersuchungen*. Saarbrücken: VDM Verlag.

Hall, J. A. (1985) *Powers and Liberties: The Causes and Consequences of the Rise of the West*. Oxford: Basil Blackwell.

Hall, J. A. (ed.) (1986) *States in History*. Oxford: Basil Blackwell.

Hawkins, M. (1997) *Social Darwinism in European and American Thought, 1860-1945*. Cambridge: Cambridge University Press.

Hintze, O. (1975) *The Historical Essays of Otto Hintze*. F. Gilber (ed.) New York: Oxford University Press.

Joas, H. (2003) *War and Modernity*. Cambridge: Polity.

Joas, H. and Knöbl, W. (2013) *War in Social Thought: Hobbes to the Present*. Princeton, NJ: Princeton University Press.

King, A. (2013) *The Combat Soldier: Infantry Tactics and Cohesion in the Twentieth and Twenty-First Centuries*. Oxford: Oxford University Press.

Konieczny, M. (2015) Ludwig Gumplowicz (1838-1909). In: A. Smith et al. (eds) *The Wiley Blackwell Encyclopedia of Race, Ethnicity, and Nationalism*. London: Wiley Blackwell, available online at: https://onlinelibrary.wiley.com/doi/abs/10.1002/9781118663202.wberen065.

Malešević, S. (2010) *The Sociology of War and Violence*. Cambridge: Cambridge University Press.

Mann, M. (1986) *The Sources of Social Power: A History of Power from the Beginning to A.D. 1760*. Cambridge: Cambridge University Press.

Mann, M. (1988) *States, War and Capitalism*. Oxford: Blackwell.

Oestreich, G. (2008) *Neostoicism and the Early Modern State*. Cambridge: Cambridge University Press.

Pocar, V. (2007) Ludwig Gumplowicz. In: S. D. D. Clark (ed.) *Encyclopedia of Law & Society: American and Global Perspectives*. London: Sage, available online at: http://sk.sagepub.com/reference/law/n294.xml.

Ratzenhofer, G. (1904) The Problems of Sociology. *American Journal of Sociology*, 10, pp. 177–88.

Rees, J. (2013) *Industrialization and the Transformation of American Life: A Brief Introduction*. Armonk, NY: M. E. Sharpe.

Shaw, M. (1988) *Dialectics of War: An Essay on the Social Theory of War and Peace*. London: Pluto Press.

Siebold, G. (2007) The Essence of Military Group Cohesion. *Armed Forces & Society*, 33(2): 286–95.

Small, A. (1905) *General Sociology: An Exposition of the Main Development in Sociological Theory from Spencer to Ratzenhofer*. Chicago, IL: University of Chicago Press.

Smith, P. (2008) *Punishment and Culture*. Chicago, IL: Chicago University Press.

Stark, W. (2013 [1962]) *The Fundamental Forms of Social Thought*. London: Routledge.

Tilly, C. (1985) War Making and State Making as Organized Crime. In: P. B. Evans, D. Rueschemeyer and T. Skocpol (eds) *Bringing the State Back In*. Cambridge: Cambridge University Press, pp. 169–87.

United States Census Bureau (1976) *Statistical Abstract of the United States: 1976* [online]. Available at: https://www.census.gov/library/publications/1976/compendia/statab/97ed.html (Accessed 10 January 2020).

Wallerstein, I. (2011) *The Modern World-System I: Capitalist Agriculture and the Origins of the European World-Economy in the Sixteenth Century*. Berkeley, CA: University of California Press.

Ward, L. F. (1907) Social and Biological Struggles. *American Journal of Sociology*, 12(3), pp. 289–99.

Ward, L. F. (1908) Social Classes in the Light of Modern Sociological Theory. *American Journal of Sociology*, 13, pp. 617–27. Available at: https://archive.org/details/jstor-2762575 (Accessed 10 January 2020).

Ward, L. F. (1914) *Pure Sociology*. London: Macmillan.

Ward, L. F. (1918) *Glimpses of the Cosmos, Volume VI: Period, 1897–1912. Age, 56–70*. New York: G. P. Putnam's Sons.

Weber, M. (1968) *Economy and Society: An Outline of Interpretative Sociology*. New York: Bedminster Press.

XI

DU BOIS

W. E. B. Du Bois was a founding figure in American sociology (Gabbidon, 1999; Green and Wortham, 2015; Morris, 2015) and has been described as the 'first sociologist of race' (Lewis, 2000: 550). Living to the age of 95, he was a prolific writer who published numerous books now collected in a 37-volume edition of his *Collected Works*. Although an advocate of sociology as a science, he combined this with a moral passion and political activism geared towards the ethno-racial, and later class, emancipation of African Americans. Adept and open to using a variety of social research tools, he was a pioneer in the development of sociological research methods.

Du Bois is also regarded as a major historian and literary figure, and his writings often move between these various fields, best illustrated in his most well-known work, *The Souls of Black Folk* (2007b [1903]). Though his contribution to sociology is often ignored, partly as a result of the endemic racism extant during his lifetime and immediately after, including within sociology, he was an influence on the urban ecological approach of the Chicago School of sociology, presaging their work by decades (Green and Wortham, 2017). He was also, later, taken up as a founding figure in the development of African American Studies and Whiteness studies.

Life and Intellectual Context

William Edward Burghardt Du Bois was born in Great Barrington, Massachusetts, on 23 February 1868. His father, Alfred Du Bois, a 'white mulatto' (of mixed race) was a barber with French–Haitian origins and died young, while his mother, Mary Silvina Burghardt, worked as a domestic. For the most part, she raised him, exercising a strong influence on his personality. Du Bois grew up in a small community of about 5,000 people of whom only between 25 and 50 were black. In his early upbringing class played as prominent a role as race. Though conscious of skin colour, he also grew up in a context where merit was important. A precocious child, in a class of 12 he was the only

African American to go to college. Following a short stint as a correspondent at the *Springfield Republican*, he acquired a scholarship and went onto receive an undergraduate degree in 1888 from Fisk University, a segregated university, located in Nashville, Tennessee. In marked contrast to his upbringing, Nashville was marked by deep racial discrimination and bigotry.

He then moved to Harvard where he undertook a further degree in philosophy, an MA in political science and then a PhD in history with a dissertation titled *The Suppression of the African Slave Trade to the United States of America* (2007a [1896]). Du Bois became the first black person to graduate with a doctorate from Harvard. During his time there he spent two years abroad from 1892 to 1894, at the University of Berlin, studying history and economics. Here he came into contact with and sat in the lectures of amongst others: Gustav Schmoller, George Simmel, Heinrich von Treitschke, Adolf Wagner and Max Weber. In Germany he learned quantitative methods and statistics, something foreign to American sociology at the time. He also attended meetings of the Social Democratic Party, the leading party of the left. Having visited at a time when Germany was relatively liberal, tolerant and open, Du Bois experienced something of a personal liberation with regard to experiencing less racism and being judged instead, on meritocratic grounds. After his return to the US, a lack of career opportunities and antipathy towards African Americans meant that he found it difficult to secure a teaching post at any major American university. Nevertheless, he found a job at Wilberforce University, in Ohio, where he taught classics. As well as marrying Nina Gomer in 1896, he published his doctoral thesis as a book. The success of the book helped him secure a new position at the University of Pennsylvania as an assistant instructor in sociology.

The Move to Atlanta

At Pennysylvania Du Bois undertook empirical research on the black population living in Philadelphia. He then moved to Atlanta University, a black university at the time, where he established a new research centre – the Atlanta Sociological Laboratory. Focusing on the socio-economic conditions of the black population, the research centre challenged everyday interpretations of the racial dynamics of inequality. Between 1896 and 1913 Du Bois edited and co-edited 17 volumes from the Annual Conferences for the Study of Negro Problems. To critical acclaim he also published *The Philadelphia Negro* (1899), the first major in-depth study of black life in an American city. It followed in the wake of empirically focused research-based studies by other writers on the living conditions of the poor by Charles Booth and the progressive work of Beatrice Webb and Jane Addams. Du Bois also travelled to the South to undertake a study of Farmville, part of Virginia's rural black community, which he published as 'Negroes of Farmville, Virginia: A Social Study' (1898) and which has been described as the first empirical study of rural sociology in the United States (Morris, 2015: 49).

He followed this with *The Black North in 1901: A Social Study* (1969 [1901]). Two years later he published arguably his best-known work, *The Souls of Black Folk* (1903), as well as writing one of the first major studies on religion *The Negro Church* (1903). Increasingly recognised, Du Bois received offers of a teaching post at Tuskegee Institute in Alabama from Booker T. Washington, which he rejected on political grounds. During this time he became progressively engaged in arguing for racial equality and acting as a central political organiser of the Niagara movement in 1905. The latter contained the country's leading black intellectual figures whom he dubbed the 'Talented Tenth' brought together to advocate political change, challenge racism and fight for greater rights for blacks. In 1908 he published a biography of the abolitionist, John Brown. Two years later he left Atlanta, and together with a number of progressive whites became part of the newly established National Association for the Advancement of Coloured People (NAACP). Here he served as a writer, polemicist, activist and critic, as well as editor of their in-house journal, *Crisis*. Du Bois's political stance led him into both a political and personal conflict with Marcus Garvey and the latter's Universal Negro Improvement Association. The following year he published his first novel, *The Quest of the Silver Fleece* (2007b [1911]).

While at the NAACP he continued to highlight US failure to recognise the contribution of black soldiers to the Great War, as well as their dire treatment. He also began to systematically challenge all forms of colonialism and imperialism, especially those in Africa. This led to the foundation of a Pan-African movement which met for the first time in Paris in 1919. As well as further historical studies including *The Negro* (2007d [1915]), his literary and artistic essays collected in *Darkwater* (2007e [1920]) played a central role in the cultural Harlem Renaissance.

In the early 1930s Du Bois began to develop stronger attachments to socialism and Marxism, leading to his departure from the NAACP in 1934. His new radical political position was expressed in *Black Reconstruction in America* (1992 [1935)]. Now back at Atlanta University, he also founded another scholarly journal, *Phylon*, and attempted to acquire funding for a massive academic project, *The Encyclopedia of the Negro*. After returning to the NAACP in 1944, he left again, following his support for Henry Wallace instead of the NAACP's preferred candidate. As well as joining Paul Robeson's Council of African Affairs, he became increasingly involved both with the Soviet Union and the International Peace movement. At the age of 83, because of his radical politics and Soviet affiliation, he was imprisoned and unsuccessfully tried by the Justice Department for acting as a foreign agent – recounted in his book *In Battle for Peace: The Story of My 83rd Birthday* (1976 [1952]). After his passport was returned in 1958 he travelled across both the Soviet Union and China where he successfully prompted Khrushchev to create an Institute of African Studies in the Academy of Sciences, and where he secured the Lenin prize in 1959. In 1961 he joined the American Communist Party.

Unhappy in the United States he renounced his American citizenship and moved to Ghana where he was on friendly terms with the new President Kwame Nkrumah, and where he began work on the *Encyclopedia Africana*. He died in Ghana on 27 August 1963 at the age of 95, and was buried in Accra.

Intellectual Influences

There were three major sources of intellectual influence on Du Bois's work in addition to Marxism: one deriving from Harvard, the other Chicago and the last from his time at Berlin. At Harvard, Du Bois came into contact with some of the leading American philosophers at the time. Here he studied with, among others, William James, learning pragmatism; Josiah Royce, learning Hegel; Georges Santayana, learning German idealism; and the historian Alfred Bushnell Hart, learning historical methods. In addition, the pioneering work of Jane Addams, especially her applied sociological work on living conditions in Hull House, and its reformist agenda, influenced Du Bois's early sociological work. According to Deegan (1988: 13) Addams was 'a close friend and colleague' of Du Bois and 'together they formed a sociological network'.

Although he may have attended Simmel's lectures while in Germany the work of Gustave Schmoller's German Historical School of Economics also played a major role in his intellectual development. The School focused on political economy, culture, institutions and values, as well as undertaking concrete empirical investigations based on inductive reasoning rather than abstract deductive thinking. This formed the basis for developing social policy prescriptions.

Historical, Social and Political Context

Slavery as an Institution

Du Bois's sociology was profoundly shaped by the 'peculiar' institution of slavery as it unfolded within the United States. With origins in the European and Atlantic slave trade and British colonisation of the United States, slavery became a central institution not only as Eric Williams argues for 'providing the capital which financed the Industrial Revolution in England' (1944: vii) but also for defining US history from at least the seventeenth century onwards. The number of slaves estimated to have been imported into the United States ranges from 10 to 20 million. Although it peaked in 1860 when approximately 34% of the entire population of the Southern United States was slaves (Potts, 1990: 39). By the time of the American Revolution every English colony in both the North and the South from Virginia to Massachusetts had slaves.

Blacks were deemed biologically and intellectually inferior as a race and seen as suited only to menial work. In his infamous 'mudhill' speech delivered to the US Senate in 1858, James Henry Hammond, a former South Carolina governor, reflected such an entrenched slave-owning ideology:

> In all social systems there must be a class to do the menial duties, to perform the drudgery of life. That is, a class requiring but a low order of intellect and but little skill... Its requisites are vigor, docility, fidelity. Such a class you must have, or you would not have that other class which leads progress, civilization, and refinement... Fortunately for the South, she found a race adapted to that purpose to her hand. A race inferior to her own, but eminently qualified in temper, in vigor, in docility, in capacity to stand the climate, to answer all her purposes. We use them for our purpose... and call them slaves. (Cited in Williams, 2014: 103)

Within a context of capitalist and colonial expansion, race became a dominant and defining frame through which to understand African American culture and life. Common-sense understandings of race were reinforced and refracted through powerful pseudo-scientific understandings that divided the world's populations into different races on the basis of phenotypical or somatic differences (Banton and Harwood, 1975). Race, it was argued, not only determined the cultural characteristics and intellectual capacities of different racialised populations, but was always hierarchically ordered with white Europeans at the apex.

According to Patterson, the slave was a non-person with no rights; this natal alienation where the slave was socially isolated from his or her heritage, and the generalised dishonour which characterised his or her condition, meant that slaves were 'socially non-persons' (1982: 5); that is, socially dead. Nevertheless, not only did the relationship between slave owner and slave vary greatly, but slavery as an institution was not found or supported everywhere. Economically, the North of the United States was generally characterised by industry while the South remained, for the most part, dominated by agriculture and farming. Although predominantly a Southern institution, even here slave distribution was not uniform with only about a third of the 8 million Southern whites owning slaves in 1860 (Remini, 2009: 132). For Northern industrial capitalists much of the cheap labour they needed was provided by a highly diverse range of European immigrants, though they also employed black workers who had migrated to the North to escape slavery. By contrast, slaves were necessary to maintain the socio-economic position of Southern plantation capitalists as a ruling aristocracy, accruing huge profits for them. In the South slaves worked in many plantations, including in strictly monitored gangs in tobacco plantations in Virginia, Maryland and North Carolina; under task systems in rice plantations in South Carolina and Georgia; in sugar plantations in Louisiana; hemp plantations in Kentucky; but most importantly in cotton production, in both North and South Carolina, Tennessee, Arkansas, Georgia, Texas and Mississippi.

Moreover, across the United States slaves were for the most part perceived by white workers as not only undermining white workers' wages but also lowering the status of the jobs they shared. White workers therefore held ambivalent attitudes towards the conferral of greater citizenship rights to blacks: on the one hand blacks would compete on an equal footing meaning white workers would lose the sense of privilege they had, yet conferring rights would also remove the ability of black workers to undercut them. Consequently, as Du Bois charts in his book *Black Reconstruction in America 1860–1880*, the working class remained divided and incapable of uniting to further its common interests against the capitalist class. Given these uneven power relations between blacks – slaves and free men – and whites, tensions, conflict, struggle and resistance were endemic in their relations.

The American Civil War

Conflicts between pro-slavery and abolitionist groups were especially evident in the political sphere. The secession of a number of Southern states from the United States in order to create the Confederate States of America led in 1861 to the American Civil War (1861–5). By 1863, slavery had become the dominant issue in American politics and Lincoln passed his Preliminary Emancipation Proclamation in 1863, declaring that all the slaves in the rebellious Confederate areas, would be freed. In the context of a sharp conflict over power and administration between the President and Congress more radical Republican forces in Congress, led by Thaddeus Stevens, pushed for more radical legislation including the Wade–Davis manifesto, allowing Congress to deal with rebellious Confederates. The devastation wrought by the Civil War – up to 3% of the population had died during the war (359,528 for the Union and 258,000 for the Confederates) – was followed by a period of 'Reconstruction' (1863–77). The latter referred to the revolutionary period of post-war rebuilding led initially by President Lincoln and, after his assassination, Andrew Johnson. It was a period marked by economic collapse, widespread disease and poverty. It also marked the end of the era of slavery and meant that some 4,000 slaves were set free. Du Bois referred to the period as 'the Second Civil War'.

During this period, not only did the question of who would dictate reconstruction – the President or Congress – emerge, but also important issues concerning who was a citizen and the relation between political and economic democracy were raised. Using the military to enforce rights given to blacks, Congress also set up the Freedman's Bureau, which aimed to smooth the transition from slavery to freedom by providing shelter and medical services to emancipated slaves as well as poor whites, as well as setting up schools and hospitals. Former slaves played a central role in reconstruction. African Americans entered into government for the first time, with approximately 2,000 holding office. However, bribery and corruption also followed from increasing economic intervention by the government.

The onset of a steep depression in 1873 saw a major run on a number of banks, the folding of thousands of businesses and the collapse of the Freedman's Savings and Trust in 1874. This effectively ended the period of reconstruction (Lemert, 2000: 230–1). Its end was politically sealed with the coming into power of Rutherford B. Hayes and the withdrawal of federal troops from the South. As Lemert notes:

> Freed men and women in the South were thrown back to feudal conditions made more severe by the crippling effects of war on an agrarian system that had lost its most valuable commodity—enslaved labor. The white South was itself divided between the poor whites who were forced to compete with freedmen in an unstable labor market and the propertied class that rose from the ashes to reassert its domination. (2000: 231)

The Rise of Jim Crow

Shortly after, Southern states began to re-implement racial segregation through Jim Crow (a pejorative term meaning negro) laws passed initially in Tennessee in 1881. Antecedent steep power relations between blacks and whites were partially restored as blacks once again experienced economic and human misery in the South. By 1892 the number of lynchings of blacks reached their highest ever figure with 235 taking place. Other states followed the Jim Crow legislation by extending a 'separate but equal' policy to all public facilities from educational institutions and workplaces to drinking fountains, a practice upheld by the Supreme Court in the case of *Plessy* v. *Ferguson*. Officially sanctioned discrimination meant that economic, social and political disadvantage reinforced interpersonal racism and white domination. Increasing electoral restrictions based on a poll tax, birth and literacy tests disenfranchised many African Americans, so that as a consequence, fewer blacks could vote. Lack of funding for black public schools and disenfranchisement also meant constrained access to juries and political office. White supremacy in the cotton belt led to many blacks migrating to the North: between 1910 and 1940 about 1.5 million migrated to cities such as New York, Chicago and Boston.

Conflicts over Political Strategy

Following Reconstruction, along with a number of African American politicians, there emerged a number of intellectuals and spokespersons calling for rights and privileges to be given to blacks within an established democracy. These included Kelly-Miller, Wells-Brown and most importantly Frederick Douglas, who Du Bois referred to as 'the greatest of American Negro leaders' (2007: 38). But it also incorporated less radical, reform-orientated black intellectuals, including Booker T. Washington, who founded the Tuskegee

Normal and Industrial Institute in Alabama in 1881, later renamed Tuskegee University Development for Black Social and Intellectual Advancement. The latter's curriculum reflected Washington's conciliatory political philosophy that blacks should accept social segregation and disenfranchisement as long as they were afforded access to education, the courts and economic opportunity. As an adviser to various presidents including Roosevelt and Taft, Washington became the leading national spokesperson for African Americans. Sometimes referred to as the 'Great Accommodator' his acceptance of white domination and surrender of demands for civic and political equality to appease politicians in the South and North, deeply angered a more radically oriented Du Bois: 'Mr Washington represents in Negro thought the old attitude of adjustment and submission' (2007: n. 38). Washington's insistence on African Americans giving up political power, civil rights and the higher education of black youth led to or facilitated the disenfranchisement of blacks, the creation of a distinct and inferior civic status, and the withdrawal of aid from institutions of higher education. Du Bois's alternative political position involved developing the 'Talented Tenth', a black professional class containing teachers, lawyers, doctors, engineers and intellectuals. As he noted:

> The Negro race, like all races, is going to be saved by its exceptional men. The problem of education, then among Negroes must first of all deal with the Talented Tenth; it is the problem of developing the Best of this race that may guide the Mass away from the contamination and death of the Worst, in their own and other races... Intelligence, broad sympathy, knowledge of the world that was and is, and the relation of men to it—this is the curriculum of that Higher Education which must underlie true life. (2007: 189)

Through political organisation, historical and polemical writing, and moral regeneration, the exceptional aristocracy of the Talented Tenth would seek to uplift the condition of African Americans. In later work, Du Bois renounced this elitist vanguardism, recognising that the Talented Tenth may not represent the interests of all blacks but only their own (the Talented Tenth Memorial Address 1948 in Gates and West, 1996: 162). During the period from the mid-1930s onwards, DuBois's work became increasingly Marxist. In his book *In Battle for Peace* (1952) DuBois argued that all strategies aimed at curtailing American capitalism were to be accepted, including those from the Soviet Union, no matter how morally questionable they appeared. But his Marxist, class-focused work was also pervaded by a radical pan-Africanism and stern critique of colonialism combining issues of race and class in a complex theoretical framework.

Ideas and Arguments

Du Bois conceived his general sociological approach in what prima facie appears to be a quasi-positivistic manner, as a science akin to the physical and natural sciences which inductively collected facts. Like them, sociology was an empirical science but, unlike them, it sought to study human actions or the regularities expressed in the 'the deeds of men'. Though seeking laws, the scope of sociology also differed from the natural sciences:

> Sociology is ... the name given to the vast field of inquiry into human action as manifested in modern organized life. It cannot study all human action under all circumstances, but that human action which by its regularity gives evidence of the presence of laws. What these laws are we hardly know, and yet we do know that there are in life curious and noticeable coincidences—rhythm in life and death, a working out of cause and effect, evidence of force, action and reaction, which cannot be ignored or neglected. (Du Bois, 1897: 3)

Sociology's focus was on human action, interaction and the structure of social relations in order to reveal the laws underpinning acts. This was in opposition both to philosophical and sociological approaches such as those of August Comte and Herbert Spencer, which examined abstract or metaphysical entities such as 'society', 'imitation' or 'consciousness of kind'. As Du Bois noted in his essay 'Sociology Hesitant' (2000 [1905]), such abstract theorising was unsound and led sociology in the wrong direction, away from grounded empirical research. Abstract theorising constituted a form of 'car-window sociology', an ungrounded approach that did not participate or engage ethnographically in the subject it was investigating. The balance between laws and regularities in human behaviour, and chance and freewill, also remained a central concern in his work: 'Sociology is the science that seeks to measure the limits of chance in human action, or if you will excuse the paradox, it is the science of free will' (1978 [1904]: 53). Part of the focus on action, as well as structure or environment, entailed an examination of how certain groups are unable to realise their group goals or ideals. The attempt to realise interests resulted in social problems emerging: 'a social problem is ever a relation between conditions and action, and as conditions and actions vary and change from group to group from time to time and from place to place, so social problems change, develop and grow' (1898, as cited in Green and Wortham, 2017: 63).

The predominant focus for much of Du Bois's sociology was 'the negro problem'. He sought to challenge the dominant way of thinking about blacks in both the everyday and academic world. Racial inequality and racism were not a biological given, an outcome of the inherent differences between superior and inferior races, but the outcome of social and historical processes. Racial domination could be understood scientifically through the precise measurement of empirical data.

The Philadelphia Negro

The concern with ethno-racial inequality is evident in his first major work, *The Philadelphia Negro* (1967 [1899]), arguably the first major sociological study of *urban* African American living conditions in the United States. Written in the context of a virulent post-Civil-War racism directed against African Americans often justified through social Darwinism, the book sought to develop conceptual themes addressed in his earlier study, 'The Negroes of Farmville, Virginia: A Social Study'. Drawing on the model of Charles Booth's *Life and Labour of the People in London* (1902) and Jane Addams' *Hull House* (1895), Du Bois combines comparative historical analysis with penetrating observation to understand the 'Negro's problem'; that is, to reveal the 'truth' of the situation facing blacks. By contrast to the earlier community studies of poverty by Booth and Addams, however, Du Bois employs a thoroughly novel and innovative sociological research methodology allowing for triangulation, combining thousands of surveys and interviews, participant observation, archival and census data, statistical analysis and ethnographic description. The data was also presented in heretofore little-used charts and diagrams to highlight the effect of race and racism on the black population, and to reveal geo-spatial processes of segregation.

Focusing on the seventh ward in Philadelphia, where the vast majority of blacks lived, the book covers four major themes: the history of blacks in the city from 1638 to 1896; their current socio-economic conditions as individuals; their condition as an organised social group; and their physical and social environment. The historical discussion is in some ways also the most important. Unlike other social analysts, Du Bois concentrates on the profound effects of slavery in shaping subsequent African American consciousness and action, despite the *de jure* freedom they had achieved after the Civil War, and in the face of the continuing prejudice against them. Demographically the majority of blacks possessed low education levels while most of the population lived either alone or in small families, characterised by relatively high mortality rates and low property-owning levels standing at 8%. Large numbers lived in slums, or segregated, overcrowded housing. These negative social attributes were compounded by a marginalised position in the labour market and relatively high crime levels. According to Du Bois, the social position of blacks in the last decade of the nineteenth century had become worse than it was in the first decade. Rather than using hereditary racial factors to account for these abject conditions DuBois looks to social, class, cultural and environmental factors, and especially ethno-racial discrimination as a causal factor. By pointing to environmental and ecological factors, Du Bois explains African American social conditions as an effect of political conditions that could be altered rather than as a given through hereditary racial traits. According to Du Bois, racial power and ideology trapped blacks in a vicious cycle of domination yet their social afflictions – crime, alcoholism, pauperism, poverty, idleness and slum living – could be alleviated through political action.

Importantly, Du Bois understood blacks in his study not as a homogeneous grouping but as stratified by class and status distinctions. Racial inequality and domination were both shaped by and intersected with class inequality, and blacks needed to be judged not in terms of the poorest groupings, but of their most successful:

> every group has its upper class; it may be numerically small and socially of little weight, and yet its study is necessary to the comprehension of the whole – it forms the realized ideal of the group, and as it is true that a nation must to some extent be measured by its slums, it is also true that it can only be understood and finally judged by its upper class. (1967 [1899]: 7)

The intersection of race and class provided racialised class formations. Du Bois identifies four class divisions within the African American population, which he places in an economic and moral hierarchy. The Negro aristocracy or talented few families with good living and high income; the respectable working class 'with a steady income and children in school'; the black poor; and the lowest class containing 'criminals, prostitutes and loafers'. Despite their privileged condition, well-off middle-class blacks had done little to help those less well-off, such as providing them with employment or moral guidance, which Du Bois believed was their duty (and which would become the basis for his thesis of developing the 'Talented Tenth'):

> Not only do blacks face intense competition from European immigrants and whites in the labour market, but their marginalization is exacerbated by a mix of their slave backgrounds, poor training, dispositions, educational backgrounds, morality, and their own poor choices which make the transition to the capitalist work ethos difficult.
>
> The competition in a large city is fierce, and it is difficult for any poor people to succeed. The Negro, however, has two especial difficulties: his training as a slave and freedman has not been such as make the average of the race as efficient and reliable workmen as the average native American or as many foreign immigrants. The Negro is, as a rule, willing, honest and good-natured; but he is also, as a rule, careless, unreliable and unsteady. This is without doubt to be expected in a people who for generations have been trained to shirk work; but an historical excuse counts for little in the whirl and battle of breadwinning. (1967 [1899]: 97–8)

These socially inherited characteristics are compounded by 'prejudice of whites' in the labour market: 'by a widespread inclination to shut against them many doors of advancement open to the talented and efficient of other races' (1967 [1899]: 98). It was this discrimination, together with their lack of education, that filtered them into certain occupations in the labour market as labourers, servants or allied personal services including shoeshine, waiters, porters or, for women, domestics and dressmakers. As he noted: 'A Negro woman has but three careers open to her in this city: domestic service, sewing, or married life' (1967 [1899]: 323).

The Negro Problem and *The Souls of Black Folk*

The issue of 'the negro problem' does not remain static in Du Bois's work but undergoes continual development including in *The Souls of Black Folk, Darkwater* and *the Gift of Black Folk*. It is, however, concisely stated in his essay 'The Conservation of Races' ([1897). In the essay, Du Bois argues that race should not be understood singularly through a biological or hereditary lens, so that physical characteristics determine cultural characteristics that can be hierarchically ranked, but instead through a social and historical lens. Though races can be understood in terms of 'common blood', race 'is a vast family of human beings, generally of common blood and language, always of common history, traditions and impulses, who are both voluntarily and involuntarily striving together for the accomplishment of certain more or less vividly conceived ideals of life' (1897: 7). For Du Bois, there exist several races in the world which cannot be ranked but all of which bring their contribution to humanity as a whole:

> they are the Slavs of eastern Europe, the Teutons of middle Europe, the English of Great Britain and America, the Romance nations of Southern and Western Europe, the Negroes of Africa and America, the Semitic people of Western Asia and Northern Africa, the Hindoos of Central Asia and the Mongolians of Eastern Asia. (1897: 8)

Many of these racial groupings had 'intermingled', producing an even greater diversity of races. Groping in an early way to look beyond biological reductionism in a context where social constructionist language was not available, Du Bois emphasises that 'the physical ... differences between men do not explain the differences of their history' (1897: 6–7).

Du Bois continues his discussion concerning 'the Negro problem' as well as black identity, spirituality and self-consciousness in *The Souls of Black Folk* (2007b [1903]). In the time since the publication of *The Philadelphia Negro*, however, both his tone and writing style changed, especially with a move away from the relatively detached sociological and scholarly stance to a more subjective, mitted, allusive and poetical style. The shift in Du Bois's perspective away from the more detached social science stance, he argues, followed the lynching of an agricultural worker, Sam Hose, by approximately 2,000 Southern whites who tortured, burnt and dismembered his body. This, he later noted, challenged his faith in rational knowledge as a foil against ignorance:

> Two considerations thereafter broke in upon my work and eventually disrupted it: first, one could not be a calm, cool and detached scientist while Negroes were lynched, murdered and starved; and secondly, there was no such definite demand for scientific work of the sort that I was doing, as I had confidently assumed would be easily forthcoming. (1984 [1940]: 603)

The book, a transdisciplinary undertaking – part autobiographical, part historical, part sociological, part literary – introduces a series of important concepts including 'the veil', 'the colour line', 'double consciousness' and 'second sight' (Rabaka, 2010: 133). Written at the very beginning of the twentieth century, it opens with his famous prophecy concerning what he calls the problem of the *colour line*:

> Herein lie buried many things which if read with patience may show the strange meaning of being black in the dawning of the Twentieth Century. This meaning is not without interest to you, Gentle Reader; for the problem of the Twentieth Century is the problem of the colour line'. (Du Bois, 2007b [1903]: 3)

The colour line refers not only to the entrenched racial segregation marking the United States, but more broadly, and reflecting the development of a more international and anti-imperialist perspective in his work, to 'the relation of the darker to the lighter races of men in Asia and Africa, in America and the islands of the sea' (Du Bois, 2007b: 15). Yet at the national level, the issue of post-slavery and post-Civil-War racism preventing black equality pervades the book. This is discussed not only through the notion of a colour line, but also through the metaphor of a veil, between the stigmatised and disempowered world of blacks, and the taken for granted and empowered world of whites. The veil implies that both whites and blacks see and perceive the world differently given their different experiences in interaction. Whites, for example, are blinded to the agency and humanity of blacks as human beings, distorting their interactions and communication. Not only does the colour line prevent black access to material equality in terms of jobs, housing, education, etc., but it also has a deleterious impact on their consciousness, it disfigures their inner being, their soul and their potential for self-realisation as self-conscious, sentient, human beings. Moreover, the power difference between the two groups results in blacks seeing themselves negatively through the discriminatory eyes of socially empowered whites, therefore preventing them from acquiring a true self-consciousness. This leads them to develop a divided, fractured personality or double form of consciousness:

> After the Egyptian and Indian, the Greek and the Roman, the Teuton and Mongolian, the Negro is a sort of seventh son, born with a veil,

> and gifted with second sight in this American world—a world which yields him no true self-consciousness, but only lets him see himself through the revelation of the other world. It is a peculiar sensation, this double-consciousness, this sense of always looking at one's self through the eyes of others, of measuring one's soul by the tape of a world that looks on in amused contempt and pity. One ever feels his two-ness—an American, a negro; two souls, two thoughts, two unreconciled strivings; two warring ideals in one dark body, whose dogged strength alone keeps it from being torn asunder. (Du Bois, 2007b: 8)
>
> [Republished with permission of Oxford University Press, from *The Souls of Black Folk,* W.E.B. Du Bois, 2007 [1903]. Reproduced with permission of The Licensor through PLSclear]

Du Bois hopes that Black Americans will ultimately resolve this schizophrenic experience, this painful dualism that pervades their consciousness towards a 'truer' reconciled self through the social transformation of an endemically racist society. This is partially predicated on their ability of becoming conscious of their predicament through an intuitive ability of 'second sight'. That is, the ability to see the world as it truly is, and recognise their distinct history and culture, including their African roots. It also requires whites – referred to as the 'Gentle Reader' – lifting their veil and recognising blacks as equals, their distinct yet valuable culture and history, and becoming conscious of the damaging effects of white privilege.

Black Reconstruction in America, 1860–1880

Written in 1935, *Black Reconstruction in America, 1860–1880* (1992) registers a marked shift in Du Bois's perspective towards Marxism. In writing the book he sets out to challenge white supremacist historians in the Dunning School of history – including William Archibald Dunning, John W. Burgess and Claude G. Bowers – who portrayed the period of Reconstruction in which blacks came to take positions of political power, as one of pervasive corruption and misgovernment resulting from the inherent docility and ignorance of blacks.

Writing during the peak of the Great Depression, Du Bois draws on an unorthodox version of Marxism to help him achieve a number of profoundly novel goals in the book. Again demonstrating a marked originality for the time, the book not only includes the voices of radical white abolitionists, various generals and politicians, but most importantly, also blacks themselves as active agents in making history – what later became termed as 'history from below'. Affirming the agency of blacks – usually marginalised in academic accounts – Du Bois recognises their central role in shaping the period of Reconstruction, deciding the outcome of the American Civil War, influencing the shape of American democracy, and structuring the subsequent development of American capitalism.

Blacks, he argued, were not docile and ignorant slaves, but an active and revolutionary proletariat. Slaves were workers, active human agents who struggled with their masters over their legal and social status, and the Civil War provided them with a rationale to escape by taking up arms, withdrawing their labour, undertaking industrial sabotage, or participating in slave revolts. Blacks freed themselves by fighting as soldiers, but just as importantly by running away from plantations where they were crucial to the functioning of a war economy. It was only the labour on plantations that allowed Southern whites to fight while necessary goods and services were produced. The withdrawal of labour formed part of what Du Bois referred to as a 'general strike', crippling the South's war effort. It was this that eventually allowed the North's victory. Consequently, it was slaves that freed themselves during the Civil War and not, as commonly assumed, the converse. With the exception of some abolition democrats, the North had no intrinsic interest in freeing slaves and instead sought to maintain the Union for the purposes of increased growth and profits.

Du Bois expands both the spatial and temporal framework within which the era of Reconstruction is ordinarily understood by including within it the history of slavery. Slavery and the position of the black worker were the underlying cause of the war. Slavery was central not just for understanding the socio-economic development of the South but also of capitalism in the North and Europe more generally. The production of tobacco, rice and, most importantly, cotton, were central to the maintenance of global capitalism. In addition to exploitation, black workers also faced racism while embedded within highly elaborate international production chains. The 'new economic system of the nineteenth century' entailed national and international class and capitalist relations, processes of imperialism and the exploitation of the 'dark proletariat' through surplus value 'filched from human beasts':

> That dark and vast sea of human labor in China and India, the South Seas and all Africa; in the West Indies and Central America and in the United States—that great majority of mankind, on whose bent and broken backs rest today the founding stones of modern industry—shares a common destiny; it is despised and rejected by race and color; paid a wage below the level of decent living; driven, beaten, prisoned and enslaved in all but name; spawning the world's raw material and luxury—cotton, wool, coffee, tea, cocoa, palm oil, fibers, spices, rubber, silks, lumber, copper, gold, diamonds, leather—how shall we end the list and where? All these are gathered up at prices lowest of the low, manufactured, transformed and transported at fabulous gain; and the resultant wealth is distributed and displayed and made the basis of world power and universal dominion and armed arrogance in London and Paris, Berlin and Rome, New York and Rio de Janeiro. (Du Bois, 1992: 15–16)

As part of his analysis Du Bois outlines the triad of core racial–class groupings and their conflicting interests that were central in structuring both the Civil

War and its outcome. Theses groupings included 4 million black workers who had been set free, and another 2 million who were already free; white workers; and plantation owners. These three formative groups in the South were connected with three major racial–class groupings in the North: black workers; white labourers; and Northern industrialists and capital. The American working class, he argues, remained divided on racial grounds, both in the North but especially in the South. In addition, whites were not a homogeneous grouping but fractured along class lines. Those whites who opposed their exploited condition migrated either to the North or to the West to gain access to 'free soil' on which to cultivate. The others, instead of throwing in their lot with black workers and recognising that an escape from their lowly exploited condition was bound up with the emancipation of slaves, preferred to work for and align themselves with plantation owners, either in the belief that they had future opportunities in a market society, or to be 'compensated in part by a sort of public and psychological wage' (1992: 700). Du Bois therefore posits both material and psychological factors in his account. The 'psychological wage' compensated white workers for their low wages, by providing a sense of public status and deference that fed their 'vanity' because it associated and aligned them 'with the masters' (1992: 12).

Slavery and emancipation played a central role in the development of the shape and contours of American democracy and its limits. Freed slaves in the South, not willing to return to work on plantations, now demanded rights and entitlements including the right to vote and access to land for self-subsistence. This was famously captured in Thaddeus Stevens' demand for 'forty acres and a mule'. The initial conferral of confiscated plantation lands to blacks, however, was later rescinded. Such demands challenged the Northern capitalists' ideological viewpoint that private property could only be acquired by working for wages or by selling one's labour power. Nor did white Northern workers sympathise with freed blacks, holding instead onto their white privilege.

The establishment of The Freedman Bureau, Abolition Acts and 14th Amendment provided a political and material basis for black reconstruction, and for the first inter-racial governments in American history:

> The Freedmen's Bureau was the most extraordinary and far-reaching institution of social uplift that America has ever attempted. It had to do, not simply with emancipated slaves and poor whites, but also with the property of South planters. It was a government guardianship for the relief and guidance of white and black labor from a feudal agrarianism to modern farming and industry. (1992: 219)

Although portrayed as inept and corrupt by the Dunning School, those black activists who participated in governing were defended by Du Bois, who argues that the historians' hostility derived from Southern whites repulsion at being ruled by blacks. By being democratically elected, active and supported by many black voters in South Carolina, Mississippi and Louisiana, blacks created a 'dictatorship of labour'.

By 1877 and in the context of a huge world recession that began in 1871, Northern capitalists and Southern plantation owners formed an alliance. Labour was suppressed, funding for the Freedman Bureau revoked and a pact developed where the new Republican President would come into office on the condition that he dismantle such radical democracy. The United States then became a 'cornerstone of that new imperialism which is subjecting the labour of yellow, brown and black peoples to the dictation of capitalism organized on a world basis' (1992: 631). However, for Du Bois, the outcome of Reconstruction was not wholly negative. The question of democracy and race was brought to the fore and the proliferation of public schools in the South provided the basis for a Talented Tenth to emerge. Although Reconstruction failed, it constituted a 'splendid failure' (1992: 708).

Applications and Influences

Although it is not always recognised, there are strong grounds for claiming that Du Bois was the founding figure of American sociology who established the first American school of sociology (Wright II, 2008). As Morris notes:

> There is an intriguing, well-kept secret regarding the founding of scientific sociology in America. The first school of scientific sociology in the United States was founded by a black professor located in a historically black university in the South. This reality flatly contradicts the accepted wisdom. (2015: 1)

Many of Du Bois's original and pioneering ideas, including his research methodology and use of triangulation, have now become commonplace in sociology.

RACE, DE-TRADITIONALISATION AND MODERNITY

The central insight of sociology is that society is collectively created. Social order is maintained by the assumptions, habits and customs that shape everyday life. While in traditional societies these were sacredly secured, in modern society they are always open to questioning. From this perspective, theories of race can be seen as expanding the critical communication consistent with modernity itself. Race theorists expose a set of hitherto taken-for-granted and purportedly *natural* relations as instead *social* relations that are normatively constituted, and so may be changed. Theories of race, therefore, extend the modern process of de-traditionalisation, as well as radicalising it in an important direction. In terms of democratisation, raising the category of race shifts the focus from the more established issue of vertical inequalities between social classes to the less acknowledged and deeper issue of horizontal inequalities between social identities. In questioning one of the most entrenched and resilient normative frameworks of modernity, race theorists challenge us all to be truly modern.

A number of sociologists in the United States were strongly influenced by Du Bois's work though they did not fully acknowledge him. These include the analyses of immigration of W. I. Thomas and Florian Znaniecki, the urban sociology of Robert E. Park and the Lloyd Warner School of Community Studies. His work was never acknowledged or recognised for its originality by many of these thinkers or the sociological community, generally (Green and Driver, 1976; Rabaka, 2010). Du Bois's first book, *The Philadelphia Negro*, which received lavish praise in the press, did not merit a review in the *American Journal of Sociology*, nor was he offered any position in any white universities at the time. According to Morris (2015), not only was Du Bois ignored and marginalised but so too were the students that he mentored and trained including Wright and Haynes. Instead, most sociological commentators have looked to the work of Park and the Chicago School as founding the discipline of sociology in the United States. Recent writers have argued that this was primarily for reasons of racism in an all-white sociological world which presupposed white superiority and black primitiveness. For Rabaka (2010: 14) this still remains the case today as the 'white sociological fraternity' continues to ignore his work, enacting a form of 'epistemic apartheid'.

More recently, Du Bois's influence was also present in the work of E. Franklin Frazier's writing on the black bourgeoisie (1957) and Manning Marable (1983, 2005). But given the transdisciplinary nature of his investigations Du Bois's influence has not just been in sociology. The Black or African Studies movement, which began in the 1960s and grew out of student struggles, has also drawn heavily on the work of Du Bois; this in particular includes the work of Cornell West and Henry Louis Gates Jr, who were central to founding the *Du Bois Review* journal at Harvard. More recently, 'Whiteness studies' drawing on the work of David Roediger (2000) and the historian Noel Ignatiev's *How the Irish Became White* (1995), as well as critical race theory, have recognised the importance of his analyses. In history, the work of Eric Foner has drawn heavily on Du Bois. Foner has described Du Bois's contribution to Reconstruction as having 'anticipated the findings of modern scholarship' (Foner, 1988: xxi).

Criticism

Du Bois has been criticised first for continuing to adhere to a notion of race and race thinking despite his criticism of racial domination (Appiah, 1985; Gooding-Williams, 2009). As Appiah notes, though Du Bois moved away from race as a biological concept to a more socio-historical one, this shift remained superficial since he continued to accept the idea and existence of a black race which had to fulfil its mission. The black race was not inferior to white races but complementary to them, as Du Bois argued in 'The Conservation of Races' (2015 [1897]). Consequently:

> what Du Bois attempts, despite his own claims to the contrary, is not the transcendence of the nineteenth century scientific conception of race ... but rather as the dialectic requires, a re-evaluation of the negro race in the face of the sciences of racial inferiority. (Appiah, 1985: 25)

However, such criticisms have been challenged by Morris, who argues that Du Bois writes with a rigorous understanding of race as socially constructed (Morris, 2015: 39).

Du Bois's *The Philadelphia Negro* has also been criticised. It has been argued that underlying his analysis is the presupposition that many of the actions that whites undertake against blacks are unintended, or effected through ignorance, misinformation or merely 'stupidity' rather than to maintain domination and privileged interests. Others have criticised Du Bois's approach in the book for his conceptual conservatism and interpretive elitism, as well as his implicit adherence to Eurocentric and Victorian values in which those in single families or living in slums are condemned for being 'backward', 'ignorant' or of 'low social grade' requiring 'guidance' and of 'widows' as having 'lax moral standards', failing to fulfil the patriarchal gender roles he normatively adhered to. Thus Rabaka (2010) refers to what he calls Du Bois's 'double consciousness' that 'frequently used white-middle class morals and culture as the criteria in which to identify and offer solutions to "Negro problems" as well as "his homespun black elitist orientation"' (2010: 72, 73). He adds, despite its methodological innovations the book is characterised by 'the fact that he was intellectually infected with Eurocentrism, elitism, assimilationism, certain elements of Social Darwinism, and a very subtle form of sexism which privileged the patriarchal conception of the African American family' (Rabaka, 2010: 76). Such elitism was also manifested in his discussion of the 'Talented Tenth' and, in later, more Marxist work, which continued to operate with the notion of a leading vanguard dubbed the 'Guiding Hundredth'.

Conclusion

Du Bois's work is evidently not of one piece but developing and changing, transcending disciplinary boundaries, but always attempting to remain politically relevant to the condition and experience of African Americans, as well as of all non-white marginalised groups across the globe. It needs to be seen in the socio-historical context within which it was developed, in terms of not only its pioneering nature, but also its profoundly important methodological and substantive analyses, including the recognition of the lingering effects of slavery and the agency of blacks in challenging it, as well as the original intersectional analysis between class and race that he developed.

References

Addams, J., (1895) (ed.) *Hull House, Maps and Papers: A Presentation of Nationalities and Wages in a Congested District of Chicago*. New York: Thomas Y. Crowell. Available at: https://archive.org/details/hullhousemapsan00unkngoog/page/n6 (Accessed 16 July 2019).

Appiah, A. (1985) The Uncompleted Argument: DuBois and the Illusion of Race. *Critical Inquiry*, 12(1), pp. 21–37.

Banton, M. and Harwood, J. (1975) *The Race Concept*. New York: Praeger.

Booth, C. (1902) *Life and Labour of the People in London*. London: Macmillan.

Deegan, M.J. (1998) *Jane Addams and the Men of the Chicago School: 1892–1918*. New Brunswick: Transaction Books

Du Bois, W. E. B. (1897) 'A Program for a Sociological Society' speech given at Atlanta University to the First Sociological Club. Available at: https://credo.library.umass.edu/view/full/mums312-b196-i035

Du Bois, W. E. B (2015 [1897]) 'The Conservation of Races'. Washington, DC: American Negro Academy.

Du Bois, W. E. B (1898) The Negroes of Farmville, Virginia: A Social Study. *Bulletin of the Department of Labour* 3 (January): 1–38.

Du Bois, W. E. B (1903) *The Negro Church*, Atlanta University Study, No. 8. Atlanta, GA: Atlanta University Press.

Du Bois, W. E. B (1969 [1901]) *The Black North in 1901: A Social Study*. New York: Arno Press.

Du Bois, W. E. B. (1976 [1952]) *In Battle for Peace: The Story of My 83rd Birthday*. Millwood, NY: Kraus-Thomson.

Du Bois, W. E. B (1978 [1904]) The Atlanta Conferences. In: D. Green and E. Driver (eds) *W.E.B. Du Bois on Sociology and the Black Community*. Chicago, IL: University of Chicago Press, pp. 53–60.

Du Bois, W. E. B. (1984 [1940]) *Dusk of Dawn: An Essay Toward an Autobiography of a Race Concept*. New Brunswick, NJ: Transaction Books.

Du Bois, W. E. B. (1992 [1935]) *Black Reconstruction in America: Toward A History of the Part Which Black Folk Played in the Attempt to Reconstruct Democracy in America, 1860–1880*. New York: Atheneum.

Du Bois, W. E. B. (1967 [1899]) *The Philadelphia Negro: A Social Study*. Philadelphia, PA: University of Pennsylvania Press.

Du Bois, W. E. B. (2000 [1905]) Sociology Hesitant. *Boundary 2*, 27(3), pp. 27–44.

Du Bois, W. E. B. (2007a [1896] *The Suppression of the African Slave Trade to the United States of America: 1638–1870*. Oxford: Oxford University Press.

Du Bois, W. E. B. (2007b [1903]) *The Souls of Black Folk*. Oxford: Oxford University Press.

Du Bois, W. E. B (2007c [1911]) *The Quest of the Silver Fleece*. Oxford: Oxford University Press.

Du Bois, W. E. B (2007d [1915]) *The Negro*. Oxford: Oxford University Press.

Du Bois, W. E. B (2007e [1920]) *Darkwater*. Oxford: Oxford University Press.

Du Bois, W.E.B (2007f [1924]) *The Gift of Black Folk*. Oxford: Oxford University Press.

Foner, E. (1988) *Reconstruction: America's Unfinished Revolution, 1863–1877*. New York: Harper & Row.
Frazier, E. F. (1957) *The Black Bourgeoisie*. Glencoe, IL: Free Press.
Gabbidon, S. L. (1999) W.E.B. Du Bois and the 'Atlanta School' of Social Scientific Research, 1897–1913. *Journal of Criminal Justice Education*, 10(1), pp. 21–38.
Gates, H. L. and West, C. (1996) *The Future of the Race*. New York: A. A. Knopf.
Gooding-Williams, R. (2009) *In the Shadow of DuBois: Afro-Modern Political Thought in America*. Cambridge, MA: Harvard University Press.
Green, D. S. and Driver, E. D. (1976) W.E.B. Du Bois: A Case in the Sociology of Sociological Negation. *Phylon*, 37(4), pp. 308–33.
Green, D. S. and Wortham, R. A. (2015) Sociology Hesitant: The Continuing Neglect of W.E.B. Du Bois. *Sociological Spectrum*, 35(6), pp. 518–33.
Green, D. S. and Wortham, R. A. (2017) The Sociological Insight of W.E.B. Du Bois. *Sociological Inquiry*, 88(1), pp. 56–78.
Ignatiev, N. (1995) *How the Irish Became White*. London: Routledge.
Lemert, C. (2000) The Race of Time: Du Bois and Reconstruction. *Boundary 2*, 27(3), pp. 215–48.
Lewis, D. L. (2000) *W.E.B. Du Bois: The Fight for Equality and the American Century, 1919–1963*. New York: Henry Holt.
Marable, M. (1983) *How Capitalism Underdeveloped Black America*. Boston, MA: South End Press.
Marable, M. (2005) *W.E.B Du Bois: Black Radical Democrat*. London: Routledge.
Morris, A. D. (2015) *The Scholar Denied: W.E.B. Du Bois and the Birth of Modern Sociology*. Oakland, CA: University of California Press.
Patterson, O. (1982) *Slavery and Social Death: A Comparative Study*. Cambridge, MA: Harvard University Press.
Potts, L. (1990) *The World Labour Market: A History Migration*. London: Zed Books.
Rabaka, R. (2010) *Against Epistemic Apartheid: W.E.B. Du Bois and the Disciplinary Decadence of Sociology*. Lanham, MD: Lexington Books.
Remini, R. V. (2009) *A Short History of the United States*. New York: Harper Perennial.
Roediger, D. R. (2000) *The Wages of Whiteness: Race and the Making of the American Working Class*. Revised edition. London: Verso.
Williams, E. (1944) *Capitalism and Slavery*. Chapel Hill, NC: University of North Carolin
Williams, H. (2014) *American Slavery: A Very Short Introduction*. Oxford: Oxford University Press.
Wright II, E. (2008) Deferred Legacy! The Continued Marginalization of the Atlanta Sociological Laboratory. *Sociology Compass*, 2(1), pp. 195–207.

XII

MEAD

George Herbert Mead is considered the founder of the symbolic interactionist tradition in sociology. Though he trained as a philosopher, his work contained a strong empirical and psychological focus. Mead was writing at a time when the disciplinary boundaries that exist today were weak. Though philosophically a pragmatist, scientifically he remained a social psychologist, yet his work has had its strongest impact in sociology. As part of a tradition of reform-orientated progressive, pragmatist philosophers, he saw philosophy as an active tradition geared towards solving problems in the world, rather than contemplating or mirroring and describing reality. In his most famous work, *Mind, Self, and Society* (1934), he elaborated upon his central concepts of the 'I' and the 'Me', which attempted to integrate dialectically and balance the relation between individual and society. The book also foregrounded the importance of humans as animals that use symbols to communicate through interactions. Although relatively unknown during his lifetime, Mead's work gained popularity and widespread diffusion through his student, Hebert Blumer, who coined this tradition of thinking as 'symbolic interactionism'.

Life and Intellectual Context

George Herbert Mead was born in South Hadley, Massachusetts, on 27 February 1863. His father, Hiram Mead, descended from a line of New England farmers and clergymen, initially worked as a Congregationalist minister but later took up a job as a professor of homilectics (the art of preaching) at the theological seminary Oberlin College in Oberlin, Ohio, in 1870. His mother, Elizabeth Storrs Billings, also valued education highly, and as well as serving as an administrator at Mount Holyoke College, also taught at Oberlin. George was the second of three children and studied classics, rhetoric and moral philosophy at Oberlin in a college steeped in New England Puritanism pervaded by progressive social ethics. He has been described as a 'shy, serious, well-behaved boy' (Shalin, 1988: 919) who was indoctrinated with the aforementioned religious values through regular prayer meetings.

Expected to follow in his father's footsteps, Mead reluctantly chose not to do so, though he always remained imbued by many Christian social values. After graduating from college in 1883 he found a job as a teacher in a school but was dismissed for sending home unruly pupils. Moving to Wisconsin in the Northwest, for three years he worked as a land surveyor for Wisconsin Central Railroad Company, and during the winter periods also worked as a tutor. However, afflicted by a crisis of conscience as a result of shunning his expected pastoral vocation, he suffered from periods of acute depression. After completing college he remained torn between pursuing a career in Christian social work or teaching philosophy. In 1887 Mead returned to Harvard. The progressive and reform-oriented social and political atmosphere there was also evident in his philosophy teachers, especially the American idealist Josiah Royce and the pragmatist philosopher, William James.

After gaining a Harvard scholarship, Mead travelled to Leipzig with his friend, Henry Castle, and Castle's sister, Helen. Here he undertook a PhD in philosophy and physiological psychology working with two experimental psychologists, Wilhelm Wundt and G. Stanley Hall, as well as the Hegelian philosopher Wilhelm Dilthey. After becoming steeped in the work of Darwin in the politically progressive, socialist atmosphere of Leipzig, he transferred to Berlin in 1889, where he became involved with activist academics engaging in German policy debates. In October 1891, he married Helen Castle and returned to the United States having secured a position in the Department of Philosophy and Psychology at the University of Michigan at Ann Arbor. There he came into contact with John Dewey – who later become the foremost philosopher in the United States, the philosopher James H. Tufts, as well as the social psychologist Charles Cooley, all of whom became close friends. It was at Michigan that Mead began to develop a physiological theory of emotions. In 1894 Dewey was offered the Chair of Philosophy at the newly emergent Department of Philosophy at the University of Chicago and brought Mead with him, as an assistant professor. The Department at Chicago became the centre of American pragmatism and Mead also remained active in the politics of the city, especially as part of the educational reform movement. He became a full professor in 1907. However, he was heavily affected by the death of his wife in 1929 and although Dewey offered him a position in Columbia where he had himself relocated, he decided to remain in Chicago where he died on 26 April 1931.

Intellectual Influences

Carreira da Silva (2007) emphasises the importance of the dialogic nature of all of Mead's work, which arose in conversation with many other thinkers including the philosophers Immanuel Kant, George Hegel and John Dewey; psychologists such as Wilhelm Wundt (1832–1920) and Sigmund Freud; and biologists including Charles Darwin (1809–82) and John B. Watson (1878–1958). Eschewing any division between philosophy and science, he saw them as integrally connected. In the time Mead was writing, the Darwinian theory of biological evolution was considered the most prominent and widespread scientific doctrine. In the work of John B. Watson, a former student, behaviourism aimed to understand all human life as an extension of animal life, or in terms of an organism and its interaction with the environment including society (Morris, 1962: ix). As Morris argues:

> Mead endeavored to carry out a major problem posed by evolutionary conceptions: the problem of how to bridge the gap between impulse and rationality, of showing how certain biological organisms acquire the capacity of self-consciousness, of thinking, of abstract reasoning, of purposive behavior, of moral devotion; the problem in short of how man, the rational animal, arose. (1962: xvi)

In this respect, Mead worked with Wilhelm Wundt, who criticised Darwin's view that gestures simply expressed emotions (Darwin, 1872). Instead, Wundt argued, we need to understand gestures within the social context within which they operated and functioned, that is as part of a wider repertoire of social acts. Equally from Wilhelm Dilthey (1833–1911) Mead drew on the argument that we cannot understand individuals outside of their social, historical and cultural contexts.

Psychology was an emerging and popular science at the time Mead was writing. However, its reductionist view of atomised individuals began to be challenged by thinkers of a more philosophical bent. They argued that it was through the co-operation of individual minds that society emerged. This included the philosopher psychologist Charles Horton Cooley (1864–1929). In his book *Human Nature and the Social Order* (1964) Cooley discussed the idea of a 'looking-glass self'. We see ourselves, he argued, as others see us, as if others were a mirror. One has an image of oneself derived from other people: 'there is no sense of "I" ... without its correlative sense of you, or he or they' (1964: 182). The idea of a looking-glass self contained three components: 'the imagination of our appearance to the other person, the imagination of his judgement of that appearance, and some sort of self-feeling, such as pride or mortification' (1964: 184). The self was a thoroughly social product which arose through interaction with others; through communication, it constituted a social self. A person's sense of self reflected the ideas that they had of themselves which they believed or attributed others held about them. According to Cooley, many 'significant' interactions took place within the context of the primary group, the family, the playgroup of children and the neighbourhood, in contrast to the distant impersonal relations found in other groups. These symbolic interactions fostered and developed human solidarity within children through the empathetic development of ties of sympathy and affection, and recognition of the needs of others.

As well as the pragmatism of Pierce and especially John Dewey, Mead was also influenced by the work of Josiah Royce, a philosopher hugely sympathetic to German idealism and romanticism. Royce, like Hegel, emphasised the social nature of the self, the importance of role-playing for children in acquiring a self, as well as morality, and the importance of social processes.

Historical, Social and Political Context

In a country characterised by huge resources tied to land and rocketing levels of immigration, rampant individualism and a philosophy of laissez-faire had become the dominant philosophy in the United States. However, massive industrial expansion led to steep levels of inequality. As Henry George, a socialist whose work was influential on the progressive movement, The Age of Reform, noted in *Progress and Poverty*:

> We plow new fields, we open new mines, we found new cities; we drive back the Indian and exterminate the buffalo; we girdle the land with iron roads and lace the air with telegraph wires; we add knowledge to knowledge, and utilize invention after invention; we build schools and endow colleges; yet it becomes no easier for the masses of our people to make a living. On the contrary, it becomes harder. The wealthy class is becoming more wealthy; but the poor class is becoming more dependent. The gulf between the employed and the unemployed is growing wider; social contrasts are becoming sharper; as liveried carriages appear, so are barefooted children. (1926 [1879]: 391–2)

Under the impetus of increasingly widespread Christian forms of socialism a number of progressive socio-political reforms attempted to challenge laissez-faire individualism. These included:

> the establishment of the Interstate Commerce Commission, the Conservation Act, the Federal Reserve Act, the food and drug law, the federal workmen's compensation program, the Adamson Act mandating an eight-hour working day on interstate railroads, the electoral reforms, including the initiative, the referendum, the direct election of U.S. senators, and women's suffrage. (Shalin, 1988: 916)

For the political right these reforms jarred against belief in the natural laws of the market, while for the revolutionary left, such piecemeal changes did not fundamentally challenge the concentration of private property. It was in this centre–left reformist space that both pragmatist philosophy and Mead's piecemeal advocacy of socialism through constitutional democracy unfolded. According to Shalin he was:

> a man of radically democratic convictions, keenly aware of social inequality, and deeply concerned with the effect of the division of labour on the working man. Like many other progressives of his time,

> Mead was engaged in a lifelong polemic with socialists. He accepted without reservation their humanitarian ends but took issue with them on the question of means, fully embracing the basic progressivist tenet that the historically unique framework of American democracy provides the best available leverage for social reconstruction. Mead's life can be seen as an attempt to prove in both theory and practice that revolutionary objectives can be achieved by essentially conservative means. (1988: 914)
>
> [Republished with permission of The University of Chicago Press, from *G. H. Mead, Socialism, and the Progressive Agenda,* D. Shalin, 1988]

The Importance of Pragmatism

Pragmatism, especially in the work of Dewey, sought to extend the principles of political and economic democracy. It emphasised the importance of protean experience which it saw as the source of growth and of the good. People, who were conceived as naturally good, could actively create a more just society through their social interactions. It therefore advocated a 'dynamic, naturalistic, anti-formal, and voluntaristic' philosophy linked to 'social reform and activism' in which actors sought value and purpose in their situations and through their experience (Alexander, 1987: 202–3). As a member of this school, Mead remained sympathetic to a humanistic socialism containing a pragmatic, non-revolutionary and undoctrinaire form. That is, he was someone committed to the ideals of a social and radical democracy.

The new philosophy department established in Chicago in 1982 under Dewey, also remained committed to confronting the social problems faced in the city, and in the United States more generally. It advocated educational upheaval and supported progressive social reforms including the development of new settlements, such as those initiated by Jane Addams' Hull House movement. Within several decades Chicago had experienced an unprecedented boom in industrialisation and growth from its former rural base. Boasting industries in meat-packing and steel – used for the American railroads – such rapid economic development brought high levels of immigration but also inequality, crime and the development of slum districts. Mead took his moral duty towards the community very seriously. He became involved in educational reform, serving as president of the School of Education's Parents' Association, as well as editing the university's educational journal, the *Elementary School Teacher* (Coser, 1974: 344–5). He advocated free progressive education for children of all social classes, providing them with culture aimed at fostering the development of more rounded, and less alienated, workers.

Recognised as a leading figure in the Chicago progressive movement, Mead also served as vice-president of the Immigrants Protective League of Chicago.

The search for developing a greater democracy was also reflected in his sociological writings. Here he sought to balance political engagement with scientific detachment. Science provided both the basis for freedom and the means by which to replace the remaining residues of the arbitrary authority of the medieval world for the rational authority characteristic of the modern world. His emphasis on social interaction reflected these political commitments. It was the ability to take on increasingly the role of others that undergirded human rationality and the development of a rational society. Interactions were the basis of moral life and moral life entailed facilitating the maximum satisfaction of individual impulses, while simultaneously retaining social cohesion.

For Mead democracy was tied to expanding the possibilities for individuals. As Shalin notes:

> Mead's pragmatist cosmology was tailor-made for the Progressive era. It envisaged the pluralistic universe whose inhabitants incessantly multiply perspectives, reinvent their selves, and reconstruct their community for the common good. No society embodies this ideal better than democracy. At its heart is a universal discourse or system of symbols binding individuals into a social whole and transparent to 'every citizen of the universe of discourse.' Democratic society never stops restructuring its perspectives and broadening its horizon of universality... Democracy makes its symbolic and material resources available to all its members... Democratic society teaches its members to place themselves in each other's shoes. More than that, it gives everyone a practical chance to experiment with new roles and selves. When it lives up to its promise, democracy approximates what Mead calls 'a universal society in which the interests of each would be the interests of all.' (2000: 335–6)
>
> [Republished with permission of Blackwell, from *The Blackwell Companion to Major Social Theorists*, G. Ritzer, 2000. Permission conveyed through Copyright Clearance Center, Inc]

Ideas and Arguments

Mind, Self and Society

Although Mead published a number of articles for journals during his lifetime, he published no books. Throughout his life, he remained a modest figure, often not seeing the fundamentally novel aspects of his work, and as a result felt unease at publishing a book. Moreover, he found writing exceptionally difficult and strained to express his original ideas in a suitable vocabulary or available conceptual language. After his death four major books were published based on stenographic notes of his lectures taken by his students.

These included: *The Philosophy of the Present* (1932) in which he examined the temporal framework and the status of objects as they occurred; *Mind, Self, and Society*, (1962 [1934]); *Movements of Thought in the Nineteenth Century* (1936) in which he traced the movements of nineteenth-century thought and science from Kant to Pragmatism beginning in the medieval period; and *The Philosophy of the Act* (1938) in which he examined the various stages of human acts. Although his writings and interests were diverse, many of the themes he discussed in these books were interconnected, including philosophy, psychology, biology, history and physics.

Mind, Self, and Society

In *Mind, Self, and Society*, Mead challenged the religious view that mind was a supernatural substance existing separately from the body often reproduced in philosophical discussions through the Cartesian notion of dualism (Miller, 1982). Instead, he argued, mind is embodied. The social experience of individuals presupposed a biological, physiological and behavioural basis, a central nervous system. By contrast to Watson's view that humans were merely animals who responded to stimuli, Mead designates his approach as a form of *social behaviourism* that does not deny the subjective self-experiences, imagery and consciousness of humans, as well as the social context within which humans operate. Moreover, his approach did not turn on the analysis of individuals. The group or whole was ontologically and epistemologically prior to the individual:

> We are not, in social psychology, building up the behavior of the social group in terms of the behavior of the separate individuals composing it; rather, we are starting out with a given social whole of complex group activity, into which we analyze (as elements) the behavior of each of the separate individuals composing it. We attempt, that is, to explain the conduct of the individual in terms of the organized conduct of the social group, rather than to account for the organized conduct of the social group in terms of the conduct of the separate individuals belonging to it. For social psychology, the whole (society) is prior to the part (the individual), not the part to the whole; and the part is explained in terms of the whole, not the whole in terms of the part or parts. (Mead, 1962 [1934]: 7)

Individual psychology can only be understood in social terms. The individual act needed to be understood as part of a social act. In this sense mind was socially constituted and located within social structures.

Social Acts and the Conversation of Gestures

Mead is concerned with analysing social acts – acts which involve more than one person – and analysing these not in terms of a single stimulus and response from an isolated individual, but dynamically and organically, as conditioned stimuli and responses between individuals effected on an ongoing basis in social situations. That is, as social acts constituting a social process.

Social acts vary from simple dyads with two people to those entailing numerous individuals, for example those operating in complex institutions. Taken together as a totality, the sum of these acts constitutes a society or social order. Such acts involve social objects – objects and things – which have a meaning for all the participants involved but are situationally bound; that is, they can have different meanings for different people in the same situation, but also across situations. Thus, a chair may be used to seat someone or as a weapon in a bar fight.

According to Mead communication between two or more individuals is central for explaining individual minds. This entails both the *conversation of gestures*, which applies to both animals and humans, and the *conversation of significant gestures*, applicable only to the latter. Gestures involve a multiplicity of movements and expressions. Mead gives the example of a dog fight in which each dog shapes its behaviour in terms of what the other dog begins to do:

> The act of each dog becomes the stimulus to the other dog for his response. There is then a relationship between these two; and as the act is responded to by the other dog, it, in turn, undergoes change. The very fact that the dog is ready to attack another becomes a stimulus to the other dog to change his own position or his own attitude. He has no sooner done this than the change of attitude in the second dog in turn causes the first dog to change his attitude. We have here a conversation of gestures. They are not, however, gestures in the sense that they are significant. We do not assume that the dog says to himself, 'If the animal comes from this direction he is going to spring at my throat and I will turn in such a way.' What does take place is an actual change in his own position due to the direction of the approach of the other dog. (1962 [1934]: 42–3)

Significant Gestures

Similar conditioned responses take place in fencing, boxing or a parent responding to an infant's cry: individuals adjust their behaviour 'instinctively' in relation to another individual; that is, such communication takes place without deliberation. The communication between biological individuals does not entail any subjective meaning to be present but exists objectively in the social situation, it is not in the mind of the participants. This can be contrasted with more advanced forms of social interaction which entail *significant gestures*; that is, vocal gestures, language or acts of meaning that employ significant symbols. Thus, for example, someone shaking their fist at you indicates an idea or gesture:

> [I]f somebody shakes his fist in your face you assume that he has not only a hostile attitude but that he has some idea behind it. You assume that it means not only a possible attack, but that the individual has an idea in his experience.
>
> When, no, that gesture means this idea behind it and it arouses that idea in the other individual, then we have a significant symbol. In the case of the dog-fight we have a gesture which calls out appropriate response; in the present case we have a symbol which answers to a meaning in the experience of the first individual and which also calls out that meaning in the second individual. Where the gesture reaches that situation it has become what we call 'language.' It is now a significant symbol and it signifies a certain meaning. (Mead, 1962: [1934]: 45–6)

Significant symbols allow individuals to adjust their behaviour to each other during interactions; they allow forms of communication to develop. The individual making the gesture 'knows' what his or her gesture will arouse in the person to whom it is addressed, so that their reaction is represented to themselves before it is aroused in the individual with whom they are interacting. It is only the ability to take the role of the other that allows this possibility. Taking on the role of the other indicates a shift from a biological individual, governed by impulses, to a minded organism governed by rationality: it is the basis of reason.

The interpersonal conversation of significant gestures forms a condition for the mind to function and emerge. Language in interaction constitutes an objective phenomenon which, when internalised by the individual, structures his or her mind as a social process. With each person taking on the role of the other we arrive at a world of common meanings in which individuals are mutually attuned to the expectations of others.

The Self

In addition to examining the mind and its presupposition of a nervous system and significant gestures, Mead also investigates the self. The development of the self, like the mind, also takes place through experience and social action. Through the ability of role taking, the self becomes 'an object to itself' (1962: 136). Here the process of self-reflexivity is central. By adopting roles and the associated attitudes and values of others, the self becomes an object of its own reflection. The notion of a reflective self, however, has huge implications. As Blumer argues:

> The possession of a self converts the human being into a special kind of actor, transforms his relation to the world, and gives his action a unique character. In asserting that the human being has a self, Mead simply meant that the human being is an object to himself. The human

> being may perceive himself, have conceptions of himself, communicate with himself, and act toward himself. (1969: 61)

For Mead the self undergoes development and he analyses the social conditions under which a self arises as an object. This includes its development through the activities of play and the game. When discussing play Mead focuses on children's role-playing, especially with imagined others:

> We find in children something that answers to this double, namely, the invisible, imaginary companions which a good many children produce in their own experience. They organize in this way the responses which they call out in other persons and call out also in themselves. Of course, this playing with an imaginary companion is only a peculiarly interesting phase of ordinary play. Play in this sense, especially the stage which precedes the organized games, is a play at something. A child plays at being a mother, at being a teacher, at being a policeman; that is, it is taking different roles, as we say... He has a set of stimuli which call out in himself the sort of responses they call out in others. He takes this group of responses and organizes them into a certain whole. (1962 [1934]: 150–1)

In this scenario of play, the child adopts one single, specific role at a time, adopting the role of the other in a sequential way. However, following a developmental phase, the child becomes able to internalise and plays the role of all others in the game, as well as their different relationships to each other and the rules of the game. That is, the child becomes capable of participating fully in common activities in a social manner. It is through the game phase that the individual achieves selfhood and adulthood. Mead refers to the internalisation of all the attitudes of others in a game, or in a community, as part of the 'generalized other':

> The organized community or social group which gives to the individual his unity of self may be called 'the generalized other.' The attitude of the generalized other is the attitude of the whole community. (1962 [1934]: 154)

He uses the analogy of a ball game in which the:

> attitudes of a set of individuals are involved in a cooperative response in which the different roles involve each other. In so far as a man takes the attitude of one individual in the group, he must take it in its relationship to the action of the other members of the group; and if he is fully to adjust himself, he would have to take the attitudes of all involved in the process. (1962 [1934]: 256)

The 'I' and the 'Me'

It is also in relation to the 'generalised other' that Mead talks of a dualistic or intra-psychic aspect of the self, the 'me' and the 'I', which constitute two parts of a whole. The self is not simply a receptacle for social attitudes and the generalised other, a socially determined product. Rather, it also contains an active side which creatively and dialectically interrogates and interprets these social attitudes. This active side is the basis of action and impulse, it is an 'I':

> The 'I' is the response of the organism to the attitudes of the others; the 'me' is the organized set of attitudes of others which one himself assumes. The attitudes of the others constitute the organized 'me,' and then one reacts toward that as an 'I.' ... the taking of all those organised sets of attitudes gives him his 'me'; that is the self he is aware of. He can throw the ball to some other members because of the demand made upon him from other members of the team... But what that response will be he does not know and knowbody else knows. Perhaps he will make a brilliant play or an error. The response to that situation as it appears in his immediate experience is uncertain, and it is that which constitutes the 'I.' (Mead, 1962 [1934]: 175)

For Mead the 'I' both 'calls out the "me" and responds to it' (1962 [1934]: 178). Moreover, although the attitudes of others that constitute the 'me', the organised community, are relatively predicatable, the 'I' is something that more or less remains uncertain, incalculable, it is a space of initiative and freedom. Taken together, the 'I' and the 'me' 'constitute a personality as it appears in social experience' (1962 [1934]: 178). In this dynamic model, the self is envisaged not as a substance or rigid structure, but as a process, entailing a dialectical relation between an autonomous 'I', within the community 'me', both embedded in a social situation. Through its actions the 'I' changes the social structure, albeit incrementally for the most part, but more comprehensively or substantially by powerful individuals such as political leaders, and these changes are in turn reflected back into the 'I'. According to Mead, individuals are both produced by and produce society. The individual self acts over time, drawing on the past, but not determined by it, so that there exist 'alternative ways of completing' what he or she has begun (1962 [1934]: 169). To the socially given attitudes of the 'me' the outcome of the response of the 'I' is always open, contingent and unpredictable. Thus, although we are born into specific social structures which constrain us in terms of language, customs and law, as individuals we still have agency through the spontaneous ability of the 'I' to react. The individual and social structure are continually adjusting in relation to one another.

Despite some agency, the 'I' always remains constrained to an extent. Through role taking, the self takes on not only the attitude of others, but also the values of others – it becomes the others. The generalised other becomes internal to the actor following long periods of socialisation into collective life and role taking. It is through the generalised other that social processes influence individual behaviour to such an extent that they operate as a form of social control by shaping the individual's thinking. Thus, the domination of the 'I' by the 'me' not only facilitates social co-ordination and the efficient operation of society, but also allows for social control.

Society

In his discussion of the third main theme in the book, society, Mead is emphatic concerning the social nature of humans as physiological organisms, as he notes: 'human nature is something social through and through' (1962 [1934]: 229). The behaviour of all living organisms has a social aspect:

> the fundamental biological or physiological impulses and needs which lie at the basis of all such behavior—especially those of hunger and sex, those connected with nutrition and reproduction—are impulses and needs which, in the broadest sense, are social in character or have social implications, since they involve or require social situations and relations for their satisfaction by any given individual organism; and they thus constitute the foundation of all types or forms of social behavior, however simple or complex, crude or highly organized, rudimentary or well developed… All living organisms are bound up in a general social environment or situation, in a complex of social interrelations and interactions upon which their continued existence depends. (1962 [1934]: 227–8)

Mead believes the family, in which vital biological activities are expressed, is central to the maintenance and reproduction of the species. It is also the unit on which other forms of social organisation are based, including clan and state.

According to Mead, society is composed of a multiplicity of generalised others, many of which are unknown to the individual. The socio-physiological tendencies which lead individuals to enter into organised societies and communities entail not only social co-operation but also social antagonism. Mead discusses the hostile impulses and attitudes aimed at the self-protection and self-preservation of competing groups, sometimes breeding feelings of superiority between them. This competition can shift from the tribe, clan or class level to the state level. The idea of a common enemy in inter-group conflict often aids intra-group solidarity uniting individuals in their opposition to other groups or states, for example in wars between states. But individuals can also develop an attitude of hostility towards their own group or the organised social organisation to which they belong, arousing a feeling of self-superiority in order to 'keep himself [*sic*] going' (1962 [1934]: 307). Thus modern complex societies contain high degrees of functional and behavioural differentiation and intricate webs of social relations, with many individuals sharing commonalities with others, but also different and sometimes antagonistic interests and goals. Moreover, these conflicts and divergences of interest can also be expressed within the self:

> A highly developed and organized human society is one in which the individual members are interrelated in a multiplicity of different intricate and complicated ways whereby they all share a number of common social interests—interests in, or for the betterment of, the society—and yet, on the other hand, are more or less in conflict relative to numerous other interests which they possess only individually, or else share with one another only in small and limited groups. Conflicts among individuals in a highly developed and organized human society are not mere conflicts among their respective primitive impulses but are conflicts among their respective selves or personalities, each with its definite social structure—highly complex and organized and unified—and each with a number of different social facets or aspects, a number of different sets of social attitudes constituting it. Thus, within such a society, conflicts arise between different aspects or phases of the same individual self (conflicts leading to cases of split personality when they are extreme or violent enough to be psychopathological), as well as between different individual selves. (Mead, 1962 [1934]: 307)

However, nations for Mead, unlike individuals, cannot as yet take the role of the other in order to participate in a morally regulated system of international relations. As a result, they often remain at war or in conflict, adjusting to one another's actions much like dogs in a dog fight as discussed above.

Applications and Influences

Many sociologists including W. I. Thomas and Robert Park, and others central in the Chicago School of sociology, were heavily influenced by Mead's work. Thomas was primarily known for his huge and pioneering work with Florian Znaniecki, *The Polish Peasant in Europe and America* (1958 [1918]). The book combined theory with newspaper cuttings, personal diaries and immigrant letters to examine the uprooted village peasant's move to urban American life. It also examined the subjective attitudes, values and experiences of these immigrants with regard to the objective changes that affect and influence them.

Drawing on Mead, Robert Park also eschewed abstract philosophical speculation to examine concrete observable processes, and develop working concepts, for example in his famous paper, 'The City: Suggestions for the Investigation of Human Behavior in the City Environment' (1915). His theoretically guided research analysed the importance of interactions and social control as 'the central fact and central problem of modern society' (cited in Coser, 1974: 358).

LABELLING THEORY

Howard Becker's *Outsiders* (1963) was pivotal in the development and popularisation of labelling theory, a prominent sociological approach to deviance in the 1960s and 1970s. Labelling theory considers two aspects in the genesis of deviance. At the societal level, labelling theory holds that deviance is socially constructed through the meaning attributed to certain individuals or actions. This involves the negative categorisation of minorities, often through stereotyping, according to the normative prescriptions of the majority. At the group or individual level, labelling theory explores how classification as deviant then affects the self-identity and behaviour of those labelled. Here, the relationship between stigmatisation, social identity and self-fulfilling prophecy are considered. As well as the categorisation of 'criminal' deviancy, labeling theory has been used to explore mental health (the 'mentally ill') and sexuality (the 'homosexual'). What are the categories of deviance deployed in contemporary society deserving exploration through labelling theory?

Other figures influenced by Mead included his former students, Ellsworth Faris (1936) and Herbert Blumer. Part of the Chicago School of sociology, which undertook a number of substantive empirical projects, it was Blumer who formulated the notion of 'symbolic interactionism' as a distinct approach to human group life and social conduct (Blumer, 1937). He did more than anyone to promote Mead's work after his death. Yet Blumer developed his own distinctive version of Mead's approach since he believed that many important aspects of symbolic interactionism were only implicitly dealt with by the latter. Nevertheless, like Mead he foregrounded the importance of symbols and meaning for actors wherein meaning arose through interaction and communication between individuals. Blumer also drew upon the pragmatist focus on the importance of empirical observation of social processes and, from Thomas, the need to foreground the actor's definition of the situation, in order to understand his or her actions. According to Blumer, symbolic interactionism is based on three central premises:

> The first premise is that human beings act toward things on the basis of the meanings that the things have for them. Such things include everything that the human being may note in his world—physical objects, such as trees or chairs; other human beings, such as a mother or a store clerk; categories of human beings, such as friends or enemies; institutions, as a school or a government; guiding ideals, such as individual independence or honesty; activities of others, such as their commands or requests; and such situations as an individual encounters in his daily life. The second premise is that the meaning of such things is derived from, or arises out of, the social interaction that one has with one's fellows. The third premise is that these meanings are handled in, and modified through, an interpretative process used by the person in dealing with the things he encounters. (Blumer, 1969: 2)

Blumer developed his approach in contrast to the diametrically opposed but dominant approaches extant at the time: quantitatively oriented sociologists concerned with understanding society through various measurements including surveys, on the one hand, and qualitative approaches which explained social life through reified notions of culture, norms and values, such as the grand theorising of Parsonian functionalism, on the other. In functionalism or psychology, he argued, the view that actors approach the world on the basis of meaning is taken for granted or ignored. Human behaviour is instead interpreted by psychologists on the basis of factors producing it, such as stimuli or unconscious motives, and by sociologists in terms of social roles or norms and values determining it. Symbolic interaction not only takes meaning seriously, but also locates the source of meaning not, as realists do, as intrinsic to the object or thing, or as psychologists do, as brought to the thing by the individual person through perceptions, sensations and feelings, but in the process of interaction between people. The use of meaning involves an interpretive process, entailing deciphering actions, values, situations and other actors. The focus was neither on the individual nor on society but on concrete social groups and their actions and interactions, of individuals engaged in living and coping in determinate life situations and whose experiences are in process. Like Mead, Blumer emphasised social processes, symbols, language and meaning, and the connections and interactions between people interpreting and adjusting their behaviour in response to others by taking on the role of the other. Social life involved individuals defining their situations and acting accordingly, aligning their actions and interpreting and responding to shifts in the actions of others. It was from the collection of these lines of actions that society is formed:

> A society is seen as people meeting the varieties of situations that are thrust on them by their conditions of life. These situations are met by working out joint actions in which participants have to align their acts to one another. (Blumer, 1969: 72)

Politically progressive, Blumer extended his interactionist approach to the analysis of race relations. In a celebrated paper 'Race Prejudice as a Sense of Group Position' (1958) he argued that to understand race prejudice sociologists needed to shift their gaze away from feelings lodged within individuals – hostility, intolerance hatred, etc. – to the relationships between groups in which they define and redefine one another, and themselves as racial groups: 'race prejudice exists basically in a sense of group position rather than in a set of feelings which members of one racial group have towards the members of another racial group' (1958: 3). A more in-depth understanding examined the processes through which racial groups form images of themselves in opposition to other racial groups, a collective process in which groups position themselves. According to Blumer, there existed four basic types of feeling that were always present in the dominant group:

> They are (1) a feeling of superiority, (2) a feeling that the subordinate race is intrinsically different and alien, (3) a feeling of proprietary claim to certain areas of privilege and advantage, and (4) a fear and suspicion that the subordinate race harbours designs on the prerogatives of the dominant race. (1958: 4)

The dominant group possessed a self-assured feeling that it was naturally superior by disparaging the qualities of the subordinate group, and applying derogatory labels to members of that group including laziness, unreliability, stupidity. The distinctive sense that the subordinate group 'is not of our kind' was also present giving rise to a sense of aversion. However, these characteristics need to be connected to proprietary claims that the dominant groups had exclusive rights and entitlements in various areas of life, such as certain jobs, membership of certain schools and positions of social prestige. One major source of race prejudice occurred in situations where a dominant group felt its social status being challenged. The final type of feeling arose from the fear that the subordinate group threatened the position of the dominant group:

> The sense of group position is the very heart of the relation of the dominant to the subordinate group. It supplies the dominant group with its framework of perception, its standard of judgment, its patterns of sensitivity, and its emotional proclivities. It is important to recognize that this sense of group position transcends the feelings of the individual members of the dominant group, giving such members a common orientation that is not otherwise to be found in separate feelings and views. (Blumer, 1958: 4)

The feelings of the dominant group did not represent the objective positions between racial groups but rather 'what ought to be' the case, not what was the case, of where the two groups belonged. Group relations and therefore feelings between the groups were also highly variable. For the most part the dominant group held an 'abstract image' of the subordinate group often fostered by social elites, intellectuals and those who had the public ear.

Blumer's students including Anselm Strauss and Howard Becker took up and expanded on many of his ideas. In his famous essay entitled 'Becoming a Marijuana User' (1953) Becker shows how the use of the marijuana drug, a natural product, is shaped in social interactions and social situations. The effects of the drug depend on their interpretation by social individuals. According to Becker, individuals have to learn from others what the effects of the marijuana are, rather than the effects emerging directly and immediately from the physical properties of the drug itself. For Becker, drug users were not a distinct group with a specific set of psychological dispositions; rather, anyone could become a drug user, by learning the techniques of drug use:

> An individual will be able to use marihuana for pleasure only when he (1) learns to smoke it in a way that will produce real effects;

> (2) learns to recognize the effects and connect them with drug use; and (3) learns to enjoy the sensations he perceives. (Becker, 1953: 235)

Human behaviour therefore cannot be understood in terms of pre-given dispositions but instead:

> the presence of a given kind of behavior is the result of a sequence of social experiences during which the person acquires a conception of the meaning of the behavior, and perceptions and judgments of objects and situations, all of which make the activity possible and desirable. Thus, the motivation or disposition to engage in the activity is built up in the course of learning to engage in it and does not antedate this learning process. For such a view it is not necessary to identify those 'traits' which 'cause' the behavior. Instead, the problem becomes one of describing the set of changes in the person's conception of the activity and of the experience it provides for him. (Becker, 1953: 235)
>
> [Republished with permission of The University of Chicago Press, from *Becoming a Marihuana User*, H. S. Becker, 1953]

Becker also continued to operate with the progressive politics that had become associated with the symbolic interactionist tradition. In his essay 'Whose Side Are We On?' (1967) he argues that we must take the side of the underdog. This is evident in his discussion of deviance and the development of what is referred to as 'labelling theory', in which he examines the notion of deviance as entailing both people who enforce rules and others who break them – dubbed outsiders. Becker argues that most ordinary members of society and sociologists have tended to focus on common-sense questions and taken-for-granted attitudes, for example asking why people break rules and whether there is something inherently deviant about acts that break social rules. According to Becker, what is of greater concern for the sociologists is why certain forms of behaviours are defined as deviant, by whom, and in relation to what social rules and norms. It is by labelling and defining certain acts as deviant that they become so. Arguing against statistical definitions of deviances as measurements of actions deviating from the norm, as pathological or an 'illness', or as the failure to follow group norms, he argues that deviance is created by society:

> that social groups create deviance by making the rules whose infraction constitutes deviance, and by applying those rules to particular people and labeling them as outsiders. From this point of view, deviance is not a quality of the act the person commits, but rather a consequence of the application by others of rules and sanctions to an 'offender.' The deviant is one to whom that label has successfully been applied; deviant behavior is behavior that people so label. (1973: 10)

Criticism

Given the disparate strands of philosophy and psychology that Mead synthesises, the publication of his lecture notes unintended as books, his interdisciplinary training in philosophy and psychology and not as a sociologist, his project should be seen as ambiguous, open and incomplete. Mead foregrounded the biological and social nature of the self, attempting to highlight simultaneously the profoundly social nature of humans and society as an emergent product of individual actions, mutually adjusting to one another. Sympathetic critics such as Coser, however, have noted the ambiguities in his discussion of the nature of social processes, especially in relation to social acts and their co-operative or conflictual nature: 'He fluctuated in his usage and definition of social acts, sometimes assuming that these are necessarily cooperative, and sometimes holding to the more realistic view that social conflict is as much a social act as is cooperation' (1974: 354). Alexander (1987) also discerns ambiguities in Mead's work which derive from a residual individualism, itself inherent and issuing from his philosophy of pragmatism. This individualism, Alexander argues, was attenuated by Blumer's excessively individualistic reading of Mead. Thus:

> There are significant places in his work where the autonomy of attitude and response is collapsed. He proclaims, in these instances, that the meaning of a gesture is determined not by a prior symbolic system but by the respondent's gesture itself, that is, by contingent and purely 'pragmatic' individual considerations. (1987: 210)

Mead's focus on meanings and reflexivity also underplays the unconscious forces operating in the social world as well as the role of habit and custom. Though he does occasionally acknowledges customs, for the most part he foregrounds a reflexive, highly conscious actor. His analysis of the development of a social order emerging from creative individuals' actions also needs to be refined.

In addition, Mead has been criticised for his failure to establish a connection between micro processes of interaction with broader, emergent macro sociological processes. The recurrent and systematic development of macrostructural patterns is for the most part left unexplained. Although he recognises social conflict, he also fails to examine issues of the endemic nature of power in social life. As Shalin notes:

> Mead's political theory also blurs the distinction between symbolic and economic resources, ignoring the power of the market in structuring uneven access to resources, and over generalising societal processes of cooperation. Although he recognises social conflicts he does not highlight processes of cultural, racial and ethnic division in his work. In that sense, his sociology not only lacks an analysis of general

macro-processes, but also contains an inadequate theory of power and conflict. (2000: 341)

Conclusion

Through his sociological analysis Mead attempts to transcend a number of sociological dualisms, between agency and structure, nature and culture, mind and matter, self and society. For example, in discussing what is now termed the relation between agents and social structures, Mead attempts to give a balance between the two through his dialectical related concepts of 'me' as representing social structure and 'I' as agency. Equally, with regard to mind and body, Mead presciently provides an embodied account of the self. As Shalin argues:

> The Meadian approach draws attention to the corporeal dimension of social institutions and invites an inquiry into authoritarian emotions, aristocratic demeanour, and the body language of democracy. Indeed polity affects our entire body. Democracy, in this sense, is an embodied institution. There is more to it than a system of constitutional checks and balances and a list of civil rights. It is also a demeanour, the practical care we take of our own and other people's bodies and selves. The body politic is the politics of the body. (2000: 341)

[Republished with permission of Blackwell, from *The Blackwell Companion to Major Social Theorists*, G. Ritzer, 2000. Permission conveyed through Copyright Clearance Center, Inc]

References

Alexander, J. C. (1987) *Twenty Lectures: Sociological Theory Since World War II*. New York: Columbia University Press.

Becker, H. S. (1953) Becoming a Marihuana User. *American Journal of Sociology*, 59(3), pp. 235–42.

Becker, H. S. (1967) Whose Side Are We On? *Social Problems*, 14(3), pp. 239–47.

Becker, H. S. (1973) *Outsiders: Studies in the Sociology of Deviance*. New York: Free Press.

Blumer, H (1937) Social Psychology. In: Emerson P. Schmidt (ed.) *Man and Society*. New York: Prentice-Hall, pp. 144–98.

Blumer, H. (1958) Race Prejudice as a Sense of Group Position. *Pacific Sociological Review*, 1(1), pp. 3–7.

Blumer, H. (1969) *Symbolic Interactionism: Perspective and Method*. Englewood Cliffs, NJ: Prentice Hall.

Carreira da Silva, F. (2007) *G. H. Mead: A Critical Introduction*. Cambridge: Polity.

Cooley, C. H. (1964) *Human Nature and the Social Order*. New York: Schocken Books.
Coser, L. A. (1974) *Masters of Sociological Thought: Ideas in Historical and Social Context*. New York: Harcourt Brace Jovanovich.
Darwin, C. (1872) *The Expression of the Emotions in Man and Animals*. London: J. Murray.
Faris, E. (1936) Review of *Mind, Self, and Society* by George H. Mead. *American Journal of Sociology*, 41, pp. 809-813.
George, H. (1926 [1879]) *Progress and Poverty: An Inquiry into the Cause of Industrial Depressions and of Increase of Want with Increase of Wealth*. New York: Garden City.
Mead, G. H. (1932) *The Philosophy of the Present*. Chicago, IL: Open Court.
Mead, G. H. (1936) *Movements of Thought in the Nineteenth Century*. Chicago, IL: University of Chicago Press.
Mead, G. H. (1938) *The Philosophy of the Act*. Chicago, IL: Chicago University Press.
Mead, G. H. (1962 [1934]) *Mind, Self, and Society: From the Standpoint of a Social Behaviorist*. C. W. Morris (ed.) Chicago, IL: University of Chicago Press.
Miller, D. L. (ed.) (1982) *The Individual and Social Self: Unpublished Work of George Herbert Mead*. Chicago, IL: University of Chicago Press.
Morris, C. W. (1962) Introduction: George H. Mead as Social Psychologist and Social Philosopher. In: C. W. Morris (ed.) G. H. Mead, *Mind, Self, and Society: From the Standpoint of a Social Behaviorist*. Chicago, IL: University of Chicago Press, pp. ix-xxxv.
Park, R. (1915) The City: Suggestions for the Investigation of Human Behavior in the City Environment. *American Journal of Sociology*, 20(5), pp. 577-612.
Shalin, D. (1988) G. H. Mead, Socialism, and the Progressive Agenda. *American Journal of Sociology*, 93(4), pp. 913-951.
Shalin, D. (2000) George Herbert Mead. In: G. Ritzer (ed.) *The Blackwell Companion to Major Social Theorists*. Malden, MA: Blackwell, pp. 302-44.
Smith, D. (1988) *The Chicago School: A Liberal Critique of Capitalism*. London: Macmillan.
Thomas, W. I and Znaniecki, F (1958 [1918]) *The Polish Peasant in Europe and America*. New York: Dover (2 vols).

INDEX